The Translator's
Grammar
of the
Textus Receptus

The Translator's Grammar of the Textus Receptus

By
Dr. Steve Combs, Th. D.

Published in the USA by
The Old Paths Publications
www.theoldpathspublications.com
and
Global Bible Translators
www.bpsglobal.org

Copyright © 2021 by *Steve Combs*

ISBN: 978-1-7376384-4-5

All rights reserved. No part of this publication may be reproduced or transmitted in any form or by any means, electronic or mechanical, including photocopy, recording, or any information storage and retrieval system, without permission from the copyright owner in writing (11-17-2021)

The Author may be contacted by writing:
bpsg.scombs@gmail.org

This grammar of New Testament Greek is based entirely on the Greek Received Text and examples are primarily taken from the New Testament with emphasis on the Gospel of John and the Book of Romans.
English Bible quotations are from the King James Version.

Cover photo obtained from a Wikipedia article on the Library of Celcus in Ephesus. The author is the Austrian Archaeology Institute. Public Domain

Published in the USA by
The Old Paths Publications
www.theoldpathspublications.com
and
Global Bible Translators
www.bpsglobal.org

Table of Contents

Chap.	Topics	Page
	Acknowledgments	11
	Author's Preface: The Purpose of this Book	15

Part 1: Introduction to the Greek New Testament

1	Inspiration, Preservation, and Authority of the Bible	21
2	History of the Text: The Traditional Text	36
3	History of the Text: The Received Text the KJV, and the UBS	66
4	A Bible Believer Asks, Why Use Greek and Hebrew?	84
5	The Great Need for Bible Translating	87

Part 2: Introduction to New Testament Greek

6	The Greek Alphabet, Its Pronunciation, and Accents	96
7	How to do a Greek Word Study in E-sword	101

Part 3: Basic Greek Grammar

8	The Gospel of John Chapter 1 in Greek and English	108
9	The Article	113
10	Verbs: Imperfect Active, Middle, and Passive Indicative; The Imperfect of Εἰμί	116
11	Nouns: The Second Declension; Uses of Nominative Case	124
12	Nouns: The First Declension; Uses of the Dative Case	129
13	Prepositions and Conjunctions; Uses of Prepositional Phrases	136
14	Verbs: Present Active Indicative, Present Middle and Passive; Indicative, and Vowel Contraction	143

15	Personal Pronouns.. 150
16	Other Pronouns:
	Demonstrative, Interrogative, Indefinite, Reflexive, and Relative 155
17	Adjectives of the First and Second Declension;
	Agreement of Adjectives; Attributive and Predicate Positions of Adjectives; Use of an Adjective as a Substantive; The Declension of πᾶς, πολύς, μέγας........ 162
18	Comparison Adjectives, Adverbs, and Genitives;
	Declension of μειζων; Adverbs of Place; and Use of ἤ... 168
19	Verb: First and Second Aorist Tense
	First Aorist Endings on Second Aorist Stems; Constructions with πιστευω; Use of the Aorist Tense; The Aorist of Εἰμί.. 174
20	The Future Active, Middle, and Passive Indicative............ 181
21	The Third Declension;
	Adjectives of the Third Declension..................................... 188
22	Present Participles;
	The Nominative of Appellation; Uses of the Genitive.... 195
23	Aorist Participles; Additional General Uses of Participles;
	Genitive Absolute; More Uses of the Genitive Case........ 203
24	The Perfect and Pluperfect Tenses; Perfect Participle...... 212
25	The Subjunctive Mood;
	Conditional Clauses; Μη Used as a Conjunction; the Subjunctive and ινα; Subjunctive of εἰμί; Review Jn. 1:6-7; Dative of Possession; Purpose Clauses; Inserted Word... 218
26	Imperatives and Infinitives
	Direct and Indirect Discourse; Review Jn. 1:8-10; Word Order in Translation; Use of Italics in Translation; Διά with the Genitive and the

	Expression of Agency.. 228	
27	General Points of Grammar I:	
	ὑπό with the genitive, The Dative of Means, The Negatives οὐ and μή, Various Cases with Verbs, Proper Names; Review Jn. 1:11-13; Pronoun Showing Possession, ἴδιος; Polysemy and the Meaning of Words.. 241	
28	Μι Verbs; Review Jn. 1:14-16;	
	The Meaning of Μονογενῆ, Only-begotten; Flexibility of the word γίνομαι.................................... 246	
29	General Points of Grammar II:	
	The Second Aorist of γινώσκω; The Article Before μέν and δέ; Aorist Participle and Leading Verb; First Aorist on Second Aorist Stems; ἕως and ἄν with Subjunctive; Review of John 1:17-20; Abstract Nouns; The Preposition εἰς; Attributive and Predicate Positions of Adjectives; Consistency in Bible Translation; Uses of ὅτι.. 254	
30	Numbers; Review of John 1:21-24;	
	Implied Information; The Article as a Pronoun............... 260	
31	Review of John 1:25-30	
	εἰ verses εἶ, the Importance of Accent; Personal Pronouns Used for Emphasis; Word Analysis-Preferred or Made; The Historical Present; Figures of Speech in Historical Context; Collocational Clash........................ 266	
32	Review of John 1:31-35	
	Flexibility in Translation; Uses of ἐν with the Dative..... 270	
33	Review John 1:36-40	
	Uses of the Conjunction δέ; Grammatical Structure and Meaning; Word Order; παρά	

	with the Genitive of Person..	274
34	Review of John 1: 41-45	
	The Foundational Method of Bible Translation; Basic Guidelines for Translating Idioms; Figures of Speech; Shifts in Verb Tense; The Word Would.........	279
35	Review of John 1:46-51	
	Adding To or Taking Away from Scripture; Ambiguities; Cultural Substitutes; Anachronisms; The Role of Teachers.............................	292
36	Summary of Greek Grammar...	305
	Abbreviations..	314
	Greek to English Lexicon...	315
	About the Author...	357
	Index...	358
	Notes..	368

4 ὁ δὲ Θεὸς, πλούσιος ὢν ἐν ἐλέει, διὰ τὴν πολλὴν ἀγάπην αὐτοῦ ἣν ἠγάπησεν ἡμᾶς, 5 καὶ ὄντας ἡμᾶς νεκροὺς τοῖς παραπτώμασι συνεζωοποίησε τῷ Χριστῷ (χάριτί ἐστε σεσωσμένοι), 6 καὶ συνήγειρε, καὶ συνεκάθισεν ἐν τοῖς ἐπουρανίοις ἐν Χριστῷ Ἰησοῦ· (Eph. 2:4-6)

How deep the Father's love for us?
How vast beyond all measure?
That He should give His only Son
To make a wretch His treasure

ACKNOWLEDGMENTS AND A SHORT BIBLIOGRAPHY

In producing this grammar, the author would like to acknowledge his debt to the following teachers and their works.

Aristarhos Matsukas. *Greek A Complete Course for Beginners.* London: Hodder & Stoughton Educational. 1997. Print.

Bagster, Samuel. *The Analytical Greek Lexicon.* London: Samuel Bagster and Sons; New York: John Wiley and Son. 1870. Google Facsimile Edition.

Beekman, John and Callow, John. *Translating the Word of God.* Grand Rapids: Zondervan Publishing House. 1974.

Betts, Gavin. *Complete New Testament Greek.* Google Books Edition: 2012.

Burton, Ernest De Witt. *Syntax of the Moods and Tenses in New Testament Greek.* Figment Publishing: figmentdigital.com. 2011. Kindle Edition: Amazon.com.

Donegan, James. *A New Greek and English Lexicon.* Boston: Hilliard, Gray, and Company. 1833. Google Facsimile Edition.

Dongell, Joseph R. *Elementary New Testament Greek.* Wilmore, Ky: Firstfruits Press. 2014. Digital Version: The Academic Open Press of Asbury Theological Seminary. Web.

Douglas Q. Adams. *Essential Modern Greek Grammar.* New York: Dover Publications Inc. 1987. Print.

Frederick Blass, Phil. *Grammar of New Testament Greek.* London: Macmillan and Company. 1898. Google Books Facsimile Edition.

G. Abbott-Smith. *A Manual Greek Lexicon of the New Testament.* New York: Scribner's Sons. 1936. Print.

Goodwin, William W. *A Greek Grammar.* Boston: Ginn and Company. 1900. Google Books Facsimile Edition.

Green, Thomas Sheldon. *A Greek-English Lexicon to The New Testament, Revised and Enlarged.* Project Gutenberg E-book. 2012. Public Domain.

Hara Garoufalia-Middle. *Conversational Greek in 7 Days.* Chicago: Passport Books. 1991. Print.

H. E. Dana and Julius R. Mantey. *A Manual Grammar of the Greek New Testament*. Ontario: The Macmillian Company. 1955. Print.

Hamilton, Henry R. *An English-Greek Lexicon*. London: John Weale. 1855. Google Facsimile Edition.

Hildebrandt, Ted. *Mastering New Testament Greek Textbook*. Grand Rapids: Baker Academic. 2003. Found online at: https://faculty.gordon.edu/hu/bi/ted_hildebrandt/New_Testament_Greek/Mastering_Books/MNTG_Textbook_2017.pdf

https://www.logosapostolic.org/greek/numerals.htm

Machen, J. Gresham. *New Testament Greek for Beginners*. Ontario: The Macmillan Company. 1951. Print.

Metzger, Bruce. *Lexical Aids for Students of New Testament Greek*. Princeton: The Theological Book Agency. 1976. Print.

Moulton, Harold K., ed. *The Analytical Greek Lexicon Revised*. Grand Rapids: Zondervan Publishing House. 1978. Print.

Packhurst, John, M.A. *A Greek and English Lexicon to the New Testament*. London: Thomas Davidson, Whitefriars. 1829. Google Facsimile Edition.

Pappas, John P. *Bible Greek Basic Grammar of the New Testament*. A companion to the video instruction found at Biblegreekvpod.com. 2016. Web.

Pappas, John P. *An Intermediate Grammar for New Testament Greek*. http://www.biblegreekvpod.com/?page_id=77. 2018. Web.

Pickering, John. *A Greek and English Lexicon*. Third edition. Boston: Hilliard, Gray, Little, and Watkins, 1832. Google Facsimile Edition.

Robertson, A. T. *A Grammar of the Greek New Testament in Light of Historical Research*. Kindle Edition. Web.

Rollinson, Shirley J. *Online Greek Textbook*. Portales, NM. Web. 1999. http://www.drshirley.org/greek/textbook02.

Smelser, Jeff. *Three Graduated Courses in New Testament Greek*. Web. ntgreek.net.

Strong, James. Greek in a Nutshell. Kindle Edition: Amazon.com. Originally entered into the Library of Congress 1876. Web.

Strong, James. *Strong's Hebrew and Greek Dictionaries*. 1890. Included in E-sword.net free Bible software download, copyright 2000-2019. Web.

Taylor, Jim. *In Defense of the Textus Receptus.* Theoldpathspublications.com. 2016. Nook Edition.

Thayer, Joseph Henry. *Thayer's Greek Definitions.* 1889. Included in E-sword.net free Bible software download, copyright 2000-2019.

Turner, Charles V. *Biblical Bible Translating.* Lafayette, In: Sovereign Grace Publishers, 2001. Print.

Vance, Lawrence M. *Greek Verbs in the New Testament and their Principal Parts.* Pensacola: Vance Publications. 2006. Print.

Zodhiates, Spiros. *The Complete Word Study Dictionary New Testament.* 2018. Included in E-sword.net free Bible software download, copyright 2000-2019.

And ...

Dr. Robert Gromacki of Cedarville University, Cedarville, Ohio: A great teacher of Greek and the Bible. 1975-1977.

Dr. Jim Taylor, Missionary in Korea, Pastor, Bible Institute Professor, Bible translator, author, and Chief Translation Advisor for Global Bible Translators: for his friendship, his many helpful suggestions, and for reviewing this volume.

AUTHOR'S PREFACE:
THE PURPOSE OF THIS BOOK

As you may have noticed from the Acknowledgments, many Greek grammars have been written. Those listed are only a few of them. Why would I write one more and further choke an already choked field? In my personal opinion, many grammars were written to turn students into critical scholars or to turn students into pastors who can become critics of the Bibles they preach in their own languages and confidently declare to their congregation, "A better translation would be …" I am not trying to create scholars. I am not trying to create doubt in the student, either in the Greek New Testament or in the English KJV. I am trying to turn students into 1) translators who can confidently, accurately, and skillfully translate the word of God into the many languages of the world, 2) to train students who want to learn the New Testament in its original language, 3) to provide a manual that will help Bible Students understand Greek grammar when they use computer Bible tools such as E-sword. After all, God inspired the New Testament in Greek and those inspired Greek words are also the Word of God.

From the start of this book, you should know some things about my use of Greek and Hebrew. First, I do not use Greek and Hebrew to criticize or try to discredit the KJV, as many do. I use these languages to explain and defend the KJV. Second, I do not believe that a Christian must know Greek and Hebrew to understand the Bible or know the will of God. The English Bible (KJV) is completely sufficient to perfect the Christian. This whole book is based on the idea that every Christian needs the Word of God in his own language and the Greek New Testament can help accomplish that. Third, I believe that the Greek New Testament Received Text and the Ben Chayim Hebrew Masoretic Old Testament are the preserved word of God in those languages. The current and accepted form of these texts is the Scrivener 1881 edition of the Received Text and the Ginsburg edition of the Ben Chayim Hebrew Old Testament. Furthermore, I can confidently say that the KJV is not only the best and most accurate English translation of the Greek and Hebrew texts, but it is a completely accurate translation, and it is, therefore, the Word of God in English.

So, now we can go back to our question. There are many grammars of the Greek New Testament. There seems to be no end to them. So, why write another one? Several distinctives in this grammar make it unique.

1. This grammar is based on the Textus Receptus Greek text and specifically uses the Global Edition (2020) of the Scrivener 1881 text. Many of the current grammars embrace modern textual scholarship,

which rejects the Textus Receptus, and their Greek grammars are based on the United Bible Societies critical Greek text or on the Westcott and Hort text.

2.   Most grammars focus on the history of the Greek language in their introductions or prefaces. The introductory section of this grammar focuses on the doctrines of the inspiration and preservation of the Bible and the history of the Greek New Testament. It details the history of the Traditional text (the majority of the ancient handwritten copies), the history of the Textus Receptus printed Greek text that came from the Traditional text (it is also called the Received Text or simply, TR), and how the King James English translation is connected to them. The KJV is included for two reasons. First, it is the only completely accurate representative of the Received Text among popular English translations. Second, the last edition of the TR, the 1881 Scrivener edition, was edited based on revisions in the TR that were made by the KJV translators. All this information (and much more) is also in my book, *A Practical Theology of Bible Translating*.

3.   This grammar is also based on the translation choices of the KJV. We can learn a great deal from the words chosen and the methods used by the KJV translators. The KJV translation team consisted of 47 outstanding scholars. These men had a level of learning and understanding of the original languages that few can rival in the current day. There is nothing known today about the meaning of Greek and Hebrew words that the KJV translators did not know or could not learn. Following the European Renaissance, the Greek learning of the sixteenth and seventeenth centuries came from the Greek speakers of Greek in the Greek Orthodox Church and the inhabitants of Eastern lands, many of whom had fled the invasion of the Muslims into Europe. Knowledge of Hebrew came from the Jews.

4.   This grammar includes the entire text of John 1 in Greek and English. The grammar is based on this chapter for the purpose of enabling translators to translate that and the remainder of the Book of John.

5.   The lessons start with John 1:1 and explain the topics raised by that and succeeding verses. The topics are drawn from the text of the New Testament, along with any additional grammatical points that apply. This necessitates that the topics are covered in a different order than is often used when teaching Greek. However, the overall teaching

will fit together nicely. From time to time, it will be necessary to deviate slightly from this path and we will skip ahead to a verse or verses that bring up topics that need to be addressed before others. Also, sometimes we will look at detailed aspects of Greek that are important but may not fit with a specific verse in John.

6. All aspects of basic grammar will be covered. This method has the advantage of allowing the student to study, understand, and translate words, phrases, and verses in the Greek New Testament quite early in the lessons.

7. Examples and exercises are drawn from the Received Greek Text with only rare exceptions.

8. It is the goal of this text to give the student all the understanding and tools he needs to accurately translate the Book of John. After that experience, he or she will be able to go on to the rest of the New Testament with the help of the Holy Spirit and the advice of the KJB.

9. The book (especially the final chapters) includes instruction on key principles of translating.

Using This Grammar with Computer Programs
Such as E-Sword or The Word

One further very important purpose of this grammar is that it can be used without a formal study of Greek. There are many Christians who would like to know how to use Greek but have not and will not have an opportunity or an inclination to study grammar. This book provides them the information and tools they need to do this.

This book provides instruction in the Robinson Morphological Codes that reveal the part of speech of each Greek word in *free* computer programs such as E-Sword, The Word, and My-Sword. This will make the grammar useful to those who have not and perhaps will not attend a formal class on Greek. It will enable the student and the translator to effectively use the Greek tools available in this free software. They will learn the meaning of different aspects of Greek grammar and how they should be translated. They will be able to identify the grammar by the coding system in e-sword. This will enable them to go beyond mere word studies and definitions and make it possible for them to use the grammar itself.

It is easy to obtain these apps. You can get E-sword at www.e-sword.net, The Word at www.theword.net, and, for Android phones, Mysword can be found by searching "mysword Bible app for android". All of these applications are free to obtain, although there are certain additional features with each that can be purchased. The free portion of the applications are extremely robust and sufficient in and of themselves. E-sword is available for PC, I-phone, I-pad, and Mac. Mysword, a very similar product, is available for Android phones and Android tablets. The Word is available for PC and Mac. Of course, all of this is available for these purposes and at these locations at the time of this writing and could change in the future.

This book is based on E-sword, but it can be used with the other two. If the student has not already downloaded E-sword, please do so with the modules that are listed at the end of this preface. E-sword not only includes Robinsons Morphological Codes, but also several lexicons for Greek and Hebrew Words. The Greek text in the Textus Receptus module, Greek NT TR+, appears as follows.

Joh 1:1 εvG1722 PREP αρχηG746 N-DSF ηvG1510 V-IAI-3S oG3588 T-NSM

The Greek word, αρχη, *arche*, means *beginning*. The number, G746, is the Strong's definition of the word. Put your cursor on the number and the definition pops up. The code, N-DSF, means that αρχη is a **N**oun-**D**ative case, **S**ingular number, **F**eminine gender. There are many such codes. The student needs to know and understand what these codes mean and ways they are translated. The student can learn these things with this book.

Pronunciation, Case System, Paradigms, Accents

The usual system of pronunciation taught in Bible colleges and seminaries is a system that evolved from the one used in the early days of printed Greek texts. However, to use the term *system* (singular) may be a misnomer. There are several systems that have been used over the years and they vary in Greek grammars. The system of pronunciation used in this grammar may also be viewed as a variation, but it has a cultural basis. The official and common Greek spoken and written in Greece today is called Demotic Greek. The system of pronunciation in this grammar is based on Demotic Greek. In other words, it is the pronunciation currently used by actual Greeks.

There are two case systems taught for Greek nouns: a five-case system and an eight-case system. When I was learning Greek at Cedarville University, I first studied from a grammar by J. Gresham Machen. He taught the five-case system. The authors of my intermediate grammar taught the eight-case system. This grammar embraces the five-case system. You should understand that the eight-case system is based on various uses of the nouns, not on actual grammatical forms. In reality, there are only *five different* grammatical noun forms. For that reason, I teach the five-case system.

Many grammars have a section in the back called "paradigms," which is a section that repeats all the declensions and conjugations without the explanatory text. This often makes it easier to look up all the various forms of Greek words. The present volume dispenses with the section on paradigms. The reason for this is that the table of contents makes it easy to find the chapter that contains the declensions and conjugations. Then, in the chapters, you will find it easy to locate the actual forms. The section on paradigms is considered unnecessary.

Greek words carry accent marks, which will be explained later. Often, grammars spend a lot of time on the rules of accent. This grammar does not. Since the emphasis of this grammar is on translating from Greek to other languages, rather than from those languages *into* Greek, it is not deemed necessary to instruct the student on how to properly accent Greek words. Therefore, only minor attention is given to that subject.

A Short History of the Greek Language

Greek is a very ancient language. Scholars have traced Greek writing back about 3500 years, according to Wikipedia.[1] That is interesting, because Javan, the son of Japheth, the son of Noah, founded Greece. Larry Pierceon, in an article written for Answers in Genesis, gave evidence that Egialeus, king of the Greek city of Sicyon, west of Corinthin Peloponnesus, began his reign in 2089 BC.[2] That was about 261 years after the Great Flood of Genesis 6-8. So, the history of the Greek language actually goes back more than 4000 years.

The form of Greek we call "Classical" was prevalent in Greece from about 500 BC to 300 BC. Classical Greek was the language in which the Greek philosophical literature of men like Plato, Epicurus, and Aristotle was written. Classical Greek was divided into several dialects.

Upon the primary foundation of the Attic dialect, a common form of Greek developed within the army of Alexander the Great, who died in 323 BC. This common Greek was spread from Greece to India in the East and to Egypt in the south. We know this common Greek by the name Koine Greek. By the First

Century A. D., it was the dominant form of Greek throughout the Roman Empire and is the language of the New Testament.

About 303 A. D., the Roman Emperor, Constantine, renamed the city of Byzantium (now Istanbul) in Asia Minor to Constantinople. In 359 A.D., it became the capital of the Eastern half of the Roman Empire. Koine was the language of the Eastern Empire at that time. After the fall of the Western half of the Empire about 500 A.D., the Eastern Empire became known as the Byzantine Empire, which lasted until its fall to the Ottoman Turks in 1453 A.D. The Greek of the period 500-1453 AD flowed from Koine and is called Medieval Greek or Byzantine Greek. It was the language of the Government, the people, the Eastern Church, scholarship, the arts, and a common trade language of people of diverse mother tongues. Eventually, Byzantine Greek developed into the current form of common Greek, now called Demotic Greek or Standard Modern Greek.

It is my prayer that this grammar will be a blessing to many and will help produce many excellent translators of the Bible, who also have confidence and trust in the Greek Received Text.

Steve Combs, 2021

CHAPTER ONE
THE INSPIRATION, PRESERVATION,
AND AUTHORITY OF THE BIBLE

All scripture is given by inspiration of God, and is profitable for doctrine, for reproof, for correction, for instruction in righteousness: (2 Tim. 3:16)
For the prophecy came not in old time by the will of man: but holy men of God spake as they were moved by the Holy Ghost. (2 Pet. 1:21)
Man shall not live by bread alone, but by every word that proceedeth out of the mouth of God. (Mat. 4:4)

The very foundation of Bible translating is a firm Biblical conviction about the nature of the Bible itself. God has an extremely high view of Scripture. Every translator must have the exalted view of Scripture that God Himself has. Everything depends on this. The accuracy and clarity of a translation depends on it.

The Bible is a book unlike any other. It gives us the knowledge of God. It is filled with wisdom, it reveals the future, it declares the will of God, and it shows us the plan of God for the salvation of mankind. Its truth makes the philosophies of mankind to appear what they are, foolish. The Bible is the greatest book on psychology ever written. When it speaks of science and history, it is never wrong. The character of the Bible screams to us that it can only come from one source: God Himself. That is what *inspiration* is all about. So, the Bible, the Scriptures, comes to us from God. He has also declared that He will preserve it word-perfect; therefore, the Bible carries the authority of God and we can read it today. This truth was expressed many years ago in the 1689 Baptist Confession of Faith and in the 1646 Westminster Confession of Faith.

> The Old Testament in Hebrew (which was the native language of the people of God of old), and the New Testament in Greek (which at the time of the writing of it was most generally known to the nations), being immediately inspired by God, and by His singular care and providence kept pure in all ages, are therefore authentic; so as in all controversies of religion, the church is finally to appeal to them. [3]

The Scriptures came into the world by inspiration, from that point they were preserved by God's singular care and providence, and they are the final appeal in all matters (authority). When the Scriptures speak, the matter is settled. They are inspired, preserved, and the final authority in all matters.

The Inspiration of the Bible

In the Greek text of 2 Timothy 3:16, the word for *inspiration* is *theopneustos,* and literally means *God breathed*. However, this makes very little sense in English and needs some explanation. It was the Greek's way of saying *inspired by God*. One thing it certainly means is that God is the origin of all Scripture. God is the only author. He used men as His instruments to write the words down, but the words were all from His heart and mind. It has been stated this way: "The perfect author of the perfect Bible is God." [4]

A clear statement of the process and product of inspiration is found in Matthew 4:4: "*Man shall not live by bread alone, but every word that proceedeth out of the mouth of God.*" The words of Scripture proceeded out of God's mouth; they were God-breathed. They may have been spoken by men, they may have been written down by men, but they came out of the mouth of God. Since God is a Spirit (John 4:24), this is a metaphor to help us understand that every word of Scripture comes from God. He is the origin and author of the words, all the words.

We often speak of *verbal plenary* inspiration. That simply means this. *Verbal* inspiration is that God inspired every single individual word. Every separate word is a Word of God. *Plenary* inspiration means all of Scripture, as a whole, is inspired. Nothing in Scripture escapes the label *inspired*. Every word of Scripture and the *whole* is inspired.

The words of God were inspired when they were "*given*" (2 Tim. 3:16). Inspiration points to the time when God first gave them to mankind in Hebrew, Aramaic, and Greek. The term does not belong to any time or period of time afterward. It does not refer to the making of copies and it does not refer to translations. Copies and translations have to do with the *transmission* of Scripture *through* history. Inspiration pertains to the *entrance* of Scripture *into* history. If 2 Timothy 3:16 applies to a copy or translation, then *every time* a translation is made, it is inspired, and *every time* a copy was made it was inspired. If *that* is true, then there would be no mistakes in any copy or translation, because God does not make mistakes. However, some copies have errors and some translations have errors, so they cannot be inspired.

I do not want anyone to misunderstand me here. When people talk about the inspiration of a translation, they are usually referring to the King James Bible. So, do not misunderstand me. I believe the KJB is the Word of God without error. Some may still misunderstand me, because they prefer to call the King James an *accurate* translation, rather than inerrant. Indeed, it is accurate. But what does that mean? The word accurate is defined as "free from error especially as the result of care." [5] If the KJB is an *accurate* translation (and it is), then, by definition, it is *without error*. However, it is not the accurate Word of God by *inspiration*. It is the accurate Word of God by *providentially guided translation* of the words that were given by inspiration and then preserved.

Some think that the KJV is inspired because 2 Timothy 3:16 uses the present tense, "*is given*." I presume, they reason that if it refers only to the first giving of Scripture, it would say "was given." Since it says "*is given*" that means *inspiration* applied when the KJB translation was "given." It stands to reason, if that is true, that inspiration applies *whenever any* copy or translation is "given" (see comment above).

However, that is not the reason why the KJB and the Greek text use the present tense. The reason is this. *At the time* Paul wrote 2 Timothy 3:16 *the canon of Scripture was not yet complete.* At the time, inspiration was still occurring. Therefore, the present tense is used. At that time, God was still planning to inspire more Scripture. For example, the Book of Revelation had not yet been written. Inspiration, then, applies to the miraculous work of God whereby He *first gave* the Scriptures in Hebrew, Aramaic, and Greek.

How did God give Scripture and how did He use men to do it? God used various methods. The Scriptures themselves give us some additional information and examples of what God did. Foremost among them is 2 Peter 1:16-21.

> *16 For we have not followed cunningly devised fables, when we made known unto you the power and coming of our Lord Jesus Christ, but were eyewitnesses of his majesty.*
> *17 For he received from God the Father honour and glory, when there came such a voice to him from the excellent glory, This is my beloved Son, in whom I am well pleased.*
> *18 And this voice which came from heaven we heard, when we were with him in the holy mount.*
> *19 We have also a more sure word of prophecy; whereunto ye do well that ye take heed, as unto a light that shineth in a dark place, until the day dawn, and the day star arise in your hearts:*
> *20 Knowing this first, that no prophecy of the scripture is of any private interpretation.*
> *21 For the prophecy came not in old time by the will of man: but holy men of God spake as they were moved by the Holy Ghost. (2 Peter 1:16-21)*

God started with holy men. The Spirit of God "moved" these men to speak words that He chose. These words were written down by an assistant who was listening. An example of this is found in Jeremiah 36.

> *1 And it came to pass in the fourth year of Jehoiakim the son of Josiah king of Judah, that this word came unto Jeremiah from the LORD, saying,*
> *2 Take thee a roll of a book, and write therein all the words that I have spoken unto thee against Israel, and against Judah, and against all the nations, from the day I spake unto thee, from the days of Josiah, even unto this day.*
> *3 It may be that the house of Judah will hear all the evil which I purpose to do unto them; that they may return every man from his evil way; that I may forgive their iniquity and their sin.*
> *4 Then Jeremiah called Baruch the son of Neriah: and Baruch wrote from the mouth of Jeremiah all the words of the LORD, which he had spoken unto him, upon a roll of a book.* (Jer. 36:1-4)

Even Paul used the speaking method. Romans 16:22 says, "I *Tertius, who wrote this epistle, salute you in the Lord.*" The letter was sent to Rome from Paul, not Tertius. Paul spoke the words of the letter and Tertius was his assistant writing it down.

However, Paul seems to have written some of his work himself. 1 Corinthians 16:1 tells us, "*The salutation of me Paul with mine own hand.*" Paul wrote the greeting himself, otherwise it appears the same procedure was used. "*Ye see how large a letter I have written unto you with mine own hand*" (Gal. 6:11). It has been suggested that Paul wrote the end of the epistle to the Galatians and used large letters because he had eye trouble (Gal. 4:15). Regardless, at times Paul wrote himself and at times he dictated to an assistant.

A similar method was used to give the law in Deuteronomy. Moses spoke all the law to Israel and Moses Himself wrote the words (Deut. 31:9).

When dealing with this subject, commentators usually reject out of hand the so-called dictation theory; that God dictated the Scriptures. Yet, that is exactly what God did for *part* of the Scriptures. For example, God dictated the ten commandments and wrote them Himself on tables of stone (Ex. 34:1). God also dictated the law and commanded it to be written down (Ex. 17:14; 24:4; 34:27; Num. 5:23). Much of the Prophecies are written from indirect dictation; dictated by God to the prophets, spoken aloud by the prophets, and written by a secretary. That was the method used in Jeremiah 36.

At other times, especially with narratives of events, God seems to have put into the hearts of the writers the words they should write. "*And Moses wrote their goings out according to their journeys by the commandment of the LORD: and these are their journeys according to their goings out*" (Num. 33:2).

In whatever way God gave the word, it was given by the miracle of inspiration. The Words were given by God. In whatever way the prophets and Apostles were "*moved*" (2 Peter 2:21), it was the Holy Spirit who moved them. They were led by the Spirit. "*The Spirit of the LORD spake by me, and his word was in my tongue*" (2 Sam. 23:2). Because of this, we must conclude that it is not just the meaning of the words that matter, it is the words themselves. When one is translating the Bible, he must be concerned about the meaning of the text and about the meaning of each word. *God cares about each of His words.*

> **Psalms 12:6** *The words of the Lord are* **pure words**
> **Psalms 119:103** *How sweet are* **thy words** *unto my taste! yea, sweeter than honey to my mouth!*
> **Psalms 119:130** *The entrance of* **thy words** *giveth light; it giveth understanding unto the simple.*
> **Psalms 138:4** *All the kings of the earth shall praise thee, O LORD, when they hear the* **words of thy mouth.**
> **Deuteronomy 4:2** *Ye shall not add unto* **the word** *which I command you, neither shall ye diminish ought from it, that ye may keep* **the commandments** *of the LORD your God which I command you.*
> **Proverbs 30:6** *Add thou not unto* **his words**, *lest he reprove thee, and thou be found a liar.*
> **John 3:34** *For he whom God hath sent speaketh the* **words of God:** *for God giveth not the Spirit by measure unto him.*
> **Revelation 17:17** *For God hath put in their hearts to fulfil his will, and to agree, and give their kingdom unto the beast, until the* **words of God** *shall be fulfilled.*
> **Revelation 22:19** *And if any man shall take away from the* **words of the book** *of this prophecy, God shall take away his part out of the book of life, and out of the holy city, and from the things which are written in this book.*

Inspiration is the miraculous work of God whereby He gave His Hebrew, Aramaic, and Greek words to men, through human instruments. He gave His words in various ways, including 1) holy men spoke the words as they were moved by the Holy Spirit and an assistant wrote the spoken words, 2) God dictated some of the words, particularly much of the Law and prophets. Moses and the prophets, who heard the words from God, spoke to them and what they said was written down or, as with Moses and the Law, they wrote the words directly from the mouth of God, 3) God gave some men the words in their hearts and they wrote them down, and 4) God even wrote some of the words Himself. God did all this in such a way that every word he gave is His, a part of Him, perfect, and carries His divine authority.

The Divine Preservation of the Scriptures

The inspiration of the Scriptures would mean nothing, and it would be impossible for mankind to live by the Words of God, if God did not *preserve* His words. This should be self-evident, but many miss it. Nevertheless, the Scriptures make it clear that God has preserved His words.

> *But continue thou in the things which thou hast learned and hast been assured of, knowing of whom thou hast learned them; And that from a child thou hast known the holy scriptures, which are able to make thee wise unto salvation through faith which is in Christ Jesus.*(2 Tim. 3:15-16)

Timothy had the Scriptures, but the copies he had were not the original writings. The original pen, paper, and ink had long since perished. Contrary to what some have said, there is no evidence Timothy was using a Greek Old Testament translation (designated LXX). Timothy had copies of the Hebrew Old Testament. Paul called these copies "holy scriptures" indicating that they had been copied accurately. God had preserved His word.

The Fact of Providential Preservation

Many have long denied that the Bible teaches the providential preservation of Scripture. Nowadays, some have adapted their teaching to include preservation. I suspect this is because of all the Bible believing voices that have been raised in its favor. However, many have limited preservation to the "message" of Scripture and have not applied it to the "words." Following are a few of the verses that teach the Biblical doctrine of the providential preservation of the Word of God.

> **1 Peter 1:23** Being born again, not of corruptible seed, but of incorruptible, by the **Word of God** which **liveth and abideth forever**.
>
> **Psalm 12:6-7** The **words** of the Lord are pure words: as silver tried in a furnace of earth, purified seven times. Thou shalt keep them, O Lord, thou shalt preserve them **from this generation forever**.

Ps. 111:7-8 The works of his hands are verity and judgment; all **his commandments** are sure. **They stand fast for ever and ever**, and are done in truth and uprightness.
Is. 40:8 The grass withereth, the flower fadeth: but the **word** of our God **shall stand for ever.**
Ps. 117:2 ... **the truth** of the Lord **endureth for ever**. Praise ye the Lord.
Ps. 119:152 Concerning thy **testimonies**, I have known of old that thou hast **founded them for ever.**
Ps 119:160 Thy **word** is true from the beginning: and every one of thy righteous judgments **endureth for ever.**
Matthew 24:35 Heaven and earth shall pass away, but **my words shall not pass away.**
Psalm 33:11 The **counsel** of the Lord **standeth forever**, the **thoughts** of his heart **to all generations**.
Psalm 100:5 For the Lord is good; his mercy is everlasting; and his **truth** endureth to **all generations**.
Ps 119:89-90 For ever, O LORD, thy **word** is settled in heaven. Thy **faithfulness** is unto **all generations**: thou hast established the earth, and it abideth.
Psalms 119:160 ¶Thy word is true from the beginning: and every one of thy righteous **judgments endureth for ever**.
Matthew 5:18 For verily I say unto you, Till heaven and earth pass, one **jot or one tittle** shall in no wise pass from the law, **till all be fulfilled**.
Isaiah 59:21 As for me this is my covenant with them, saith the Lord; My spirit that is upon thee, and my words which I have put in thy mouth, **shall not pass** out of the thy mouth, nor out of the mouth of thy seed, nor out of the mouth of thy seed's seed saith the Lord, from henceforth and forever.

These are just a few verses that prove providential preservation is a fact. What do we learn from these verses? We learn His Word is kept for all generations (Psalm 33:11; Psalm 100:5; Ps 119:89-90). His Word has been kept for *us*, for our good (Is. 59:21). The preservation of the Word of God is a series of supernatural acts by the Lord Himself (Ps. 12:6-7). The Word is alive, with the life of God, which is forever (1 Peter 1:23; Heb. 4:12). Perhaps it would be more easily understood if we viewed in graphical form. Below is a chart that presents the doctrinal foundation of providential preservation in just such a manner.

References	What will be preserved?	How long?
1 Peter 1:23; Is. 40:8 Ps. 119:160; Ps. 119:89-90	The Word of God	Forever
Mt. 24:35	Christ's Words	Never pass away
Ps. 12:6-7; Is. 59:21	God's Words	Forever
Ps. 111:7-8	His Commandments	Forever and ever
Ps. 119:152	His Testimonies	Forever
Ps. 33:11	His Counsel	Forever
Ps. 33:11	His Thoughts	To all generations
Ps. 100:5	His Truth	To all generations
Ps.119:160	His judgments	Forever
Mt. 5:18	Every Jot and Tittle	Till all be fulfilled
Ps. 119:89-90	His Faithfulness	To all generations

Fig. 1

Finally, some point to Psalms 119:89, "*For ever, O LORD, thy word is settled in heaven,*" and say that preservation is only in Heaven. However, Isaiah 59:21 counters that idea by explaining "*my words which I have put in thy mouth,* **shall not pass out of the thy mouth, nor out of the mouth of thy seed**, *nor out of the mouth of thy seed's seed* saith the Lord, from henceforth and forever." God's Words will not only be in Heaven, but they will be *in the mouth of people* forever. The Words of God are for us to live by. "*And* **these words**, *which I command thee this day,* **shall be in thine heart**" (Deut. 6:6).

The Definition of the Biblical Doctrine of the Providential Preservation of the Word of God

Providential Preservation is a Biblical doctrine, and it is proved by the Scriptures I have listed, along with many others. The Doctrine of Providential Preservation states:

> God has *promised* to *miraculously preserve forever* all of His Word, His individual words, and all His teachings with the words in which they are expressed. He has further promised to make them available to mankind for our good and for our lives. He has determined to do this in His own way depending on Himself alone. (Author)

We may not understand how God has done this. We may be confused by all the unbelieving statements made by modern textual critics. Nevertheless, our responsibility is to *"Trust in the LORD with all thine heart; and lean not unto thine own understanding"* (Prov. 3:3). We may not be able to see how God has preserved each of His Words, but we can rest assured that He has done so, based on His own statements and promises.

Just as the Bible teaches verbal plenary inspiration, these verses teach *verbal plenary preservation*. Each individual word is preserved and the entire body of the 66 books of Scripture is preserved.

Take special note of *what words* have been preserved. The words that were inspired were Hebrew, Aramaic, and Greek words. They were not English, German, Spanish, or any other language. When God made the promises of preservation, the words He promised to preserve were Hebrew, Aramaic, and Greek words. He did not promise to preserve English, Spanish, German, or any other language words. This is evident by the Scriptures themselves: *"Till heaven and earth pass, **one jot or one tittle** shall in no wise pass from the law, till all be fulfilled"* (Mt 5:18). The jot (yod) is the smallest Hebrew letter, and the tittle is a small part a Hebrew letter. The promise in Matthew 5:18 is to preserve words of Scripture in the Hebrew language. Clearly the Lord's promise is to preserve the Hebrew, Greek, and Aramaic words he inspired.

> Jesus taught that the same Divine providence which had preserved the Old Testament would preserve the New Testament ... The Holy Spirit providentially guided churches to preserve His Words during the manuscript period. **First,** faithful scribes produced many trustworthy copies of the original New Testament manuscripts. **Second,** these trustworthy copies were read and recopied by true believers down through the centuries. **Third,** untrustworthy copies were not so generally read or so frequently recopied. Although they enjoyed some popularity for a time, yet in the long run they were laid aside and consigned to oblivion. Thus, as a result of this special providential guidance, the true text won out in the end, and today the believer may be sure that the text found in the vast majority of the Greek New Testament manuscripts, preserved by the God-guided usage of the Greek churches, is a trustworthy reproduction of the Divinely inspired original. Some have called it the Byzantine text, thereby acknowledging that it was the text in use in the Greek churches during the greater part of the Byzantine period (452-1453). It is much better, however, to call this text

the Traditional Text because this text, which is found in the great majority of Greek New Testament manuscripts, has been handed down ... to the present day.[6]

The Authority of the Scriptures

The Word of God came from God. It had its origin in Him. Therefore, it was perfect when it was inspired, because God is perfect and makes no mistakes. Finally, God has preserved it, and because He never fails, it has been preserved perfect. Notice how God exalts the Word.

> *I will worship toward thy holy temple, and praise thy name for thy lovingkindness and for thy truth:* ***for thou hast magnified thy word above all thy name.*** *(Psalms 138:2)*

> *O LORD our Lord, how excellent is thy name in all the earth! who hast set thy glory above the heavens.* (Psalms 8:1)

If God has exalted His Word above His name, then His view of the Word is so high it is immeasurable. The glory of His name is especially important to God, but His Word is in a higher place. Consider that. His glory is above the Heavens! His Word is higher! How much must we exalt His Word and hold it precious? How much ought we to support efforts to translate His Word into every language?

Consider this. There was a time in history when people held their reputation to be of highest importance. When they gave their word, they kept their word. If they broke their word, their reputation would be lost. "A good name is rather to be chosen than great riches" (Proverbs 22:1).

Consider this. The glory of God's name depends on Him keeping His Word.

Consider, the nature of God's Word.

> *And **the scripture, foreseeing** that God would justify the heathen through faith, **preached** before the gospel unto Abraham, saying, In thee shall all nations be blessed.* (Gal. 3:8)

> *For the scripture **saith unto Pharaoh**, Even for this same purpose have I raised thee up, that I might shew my power in thee, and that my name might be declared throughout all the earth.* (Romans 9:17)

*For the Word of God is **quick**, and powerful* (Heb. 4:12)

There are some important truths I want to note from these verses.

There was no written Scripture when God gave the message in Galatians 3 and Romans 9 to Abraham and Pharaoh. The Scriptures had not been written, except possibly the Book of Job. Yet, Paul said it was the Scriptures which spoke. It was God who spoke. The word *Scriptures* was substituted for the word *God*. This indicates that whenever God speaks to men in words that will eventually be written, His voice and words are Scripture. They proceed out of His mouth. They are God-breathed. The Scriptures are part of God. Therefore, the Scriptures are as true as God is, and the Scriptures are as authoritative as the "King of kings and Lord of lords."

The Scriptures are given the characteristics of God. In Galatians 3:8, the Scriptures exhibit foreknowledge and prophecy. In Romans 9:17, the Scriptures raise a man up, have a purpose, and glorify God's name. In Hebrews 4:12, the Word of God is alive (the word *quick* means *alive*) and powerful. Where does it get its life and power? Obviously, the Scriptures have all these characteristics because they are *part of God*. Sure, we know that it was God who said and did these things. However, by using the word "Scripture," God is showing the greatness and uniqueness of His words. They are not only *from Him*, but they are *a part of Him*, of who and what He is; just as your words are part of you.

Perhaps this should be enough to convince one and all that the Word of God carries God's authority, but there is much more. God's Word must be handled with great care, faith, respect, honor, and submission. This is the only safe way to handle God's Words. We should have this attitude toward every single Word of God. We must not treat God's Words flippantly.

There are many English versions that do treat God's Words flippantly. Let me give you an example from Psalm 138:1-3 in an English translation called *The Message*.

(**KJB**) I will praise thee with my whole heart: before the gods will I sing praise unto thee.
2 I will worship toward thy holy temple, and praise thy name for thy lovingkindness and for thy truth: for thou hast magnified thy word above all thy name.
3 In the day when I cried thou answeredst me, and strengthenedst me with strength in my soul.

(**Message**) Thank you! Everything in me says "Thank you!" Angels   listen   as   I   sing   my   thanks.

> I kneel in worship facing your holy temple and say it again: "Thank you!"
> Thank you for your love, thank you for your faithfulness;
> Most holy is your name, most holy is your Word.
> The moment I called out, you stepped in; you made my life large with strength.

The Message is a complete adulteration of the Words of God. There is no correlation with the exactly translated words of the KJV. words of the message came from human imagination. The Message (along with other versions) has substituted the uninspired words of men in place of the Words of God. By doing this, they are hiding the Words God chose to use from people. We must always handle the words that God inspired with great reverence. When we translate them, we must take care to determine the exact translation of every word.

God's Word is truth. Jesus said, *"Thy word is truth."* Everything God has said is true from beginning to end. Some have said that the Bible has errors of fact, but it is still the Word of God. Poppycock! If anything is an error of fact, it is not God's Word. When men say that they value the word of men more than the Word of God. No matter what subject the Bible speaks on, be it any discipline of science, psychology, medicine, dietary advice, history, government, religion, or any other subject, it is true.

Some Christian leaders water down the Bible's authority. I ran across two quotes that show, in some measure, how far we have departed from the authority of the Bible. This preacher seems to be advising us to not reference the chapter and verse when we quote Scripture. Rather, he thinks it is better to simply say, "Jesus says" or "Paul says."

> I would ask preachers, pastors, and student pastors in their communication to get the spotlight off the Bible and back on the resurrection. Let's get people's attention back on Jesus as soon as possible, that the issue for us is always who is Jesus, [and] did He rise from the dead? And that we would leverage the authority we have in the resurrection as opposed to Scripture, not because I don't believe Scripture's inspired in terms of reaching this culture. [7]

It's time to stop saying, "the Bible says." At least according to Andy Stanley.

At Exponential, a church-planting conference attended by 5,000 in late spring (with another 20,000 watching via video), the senior pastor of North Point Community Church in Alpharetta, Georgia, said pastors should instead use phrases like "Paul says" and "Jesus says" when citing Scripture. [8]

All the authority of a preacher, the authority of Paul and Peter, was derived solely from the Bible. If you denigrate the Bible, you undermine your own authority. If you weaken the Bible's authority, you lose your own authority to preach, because that's where you got your commission. God's Word is His written authority on earth.

The following verses teach a number of truths about the sufficiency of God's Word:

1) God's Word is to be obeyed

   9 Wherewithal shall a young man cleanse his way? by taking heed thereto according to thy word.
   10 With my whole heart have I sought thee: O let me not wander from thy commandments.
   11 Thy word have I hid in mine heart, that I might not sin against thee. (Ps. 119:9-11)

2) The Word of God sheds light on our path.

   Thy word is a lamp unto my feet, and a light unto my path. Ps. 119:105

3) Those who walk according to God's Word are blessed.

   Blessed are the undefiled in the way, who walk in the law of the LORD.
   2 Blessed are they that keep his testimonies, and that seek him with the whole heart.
   3 They also do no iniquity: they walk in his ways. (Ps 119:1-3)

4) It should be the desire of our hearts to learn his word.

   Blessed art thou, O LORD: teach me thy statutes. (Ps. 119:12)

5) His Word should be a joy to our hearts.

   I have rejoiced in the way of thy testimonies, as much as in all riches. (Ps. 119:14)

> *Thy words were found, and I did eat them; and thy word was unto me the joy and rejoicing of mine heart: for I am called by thy name, O LORD God of hosts.* (Jer. 15:16)

Before we conclude this chapter, let's go back to 2 Timothy 3:16 and quote it again along with verse 17.

> 16 *All scripture is given by inspiration of God, and is profitable for doctrine, for reproof, for correction, for instruction in righteousness:*
> 17 *That the man of God may be perfect, throughly furnished unto all good works.*

The Word of God is profitable for four things: doctrine, reproof, correction, and instruction in righteousness.

It is profitable for doctrine. That is, it teaches you what is real and right, thereby helping you to make sense of the world around you, even when that world is in a mess. It teaches what is true and false and thereby, enables you to escape deception. It teaches you the will of God, thereby helping you choose the right path on which to walk, to know what is right, and to avoid the traps of sin. It makes you to understand God, who He is and what He is like. It helps you get to know Him.

It is profitable for reproof. None of us does the right thing all the time. Sometimes we fail and we need to be rebuked for it. "For the commandment is a lamp; and the law is light; and reproofs of instruction are the way of life" (Prov. 6:23). Starting as a child, it seems we always have someone telling us we are wrong. This is the way of life and it is good, especially if the rebuke comes from God's Word. "He is in the way of life that keepeth instruction: but he that refuseth reproof erreth" (Prov. 10:17). "Preach the word; be instant in season, out of season; reprove, rebuke, exhort with all longsuffering and doctrine" (2 Tim. 4:2).

It is profitable for correction. When you are wrong, the Word of God sets you right. "My son, despise not the chastening of the LORD; neither be weary of his correction" (Prov. 3:11). "Correction is grievous unto him that forsaketh the way: and he that hateth reproof shall die" (Prov. 15:10). The Word of God shows you where you went wrong (reproof) and it shows you how to get right with God again and keep on walking with Him. "For a just man falleth seven times, and riseth up again: but the wicked shall fall into mischief" (Prov. 24:16).

It is profitable for instruction in righteousness. "Teach me good judgment and knowledge: for I have believed thy commandments" (Ps. 119:66).

"Make thy face to shine upon thy servant; and teach me thy statutes" (Ps. 119:132). "Teach me to do thy will; for thou art my God: thy spirit is good; lead me into the land of uprightness" (Ps. 143:10). "The fear of the LORD is the beginning of knowledge: but fools despise wisdom and instruction" (Ps. 1:7).

The Navigators have a good way of explaining these things:

> ***Doctrine*** – The Bible teaches us what the right path is.
> ***Reproof*** – The Bible tells us when we have gotten off the right path.
> ***Correction*** – The Bible tells us how to get back on the right path.
> ***Instruction in righteousness*** – The Bible tells us how to stay on the right path.

Conclusion

The Bible is God's book. It is full of God's Words. The Words of God entered history through the miraculous process of inspiration. Those words were given in Hebrew, Aramaic, and Greek. Eventually the writings were gathered into scrolls and books. The writings, the Scriptures, were perfect when God inspired them and had them written down. The writings were perfect. God has preserved them throughout history in the same perfect condition in which they were given. All the words of God have survived, and God has made them available to us. We know this because He said that we must "live by every word that proceedeth out of the mouth of God." The Word of God, given by inspiration and kept pure by preservation, is our authority and guide in all issues and matters of life.

The Bible is clear on the power and importance of God's Word. All His words are powerful, precious, and exalted. A translator must bear that in mind when he translates the Bible. Remember, these are the words that God has chosen. He does not take it lightly when you change them or substitute other words for what he has said.

CHAPTER TWO
THE TRADITIONAL GREEK TEXT OF THE NEW TESTAMENT

8 The words of the LORD are pure words: as silver tried in a furnace of earth, purified seven times.
7 Thou shalt keep them, O LORD, thou shalt preserve them from this generation for ever. (Ps. 12:6-7)

The KJB was translated from the Received Greek Text. The Received Text (or Textus Receptus in Latin) is a printed Greek New Testament that is based on the vast majority of ancient hand-written New Testament manuscripts. That vast array of evidence is called the Traditional Text.

The Traditional New Testament Text

The last New Testament book, the Book of Revelation, was written by the Apostle John under the inspiration of God in about 98 AD. In the following centuries, the New Testament books were copied and recopied by hand many times. They were also translated into several languages. Now, we have over 5,700 pieces of New Testament evidence copied at various times over the centuries from about 100 AD to 1600+ AD. These pieces of evidence are all handwritten and range from fragments to nearly complete copies of the New Testament. They also include ancient lectionaries (guides used in church services that contain Scripture). In addition, there are ancient translations and Scripture quotations by early church writers. About 94% of the evidence agrees and the manuscripts in this category are called the *Traditional Text* or the *Byzantine Text* or the *Majority Text*. It is called the Traditional text because it can be traced back to about 100 AD. in the early writers, lectionaries, fragments found, and in ancient versions, such as the Syriac Peshitta Version (150 AD) and the Old Latin (120-150 AD). These ancient documents trace the existence of the Traditional Text continuously from very close to the lives of the Apostles to about 1600. Since there are translations from the Traditional Greek Text dated at 150 AD, the text must have existed for a considerable time before that. This strongly indicates that the traditional Greek text is the true text penned by the Apostles and their associates.

Currently we are in the middle of a great conflict between two major textual traditions. One is the Traditional text, which is our subject in this chapter. The other, opposing tradition, is the Alexandrian Text, which represents many of the remaining ancient manuscripts. The outstanding examples of the Alexandrian Text are Codex Vaticanus and Codex Sinaiticus. Another Alexandrian manuscript is Codex Alexandrinus, which is a mixed type, having readings from both the traditional Text and from the Alexandrian. Vaticanus and Sinaiticus have been dated about 350 AD. It is said they are the oldest nearly complete manuscripts of the New Testament, and, therefore, they are closest to the originals and that makes them the best. In actuality, they are not the oldest witnesses to the New Testament text, as I pointed out in the previous paragraph.

One of the greatest champions of the Traditional Text was John W. Burgon (1813-1888), Dean of Chichester Cathedral in England. When Dean Burgon died in 1888, he left a certain amount of his work unfinished. His associate, Edward Miller, gathered his materials and edited them to produce the book, *The Traditional Text of the Holy Gospels Vindicated and Established*. He espoused certain principles for the examination of ancient documents of the Bible. These were Bible believing principles. They sharply contrasted with the principles of his contemporaries, Westcott and Hort, who thought that older is better and treated the Bible like it is any other ordinary book. The list of the principles is as follows:

1. Antiquity;
2. Consent of Witnesses, or Number;
3. Variety of Evidence;
4. Respectability of Witnesses, or Weight;
5. Continuity, or Unbroken Tradition;
6. Evidence of the Entire Passage, or Context;
7. Internal Considerations, or Reasonableness. [9]

The Traditional Text and Its Antiquity

Antiquity has to do with how far back in history a particular text can be traced. This is an important consideration, but it is not the only one and, alone, it does not settle the matter. Even though, we can't depend on age alone, there are other factors and, when they are taken along with age, they can settle the issue.

The reason age alone is not sufficient is because of 2 Corinthians 2:17, *"For we are not as many, which corrupt the word of God."* Manuscripts bearing severe heretical corruptions appeared early in Church history. Therefore, the oldest manuscript in existence may not be the best. In addition, the true New Testament text would be available to Christians all through the church age. It would not show up magically 1800 years after the birth of Christ. As we have seen, God inspired the New Testament to win people to Him and teach us how to live. Therefore, we must have it in every stage of history. As Jesus promised to be with us every day until the end of the world (Mt. 28:19-20), we need His Word every day to know His will. Remember, God has preserved every word, every day, all the way through history. In addition, He preserved them for our use. Therefore, they have been available to believers all along, not left lying in some hidden, dusty, moldy manuscript recently brought to light. So, a massive and widespread testimony of agreeing manuscripts stretching over a span of centuries and showing up in a variety of sources all displaying consistency is a powerful testimony to authenticity.

Nevertheless, antiquity is the first consideration. Scholars have divided ancient manuscripts into several "types." The main divisions are Alexandrian (the source is Egypt), Western (used in Rome), and Traditional (also called Byzantine or Majority Text). Generally, scholars say the Alexandrian text is best (this idea was promoted by the Westcott and Hort). These types are based on distinctive and different words and phrases (readings) in various verses. For example, the Traditional Text manuscript says, "only begotten son" in John 1:18 and another text says, "only begotten god." Today, Western and Alexandrian readings have been combined to help create the Nestles and United Bible Societies Greek texts, which are generally called "Alexandrian," because that influence is greater.

It must also be noted that many ancient manuscripts are of a "mixed" type. Many of these "mixed" manuscripts are placed in the Alexandrian category by scholars. In my opinion, this is due to their personal prejudice that the Alexandrian is best. One of those mixed manuscripts is Codex W of the Gospels, which is dated in the 4th or early 5th century. The Book of Matthew and the last two-thirds of Luke are of the Traditional type. This is significant because Westcott and Hort popularized the theory that a group in Antioch constructed the Traditional text in the 4th century.

> The discovery of W tends to disprove the thesis of Westcott and Hort that the Traditional Text is a fabricated text which was put together in the 4th century by a group of scholars residing at Antioch. For Codex W is a very ancient manuscript. B. P. Grenfell regarded it as "probably fourth century." (3) Other scholars have dated it in the 5th century. Hence W is one of the oldest complete manuscripts of the Gospels in existence, possibly of the same age as Aleph (Sinaiticus-Author). Moreover, W seems to have been written in Egypt, since during the first centuries of its existence it seems to

have been the property of the Monastery of the Vinedresser, which was located near the third pyramid. If the Traditional Text had been invented at Antioch in the 4th century, how would it have found its way into Egypt and thence into Codex W so soon thereafter? Why would the scribe of W, writing in the 4th or early 5th century, have adopted this newly fabricated text in Matthew and Luke in preference to other texts which (according to Hort's hypothesis) were older and more familiar to him? Thus the presence of the Traditional Text in W indicates that this text is a very ancient text and that it was known in Egypt before the 4th century. [10]

Antiquity and the Papyri

Other evidence also supports the existence of the Traditional type of text early in church history. Another mixed text is the Chester Beatty Papyri (200-250 AD). Dr. Hills said, "When the Chester Beatty Papyri were published (1933-37), it was found that these early 3rd century fragments agree surprisingly often with the Traditional (Byzantine) Text against all other types of text." [11]

Even Codex Alexandrinus (Codex A) is a witness to the Traditional Text in the Gospels. It is dated in the 5th century and was written in Egypt. So, the text witnesses to the fact that the Traditional Text was in Egypt at an early date.

Another example of a mixed text is Papyrus 90, dated 2nd century AD, somewhere between 100 and 200 AD. The scholars have classified P 90 as Alexandrian, but it is as much Traditional as it is Alexandrian. [12]

Then there is the Magdalen Papyrus 64, fragments of Matthew 26. P 64 consists of three small fragments acquired in 1901, in Luxor Egypt, by Egyptologist Charles Bousfield Huleatt. He presented them to the Magdalen College, Oxford. The fragments contain part of Matthew 26:7, 8, 10, 14, 15. **The fragments are dated 50 AD.** These fragments are categorized as Alexandrian. It is said, "Without any variant of the text Eberhard Nestle and Kurt Aland." [13] However, I have examined the fragments and compared them to the Received Text. *P 64, 50 AD, is a perfect match to the Textus Receptus!*

Next, let's take a look at Papyrus 52 from the John Rylands Library. P52 is a piece of the Gospel of John written on front and back containing John 18:31-33 and John 18:37-38. Once again, P 52 was found in Egypt. There is a disagreement among scholars as to what date to assign P52. Some say it is dated 100-150 AD. Others think it should be 125-175 AD. In either case, it is assigned to the second century.

So, what do we find with P 52? My conclusions here are based on my own comparison of P 52 with the Received Text. I will start with a base conclusion that there are differences between P 52 and the Received Text. There are three differences. Does that mean P 52 is a different kind of text? No, but the scholars have left P52 uncategorized. The three differences are as follows.

Verse	P 52	Received Text
1-18:31	Emein	Emin
2-18:32	iselthein	Eiselthen
3-18:33	O P (following prait**or**ion)	praitorion palin o pilatos

Fig. 2

The first two differences are clearly different spelling, but they are the same words. The third instance is unclear. The scholars think the "O P" are part of "o pilatos." This would mean P 52 left out or the TR added "palin." However, the simplest conclusion is that O P was for "o palin," not "o pilatos." That would mean, the scribe misplaced the "O." Both possibilities are equally plausible. This kind of error would not be unusual in handwritten manuscripts. That sort of thing obviously happens. In the space of this small paragraph, I have made several errors and had to correct them. 1800 years ago, when one was writing with pen and ink on papyrus, corrections were not easy to do. *My conclusion is that the spelling differences are inconsequential and the third may be a scribal error. There is as much reason to believe P 52 is Traditional text as Alexandrian.*

I will give you one more example of the Papyri. **Papyrus 32** is also in the John Rylands University Library. It contains Titus 1:11-15 and 2:3-8. It is classified as Alexandrian. The scholars think it shows agreement with Sinaiticus. I also checked P32 against the Received Text. Except for one spelling difference the two are *exactly the same*. The spelling difference consists of one letter, a nu (N) instead of a Rho (P), which could easily be a scribal error. *In other words, there is as much reason, maybe more, to believe P 32 is Traditional Text as there is to think it is Alexandrian.* P32 is dated 200 AD.

Other Evidence of Antiquity

We have also seen that evidence from ancient translations also supports the Traditional Text. The Peshitta Syriac is dated about 150 AD and has a Traditional type text for the most part. The Sinaitic Syriac is traditional in type and is dated in the 3rd century. The Gothic version was based on the

Traditional Text and translated about 350 AD. All of this proves that the Traditional Text is a very early text.

Dr. Edward Hills studied the textual criticism of the New Testament. He graduated from Yale University, Westminster Theological Seminary, Columbia University, and Harvard University (under the supervision of the famous textual scholar, Kirsopp Lake). Having studied textual criticism, he came to this conclusion.

> The making of these two texts (Western and Alexandrian-author) proceeded, for the most part, according to two entirely different plans. The scribes that produced the Western text regarded themselves more as interpreters than as mere copyists. Therefore they made bold alterations in the text and added many interpolations. The makers of the Alexandrian text, on the other hand, conceived of themselves as grammarians. Their chief aim was to improve the style of the sacred text. They made few additions to it. Indeed, their fear of interpolation was so great that they often went to the opposite extreme of wrongly removing genuine readings from the text ...
>
> As all scholars agree, the Western text was the text of the Christian Church at Rome and the Alexandrian text that of the Christian scribes and scholars of Alexandria. For this reason these two texts were prestige-texts, much sought after by the wealthier and more scholarly members of the Christian community. The True Text, on the other hand, continued in use among the poorer and less learned Christian brethren. These humble believers would be less sensitive to matters of prestige and would no doubt prefer the familiar wording of the True Text to the changes introduced by the new prestige-texts ... And since they were poor, they would be unable to buy new manuscripts containing these prestige-texts.
>
> For all these reasons, therefore the True Text would continue to circulate among these lowly Christian folks virtually undisturbed by the influence of other texts. Moreover, because it was difficult for these less prosperous Christians to obtain new manuscripts, they put the ones they had to maximum use. Thus all these early manuscripts of the True Text were eventually worn out ... None of them seems to be extant today. The papyri which do survive seem for the most part to be prestige-texts which were preserved in the libraries

of ancient Christian schools. According to Aland (1963), both the Chester Beatty and the Bodmer Papyri may have been kept at such an institution. But the papyri with the True Text were read to pieces by the believing Bible students of antiquity. In the providence of God they were used by the Church. They survived long enough, however, to preserve the True (Traditional) New Testament Text during this early period and to bring it into the period of triumph that followed.[14]

The Traditional Text and the Number of Manuscripts

The modern textual critics, who learned their profession from Westcott and Hort, belittle the importance of the number of manuscripts that support the Traditional Text. They have often said that manuscript witnesses must be "weighed" not counted. However, we would expect the text that was most used to be the majority text. We would expect the text that was preserved and promoted by the Spirit of God to be the one that is most often copied.

The KJB is an example of this principle. It was first published in 1611, and we believe it is the correct English Bible coming from the Traditional Text and the Received Text. Every year for hundreds of years it has been a best seller. Even now, without any special marketing strategies, it is still a best seller. This is true even though its competitors (NIV, NKJV, NASV, CEV, ESV, etc.) have been all promoted with modern mass media marketing techniques. This is highly significant. The KJB has nothing like their marketing efforts, yet it is still a best seller. It is promoted by the Spirit of God.

So, number is a key ingredient to finding the truth according to the Scriptures. A factual testimony can only be established with two or three witnesses. One will not do.

> *But if he will not hear thee, then take with thee one or two more, that in the mouth of two or three witnesses every word may be established.* (Matthew 18:16)
> *This is the third time I am coming to you. In the mouth of two or three witnesses shall every word be established.* (2 Corinthians 13:1)
> *Against an elder receive not an accusation, but before two or three witnesses.* (1 Timothy 5:19)
> *He that despised Moses' law died without mercy under two or three witness* (Hebrews 10:28)

Dr. Jim Taylor investigated the overall evidence and what it suggested in his book, *In Defense of the Textus Receptus*.

> As you can see from what we have just discussed, the majority of all the existing manuscript evidence is in agreement with the Textus Receptus. Only a very small fraction of manuscripts disagree. It is often said that the remaining manuscripts fall into another "family" or grouping, but in actuality, the differences between them are so radical that each manuscript would have to be in a family of its own! Let's try to summarize this a bit. If we include the lectionaries, we have a total of 5,773 extant manuscripts. 5,369 support the Textus Receptus in full or in part. 207 manuscripts support the Critical text (Alexandrian-UBS text-Author) in full or in part. Another 226 manuscripts are either mixed texts which have been thrown in to other so-called "families" or else unclassified for one reason or another. 5369 Byzantine manuscripts versus 207 Alexandrian manuscripts. It's pretty clear which one was favored. [15]

Dean Burgon presented this reasonable view of the number of textual witnesses.

> There exists no reason for supposing that the Divine Agent, who in the first instance thus gave to mankind the Scriptures of Truth, straightway abdicated His office; took no further care of His work; abandoned those precious writings to their fate ... I am utterly disinclined to believe—so grossly improbable does it seem—that at the end of 1800 years 995 copies out of every thousand, suppose, will prove untrustworthy; and that the one, two, three, four or five which remain, whose contents were till yesterday as good as unknown, will be found to have retained the secret of what the Holy Spirit originally inspired. I am utterly unable to believe, in short, that God's promise has so entirely failed, that at the end of 1800 years much of the text of the Gospel had in point of fact to be picked by a German critic (Tischendorf-Author) out of a waste-paper basket in the convent of St. Catherine; and that the entire text had to be remodelled after the pattern set by a couple of copies which had remained in neglect during fifteen centuries, and had

probably owed their survival to that neglect; whilst hundreds of others had been thumbed to pieces, and had bequeathed their witness to copies made from them. [16]

Strange as it may appear, it is undeniably true, that the whole of the controversy may be reduced to the following narrow issue: Does the truth of the Text of Scripture dwell with the vast multitude of copies, uncial and cursive, concerning which nothing is more remarkable than the marvellous agreement which subsists between them? Or is it rather to be supposed that the truth abides exclusively with a very little handful of manuscripts, which at once differ from the great bulk of the witnesses, and—strange to say—also amongst themselves? [17]

The Traditional Text and the Variety of Evidence

This important consideration focuses on the fact that Traditional Text manuscripts were scattered geographically all over the Christian world from 100 to 1600 AD. Few can say it better than Dean Burgon.

> Now those many MSS. were executed demonstrably at different times in different countries. They bear signs in their many hundreds of representing the entire area of the Church, except where versions were used instead of copies in the original Greek. Many of them were written in monasteries where a special room was set aside for such copying. Those who were in trust endeavoured with the utmost pains and jealousy to secure accuracy in the transcription. Copying was a sacred art. And yet, of multitudes of them that survive, hardly any have been copied from any of the rest. [18]

> Speaking generally, the consentient testimony of two, four, six, or more witnesses, coming to us from widely sundered regions is weightier by far than the same number of witnesses proceeding from one and the same locality, between whom there probably exists some sort of sympathy, and possibly some degree of collusion. [19]

> No one can doubt, for it stands to reason, that Variety distinguishing witnesses massed together must needs constitute a most powerful argument for believing such

evidence to be true. Witnesses of different kinds; from different countries; speaking different tongues:—witnesses who can never have met, and between whom it is incredible that there should exist collusion of any kind:—such witnesses deserve to be listened to most respectfully. Indeed, when witnesses of so varied a sort agree in large numbers, they must needs be accounted worthy of even implicit confidence. Accordingly, the essential feature of the proposed Test will be, that the Evidence of which "Variety" is to be predicated shall be derived from a variety of sources. Readings which are witnessed to by MSS. only; or by ancient Versions only: or by one or more of the Fathers only:— [20]

The Traditional Text and Respectability

Dean Burgon speaks of "respectability" as a part of the weight a manuscript is given. He said:

In the first place, the witnesses in favour of any given reading should be respectable. "Respectability" is of course a relative term ... Some critics will claim, not respectability only, but absolute and oracular authority for a certain set of ancient witnesses,—which others will hold in suspicion ... We listen to any one whose character has won our respect: [21]

The thousands of manuscripts of the New Testament and NT quotes from the early church "fathers" and lectionaries date from the second century to the 1600's. They are all witnesses to the text of the original inspired New Testament. If witnesses are called to court they have credibility or respectability only if they agree. Two or three witnesses may establish the facts, but the witnesses must agree. This is illustrated from the trial of the Lord Jesus.

55 And the chief priests and all the council sought for witness against Jesus to put him to death; and found none.
56 For many bare false witness against him, but their witness agreed not together.
57 And there arose certain, and bare false witness against him, saying,
58 We heard him say, I will destroy this temple that is made with hands, and within three days I will build another made without hands.

59 But neither so did their witness agree together.
(Mark 14:55)

When Dean Burgon said, "Some critics will claim, not respectability only, but absolute and oracular authority for a certain set of ancient witnesses," he was writing about Vaticanus and Sinaiticus and certain other Alexandrian manuscripts like them, all of which were promoted by Westcott and Hort and most modern scholars today. This group of manuscripts generally opposes the Traditional text. However, like the witnesses in Jesus' day, "Their witness agreed not together." They do not represent a single unified text, but they greatly disagree with one another. Dr. D. A. Waite summarized the agreement of these manuscripts.

> Any witnesses, such as "B" (Vatican) and "Aleph" (Sinai), which disagree one with the other in over 3,000 substantial places in the Gospels alone would certainly not be respectable witnesses. Certainly such false witnesses cannot be "respectable" by objective standards.[22]

On the other hand, the Traditional Text is recognized as one unified text. Most of its manuscripts have not been copied from any of the other manuscripts. They each stand alone as thousands of independent witnesses. According to Dean Burgon this is not true with the Alexandrian manuscripts.

> If one Codex (z) is demonstrably the mere transcript of another Codex (f), these may no longer be reckoned as two Codexes, but as one Codex. It is hard therefore to understand how Tischendorf constantly adduces the evidence of "E of Paul" although he was perfectly well aware that E is "a mere transcript of the Cod. Claromontanus" or D of Paul. Or again, how he quotes the cursive Evan. 102; because the readings of that unknown seventeenth-century copy of the Gospels are ascertained to have been derived from Cod. B itself.[23]

However, it has often been proclaimed that no two Traditional Text manuscripts agree 100%. It is a mystery to me how this can be known as a fact by those who say it. I seriously doubt that they have any proof of it beyond having heard it from someone else. Furthermore, I seriously doubt that *any* of them have examined *all* the 5300+ plus manuscripts of the Traditional Text.

The collation efforts of Wilbur Pickering demonstrated evidence that it is *not* true that every Traditional Text manuscript has errors. The Traditional

Text is categorized into families. Pickering collated the manuscripts in Family 35. He had some amazing results.

> Notice that of twenty-one MSS, eleven of their exemplars (over half) were 'perfect', and another five were off by only one variant (the worst was only off by six, for two books) ... I conclude that all twenty-one MSS were independent in their generation, and I see no evidence to indicate a different conclusion for their exemplars ... I now invite attention to location and date. The MSS come from all over the Mediterranean world. The six Mt. Athos MSS were certainly produced in their respective monasteries (five). Ecclesiastical politics tending to be what it tends to be, there is little likelihood that there would be collusion between the monasteries on the transmission of the NT writings—I regard the six as representing independent lines of transmission (five of the exemplars were not identical). MSS from Trikala, Patmos, Jerusalem and Sinai were presumably produced there; 18 was certainly produced in Constantinople; 35 was acquired in the Aegean area. The MSS at the Vatican and Grottaferrata may very well have been produced there ... The implications of finding a perfect representative of any archetypal text are rather powerful. All the 'canons' of textual criticism become irrelevant to any point subsequent to the creation of that text (they could still come into play when studying the creation of the text). For MS 18 to be perfect, all the generations in between had to be perfect as well. Now I call this incredibly careful transmission. Nothing that I was taught in Seminary about New Testament textual criticism prepared me for this discovery! Nor anything that I had read, for that matter. But MS 18 is not an isolated case; all the twenty-one MSS in the chart above reflect an incredibly careful transmission—even the worst of the lot, minuscule 201 with its 6 variants [the 'singulars' in 1893 and 1248 are careless mistakes (unhappy monks), is really quite good, considering all the intervening generations. [24]

Nevertheless, I concede that there are some disagreements among many of these copies. Scribal mistakes do occur. Many of the various kinds of disagreements in the Traditional text are minor. I have illustrated some of them in the following chart. This chart does not show actual variances. It is merely illustrative of the types of errors found and is based on Mark 7:23.

MSS	TEXT	ERROR TYPE
1	All these evil things from within **come**, and defile the man.	Wrong word order
2	These evil things come from within, and defile the man.	Omit word
3	All **of** these evil things come from within, and defile the man.	Add word
4	All these evil things come from **without**, and defile the man.	change word
5	All these evil things come from within, and **defl** the man.	Misspelling
6	All these evil things come **form** within, and defilethe man.	Misspelling
7	All these evil things come from within	Leave out phrase

Fig. 3

The importance of this illustration is that the correct readings are easily seen when all six copies are compared. The first manuscript has the wrong word order, but the other five have it correct, so the right word order is evident. Two of the manuscripts have misspellings, but the other manuscripts reveal the true spelling. Even if a word or phrase is omitted in one of them, the others reveal that fact. The same is true for a word added or changed.

The Traditional Text and Continuity

If the manuscripts of a textual tradition could be traced throughout the manuscript period (50-1600 AD), it would be a powerful testimony to its genuineness. The Traditional Text has just this history. There are a high number of Traditional text manuscripts (over 5,000) and they were found over a widespread area and though the entire period. This tells us that they both *existed*, and they were *used*. The chart below (Figure 4) shows that the Traditional text was present continually throughout church history.

There is evidence in the Papyri for an early Traditional Text date. Papyrus was like a cheap paper made from the Papyrus plant. It decayed easily. It fell apart quickly. On the next page is a chart that shows that the Traditional text existed continually from an early date in Christian history.

The Continual Existence of the Traditional Text 50-1600 AD

Sign	Name	Date/ Century
P64 *	Magdalen Papyrus 64	50 AD
P52 *	Papyrus 52	100-175 AD
P66	Papyrus Bodmer II P66 (see below)	125 AD
P32 *	Papyrus 32	200 AD
A (02)	Codex Alexandrinus	5th
C (04)	Codex Ephraemi Rescriptus	5th
W (032)	Codex Washingtonianus	5th
Q (026)	Codex Guelferbytanus B	5th
061	Uncial 061	5th
N 022	Codex Petropolitanus Purpureus	6th
0103	Uncial 0103	7th
E^e (07)	Codex Basilensis	8th
F^e (09)	Codex Boreelianus	9th
G^e (011)	Codex Seidelianus I	9th
H^e (013)	Codex Seidelianus II	9th
L (020)	Codex Angelicus	9th
V (031)	Codex Mosquensis II	9th
Y (034)	Codex Macedoniensis	9th
Θ (038)	Codex Koridethi	9th
0142	Uncial 0142	10th
8	Minuscule 8	11th
1241	Minuscule 1241	12th
6	Minuscule 6	13th
11	Minuscule 11	14th
30	Minuscule 30	15th
90	Minuscule 90	16th

Fig. 4 [25] * Included based on my own comparisons.

There is not much New Testament written on papyrus remaining. In addition to P64, P52, and P32, the early existence of the Traditional Text was confirmed by the discovery of Papyrus Bodmer II P66. It is the Gospel of John consisting of 75 leaves and 39 unidentified fragments. It was dated 200 AD, but many now are dating it at 125 AD. It is usually classified as Alexandrian. In reality, it is a mixed text. Dr. David Brown commented on P 66 and shared the examples in the following chart.

Further, I find it very encouraging that more recently discovered papyrus fragments have confirmed the Majority Text. "Nineteenth-century biblical scholars claimed that much of the first fourteen chapters of the Gospel of John was corrupted by scribes in the later Byzantine Era. This claim was shown to be utterly false by the discovery of Papyrus Bodmer II (also called P66). Dated about A.D. 200, (now by many at 125 A.D.) prior to the commencement of the Byzantine Era, this Papyrus verified many of the disputed passages attributed to late Byzantine copyists and demonstrated that these passages were present in very early manuscripts." (Modern Bible Translations Unmasked by Russell & Colin Standish; p.37-38). Dr. Gordon Fee has shown that in John chapter 4, P66 agrees with the Traditional Text (and thus the King James Bible) 60.6% of the time when there are textual variations (Studies in the Text and Method of New Testament Textual Criticism, by Epp and Fee). While P66 is a mixed text it does demonstrate so called "Byzantine readings well before that era. [26]

In the places listed in the table below and others, P66 sides with the Traditional Text.

Ref.	P66/Traditional	Vs. Alexandrian
John 4:1	κυριος (Lord)	Ιεσους (Jesus)
John 5:9	καιευτηεος (and immediately)	omitted
John 5:17	δεΙεσους (but Jesus)	δε Ιεσους Κυριος (but Jesus Christ)
John 6:36	με (me)	omitted
John 6:46	και την μετερα (and the mother)	omitted
John 6:69	ο Χριστος (the Christ)	omitted
John 7:10	αλλ ος (but as)	αλλ (but)
John 7:39	πνευμα αγιον (Holy Spirit)	πνευμα (Spirit)

Fig. 5

An early date and the continuity of the Traditional Text is supported by the early church writers. The early Christians who left writings behind (so-called church fathers) often quoted the Traditional text. The table below has a few specific examples of writers who quoted the Traditional Text and what passages they quoted. This information comes from the same source as the quote above, Dr. David Brown and also Dr. Thomas Strouse. In these, the Traditional Text reading which was quoted by the writers is designated (T) and the Alexandrian reading is designated by (A).

The following list could go on and on. There are many of these writers who quoted specific Traditional Text readings. When I put in the chart "quoted (T) but omitted (A)," I mean that the verse, word, or phrase shown is quoted by at least one church father (but not limited to one), and it is omitted in the Alexandrian text.

Name and Dates	Ref.	Quote
Irenaeus (130-202)	Mark 1:2	"prophets"(T) - "prophet" (A)
Irenaeus	Mark 16:19	quoted (T) but omitted (A)
Justin (100-165)	Luke 22:44	quoted (T) but omitted (A)
Ireneaus	John 1:18	"begotten son"(T) "god" (A)
Hyppolytus (170-236)	John 3:13	"the Son of man which is in heaven" (T) – omitted (A)
Tertullian (160-221)	John 5:3-4	quoted (T) but omitted (A)
Cyprian (200-258)	1 John 5:7-8	quoted (T) but omitted (A)

Fig. 6

Several excellent summary charts are included in *The Traditional Text of the Gospels*, dividing the fathers by the era in which they lived. See below for a reproduction of some of this information giving the name, date, how many times the Traditional Text was quoted in the gospels, and how many times the Alexandrian or another type text was quoted in the gospels.

The Early Church Writers 100-250 AD (Apostolic Fathers)

Name	Date	Traditional	Other
Didachè (document)	50-100	11	4
Clement of Rome *	died in 99	18	7
Epistle to Diognetus	c. 50-200	1	0
Papias (Heirapolis, Turkey)	c. 60-160	1	0
Hegesippus (Palestine)	c. 110-180	2	0
Justin Martyr (Rome)	100-165	17	20
Athenagoras (Athens)	133-190	3	1
Irenaeus (Greece/France)	130-202	63	41
Hippolytus (Rome)	170-236	26	11

Fig. 7 [27] (*Clementine Homilies)

Later Ante-Nicene and Nicene Writers 200-400 AD

Name	Date	Traditional	Other
Gregory Thaumaturgus (Pontus)	c. 213-270	11	3
Cornelius (Rome)	Died 253	4	1
Gregory of Nazianzus (Turkey)	c. 329-390	18	4
Methodius (European Slavs)	Died c. 311	14	8
Titus of Bostra (Arabia)	Died c. 378	44	24
Basil (Cappadocia, Turkey)	c. 329-379	272	105
Eusebius of Caesarea	c. 260-339	315	214
Cyril of Jerusalem	313-386	54	32
Ambrose of Milan	c. 337-397	169	77
Lucifer of Cagliari, Sardinia	Died c. 370	17	20

Fig. 8 [28]

Alexandrian and African Writers 100-400 AD

Name	Date	Traditional	Other
Cyprian	c. 200-258	100	96
Tertullian	c. 155-240	74	65
Novatian	c. 200-258	6	4
Didymus	c. 313-398	81	36
Clement of Alexandria	c. 150-215	82	72
Dionysius	Died 264	12	5
Origen Adamantius	c. 184-253	460	491
Alexander of Alexandria	Died c. 328	4	0
Athanasius of Alexandria	c. 296-373	179	119

Fig. 9 [29]

The information in these examples is similar for the writers not listed. There are a total of 76 listings of writers in *The Traditional Text* with similar statistics to those in these charts. These statistics give us some strong information and implications about the existence, location, and use of the Traditional text from the earliest of times.

The first and foremost thing we learn is that the Traditional text **existed** *in the first century.* The Didache predominantly quoted it in the first century. There is also Clement of Rome who died in 99 AD, who quoted the Traditional text 18 times out of 25. The Traditional Text existed in the days of the Apostles.

Corruptions of the Word of God were insinuating themselves into copies in the first century. We learn this from Clement, who quoted some other text 7 times, and others. The corruptions of the Word of God Paul talked about (2 Cor. 2:17) were making their way around the Mediterranean area.

The charts also indicate the early dominance of the Traditional text. The early church writers used the Traditional text far more often than they used anything else. Even though corruptions were present in the early days and grew stronger later, the traditional Text was dominant. The traditional Text continued to be the most used text all the way to 400 AD. There is absolutely no indication that an official revision was done in Palestine in the fourth century. The witness to the Traditional text was continuous.

The corruption of the text was worst in Alexandria. As you can see, those who were in Alexandria or elsewhere in Africa (such as Carthage) used the Alexandrian text more than most of the others. However, they were all mixed, because they also used the Traditional Text. That shows that the Traditional Text was also in Egypt from an early time. The Traditional was both present and frequently used. Therefore, it existed, was strong, and popular.

The Alexandrian leader, Origen (182-254 AD), moved from Alexandria to Caesarea in Palestine, being strongly welcomed by the Bishops in Palestine. Origen spent a great deal of time writing and working with New Testament manuscripts. He was half preacher and half Greek philosopher. When he came to Palestine, he started the library at Caesarea. His influence among the Bishops in Palestine was powerful. He brought his Alexandrian Scripture scrolls with him when he came from Alexandria. There followed later many who were influenced by him. These included Eusebius, Bishop of Caesarea, Basil, Cyril of Jerusalem, and probably Titus of Bostra. These used Origen's Bible material and quoted often from the Alexandrian Text. Apparently, in Palestine and Asia Minor of that time, the Traditional Text and the Alexandrian Text were in stiff competition (just as they are today).

Rome and at least part of Italy was also strongly affected by the Alexandrian Text. Justin Martyr lived there and Ambrose lived in Milan, not far from Rome.

An early date for the Traditional Text is supported by the ancient translations. Here is a table for you showing some translations and their dates in Fig. 10.

Date	Translation
150 AD	The Old Syriac Peshitta
120-150 AD	The Old Latin or Itala
350 AD	The Gothic
300 AD	The Ethiopic

The Bible of the early Greek Church and the modern Greek Orthodox Church was predominantly the Traditional Greek Text, showing its continual use through the centuries. The Traditional Text prevailed in the Eastern half of the Roman Empire and continued to be the Bible of the Greek churches throughout the Middle Ages and on into modern times. The Greek Bible of the Greek Orthodox Church published in 1904 has 1 John 5:7, a passage which is strenuously rejected by those who believe in the Alexandrian Text. On the other hand, the Latin Vulgate, translated about 382 by Jerome, became the Bible of the West and the Catholic Church. Rome nearly abandoned the Greek New Testament altogether. Previously, in the early centuries, the Alexandrian text prevailed in Africa and influenced Rome. As a result, the Latin Vulgate has a distinct Alexandrian flavor.

This continuity did not exist with the Alexandrian Text. Part of Jerome's basis for translating his Latin Version in 382 AD was the Alexandrian Text. The Roman Catholic Church quit using the Greek manuscripts and embraced the Latin Vulgate as its official Bible. It took several hundred years before the people also embraced it. So, the Alexandrian Greek Text did not have much influence in Europe in the Middle Ages and the Renaissance/Reformation period. It was a little used text. That is probably why Vaticanus survived. It was hidden in the library. God did not use it or its sister manuscripts very much, if any.

Where are the 2nd 3rd and 4th Centuries Greek Manuscripts?

There are definite historical reasons why there are so few purely Traditional Text papyri from the second through the fourth centuries. There are reasons why so many manuscripts from that time are mixed texts or no longer in existence

Heresy is one of the greatest reasons for the presence of mixed and alternative texts. Remember the statement of the Apostle Paul that the Word of God was being corrupted in his time. Many of the heresies were built around the Greek philosophies, such as Gnosticism, and were centered in Alexandria, Egypt.

> *For we are not as many, which corrupt the word of God:*
> (2 Cor. 2:17)

Paul said ***many*** were busy corrupting the Word of God in his day. There is no reason to suppose that the corrupting activity stopped with Paul's death. Chances are it increased. Remember, how Paul told the Ephesian elders...

> For I know this, that after my departing shall grievous wolves enter in among you, not sparing the flock. Also of your own selves shall men arise, speaking perverse things, to draw away disciples after them.
> (Acts 20:29-30)

You don't suppose they stopped with simply *speaking* perverse things, do you? This is especially true, since many were already busy corrupting God's word? Paul was speaking of the corrupting influence in *Ephesus*. So, the corruption was not confined to Alexandria, although it was strong there.

> It is no less true to fact than paradoxical in sound, that the worst corruptions to which the New Testament has ever been subjected, originated within a hundred years after it was composed; that Irenaeus and the African Fathers and the whole Western, with a portion of the Syriac Church, used far inferior manuscripts to those employed by Stunica, or Erasmus, or Stephen, thirteen centuries after, when moulding the Textus Receptus. [30]

Numerous heresies were dealt with in the New Testament. 1 John 4:2 seems to point directly at Docetism (Jesus did not have a real physical body, so he did not die on the cross and the resurrection was not real). The denial of the deity of Christ taught by Marcion in the 2nd Century is answered in 1 Timothy 3:16. That verse was probably changed in the Alexandrian text by Marcion or someone who thought like him. Marcion was certainly busy corrupting the Scriptures. The heresy that salvation is by works is debunked in Romans. The influence of the Judaizers, who wanted to put Christians under the law, is fought in Galatians. Antinomianism, the denial that Christians have any moral obligations is taught against everywhere in the New Testament. Finally, Gnosticism is dealt with in Colossians and 1, 2 John. Just as a certain prominent heresy of today translated the *New World Translation* to back up their heresy, many of these false teachers had interest in changing Scripture.

Another reason papyri are hard to find in the Roman Empire is climate. The northern coasts of the Mediterranean, Syria, Turkey, Greece, and Italy are very moist. Papyrus is such a fragile material that it simply does not last. Most Papyri that still exist are found in southern Palestine and Egypt, where the Alexandrian text prevailed early. Egypt and Southern Palestine are dry. Everywhere in the Roman Empire Christians lived from 100 to 300 AD had a climate that made papyrus rot and disintegrate quickly, except Africa and Southern Palestine.

A further reason for the scarcity of Traditional manuscripts is that parchment, or vellum, tended to be reused. Parchment was a more expensive writing material and sometimes it was hard to get. The solution was to scrape the used parchment and gently wash off the ink. Then they would write over the old text. The old writing would usually become faint, but it would still be there. A reused piece of parchment is called a palimpsest. Below is Codex Nitriensis, a 6th Century palimpsest manuscript, with Syriac text.

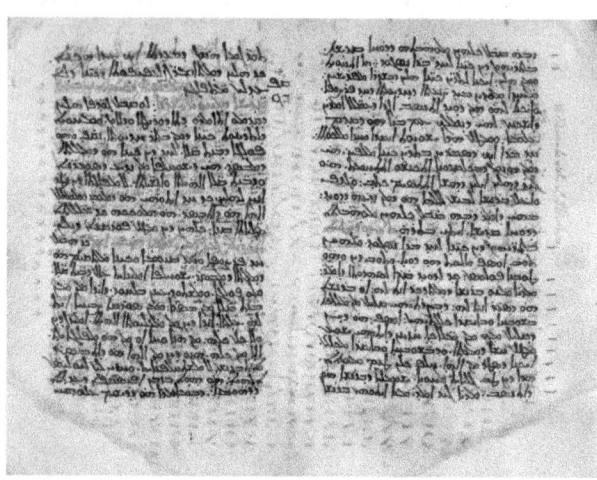

Fig. 11

Traditional Text manuscripts were the most frequently used manuscripts by common Christians and papyrus copies simply wore out from use. I have worn out some Bibles in my lifetime. Today, the most well-made Bible will not last a hundred years of constant use. It is the least used Bible that lasts the longest. In the first and second centuries, Bibles had to be copied by hand. That was a long painstaking process. It was no doubt done carefully and when finished the Bibles were cared for. Nevertheless, they were well used. At first, Bibles were written on cheap papyrus, so the oldest fragments are papyrus. Much later parchment (called vellum) was used. That was a much longer lasting material, but even that got old, worn, and torn. Due to use and quality of materials, the Traditional Text had few first through fourth Century papyrus New Testament fragments survive.

Few Traditional Text copies exist from the second through the third centuries because of Roman persecution. The tenth imperial persecution of the church was especially devastating. It was ordered by Roman Emperor Diocletian and his Co-Emperor, Galerius, and began in 303 AD.

> The fatal day fixed upon to commence the bloody work, was the 23d of February, A. D. 303, that being the day in which the Terminalia were celebrated, and on which, as the cruel pagans boasted, they hoped to put a termination to Christianity. On the appointed day, the persecution began in Nicomedia, on the morning of which the prefect of that city repaired, with a great number of officers and assistants, to the church of the Christians, where, having forced open the doors, they seized upon all the sacred books, and committed them to the flames ... This was followed by a severe edict, commanding the destruction of all other Christian churches and books; and an order soon succeeded, to render Christians of all denominations outlaws ... A general sacrifice was commenced, which occasioned various martyrdoms. No distinction was made of age or sex; the name of Christian was so obnoxious to the pagans, that all indiscriminately fell sacrifices to their opinions. Many houses were set on fire, and whole Christian families perished in the flames; and others had stones fastened about their necks, and being tied together were driven into the sea. The persecution became general in all the Roman provinces, but more particularly in the east; and as it lasted ten years, it is impossible to ascertain the numbers martyred, or to enumerate the various modes of martyrdom. [31]

Part of this great general persecution was the burning of Christian books, including the Bible. The persecution took place in all parts of the empire, but particularly in the eastern provinces, which is where most of the Traditional Text copies were being made. Many pure manuscripts perished during that time. Since the persecution arose at the beginning of the fourth century, it was first, second, and third century manuscripts that were destroyed. Copies then were few compared to now.

> Christian leaders and Christian Scriptures were especially targeted. Embedded in a text from AD 320 called the *Gesta Apud Zenophilum,* there is an account of Roman persecution of Christians that occurred on May 19, 303, in Cirta, a city in Numidia. (The History of Information website also has some data about it.)

How many manuscripts were seized by the Romans in Cirta, Numidia, in one day, in 303? Under Roman interrogation, Catullinus the Deacon initially handed over just one very large codex. But as the interrogation continued, more codices were surrendered: a man named Eugenius was confronted at his house, and he handed over four codices. Felix the Lector handed over five codices. Victorinus, another lector, was also confronted at his house, and he handed over eight codices. Next, Projectus the Lector handed over five large codices and two small codices. Victor the Grammarian was confronted at his house, and he handed over two codices, and four quinions (that is, loose book-sections consisting of five parchment sheets folded together). The Romans also confronted Euticius of Caesarea, who denied having any manuscripts. The Romans went on to the house of Coddeo, who, it seems, was not at home, but his wife was present, and she handed over six codices.

The total: **33 codices, and four segments of codices**. Needless to say, if we had those manuscripts from 303, our textual apparatuses would look very different. And that's just one city in Numidia. Nicomedia (an early target of the Diocletian persecution, in what is now Turkey) had many more manuscripts than that, and so, I suspect, did the churches in Corinth, Ephesus, Rome, Athens, Philippi, Berea, Smyrna, Pergamum, and throughout Turkey (Asia, Bithynia, Lydia, Galatia, Pamphylia, Cilicia, Cappadocia, etc.). My point here is not that those 34 manuscripts (and the multitudes of other manuscripts destroyed during the Diocletian Persecution) **must** have had the Byzantine Text written on their pages, but simply that the repetition of similar scenes throughout the Roman Empire explains, to a large extent, our lack of New Testament manuscript-evidence from large swaths of Roman territory. [32]

Following this tenth and last Roman imperial persecution, there was a short period of ascendency of the Alexandrian Greek text in the Western Roman Empire. Constantine the Great became the emperor in Rome in 306 AD and professed Christianity. He finally defeated his last rival for the throne in 324. In the meantime, he issued the edict of Milan in 313, which ended Roman persecution of the Church and elevated it to a status of "tolerated religion." He asked Bishop Eusebius of Caesarea for fifty Greek Bibles in 331. Eusebius got his material for these Bibles from the Library in Caesarea where Origen of Alexandria had left all his Biblical materials (the library suffered in the persecution but was able to be repaired by the Caesarean bishops). Origen's biblical materials as judged by his writings were Alexandrian or mixed in nature. This hindered the Traditional text in the Western Empire in the fourth century. However, Traditional Text copies were growing in number and by the fifth century, they completely dominated the Christian world.

The Traditional Text and Context

Context has to do with how a verse, phrase, or word fits with the words before and after it. Context also includes the larger teaching of Scripture. Does a manuscript have a reading which is out of place with the context closest to it or is it out of harmony with the teaching of the Bible in general? Dean Burgon explained it this way.

> A word,—a phrase,—a clause,—or even a sentence or a paragraph,—must have some relation to the rest of the entire passage which precedes or comes after it. Therefore it will often be necessary, in order to reach all the evidence that bears upon a disputed question, to examine both the meaning and the language lying on both sides of the point in dispute. [33]

Examples would be helpful to understand this. For that purpose, I will give two.

1. **1 Corinthians 13:5**

   <u>Vaticanus</u>: "Charity does not seek what does not belong to it." In Greek –"to me eautes" (τὸ μὴ ἑαυτῆς)
   <u>Trad. Text</u>: "Charity does not seek her own"-"ta eautes" (τὰ ἑαυτῆς)

   The sentiment of Vaticanus is directly opposite the sentiment of 1 Corinthians 13, as a whole. The context is teaching that charity seeks the good of others. That is what is meant by the Traditional Text reading, "Charity does not seek its own." It does not seek its own good, but it seeks the good of others. However, the way it is put in Vaticanus states, "I only seek the good of what belongs to me." [34]

2. **The rich young ruler: Matthew 19:16-17; Mark 10:17-18; Luke 18:18-19**.

   The young man came to Jesus and called Him, "Good Master." Vaticanus and the Traditional Text record two different responses of Jesus to what the young man called Him.

   Trad. Text: "Why do you call me good?" (τί με λέγεις ἀγαθόν)
   Vaticanus: "Why do you ask me concerning the good?" (τί με ἐρωτᾶς περὶ τοῦ ἀγαθοῦ)

   The rich young ruler's full question was, "*Good Master, what shall I do that I may inherit eternal life?*" It should be obvious that an inquiry about "the good" has nothing to do with the question Jesus was asked. Apparently, it isn't so obvious, because in Matthew 19:16-17 the United Bible Societies Greek Text has the answer as it is in Vaticanus. The UBS Text, just as Vaticanus did, even leaves out "good" in "Good Master." That puts it further out of context, because it takes away *any* reference to *anything* the young man said regarding *anything* "good." Also, in the UBS the two other references to this story (Mk. 10:17-18; Luke 18:18-19) have Jesus' statement as it is in the Traditional Text. This creates a serious conflict when the reader is comparing different Gospel accounts of the incident. There is also a cultural context to this. The concept of "the good" was a subject of Greek philosophical discussions. Remember, there were those in Alexandria who wanted to reconcile Christianity with Greek Philosophy. This is one such attempt.

The Traditional Text and Internal Evidence

There are many differences between the Traditional Text and the Alexandrian and Western texts. Some whole verses are missing in the Alexandrian. Others consist of phrases, single words, incorrect geographical references, or even spelling. However, never think that these are minor. Every word of God is indispensable. So, we want to know that we have every word. Internal considerations deal with these detailed items, like spelling and grammar and wrong use of words. Below are some examples of these issues.

1. **Luke 19:37**

   Alexandrian, Vaticanus: Panton on eidon dinameon (παντῶν ὧν εἶδον δυνάμεων)

<u>Trad. Text:</u> Pason on eidon dinameon (πασῶν ὧν εἶδον δυνάμεων)

As you can see, the only difference is *panton* and *pason*. Both are the same word. In English it means "all," and they both are adjectives modifying dinameon (mighty works). However, they are different grammatical parts of speech. *Pason* matches *dinameon* grammatically, as both are feminine. *Panton* does not, since it is neuter or masculine. Therefore, it is impossible for *panton* to be correct, and it must be rejected. [35]

2.   **1 John 5:7-8**

The previous example does not affect doctrine, but that is not always the case. This one affects the doctrine of the trinity. The Alexandrian Text, the UBS Text, and most modern versions leave out the phrase, "in heaven, the Father, the Word, and the Holy Ghost: and these three are one. And there are three that bear witness in earth." This leaves the two verses to simply say, "For there are three that bear record the Spirit, and the water, and the blood: and these three agree in one." The Trinity is left out. In English, the rest of the verse, after the objectionable words are removed, is proper grammatically, but not in Greek. The Received Text has this correct, but the MSS that leave out the words do not. I will let Dr. Edward F. Hills explain it to you.

In the third place, the omission of the *Johannine* comma involves a grammatical difficulty. The words *spirit, water,* and *blood* are neuter in gender, but in 1 John 5:8 they are treated as masculine. If the Johannine *comma is* rejected, it is hard to explain this irregularity. It is usually said that in 1 John 5:8 *the spirit, the water, and the blood* are personalized and that this is the reason for the adoption of the masculine gender. But it is hard to see how such personalization would involve the change from the neuter to the masculine. For in verse 6 the word Spirit plainly refers to the Holy Spirit, the Third *Person* of the Trinity. Surely in this verse the word *Spirit* is "personalized," and yet the neuter gender is used. Therefore, since personalization did not bring about a change of gender in verse 6, it cannot fairly be pleaded as the reason for such a change in verse 8. If, however, the *Johannine comma* is retained, a reason for placing the neuter nouns *spirit, water,* and *blood* in the masculine gender becomes readily apparent.

It was due to the influence of the nouns *Father* and *Word*, which are masculine. [36]

3. Mark 1:2-3

   Vaticanus, UBS, Alexandrian: "Isaiah the prophet" (Καθὼς γέγραπται ἐν τῷ Ἡσαΐα τῷ προφήτῃ)
   Traditional Text: "prophets" (Ὡς γέγραπται ἐν τοῖς προφήταις)

   KJB: As it is written in the prophets
   NIV: as it is written in Isaiah the prophet

   The difference in these verses is obvious. The Alexandrian text, Vaticanus, Sinaiticus, the UBS text, the Nestle-Aland Text, and nearly every English translation put it like the NIV. They have all incorporated a lie into the Scriptures. What follows the word "prophet" in the Alexandrian text is an Old Testament quote. However, the quote is only partly from Isaiah. The rest of it is from Malachi. That's *TWO* prophets, not one.

   Malachi 3:1 Behold, I will send my messenger, and he shall prepare the way before me
   Isaiah 40:3 The voice of him that crieth in the wilderness, Prepare ye the way of the LORD, make straight in the desert a highway for our God.
   Mark 1:2-3 As it is written <u>in the prophets</u>, Behold, I send my messenger before thy face, which shall prepare thy way before thee. The voice of one crying in the wilderness, Prepare ye the way of the Lord, make his paths straight.

   Someone, in early church history changed the text from "prophets" to "Isaiah the prophet." Whoever it was no doubt did not understand that the source of part of the statement was Malachi and thought it was an error. Regardless of how it happened, a lie was introduced in the Alexandrian copies. It was embraced by today's Alexandrian scholars.

   These are in the same scholarly tradition that thought Elhanan rather than David, killed Goliath the Gitite (see 2 Sam. 21:19 in the NASB, RSV, NRSV, ESV, ASV, CSB, CEV, God's Word Translation, the Message, and others) despite the story in 1 Samuel 17.

Verifying there *WAS* a Traditional "Text" and an Alexandrian "Text"

A young man used to live in my garage. His name was Bob; no last name, simply Bob. I used to go to the garage at various times and *beat the living daylights* out of "Bob." I didn't need a provocation, but I could beat on "Bob" anytime I wanted. Bob was a punching dummy. My son put him there so we could "use" him anytime we wanted. Bob is like some of the arguments given against the Traditional text – just dummy arguments. Sometimes, we call them "straw-man" arguments.

One of these straw man arguments goes like this: You keep talking about "readings" (words, phrases, and verses), but you don't show us a "text." Where is the text? There is no "text." This is a true straw man argument. First, what are texts, if not collections of words, phrases, and sentences? Nearly all scholars recognize that there is a difference between Traditional and Alexandrian readings and texts. All these readings that are available had to be copied from somewhere. In the earliest times, the Bible books of the New Testament were not placed together in one book but were copied individually. A writer may have the four gospels in the Traditional Text on his desk (in separate books or scrolls) and the rest of the NT books (separately) in the Alexandrian Text at the same time. When he copied them and bound them together in a codex, he just produced Codex Alexandrinus, with the gospels copied from Traditional Text scrolls and the rest copied from Alexandrian Text scrolls. If he writes a letter, his letter may have Traditional quotes from Mark and John, but Alexandrian quotes from Romans, because those are the types of manuscripts he has. Have you not seen how writers today will quote several different versions in one chapter of one book? Does that mean there is no "text" to back them up? They are just "readings?"

If we say there is no actual Traditional Text, we may as well say there was no Alexandrian Text, either. Scholars are fond of classifying manuscripts as "Alexandrian," but many "Alexandrian" manuscripts of the first four centuries are actually *mixed*. We see that also with the church "fathers."

The surest proof that there were and are both a Traditional Text and an Alexandrian Text is the result of their transmission through history: our present day printed "texts." Two primary streams of Bibles have come down to us and have resulted in the creation of two major competing printed Greek New Testaments that are different in about 8,000 places: The Textus Receptus or Received Text (TR) and the United Bible Societies Greek (UBS) Text, which grew out of the Westcott and Hort text of the 1880's. There is also the Nestle-Aland Greek Text, but it has the exact same text as the UBS. The character of the TR is recognized to be the Traditional Text. The UBS is clearly Alexandrian in character and scholars recognize it to be so.

The Majority Text

Finally, I will mention, and *dismiss,* the more minor printed Greek text called *The Majority Text.* Actually, there are two *different* "majority texts:" 1) *The Greek New Testament According to the Majority Text,* by Zane Hodges and Arthur Farstad, and 2) *The New Testament in the Original Greek According to the Byzantine / Majority Text form,* by Maurice Robinson and William Pierpont. First off, neither of these is "according to the majority text." Neither of them collated *all* the manuscripts of the Traditional Text to produce a true "majority" text. They got their text from a man named Von Soden, who had collated about 400 manuscripts. These texts differ from one another, and they differ from the Received text about 1,000-1,500 times. Furthermore, until Baptist Mid-missions started using the "majority text" for translation work, they remained barely alive in the library. God wasn't using them much (if any). I wonder, would God wait until the church was nearly 2,000 years old before giving it a pure New Testament? Let's hear from Robinson and Pierpont.

> It is an awesome task to attempt to present the Greek New Testament in its greatest possible integrity. **Faithful scribes** through the centuries have labored to preserve and transmit the written Word as originally given by inspiration of God. Building upon this tradition, the **textual critic** seeks not to produce a merely "good" text, nor even an "adequate" text, but instead to establish as nearly as possible the precise form of the written Word as originally revealed. (author's emphasis) [37]

The credit for preserving the New Testament text is given to "faithful scribes" and to "textual critics." It doesn't go to God Almighty? He is the one who promised to preserve it, and He is the one who takes the responsibility. Well, maybe that's not what they meant. So, let's see, how the scribes and textual critics have been doing.

> For over four-fifths of the New Testament, the Greek text is considered 100% certain, regardless of which text type might be favored by any critic. [38]

About One-fifth of the New Testament remains less than certain? One-fifth of the New Testament equals 5.4 *whole books* or 1,594.4 *whole verses*! The scribes and textual critics don't seem to be doing very well do they? Well, apparently, they don't think God has done very well either.

What unbelief!

The fact remains that it was the Received Text that was put together from Traditional Text manuscripts. It was the Received Text God used to start the Reformation and to accomplish every major move of the Holy Spirit to beyond the mid 1900's. It was the Received Text that was blessed and approved by God almighty for the last 500 years. It still is.

CHAPTER THREE
THE RECEIVED TEXT, THE KJB, AND THE UBS

Now go, write it before them in a table, and note it in a book, that it may be for the time to come for ever and ever (Is. 30:8)

Seek ye out of the book of the LORD, and read: no one of these shall fail, none shall want her mate: for my mouth it hath commanded, and his spirit it hath gathered them. (Is. 34:16)

The Received Greek Text was based on the Traditional Greek Text that existed from the days of the Apostles. The text is the printed version of the Traditional text. They are one and the same. It is fundamentally a different text than the United Bible Societies Greek Text.

According to Dr. Edward Hills, the origin and development of the Received Text was guided by the common faith in the 14-1500's. He described the common faith this way:

> This common view remained a faith rather than a well articulated theory. No one at that time drew the logical but unpalatable conclusion that the Greek Church rather than the Roman Church had been the providentially appointed guardian of the New Testament text. But this view, though vaguely apprehended, was widely held, so much so that it may justly be called the common view. Before the Council of Trent (1546) it was favored by some of the highest officials of the Roman Church, notably, it seems, by Leo X, who was pope from 1513 to 1521 and to whom Erasmus dedicated his New Testament. Erasmus' close friends also, John Colet, for example, and Thomas More and Jacques Lefevre, all of whom like Erasmus sought to reform the Roman Catholic Church from within, likewise adhered to this common view. Even the scholastic theologian Martin Dorp was finally persuaded by Thomas More to adopt it. [39]

There were textual errors and printing errors in the Received Text when it was first printed. These and other readings were corrected in subsequent editions of the printed text. The history of the text from 1516 through 1881 is a history of purification and each edition of the Received text brought it closer to perfection. These editions represented steps in the process of God's preservation of His pure words.

Some may object to the previous statement on the grounds that if God preserves His words He did not need to purify or perfect them. It is true that His words in Greek are pure and perfect, already. However, it was not the words He was perfecting, but rather a *printed* Greek text that brought all the words of God in the New Testament together into one printed book. This is something that had never before existed. Printing was a new thing. Hand-written copies of the New Testament were often incomplete and sometimes had errors. All of this had to be looked at carefully and decisions made as to what was the correct reading. This is not the same as the process of textual criticism going on today among doubting and unbelieving scholars. This all took place in a context of faith in God's preservation of His words.

The conquests of the Muslims in Turkey had caused many eastern scholars and churchmen to move into Central and Western Europe. With them, they brought many manuscripts and the knowledge of Greek by those who spoke it. Some became teachers. Western Europeans learned Greek from those who knew it as a living language. One who learned Greek well was the scholar, Erasmus.

Desiderius Erasmus (1466-1536)

Desiderius Erasmus (1466-1536) was one of the most famous scholars of the Renaissance and Reformation. He traveled widely in Europe during his lifetime and collected a number of New Testament manuscripts. Among these were the following with their designations on the Gregory-Aland list:

1) 1-an 11th century manuscript of the Gospels, Acts, and the Epistles. (Still designated 1)
2) 2^e-an 11th or 12th century manuscript of the Gospels. (Now designated 2)
3) 2^{ap}-a 12th century manuscript of Acts and the Epistles. (Now designated 2815)
4) 4^{ap}-a 15th century manuscript of Acts and the Epistles. (Now designated 2816)
5) 1^{rk}-a 12th century manuscript of Revelation. (Now designated 2814)
6) 7-a 12th century manuscript of the Gospels. (Still designated 7)

7) 817-a 15th century manuscript of the gospels. (Still designated 817)
8) 3-a 12th century manuscript of the entire New Testament except Revelation (Still designated 3). This was used in Erasmus' second edition.
9) The Complutensian Polyglot in his later editions.

Erasmus issued five editions of the Greek text: 1516, 1519, 1522, 1527, and 1535.

Erasmus had access to many more manuscripts than this. He traveled Europe and devoured libraries. The Papal Librarian, Paulus Bombasius, gave him many variant readings and offered the entire Vaticanus manuscript to him to use. Erasmus rejected Vaticanus. Regardless, the manuscripts he used were Traditional Text manuscripts and were consistent with the wide variety of other Traditional Text manuscripts.

J.H. Merle D'Aubigne, the historian of the early nineteenth century, also had this opinion as expressed in his book, *History of the Reformation of the Sixteenth Century*.

> Nothing was more important at the dawn of the Reformation than the publication of the Testament of Jesus Christ in the original language. Never had Erasmus worked so carefully. 'If I told what sweat it cost me, no one would believe me.' He had collated many Greek MSS of the New Testament, and was surrounded by all the commentaries and translations, by the writings of Origen, Cyprian, Ambrose, Basil, Chrysostom, Cyril, Jerome, and Augustine. ... He had investigated the texts according to the principles of sacred criticism. When a knowledge of Hebrew was necessary, he had consulted Capito, and more particularly Ecolampadius. Nothing without Theseus, said he of the latter, making use of a Greek proverb.[40]

In addition, Edward Hills reasoned this to be true based on Erasmus' knowledge of all the important textual variants.

> Through his study of the writings of Jerome and other Church Fathers Erasmus became very well informed concerning the variant readings of the New Testament text. Indeed almost all the important variant readings known to scholars today were already known to Erasmus more than 460 years ago and discussed in the notes (previously prepared) which he placed

after the text in his editions of the Greek New Testament. Here, for example, Erasmus dealt with such problem passages as the conclusion of the Lord's Prayer (Matt. 6:13), the interview of the rich young man with Jesus (Matt. 19:17-22), the ending of Mark (Mark 16:9-20), the angelic song (Luke 2:14), the angel, agony, and bloody seat omitted (Luke 22:43-44), the woman taken in adultery (John 7:53-8:11), and the mystery of godliness (1 Tim. 3:16). [41]

Erasmus was provided with 365 readings from Codex Vaticanus by Juan Ginés de Sepúlveda (1490-1573), a Roman Catholic philosopher and theologian, who wrote to Erasmus in 1533-1534 about the differences between Vaticanus and Erasmus' Greek text. [42] An article on the web site, AV1611, has the following to say regarding this. In doing so, they cite Samuel Prideaux Tregelles, a well-known nineteenth century scholar, in his book, *An Account of the Printed Text of the Greek New Testament with Remarks on Its Revision upon Critical Principal Together with a Collation of Critical Texts,* along with two other books.

> Furthermore, Erasmus was in regular correspondence with Professor Paulus Bombasius, the Papal librarian, who sent him any variant readings which he desired. In fact, in 1533, a correspondent of Erasmus (a Catholic priest named Juan Sepulveda) sent Erasmus 365 selected readings from Vaticanus B as proof of its superiority to the *Textus Receptus*. He offered to make the entire document available to Erasmus for use in his latest edition of the TR. [43]

Finally, the manuscripts used by Erasmus were Traditional Text manuscripts that followed the vast majority of all manuscripts, which we have discussed before. Bishop Ellicott (1819-1905), contemporary of Dean Burgon and Westcott and Hort, member of the English Revised Version translation committee in the late nineteenth century, wrote the following.

> The manuscripts which Erasmus used differ, for the most part, only in small and insignificant details, from the great bulk of the cursive MSS. The general character of their text is the same. By this observation the pedigree of the Received Text is carried up beyond the individual manuscripts used by Erasmus ... That pedigree stretches back to remote antiquity. The first ancestor of the Received Text was at least contemporary with the oldest of our extant MSS, if not older than any one of them. [44]

The Complutensian Polyglot

While Erasmus was laboring in Central Europe, a group of scholars in Spain was working on an edition of the whole Bible. The effort was led by Cardinal Francisco Jiménez de Cisneros (1436–1517), called Cardinal Ximenes. The Complutensian Polyglot was a Bible in Greek, Latin, Aramaic, and Hebrew. Cardinal Ximenes collected a number of Greek manuscripts. The work went on from 1502 to 1517. The Greek New Testament was printed in 1514, but not issued. However, Erasmus' Greek New Testament was published and issued first. The Complutensian Polyglot was not in circulation until 1522.

Although it is not historically known what specific sources he used, it is clear that many of the Greek copies Ximenes gathered were of the Traditional Greek type, which was the same type of manuscripts that produced the Received Text. This seems evident, because the KJB translators relied on the Complutensian New Testament as one of their sources. However, it also had some corrupt sources as well, seeing they used Jerome's Latin Vulgate (400 AD), the official Bible of the Roman Catholic Church. However, according to F.F. Bruce, it does not appear that the manuscript *Vaticanus* was a source for the Polyglot. Regardless, it was good enough to become a resource for the coming editions of the Received Text and, as we will see, for the King James translation.

God is the God of History

We should take a close look at what God was doing at this time. God was not merely sitting in Heaven watching the antics of some men who styled themselves as scholars. No, He was making preparation for a major change in history. Some have said that Erasmus was in competition with Ximenes to get his New Testament published first. I see it differently. It was God who was in competition with Ximenes, because He wanted Erasmus' text published first, so that it would be available to be used in the upcoming Reformation, when Europe rebelled against the Catholic Church. If a text produced by a Catholic Cardinal won first place, the Reformation may never have happened. Erasmus was forced to become a priest, but he never performed in the priesthood. Erasmus' first edition was published in 1516. The Reformation began the following year, 1517, when Martin Luther posted his ninety-five theses to the door of the church in Wittenberg, Germany. Erasmus' second edition in 1519 became the basis of Martin Luther's German translation. This was all before the Polyglot was published in 1522. Martin Luther's German New Testament was published the same year, 1522. God made a deliberate choice of the Received

Text over the Complutensian Polyglot. Nevertheless, the Polyglot became an important source for the further purification of the Received Text.

The Complutensian Greek text became the basis for the Greek New Testament of the polyglot printed in Antwerp in 1568-72 by Christopher Plantin.

Robert Stephanus (1503-1559) and Simon Colinaeus

Robert Stephanus (1503-1559) and his stepfather, Simon Colinaeus, were the next editors of the Received Text. They were French printers in Paris. Colinaeus issued an edition of the TR in 1534. The editions of Robert Stephanus (Estienne in French) were issued in 1546, 1549, 1550, and 1551. His editions of the Received Text aroused the opposition of the Catholic Church so much that he had to flee Paris in 1550 and settle in Geneva, Switzerland. His last edition was from Geneva and was the first to be divided into chapters and verses. The third edition was known as the "royal edition" or "editio regia," and it was the first to use a critical apparatus, referring to manuscript sources. Stephanus used the Complutensian Polyglot and had manuscript evidence beyond that listed above as used by Erasmus. This included:

1) Codex Bezae-a 5th century manuscript including most of the four Gospels and Acts and a small fragment of 3 John. (Now designated D^{ea} or 05)
2) Codex Regius-an 8th century manuscript containing most of the four Gospels. (Now designated Le or 019)
3) 4-a 13th century manuscript with an almost complete copy of the four gospels.
4) 5-a 13th century manuscript of the entire New Testament except Revelation.
5) 6-a 13th century manuscript of most of the New Testament except Revelation.
6) 7^{pk}-a 12th century manuscript of nearly all of Paul's epistles (now designated 2817).
7) 8-an 11th century manuscript of the entire four Gospels.
8) 9-a 12th century manuscript of the entire four Gospels.

Theodore Beza (1519–1605)

Theodore Beza (1519–1605), of Geneva, started with the third edition of Stephanus (1550) and published editions nine times from 1565-1604. A tenth edition was published after his death. In his 1582 edition, Beza listed some additional materials he used. Some of these were not Greek New Testaments. They included a Syriac version, an Arabic version translated into Latin, D (Codex Bezae), and D2 (Codex Claromontanus). However, he rarely changed anything from the fourth edition of Stephanus. God was always in control.

None of these editors differed with one another more than about 250 times and many of these were spelling, accent marks, breathing marks, word order, and other minor differences.

The Authorized Version (KJB)

The King James Bible translators used more than one edition of the Received Text for their translation. In 1603, the Received text was still developing, so the translators were open to the possibility that the text may still need to be edited. According to Frederick Scrivener (1813-1891), it is reasonable to determine that their primary source text was Beza 1598, because the KJV is almost an exact match for it.

> In considering what text had the best right to be regarded as "the text presumed to underlie the 'Authorized Version," was necessary to take into account the composite nature of the Authorized Version, as due to successive revisions of Tyndale's translation. Tyndale himself followed the second and third editions of Erasmus' Greek text (1519, 1522). In the revisions of his translation previous to 1611 a partial use was made of other texts; of which ultimately the most influential were the various editions of Beza from 1560 to 1598 ... Between 1598 and 1611 no important edition appeared; so that Beza's fifth and last text was more likely than any other to be in the hands of King James's revisers, and to be accepted by them as the best standard within their reach. It is moreover found on comparison to agree more closely with the Authorized Version than any other Greek text ... [45]

Dr. Scrivener compared every verse of the KJB New Testament with Beza's 1598 text. He found about 190 differences (variances). All these are listed in the book described in note 45.

How did the KJV translators decide what edits to make to the TR? They certainly arrived at their conclusions by divine guidance. They started with Beza 1598, but they also used the other editions of the TR, the Complutensian Polyglot, and other language translations, such as Martin Luther's German, the

Reina-Valera Spanish, and the Erasmus and Beza Latin translations. In the final analysis, the adjustments they made were ***the pinnacle of the edits made to the TR text***. However, the edits of the KJB translators to the Received Text of Beza were made in English, not Greek. Their edits to the Received Text of Beza were incorporated into the Greek Text by Scrivener. The KJV translation and its suggested changes to Beza's 1598 text was an important step toward a completely pure Greek text.

The Elzevir Editions

The Elzevir Editions were published after the publication of the King James Version. The Elzevirs were a Dutch family of printers. They published two editions in 1624 and 1633. There was a statement in the preface of the 1633 edition that declared this text was now the Greek text received by all. Hence, the name Received Text or, in Latin, Textus Receptus, is applied to the entire Greek text tradition starting in 1516 with Erasmus' first edition up the 1881 edition of Frederick Scrivener.

The 1689 Baptist Confession of Faith

The 1689 Baptist Confession of Faith confirmed the general attitude toward the Received Text. The 1646 Westminster Confession of Faith agreed with it.

> The Old Testament in Hebrew (which was the native language of the people of God of old), and the New Testament in Greek (which at the time of the writing of it was most generally known to the nations), **being immediately inspired by God, and by his singular care and providence kept pure in all ages, are therefore authentic**; so as in all controversies of religion, the church is finally to appeal to them. But because these original tongues are not known to all the people of God, who have a right unto, and interest in the Scriptures, and are commanded in the fear of God to read and search them, therefore they are to be translated into the vulgar language of every nation unto which they come, that the Word of God dwelling plentifully in all, they may worship him in an acceptable manner, and through patience and comfort of the Scriptures may have hope. [46] (Emphasis mine-Author)

This is the true Bible-believing attitude. As mentioned above, the text accepted and received by all, at this time, was the Textus Receptus. Therefore, it is certain that the tesxt meant in the confession is the Textus Receptus.

The Scrivener edition

Frederick H. A. Scrivener (1813-1891) issued an edition of the Received Text in 1881, which was reprinted by the Trinitarian Bible Society in 1894. It is usually ignored by liberal and liberal leaning scholars. Even some KJB Bible believers ignore it. However, it is a valid edition of the text and a further purification. It is entirely based on the Beza 1598 edition with the edits made by the King James translators. When it was published in 1881, it was said to be "According to the text followed in the Authorized Version." Scrivener used a process to find and adjust the differences between Beza's text and the KJV.

1) First, Scrivener compared each verse of the KJB New Testament with Beza 1598 to see if they matched.
2) He found about 190 places where they were different.
3) For each difference, he looked for the Greek manuscript evidence or Greek text that had the necessary reading. He would not make a change in Beza without Greek authority.
4) He made changes in the 190 places based on what he found in the Greek evidence.
5) He corrected printer errors in the Beza text.
6) He corrected Beza for inconsistent and incorrect Greek spelling.
7) He adjusted the paragraphs and punctuation.

Scrivener's labors were comparable to those of any other TR editor. Erasmus may have labored more because he put the text together in the first place. Stephanus may have labored more because he divided the text into verses and chapters in his fourth edition. However, the labors of Scrivener rise to their level of scholarship and intensity.

A Specific Example of the Scrivener Edits

A specific example of the Scrivener edits is Revelation 7:14.

Revelation 7:14-(KJV) And I said unto him, Sir, thou knowest. And he said to me, These are they which came out of great tribulation, and have washed their robes, and made **them** white in the blood of the Lamb.

(**Beza**) And I said unto him, Sir, you know. And he said to me, These are they which came out of great tribulation, and have washed their robes, and made **their robes** white in the blood of the Lamb.

(**Scrivener**) And I said unto him, Sir, you know. And he said to me, These are they which came out of great tribulation, and have washed their robes, and made **them** white in the blood of the Lamb.

Scrivener found the correct reading in the Greek text of the Complutensian Polyglot. Therefore, the Scrivener Edition of the TR has the right reading.

A Perspective

The KJV translators helped to make an excellent text better, by choosing alternative readings that already existed in the historic Traditional Greek Text that the Biblical church had used since the first century. God has preserved all His inspired Greek words. They were already pure (Prov. 30:5) and are available.

So, on the one hand, the men of the KJB translated God's Words that had been in existence since the days of the Apostles. On the other hand, the King James translators were also editors of the Received Text. Their edits were made in English, rather than Greek. It was Dr. Scrivener, who placed those edits into the Greek Received Text after searching for the Greek source of the edits. Then, he produced the "Greek text that underlay the KJV." It should be noted that the edits in the Received Text made by the translators of the King James Bible *were the final edits made to the Received Text.* Elzevir's edits did not flow into the Scrivener text. The KJV translators' edits did. God, who is sovereign in history, did not make a mistake here. The God of history led the work that was done on the TR by Dr. Scrivener. His edition was the final edition of the TR.

Other Reasons to Believe the Received Text is the Word of God

When we examine history, we can see the choices God has made. When we see the work of God, we are given a chance to walk in harmony with Him. The Received Text is a continuation of Traditional Text history. It has a consistent history from the first century. But, there are other reasons to believe it to be the Word of God.

For example, God could have chosen to base the entire Reformation on the Complutensian Polyglot, produced by a Roman Catholic Cardinal, but He did not. *God deliberately chose the Received Text and the Hebrew Ben Chayim Masoretic Text to be the foundation and power of the Reformation.* The cry of the Pope rejecting Reformers was, "Sola Scriptura!" ("Only Scripture!"). The Bible they embraced was the Received Text and the Masoretic Text. God clearly led them to do this. Many modern scholars and historians recognize that the Reformation was from God, but they will not acknowledge the Bible of the Reformers. God did not make a mistake when He began to free His church from the overbearing hand of Rome. He certainly did not make a mistake when He chose which Bible He would use to do it.

The Received text that God chose came from manuscripts of the Traditional Text. That text is the type of text found in over 90% of all the available ancient manuscript evidence that goes back to 150 AD or earlier in Greek manuscripts. It goes back at least as far in the ancient translations into Syriac and Latin. It goes back to the first century in the quotes of the church "fathers." It has been the New Testament of the Greek churches for many centuries. The Traditional text rests upon solid evidence greater than that of the UBS text. The Traditional text has been available from the days of the apostles to now.

As I have pointed out, corrupters of the Scriptures were at work in the days of the apostle Paul. It is no wonder, because the Devil has attempted to imitate everything God has done (2 Cor. 11). Some of those corrupt manuscripts are still around. Two of them are Vaticanus and Sinaiticus. The UBS text is based on weak corrupt sources and was edited by men who were unbelievers in the inspiration, preservation, and authority of the Word of God (blind leaders of the blind).

The following are some further reasons to embrace the Masoretic text of Ben Chayim and the Greek Received Text.

The Received Greek and Hebrew Texts were the cause of the great evangelistic movements that took place in Europe from 1500 to 1950. It began with the 1516 publication of the Received Text, and Martin Luther's translation into German from the TR and Hebrew. A flurry of new translations from the same sources followed over the next century. These translations started a movement of evangelism and teaching that lasted into the 1900's. We are still going on the momentum of that movement. Throughout this period, the liberals and textual critics were on the outside of the movement.

The Received Greek and Hebrew Texts and the translations they produced started the greatest foreign missions movement in history. This began with the Moravian mission movement in the 1600's and 1700's. It finally broke forth in the 1790's with the worldwide mission movement led by William Carey, who went to India from England. He was convinced from the Scriptures that we must commit ourselves to foreign missions. This movement is still going on. It began and was carried on under the Word of God in the form of the Received text and translations from it.

The Received Greek and Hebrew Texts with their translations have been responsible for the Reformation and every great revival since. There have been numerous revivals acknowledged by historians since the Reformation: the Great Awakening, the Cumberland Valley Revival, almost continual revival in 1800's America, and revival under evangelists like Dwight Moody, Billy Sunday, Mordecai Ham, and a host of others. Even Billy Graham "typically used the King James Version when preaching." [47]

On the other hand, the new versions of the English Bible, not translated from the Received Texts, have slowly taken over the Christian landscape since the 1950's. In doing so, they have presided over decay in the churches, weakness in our influence on our culture, general unbelief in the Bible as the Word of God and rejection of the Bible in our culture, and over a society that has progressively become more and more rebellious against God and filled with ungodliness. Look at the downward fall in Romans 1:21-32. The United States has exactly followed that course since the mid-20th century, at the same time the modern English versions have prevailed.

The Greek and Hebrew Texts the King James Bible was translated from are like the Jews. The children of Israel, the Jews, have survived for centuries no matter what has been thrown against them. They have survived, because God wanted them to survive and promised that they would. He has a plan of greatness and prosperity for them. Nothing can destroy the Jews. Likewise, in spite of over one hundred new English translations and the modern marketing techniques that have been used to promote them, they still have not destroyed the King James Bible. The KJB continues to survive and be a best seller, without the special marketing techniques. The KJB continues to enjoy a large popularity that can only be attributed to God. Not only that, but it has been reported by the Trinitarian Bible Society that the Scrivener edition of the TR is the most popular edition.

The United Bible Societies Text and Its Forebears

Of course, it is not the Devil's nature to sit still while God is inspiring a New Testament and preserving both Testaments. Paul explained the work of the Devil in 2 Corinthians 11:3-4, 13-14.

> *3 But I fear, lest by any means, as the serpent beguiled Eve through his subtilty, so your minds should be **corrupted from the simplicity** that is in Christ.*

> 4 For if he that cometh preacheth **another Jesus**, whom we have not preached, or if ye receive **another spirit**, which ye have not received, or **another gospel**, which ye have not accepted, ye might well bear with him.
> 13 For such are **false apostles, deceitful workers**, transforming themselves into the apostles of Christ.
> 14 And no marvel; for **Satan himself is transformed into an angel of light**.
> 15 Therefore it is no great thing if **his ministers also be transformed as the ministers of righteousness**; whose end shall be according to their works.

Satan is revealed in these verses as having his own false ministers, false apostles, and false workers who present another Jesus, impart another spirit, and preach another gospel. Certainly, then, Satan will create another Bible, maybe many other Bibles. That is exactly what he has done, and he began the work in the days of Paul (2 Cor. 2:17).

In the 21st century, there are primarily two competing *printed* Greek New Testaments. One is the Received Text (TR), which is based on the Traditional Greek Text manuscripts. The second, is the United Bible Societies Greek Text (UBS). They cannot both be the true text, because they differ in about 8,000 places. The UBS text is based on about 6% of the ancient evidence, but primarily on two manuscripts that contain most of the New Testament: Vaticanus and Sinaiticus. The United Bible Societies is an association of over 150 Bible Societies scattered around the globe. Its headquarters is in London. It began in 1946 with the British and Foreign Bible Society (1804) and the American Bible Society (1816) among its founding members. The UBS coordinates the work of its member societies. They are involved in Bible translation and distributing Bibles and other literature. The United Bible Societies is an apostate organization. Let me show you why I say that.

The United Bible Societies and Apostasy

These societies have been characterized by apostasy from the very beginning. This includes the British and Foreign Bible Society (BFBS) before it helped found the UBS. When the BFBS started, it immediately began to cooperate with Catholic priests including helping a priest in his translation of a new German New Testament. It would be well to note that the Catholic Church has always promoted its own version of the Bible, which is different from the protestant Bibles (based on the Received Text) in thousands of places. They have always condemned purely protestant versions translated from the Received Text.

> The policy of the United Bible Societies regarding the Apocrypha and interconfessional co-operation with Roman Catholic scholars on Bible translations was outlined in a booklet published by the American Bible Society in 1970 ... Referring to the interdenominational character of the Bible societies, [the booklet] states that Roman Catholics participated in the founding of some Bible societies in Europe, and that "the British and Foreign Bible Society from the beginning co-operated with Roman Catholic groups." It is also acknowledged that Roman Catholic churchmen were invited to participate in the founding of the American Bible Society in 1816. [48]

> The work of joint Bible translation and distribution between Protestants and Catholics was encouraged by the Driebergen conference of Bible societies in June 1964, which was attended also by Roman Catholics. The chief recommendations of the conference were: to prepare a "common text" of the Bible in the original languages, acceptable to all Churches, including Roman Catholics; and to explore the possibility of preparing a "common translation" in certain languages, which could be used by Protestants and Roman Catholics alike. It was further recommended that the Bible societies should consider translating and publishing the Apocrypha when Churches specifically requested it. [49]

In addition to cooperating with the Roman Catholic Church, the BFBS also included Unitarians, who deny the deity of Jesus Christ.

> When the constitution of the British and Foreign Bible Society was first formulated, it was understandably not foreseen that the question of Unitarianism would have much relevance to the society's work. Before long, however, Unitarians gained substantial influence upon the affairs of The Bible Society, particularly in Europe, where some auxiliary societies were run almost exclusively by persons of Unitarians beliefs. [50]

This precipitated an argument so intense that it finally resulted in a split in the BFBS. In 1831, a large number of delegates broke away and formed the Trinitarian Bible Society which is faithful to the Trinity, as well as the KJB and the Received Text to this day.

The UBS Greek Text was produced by liberal heretics. Both the Nestle-Aland Text in Germany and the United Bible Societies Greek Text were originally based on the Westcott and Hort Text, which was used to translate the Revised Version in England (1881).

> The international committee that produced the United Bible Societies Greek New Testament, not only adopted the Westcott and Hort edition as its basic text, but followed their methodology in giving attention to both external and internal consideration.[51]

B. F. Westcott and J. F. A. Hort, the Anglican scholars of the nineteenth century, learned liberal beliefs and thinking from a century of liberal thought coming from Germany. They hated the Textus Receptus (on which the KJV was based). They sought to turn the examination of the Biblical text (which was called "textual criticism") into a purely scientific thing that treated the Bible as if it was the same as any other book and dismissed inspiration and the providential preservation of the text altogether.

> Eighteenth century German textual scholars, Johann Griesbach and Johann Bengel, spurred the modern textual critical theory of re-examining the Textus Receptus and introduced a number of "scientific" criteria for determining authentic New Testament readings. In the late nineteenth century, English Churchmen Brooke Westcott and Fenton Hort adopted many of these criteria ... The establishment of these "scientific" criteria for textual criticism caused the divine work of biblical preservation to become a merely naturalistic enterprise. If the only criteria to determine the authentic readings are to determine what manuscripts are the oldest and what readings are supposedly less "improved" and "smooth", then where does one's faith fit in? [52]

This kind of approach to choosing what reading should go into the New Testament text actually led to a methodology that boiled down to little more than mere educated guesses! Should you trust a text that was put together based on the educated guesses of a bunch of theological liberals? Westcott and Hort described this approach.

The first impulse in dealing with a variation is usually to lean on Intrinsic Probability, that is, to consider which of two readings makes the best sense, and to decide between them accordingly. The decision may be made either by an immediate and as it were intuitive judgment, or by weighing cautiously various elements which go to make up what is called sense, such as conformity to grammar and congruity to the purport of the rest of the sentence and of the larger context; to which may rightly be added congruity to the usual style of the author and to his matter in other passages. (intrinsic probability and intuitive judgment = make your best guess-Author) [53]

The first edition of the UBS Text was published in 1966. The text is in its fifth edition, which was published in 2014. The third edition (1975) introduced more than 500 changes in the text of the New Testament. This third edition and the 26th edition of the Nestle-Aland Greek New Testament established a single text for them both. The fourth Edition (1993) and the fifth edition extensively revised the included critical apparatus, but did not change the text. The UBS Greek New Testament and the Nestle-Aland continue to share an identical text.

The Editors of the UBS Text

The first, second and third editions were edited by Kurt Aland, Matthew Black, Carlo M. Martini, Bruce M. Metzger, and Allen Wikgren. The fourth and fifth editions were edited by Barbara Aland, Kurt Aland, Johannes Karavidopoulos, Carlo Martini, and Bruce Metzger. Among these names are individuals who deny that the Bible is verbally inspired and infallible. I will take special note of some of them below.

Bruce Metzger (1914-2007) was George L. Collard Professor of New Testament Language and Literature at the theologically liberal Princeton Theological Seminary. He was the head of the continuing Revised Standard Version translation committee, was the lead catalyst in the translation of the New Revised Standard Version and was involved in the production of the condensed Reader's Digest Bible. Bruce Metzger was an unbeliever in the literal inspiration, preservation, and inerrancy of the Bible. [54] He denied the Mosaic authorship of the Pentateuch (the first five books of the Bible), he believed the Book of Daniel was written after the events the book prophesies, he denied Paul's authorship of some of his New Testament epistles and questioned the authenticity of other New Testament books. [55] He believed that much of the

Old Testament was drawn out of a matrix of myth and legend.[56] He did not believe the story of the Genesis flood. Job was a folktale. Jonah was a legend. Peter did not write 2 Peter and the opening chapters of the Old Testament are not history. [57] Jesus said, "For had ye believed Moses, ye would have believed me: for he wrote of me. But if ye believe not his writings, how shall ye believe my words?" (John 5:46-47)

Kurt Aland was also editor of the Nestle-Aland Text which, as we have said, now matches the UBS text exactly. He rejected verbal inspiration and he did not believe in an authoritative, settled canon of Scripture. He rejected the traditional authorship of the four gospels and other NT books. Dr. Kurt Aland did not believe in the inspiration and infallibility of the Bible. He did not believe in the inerrant preservation of the Bible. [58]

Finally, Carlo Martini is a Roman Catholic Jesuit priest and Cardinal. He was Archbishop of Milan and Professor of New Testament Textual Criticism at the Pontifical Biblical Institute in Rome. [59]

The UBS text has been a completely modernist pro-Catholic production from start to finish. In the Introduction to the Nestle-Aland: Novum Testamentum Graece, 27th edition, page 45, the editors say this about the relationship of the UBS to the Roman Catholic Church.

> The text shared by these two editions was adopted internationally by Bible Societies, and following an agreement between the Vatican and the United Bible Societies it has served as the basis for new translations and for revisions made under their supervision. This marks a significant step with regard to interconfessional relationships. [60]

Those who follow this text are following blind leaders who deny the verbal inspiration of Scripture, the veracity of Scripture, and the verbal plenary preservation of the Scriptures. These editors are blind spiritually and those who follow them often do it out of ignorance. If the blind follow the blind ...?

The UBS Text differs greatly from the Received Text. There are thousands of word differences between the two. Everett W. Fowler evaluated the third edition of the UBS Greek Text compared to the Received Text, which, as mentioned before, is the same text as the fourth and fifth editions. He published the results in *Evaluating Versions of the New Testament*. [61] Figure 12 enumerates the whole verses and partial verses missing from the UBS text as compared to the TR.

Number of whole verses missing in UBS	17
Omissions of whole and partial verses	1309

Fig. 12

The total word differences were categorized as follows. These do not include differences in spelling of proper nouns. The category of "words classed as different words" does not include "spelling variations shown in Greek lexicons as accepted ways of spelling words which have identical meanings, but which are not listed as different words (for example: labor=labour)."

Words in the Received Text omitted from UBS	3602
Words classed as different words	3146
Words in UBS not in the Received Text	976
Words spelled different, but not different words	950
Total word differences	8674

Fig. 13

Why do we have such concern over individual words, even if some of them do not materially affect the translation? There are a total of 8,674 word differences between the Received Greek Text and the UBS Greek Text. The New Testament was inspired in Greek and every Word of God is important. As we have seen before that God, Himself, emphasizes the importance of every word.

The United Bible Societies Greek text was produced by spiritually blind men. Those who follow the work of these men have blind spots, as well. "If the blind follow the blind ..."

Why the Received Greek Text and the Received Hebrew Masoretic Text? The answer is quite simple. The Received Texts have always been God's choice and He is certainly a lot smarter than you and I. I would rather be on the side of what God has chosen than on the side of modernistic scholarship.

CHAPTER FOUR
A BIBLE BELIEVER ASKS,
WHY USE GREEK AND HEBREW?

Not so long ago, I talked to two Pastors about the source texts for Bible translating. The first asked me, "Why don't you just use the King James Bible to translate?" The second told me not to say much in his church about the Greek New Testament, because his people did not like it. I understand where these questions come from. For many years, I have run in circles that included quite a number of Pastors who saw things this way. The viewpoint is that the King James Bible is the word of God in English. It has no errors. Therefore, it should be sufficient for translation work. Also, for decades, scholars have used "the Greek" to attempt to discredit the KJB. Therefore, some look on Greek as an enemy. Some of these Pastors believe the KJB is inspired, and some believe it has superseded the Greek and Hebrew Bible. My view is this: I believe the KJV is an accurate translation and is the word of God without error in the English language and I do not use the Greek text (the TR) to criticize the KJV. At the same time, God promised to preserve His words in Greek and Hebrew, and He has done so.

There are a number of reasons why I believe a translator must either 1) translate direct from the Greek and Hebrew received texts (while using the KJV as a translation guide), or 2) make strong reference to these languages in the process of translating by using the Greek and Hebrew tools that are available. Please, allow me to explain below why it is valid to use the true Greek and Hebrew texts.

It is the method used by the King James translators. On the title page of any King James Bible it says. "Newly translated out of the original tongues and with the former translations diligently compared and revised ..." Notice that the first thing mentioned is that the King James Bible is a translation from the original languages ("tongues"), that is, from Hebrew, Aramaic, and Greek. The translators based their work on the inspired Words of God. God promised to preserve those words and the KJB translators professed to have them. There had been several previous English translations. They used them as additional resources but changed them based on their own translation of the original languages ("diligently compared and revised"). They could have based their translation on Tyndale's translation alone, but they did not. Tyndale's translation had a great influence on the KJB translators, but they translated direct from Hebrew, Aramaic, and Greek. This was their method.

The Hebrew, Aramaic, and Greek words are the only inspired words of God. I have often repeated this. Therefore, these inspired Hebrew, Aramaic, and Greek texts are *the word of God.* Every word came from God. They are His words. The Greek and Hebrew Bible is the Word of God as much as the King James Bible is the word of God. *So, the words of the Greek New Testament and the Hebrew/Aramaic Old Testament were given by God, they are inspired words, and, therefore, they are perfect words. They ARE the Word of God.*

God is perfect. There is no fault or blemish in Him. As such, all He does is perfect and without error. *"As for God, his way is perfect; the word of the LORD is tried: he is a buckler to all them that trust in him"* (2 Sam. 22:31). So, God's way, all He does, is perfect. Part of what God has done is to give us His words. It follows, then, that when He gave His words, those words in Greek, Hebrew, and Aramaic were perfect, without error, and infallible. *And, they still are.*

God has preserved the Hebrew, Aramaic, and Greek words He inspired. The King James translators apparently believed they had those words and, truly, they did. The inspired words were not lost at any time in the past. The King James translators had these Hebrew, Aramaic, and Greek words and the words haven't gotten lost in the last 408 years since. Today, I can pick up the New Testament in Greek and read the inspired Greek words of God. I have them on my bookshelf, in my phone, on my computer, and on my Android pad. I also have the Hebrew and Aramaic. God has kept His promise to preserve His words. We still have the original inspired words. We ought to feel perfectly free to use them if we wish.

There is great value in a multitude of counselors. "Where no counsel is, the people fall: but in the multitude of counsellors there is safety (Prov. 11:14). "Without counsel purposes are disappointed: but in the multitude of counsellors they are established" (Prov. 15:22). The King James translators knew the value of many councilors in their translation work. They had all the former English translations available. From those, they saw all the word choices of those translators. They also had foreign translations: the Martin Luther German, the Reina-Valera Spanish, the French, the Latin Vulgate, the Erasmus Latin translation, and the Beza Latin translation. They also had the Complutensian Polyglot. A translator needs all the help he can get. The Greek New Testament and the Hebrew Old Testament are key councilors for the translation of the Bible into any language.

The Greek and Hebrew words are perfect and pure. "The words of the LORD are pure words (Ps. 12:6). "The law of the LORD is perfect" (Ps. 19:7). The words He was talking about were Hebrew words at the time He said it. His statements clearly apply to the Greek words of the New Testament, as well. We apply the same truths to His English words. My father was a master carpenter. He taught me a few tricks of the trade. If I wanted to cut several pieces of board the same length, I would measure the first one exactly and cut it. Then, I would use the first board, measured exactly, to mark the following boards, so that I could cut them to the exact same length as the original. The Greek and Hebrew texts are the original inspired Words of God for the New and Old Testaments. They are the standard by which all translations are measured. If a translation does not meet that standard, it should be rejected or revised. This was a generally accepted principle when the KJB was translated. There is reason to believe that has changed. Men like William Carey and Adoniram Judson and their associates knew that. The King James translators knew it and acted accordingly by translating that standard accurately. In these last days, we have lost sight of it.

A Word About Lexicons

A Greek or Hebrew dictionary is called a *lexicon*. These days, there are some who feel that a lexicon is dangerous thing to use. For example, the Greek dictionary by Henry Thayer is considered biased, because Thayer was a Unitarian. He denied the deity of the Lord Jesus Christ. It is possible that Thayer was biased in a few of his entries. I use Thayer ... carefully. I also sometimes use lexicons from the early nineteenth century. I do this in the hope that early lexicons will be less affected by liberal textual criticism and bad doctrine. However, this is also why you should use more than one lexicon. In the multitude of counselors, there is safety. You will find that most lexicons, even the early ones are in agreement on most words.

If you download the "e-sword" program (which I highly recommend) or "the Word" program, you will find that they have a module called "King James Concordance" (KJC). The KJC is linked to the numbering system in Strong's Concordance. The KJC lists all the Greek words used in the King James Bible and the various ways the KJB translated those words. The King James translators did not tie themselves to uniformly translate each Greek word by the same English word every time. They made extensive use of synonyms. However, at the same time, they translated consistently with the definitions of the Greek words. The result of this is the KJB is a very good Greek lexicon all by itself. I have found, in the many times I have looked up words, that the various ways a Greek or Hebrew word is translated gives me a very helpful understanding of that word. The KJC is not 100% accurate, but it still provides a great deal of useful information. In my opinion, lexicons ought to still be used, because they can provide additional information. For example, there are some Greek words used only one time in the NT. A lexicon can help in those and other cases.

CHAPTER FIVE
THE GREAT NEED FOR BIBLE TRANSLATING

Most Christians are familiar with the Great Commission. Jesus told us to go and teach all nations (Mt. 28:20). That command has never been fulfilled. We have not yet reached all nations. We may, indeed, have reached into every country, but we have not yet reached every nation. What is a Biblical nation? Whatever it is, it is not a geopolitical country as we think of nations today. A Biblical nation is much more ethnically based. In fact, the Greek word for nation is *"ethnos."* It is the source from which we get our word "ethnic."

What is a Biblical nation? Charles Turner defines a nation in his book, Biblical Bible Translating, by using four criteria: lineage, language, laws, and land. His definition is summarized below:

> 1. Lineage: In Gen. 12:2 God promised to make Abraham a great nation. The nation of Israel was descended from Abraham. Therefore, they had a common ancestry. In Gen. 12:7, God said that He would give the land of Canaan to Abraham's seed. The word "seed" refers to descendants or lineage. Abraham's son was Isaac and Isaac's son was Jacob and Jacob's sons were the twelve patriarchs who begat the twelve tribes of the nation of Israel. The nation was primarily a people with a common ancestry.
>
> 2. Language: Gen 14:13 calls Abraham a Hebrew. He was called a Hebrew for three reasons. First he was descended from a man named Eber (Gen. 11:14-16). The second is that he lived near Hebron at that time, but the other is that he spoke a distinct language that became the language of the Hebrew people and was called by that name. A Biblical nation is a people who speak a language that is distinct from others and is generally not understood by people outside the common lineage.
>
> 3. Laws: A Biblical nation must be bound together in a community governed and organized by laws. God called Israel to receive their law in Ex. 24:12.
>
> 4. Land: A Biblical nation normally has a geographic boundary in which they live. In Gen. 12:7, God promised Israel the land of Canaan

as an inheritance. Each of the tribes was given distinct geographical portions of the inheritance. [62]

Brother Turner says, "Any group of people who recognize themselves as having a common lineage, who speak a distinct language, who have common laws (written or oral), and who live in a prescribed area of land, are a nation in the sight of God." [63]   The Great Commission commands us to take the word of God to every single one of these nations. That is a much bigger job than simply planting a church within every geopolitical state or country, because most countries have more than one Biblical nation.

The Bible also provides us with other names of people groups. In Gen. 12:3 the scriptures said to Abraham, "and in thee shall all families of the earth be blessed." We are told in Rev. 5:9, "And they sung a new song, saying, Thou art worthy to take the book, and to open the seals thereof: for thou west slain, and hast redeemed us to God by thy blood out of every kindred, and tongue, and people, and nation." Here we have references to tongues, families, kindreds, and people. What are these? What is the Biblical definition of these people group terms?

The term, *tongue,* refers to languages (see 1 Cor. 13:1-3). The verse says "every" tongue or language. So, in heaven there will be representatives of every spoken language on earth.

The first use of the term, *families,* is in Gen. 10. The Scriptures tell us, "By these were the isles of the Gentiles divided in their lands; everyone after his tongue, after their families, in their nations." If we look in verses 2-4, we find that the sons of Japheth produced seven nations, all of whom are named. In verses 3 and 4, the descendants of two of these sons are named. The descendants of the sons of Japheth were the families that made up the seven nations. In other words, a family is a smaller division of a nation that is made up of related peoples, but much larger than our "nuclear family." In Gen 36:40-43, we have a description of the nation of Edom. Esau (or Edom) founded the nation and his sons, who are listed, produced the families. Study Numbers 26.

The nation of Israel (all descendants of Jacob or Israel) were divided by tribes (Reuben, Levy, Judah, etc., descendants of Israel), which were finally divided into families (descendants of the sons of Israel). A family can be traced back to a common ancestor and is a group that feels a distinct identity while also being identified as a part of the whole nation (see 2 Chron. 35:5). The New World Dictionary of American English defines it this way: "all those claiming descent from a common ancestor." [64]   While different nations usually speak different languages, families within a nation may also speak a dialect of the nation's language, or they may speak the common language of the nation.

The word *kindred* is similar to the term *family* and refers to related people and can refer to people related across families. *People* is a general term for a large group of distinct ethnically related individuals with a distinct identity similar to *nations*.

> This is how God looks at the world. Geopolitical countries are secondary. Noah Webster agreed to this definition in his 1828 dictionary. Nation, as its etymology imports, originally denoted a family or race of men descended from a common progenitor, like tribe, but by emigration, conquest and intermixture of men of different families, this distinction is in most countries lost. [65]

Noah Webster died in 1843. That was about fifty years after the start of the great missionary movement that began with William Carey going to India in the 1790's. Perhaps Webster did not know what the missionaries were discovering, because he was wrong about the distinction being lost. The great missionary movement has clearly revealed that the "family or race distinctions" have absolutely NOT been lost. They are very much alive in Africa, Asia, Central America, and South America. The distinctions are very much alive in Europe and North America with the immigration of ethnic groups that identify with one another more than with the political country they occupy.

Jesus said, "Look on the fields." (John 4:24) The original nations of Genesis 10 have divided many times and many families have become nations themselves with distinct languages and families. Modern mission leaders have proposed various ways of looking at the nations in order to clarify the targets for evangelism.

In June 2000, Mission Frontiers magazine included an article entitled "Finishing the Task." After it explains how the Gospel has made amazing progress over the previous 20 centuries, it tells us that two billion people still live outside the influence of the Gospel.

> The fact is that the Gospel often expands within a community but does not normally "jump" across boundaries between peoples, especially boundaries that are created by hate or prejudice. People can influence their "near neighbors" whose language and culture they understand, but where there is a prejudice boundary, religious faith, which is almost always bound up with many cultural features of the first group, simply does not easily "jump" to the next group, unless that group desires to adopt the other's culture in preference

to its own....If all the members of every church in the world were to bring every one of their friends and relatives within the same cultural group to obedient faith in Christ, and they in turn were able to bring all their friends and relatives to Christ and so on, no matter how much time you allow, there would still be billions who would never come to faith. They would be held at a distance from the Gospel by boundaries of prejudice and culture. The church does not readily grow within peoples where relevant churches do not exist. One-third of the individuals in the world live within people groups with no church.

This article suggests some practical ways to look at the unreached nations and families of earth. The article first lists six major cultural blocks where we find unreached peoples: Muslim, Hindu, Buddhist, Chinese, Tribal, and other. Then it gives twelve major affinity blocks: African Sahel, Cushitic, Arab World, Iranian, Indo-Iranian, Turkic, Tibetan, East Asian, Southeast Asian, Malay, Eurasian, and Jewish. Finally, we are given two more: ethnolinguistic peoples and unimax peoples. The ethnolinguistic people group concept is a Biblical way to look at the nations.

Ethnolinguistic Peoples for Mobilization and Preparation

An ethnolinguistic people is an ethnic group distinguished by its self-identity with traditions of common descent, history, customs, and language.

The Laz people from the Black Sea region of Turkey, for example, are easily identified by other Turks not only by their distinctive facial features but also by their unique "romantic" pronunciation of Turkish.

Sometimes what appears initially to be a single ethnolinguistic group turns out, in fact, to be many more...Recent cooperative efforts among mission researchers have produced fairly comprehensive lists of ethnolinguistic peoples. These lists have given a great boost to the cause of frontier mission. Much of the information is being used to make profiles and other relevant information widely available through printed media and the world-wide web. People blocs and ethnolinguistic lists give us a simple way to identify peoples and make the larger body of Christ aware of their existence and the need to reach them. The ethnolinguistic approach stimulates prayer and initial planning for specific peoples leading to serious strategic efforts to evangelize them.

Unimax Peoples for People Movements to Christ

A unimax people is the maximum sized group sufficiently unified to be reached by a single indigenous church planting movement. "Unified" here refers to the fact that there are no significant barriers of either understanding or acceptance to stop the spread of the Gospel. [66]

In 1982, mission leaders hammered out a useful definition for a "people group." For evangelistic purposes [a people group] is "the largest group within which the Gospel can spread as a church planting movement without encountering barriers of understanding or acceptance."[67]

The term *unreached* needs some definition. The meaning of this term describes the essential missionary task. That is, it tells us what must be done in order for indigenous Christians to finish the evangelization of their own nation. For this purpose we can <u>define</u> *unreached* by rather defining what a *reached* people is. A reached people is a people among whom "a viable indigenous church planting movement that carries the potential to renew whole extended families and transform whole societies" has been established. "It is viable in that it can grow on its own, indigenous meaning that it is not seen as foreign, and a church planting movement that continues to evangelize the rest of the people group." [68] Many have settled on a simple way to judge this. An unreached people is any group which is less than 2% evangelical or born again.

Many of these people groups do not have a Bible translation in their own language. They cannot read or study the Bible to grow strong spiritually as you can. They cannot quote the Bible to their neighbors in order to win them to Christ, as you can. We take the word of God for granted, sometimes leaving the Bible lay on a table until it collects dust, but these people have no Bible at all.

A View of the World

One of the premier organizations compiling people group statistics is the Global Research section of the International Mission Board (www.peoplegrpups.org). They have amassed information on over 11,000 ethnolinguistic groups. These nations are listed by continent and by country.

Thus, over seven billion people are catalogued as summarized in Fig. 14 as of March 31, 2020.

Continent	Number Countries	Total Nations	Total Population
Africa	58	3017	1,267,540,840
Asia	50	4630	4,576,859,950
Oceana	29	1321	33,272,315
Europe	52	883	749,267,975
Americas	51	1878	1,033,082,930
Total	240	11729	7,660,024,010

Fig. 14 [69]

The information in fig. 14 varies slightly year by year as research continues, but it represents a monumental effort on the part of this mission support organization. World surveys are still going on; there may be many more peoples out there than we know. The Toulambi people of Papua New Guinea, for example, were first contacted in 1993. [70] Nevertheless, it gives a very clear picture of the vast job that is worldwide missions.

The following table (fig. 15) summarizes those people groups that are considered to be *unreached*. These groups fall into one of four categories, 0) no evangelical Christians or churches-no major resources, 1) less than 2% evangelical-no church planting in the last two years-some resources available, 2) less than 2% evangelical-initial church planting in last two years, or 3) less than 2% evangelical-widespread church planting in last two years.

Unreached Biblical Nations

Continents	Unreached Nations	Unreached Population
Africa	2071	850,618,690
Asia	3346	2,908,331,900
Oceana	141	10,285,475
Europe	756	678,703,150
Americas	762	67,597,030
Totals	7076	4,515,536,245

Fig. 15 [71]

These peoples are the "last frontier" of missions. More than one half of the global population lives in unreached nations and families! This doesn't include the unsaved, who live in reached nations. This sad state of affairs is shown to be even worse by the fact that many of these nations do not have any missionary church planting teams of any denomination. *People Groups* lists nations among whom there is no active church planting in the last two years, as far as is known. These nations are considered unreached and *unengaged*. That is categories 0 and 1. The following table (Fig. 16) summarizes those peoples.

Unreached/Unengaged Biblical Nations

Continent	Unengaged Unreached Nations	Unengaged Unreached Population
Africa	728	104,926,415
Asia	1585	138,639,800
Oceana	59	760,025
Europe	303	14,718,575
Americas	428	6,557,830
Totals	3103	265,602,645

Fig. 16 [72]

This is absolutely incredible! No church planting team for almost five thousand unreached nations and families! 265 million human beings with little or no gospel preaching! I am reminded of the rebuke given by the Apostle Paul to the Corinthian believers: "Awake to righteousness, and sin not; for some have not the knowledge of God: I speak this to your shame." (1 Cor. 15:34). We have been at this task for 2000 years. The job the Lord gave us in Mt. 28:19, "Go ye therefore, and teach all nations" is far from fulfilled. Each of the peoples represented by fig. 16 are pioneer mission fields. They are named, identified, and located in the Global Research data found at www.peoplegroups.org.

What about the need for Bible translations among the nations of the world? The statistics in the next table (Fig. 17) were compiled by Wycliffe Bible Translators. The table shows how many languages have the whole Bible, the New Testament only, portions (such as the Gospel of John), and how many languages have no published Scripture.

Bible Translation Statistics of the World's Languages as of October 2019:

Continent	Total Languages	Bible	NT Only	Portions	No Published Scripture
Africa	2188	265	420	404	1099
Asia	2412	232	405	313	1462
Oceana	1341	54	335	192	760
Europe	312	73	47	71	121
Americas	1100	73	343	163	521
World	7353	697	1550	1143	3963

Fig. 17 [73]

So, there are at least 3963 languages with no known published Scripture. This amounts to 53.9 % of all languages. Moreover, this involves over 200 million individual souls! They have no Bible, nor a New Testament, and not even the Gospel of John to read. How can we turn our backs on these?

Moreover, the problem is greater than that. We have worked with languages spoken in China, Korea, Thailand, India, Togo, Ghana, Germany, Ecuador, Philippines, and Paraguay. In most cases, the language in question already had a Bible in that language ... but it was not a good translation. This is a very large, wide-spread problem. The translations are from the wrong Greek text, poorly translated (at least in significant ways), or both.

The Most Utter of the Uttermost

Finally, some nations are in triple jeopardy, so to speak. The are not reached, they are not engaged, and they do not even have a Bible translation. They have no church or a small weak church. They have no preachers, and they have no published Scripture.

The chart below summarizes these nations. In Acts 1:8, The Lord gave us the plan for this age. The progress of the gospel was to start at Jerusalem and end at the uttermost part of the earth. The nations we are discussing are in the uttermost part of the earth. It seems to me that those nations, which are unreached and without the word of God are the most-utter of them all. They are truly in a dire condition.

The Most Utter of the Uttermost

Continent	Unengaged Unreached Bibleless Nations	Unengaged Unreached Bibleless Population
Africa	451	15,575,150
Asia	511	38,349,380
Oceana	47	115,025
Europe	42	2,239,000
Americas	104	2,061,615
Totals	1155	58,340,170

Fig. 18 [74]

Regardless, of how one thinks of Wycliffe and other agencies involved in Bible translating that are using the wrong Greek text, it cannot be denied that they have seen the need and are responding. They have looked on the fields and the information that they have gathered should startle us, burden us, and motivate us to action. We should determine to be a part of the great increase in translations they are working so hard toward. As Jesus commanded, we should first respond by prayer (John 4:34-37; Mt 9:37-38). The prayer was to specifically be that the Lord will send forth laborers. Perhaps, God would have you labor as a translator and church planter. Perhaps, God would have you partner with a mission agency that seeks to recruit missionary translators and remains faithful to the King James Bible.

CHAPTER SIX
THE GREEK ALPHABET

I. The Alphabet-Pronunciation per Modern Common Greek

Capital	Lower	Name	Sound
Α	α	alpha	a as in father
Β	β	vita	v as in victor
Γ	γ	gamma	g or y *
Δ	δ	delta	th as in this
Ε	ε	epsilon	e as in pet
Ζ	ζ	zita	z as in zebra
Η	η	ita	ee as in seek
Θ	θ	thita	th as in thigh
Ι	ι	yota	ee as in seek; y before α, o
Κ	κ	kapa	k as in keep
Λ	λ	lambda	l as in look
Μ	μ	mi	m as in me
Ν	ν	ni	n as in no
Ξ	ξ	ksi	x as in mix
Ο	ο	omicron	o in fog
Π	π	pi	p as in pet
Ρ	ρ	ro	r as in red
Σ	σ/ς	sigma	s as in sign
Τ	τ	taf	t as in top
Υ	υ	ipsilon	ee as in seek
Φ	φ	fi	f as in fire
Χ	χ	ki	hy as in human or h**
Ψ	ψ	psi	ps as in collapse
Ω	ω	omega	like oh or olive

* Γ γ is a y (as in yet) sound before ε, αι, η, ι, υ, ει, οι, υι that is before all ee and eh sounds
it is a g as in brag everywhere else

**Like H in hand before ε and ι/ otherwise like hy as in human or ch in the back of the throat

Diphthongs

αι	Like e in hen
οι	Like ee in meet
ει	Like ee in meet
αυ	like af before π, τ, κ, φ, θ, χ, σ, ξ and ψ
	Like av everywhere else
ευ	like ef before π, τ, κ, φ, θ, χ, σ, ξ and ψ
	Like ev everywhere else
ου	Like oo in boot

Consonant Combinations

μπ	Like b in bed at the beginning of a word
	Like mb in lamb in the middle of a word
ντ	Like d as in door at the beginning of a word
	Like nd as in end in the middle of a word
γκ	Like g as in get at the beginning of a word
	Like ng as in sing in the middle of a word
γγ	Like ng as in sing
τσ	Like ts as in bits
τζ	Like tz as in pizza

Double consonants sound as if they are one.

Diaresis: In the NT, you may see the diaresis symbol (¨) when two vowels come together. It means they are pronounced separately, not as a diphthong.

IV Rules of Contraction

The rules of contraction apply in general to words where two vowels or a vowel and a diphthong come together. The rules of contraction are as follows:

A. Rules for Contracting Vowel with Vowel

1) The open vowels are α, ε, and ο. The close vowels are ι and υ.

2) When an open vowel comes first, followed by a close vowel, the two are united in a diphthong composed of the two vowels. For example, ε-ι combines into ει.
3) But if the close vowel comes first, the two vowels make two syllables, never a diphthong.
4) Two like vowels form a common long vowel. For example: α-α makes α; ε-η makes η; ο-ω makes ω.
5) The next rule is an exception to rule 4; ε-ε makes ει and ο-ο makes ου.
6) The vowels ο and ω overcome α, ε, and η making ω. It does not matter whether the ο and ω come first or second. Examples are α-ο makes ω and ε-ω makes ω.
7) An ε-ο and ο-ε makes ου. This rule is an exception to rule 6.
8) When α and ε or η come together, what comes first overcomes the other and forms its own long vowel. For example: α-ε and α-η make α; ε-α makes η.

B. Rules for contracting a vowel with a Diphthong

1) If a vowel comes before a diphthong and it is the same as the first vowel of the diphthong, it is absorbed by the diphthong. For example: ε-ει makes ει; ο-ου makes ου.
2) If the vowel comes before a diphthong and it is different from the first vowel of the diphthong, it contracts with the first vowel and the second vowel of the diphthong disappears unless it is ι, which become subscript.

Examples:

a) α-ει becomes ᾳ (α is contracted with ε according to rule A8 and then ι becomes subscript according to rule B2.)
b) α-ου becomes ω (α is contracted with ο according to rule 6 and υ disappears).

3) However, ο-ει and ο-η makes οι.

These rules are repeated in chapter fourteen.

V There are two breathing marks on vowels and ρ that begin words:

᾿ Smooth Breathing. This is silent at all times.
῾ Rough Breathing. In scholarly Greek, it has a "H" sound. In Modern Greek it is silent. Currently, Greece has eliminated the breathing marks.

VI There are three accent marks. They show which syllable is emphasized:

ῆ-circumflex
ί-accute
ὶ-grave

Currently, Greece has eliminated the grave and circumflex accents.

VII Iota Subscript:

Sometimes an ι is printed below α, η, and ω, especially in the dative case. It has no effect on the pronunciation.

VII Long and Short Vowels

SHORT	LONG
α	α
ε	η
ι	ι
ο	ω
υ	υ

VIII A Note about open and closed vowels.

The first vowel of a diphthong (a combination of vowels) is always considered an "open vowel" and the second vowel is a "close vowel," except in the case of υι, both of which are close vowels. This information is important in certain matters of grammar.

IX A Note About accents

Accents are important in Koine Greek and on rare occasions the accent determines the meaning of a word. Accent rules will sometimes be mentioned, but not emphasized in this grammar. Therefore, not all the accent rules will be included.

X Punctuation

When the Scriptures of the New Testament were first written, all the letters ran together and there was no punctuation. The first attempts at punctuation seems to have been in the fifth or sixth century, although there may have been some markings earlier. The following is the punctuation used in modern printed Greek New Testaments.

, comma, corresponding to an English comma

. period, corresponding to an English period

· a dot above the line, corresponding to an English colon

; a semi-colon corresponding to an English question mark (?)

CHAPTER SEVEN
HOW TO DO A GREEK WORD STUDY

The purpose of a Greek or Hebrew word Study is to understand the full meaning of a word before you translate it. Although the principles of doing a word study are the same regardless of the tools used, here we will apply those principles to the free computer software "E-sword," at www.e-sword.net. At the end of this chapter, there is a list of the E-Sword modules we recommend that you download and install. E-Sword is available for I-Pads and I-phones. For Android phones, a similar software is "My-Sword."

Step 1. Choose the word you want to study.

Below we are looking at the "Bibles" section of E-sword. This is the "Parallel" view showing the KJV with Strong's numbers (downloaded module KJV+) next to the Scrivener edition of the Received Text with Strong's numbers and parsing codes (downloaded module GNT-TR+). For our example, we will choose χαρις (charis) as in Romans 1:7 below. Notice on the KJV side the translation corresponding to χαρις (charis) is *grace*.

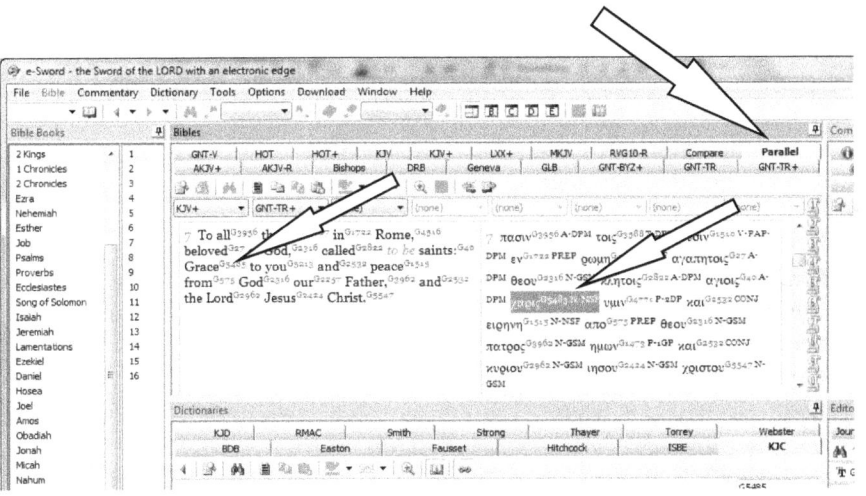

Step 2. Find the Various Ways the Word was Translated.

Click on the Strong's number next to the Greek word, χαρις. Several options will light up in the "Dictionaries" section.

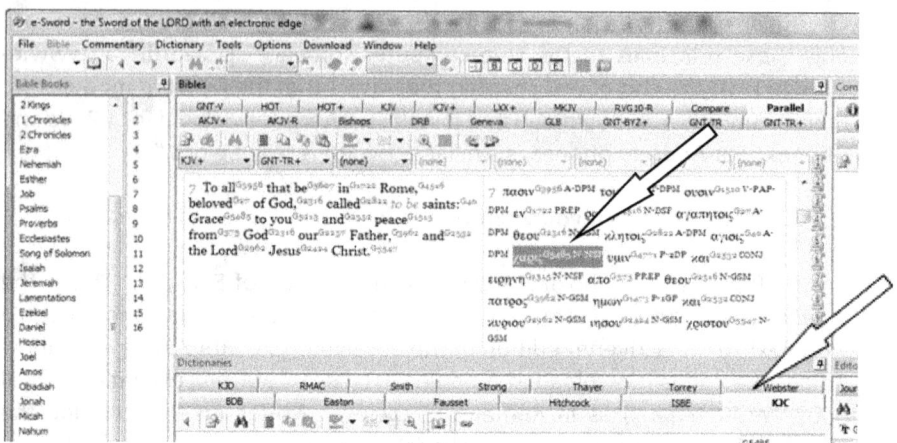

In the *Dictionaries* section choose KJC (King James Concordance). This will open the entries in the KJC for that Greek word. The KJC is designed to show every use of that word in the New Testament and the various ways it was translated in the KJV. By hovering your cursor over a verse reference, the verse itself will pop up and you can read how the word is used. By clicking on the verse reference the Bible section will go to that verse, allowing you to see the grammar of the Greek text.

The image above shows how the KJC tab will show in the *Dictionaries* section. The first image on the next page shows what appears in the *Dictionaries* section when you click on *KJC*. It will show the Greek word. Below that will be an English transliteration of the Greek word. Next, you will learn how many times the word is used in the New Testament. In the example using grace, it tells us χάρις is used 156 times in the New Testament. Finally, the various ways the Greek word are translated is shown with the verse references where they are translated using that word, as explained below. The first way χάρις is translated is *grace* and we are told that it is translated that way 130 times. Unfortunately, the KJC occasionally makes mistakes in that it includes words the KJV did not use to translate a Greek word. The KJC is, perhaps, 98% accurate.

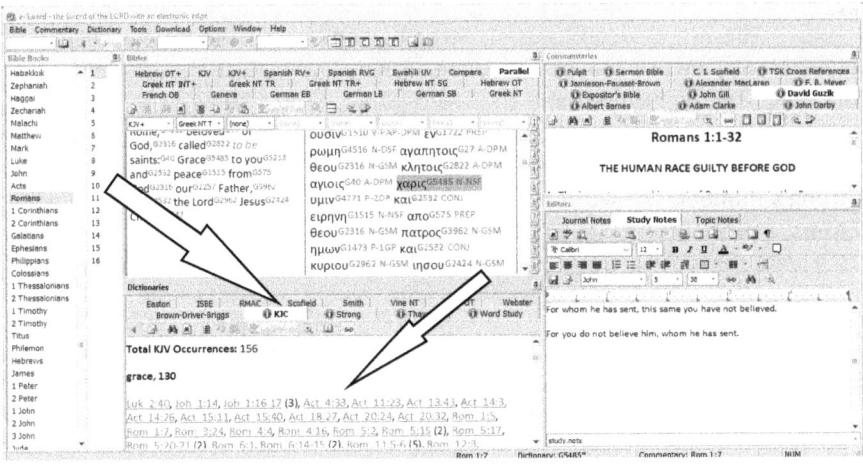

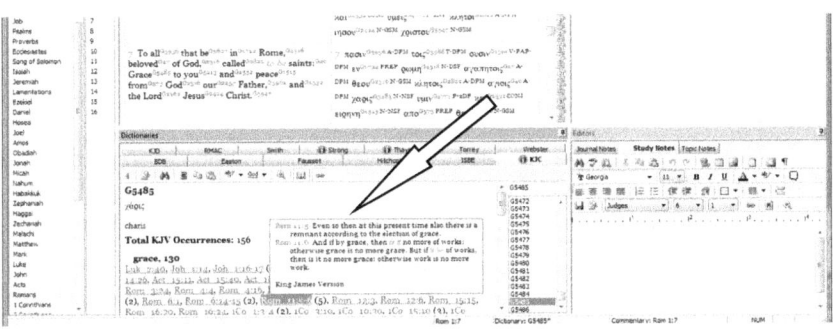

Using the copy/paste function, you can copy the entire dictionary information and paste it into a Word document to record your findings, if you wish. Examining the verses where these words are used will give you a clearer view of their meaning in the context and will expand your understanding of the Greek word.

This step shows you how the KJV translated the word and the verses where these various translations occurred. We find that translations related to χάρις are *grace, favor, thank, thanks, pleasure, acceptable, benefit, gift, gracious, joy, liberality, thanked* and *thankworthy*. Thus, the KJC is, itself, a lexicon showing the meaning of Greek words.

THE TRANSLATOR'S GRAMMAR OF THE TEXTUS RECEPTUS

Step 3. Look up the Meaning of the Word in Two or More Greek Lexicons:

The first Lexicon to use is Strong's and the second is your choice. In our example, we use Thayer's. You are already in the "Dictionary" section with the "KJC" tab highlighted and the word χάρις, charis, showing in the display block. Next click on the "Strong" tab and you will see the information from Strong's Exhaustive Concordance. Here you find six pieces of information, the Strong's number, the word in Greek letters, the word in transliterated English letters, a pronunciation guide, the definition of the word and (after the symbol ":-") ways the word is translated in the KJV listed in alphabetical order.

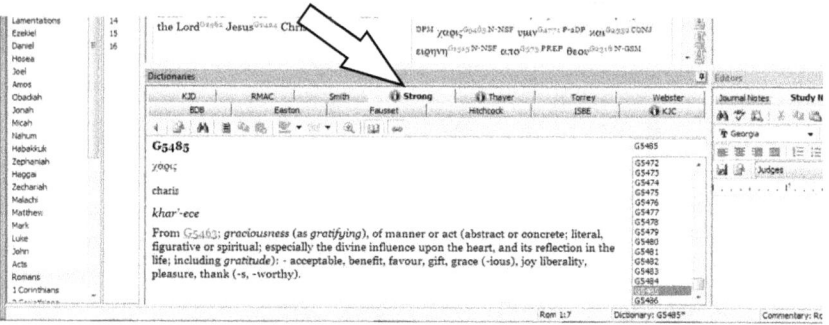

Next click the "Thayer" tab to display the information in Thayer's Greek Dictionary. In Thayer you will find the same type of information (except for how the word is translated) and sometimes you will find more information than in Strong.

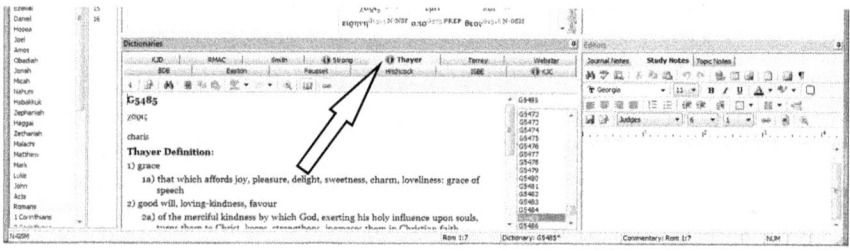

Step 4. Look up the KJV Word and the Various English Words Revealed in Step 2 in Webster's 1828 Dictionary:

Using the 1828 edition of Webster's English Dictionary has the advantage of seeing definitions that are closer to the meaning of the KJV words. Sometimes Webster 1828 has fuller definitions than many modern dictionaries.

To do this, click the "book" icon next to the search glass (if the look-up box is not there) and click on the "Webster" tab in the dictionaries section of E-sword. Then write the English word (in this case "Grace") in the look up box on

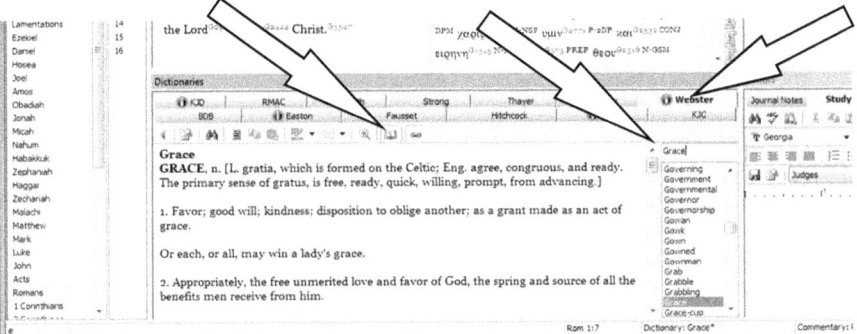

the right side. The definition will automatically appear in the information box. Other dictionaries may also be used.

Step 5. Check Several Commentaries for some of the Verses where the Word is Used:

There are several commentaries available with E-Bible. Download as many as you think you may need. If you have other commentaries, use them as well. As with all commentaries, be careful. No commentator has all the answers, and they are subject to errors, just as we all are. Choose a verse where you find the word you are studying, such as the verse we started with, Rom. 1:7. Click on the verse reference in the Bible section of E-Sword. This will highlight the commentaries where information can be found. In the "Commentaries" section, click on the commentary you want to start with, such as John Gill's commentary, "Gill". The place in the commentary relating to the highlighted verse will automatically appear.

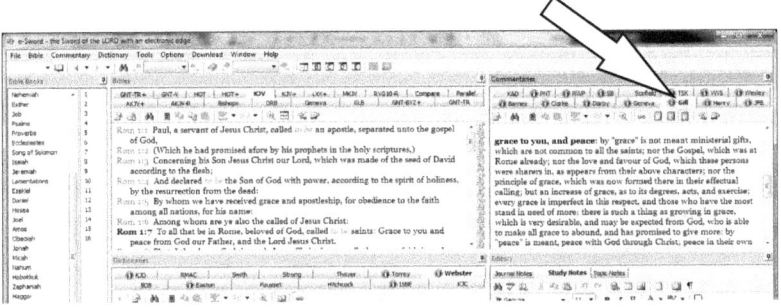

Step 6. Record your notes and Findings in the "Editor's" section of E-sword:

E-sword allows you to keep journal notes, study notes and topic notes tied to specific Bible verses. You can copy and paste from the other three sections, Bibles and commentaries and Dictionaries.

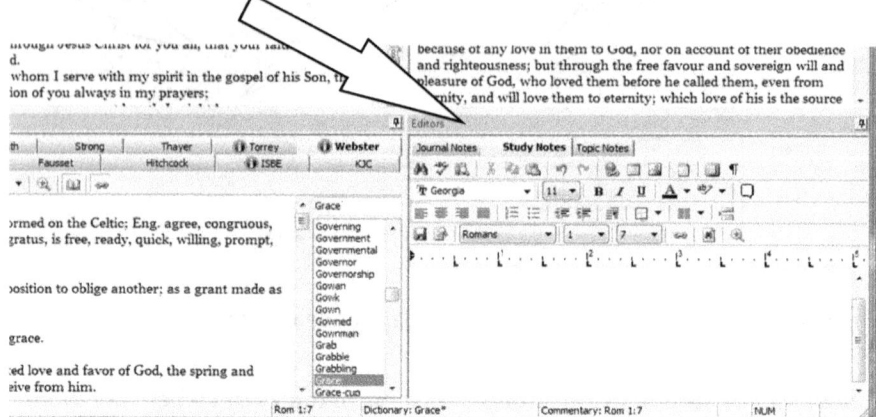

Step 7. Examine Your Findings and Write a Definition of Your Word that fits the Bible context you are studying:

The final step is to draw some conclusions based on your research. After looking at all the information you have collected you may understand the word better than most scholars. *You* have done the work, and they may not have. It is best that you write down your conclusions and, perhaps, why you came to them, so that you can refer to them again in the future.

E-Sword (www.e-sword.net) with the following free modules:

KJV
KJV with Strong's numbers
Greek TR with Strong's Numbers
Hebrew Text with Strong's Numbers
King James concordance
Albert Barnes Notes
Jamieson, Faussett and Brown Commentary
John Gill's Synopsis
John Wesley's Notes on the Bible
Matthew Henry's Commentary
Brown-Driver-Briggs Hebrew Definitions

Scofield Reference Notes
Easton's Bible Dictionary
Fausset's Bible Dictionary
International Bible Encyclopedia
Robinson's Morphological Analysis Codes
Webster's Dictionary of the English Language 1828

The following are not free, but there are important:

Vine's Expository Dictionary of New Testament Words
Vine's Expository Dictionary of Old Testament Words
The Word Study Dictionary

CHAPTER EIGHT
THE GOSPEL OF JOHN CHAPTER 1

ΕΥΑΓΓΕΛΙΟΝ ΤΟ ΚΑΤΑ ΙΩΑΝΝΗΝ

THE GOSPEL OF JOHN

ΙΩΑ Chapter 1

John 1

1 Ἐν ἀρχῇ ἦν ὁ λόγος, καὶ ὁ λόγος ἦν πρὸς τὸν Θεόν, καὶ Θεὸς ἦν ὁ λόγος.
2 οὗτος ἦν ἐν ἀρχῇ πρὸς τὸν Θεόν.

3 πάντα δι' αὐτοῦ ἐγένετο, καὶ χωρὶς αὐτοῦ ἐγένετο οὐδὲ ἓν ὃ γέγονεν.
4 ἐν αὐτῷ ζωὴ ἦν, καὶ ἡ ζωὴ ἦν τὸ φῶς τῶν ἀνθρώπων,
5 καὶ τὸ φῶς ἐν τῇ σκοτίᾳ φαίνει, καὶ ἡ σκοτία αὐτὸ οὐ κατέλαβεν.

6 ἐγένετο ἄνθρωπος ἀπεσταλμένος παρὰ Θεοῦ, ὄνομα αὐτῷ Ἰωάννης
7 οὗτος ἦλθεν εἰς μαρτυρίαν, ἵνα μαρτυρήσῃ περὶ τοῦ φωτός, ἵνα πάντες πιστεύσωσι δι' αὐτοῦ.
8 οὐκ ἦν ἐκεῖνος τὸ φῶς, ἀλλ' ἵνα μαρτυρήσῃ περὶ τοῦ φωτός.
9 ἦν τὸ φῶς τὸ ἀληθινόν, ὃ φωτίζει πάντα ἄνθρωπον ἐρχόμενον εἰς τὸν κόσμον.
10 ἐν τῷ κόσμῳ ἦν, καὶ ὁ κόσμος δι' αὐτοῦ ἐγένετο, καὶ ὁ κόσμος αὐτὸν οὐκ ἔγνω.
11 εἰς τὰ ἴδια ἦλθε, καὶ οἱ ἴδιοι αὐτὸν οὐ παρέλαβον.
12 ὅσοι δὲ ἔλαβον αὐτόν, ἔδωκεν αὐτοῖς ἐξουσίαν τέκνα Θεοῦ γενέσθαι, τοῖς πιστεύουσιν εἰς τὸ ὄνομα αὐτοῦ·

1 ¶In the beginning was the Word, and the Word was with God, and the Word was God.
2 The same was in the beginning with God.
3 All things were made by him; and without him was not any thing made that was made.
4 In him was life; and the life was the light of men.
5 ¶And the light shineth in darkness; and the darkness comprehended it not.
6 There was a man sent from God, whose name *was* John.
7 The same came for a witness, to bear witness of the Light, that all *men* through him might believe.
8 He was not that Light, but *was sent* to bear witness of that Light.
9 *That* was the true Light, which lighteth every man that cometh into the world.
10 He was in the world, and the world was made by him, and the world knew him not.
11 He came unto his own, and his own received him not.
12 But as many as received him, to them gave he power to become the sons of God, *even* to them that believe on his name:

13 οἳ οὐκ ἐξ αἱμάτων, οὐδὲ ἐκ θελήματος σαρκός, οὐδὲ ἐκ θελήματος ἀνδρός, ἀλλ' ἐκ Θεοῦ ἐγεννήθησαν.
14 καὶ ὁ λόγος σὰρξ ἐγένετο, καὶ ἐσκήνωσεν ἐν ἡμῖν, (καὶ ἐθεασάμεθα τὴν δόξαν αὐτοῦ, δόξαν ὡς μονογενοῦς παρὰ πατρός), πλήρης χάριτος καὶ ἀληθείας.
15 Ἰωάννης μαρτυρεῖ περὶ αὐτοῦ, καὶ κέκραγε λέγων, Οὗτος ἦν ὃν εἶπον, Ὁ ὀπίσω μου ἐρχόμενος ἔμπροσθέν μου γέγονεν· ὅτι πρῶτός μου ἦν.
16 καὶ ἐκ τοῦ πληρώματος αὐτοῦ ἡμεῖς πάντες ἐλάβομεν, καὶ χάριν ἀντὶ χάριτος
17 ὅτι ὁ νόμος διὰ Μωσέως ἐδόθη, ἡ χάρις καὶ ἡ ἀλήθεια διὰ Ἰησοῦ Χριστοῦ ἐγένετο.
18 Θεὸν οὐδεὶς ἑώρακε πώποτε· ὁ μονογενὴς υἱός, ὁ ὢν εἰς τὸν κόλπον τοῦ πατρὸς ἐκεῖνος ἐξηγήσατο.
19 Καὶ αὕτη ἐστὶν ἡ μαρτυρία τοῦ Ἰωάννου, ὅτε ἀπέστειλαν οἱ Ἰουδαῖοι ἐξ Ἱεροσολύμων ἱερεῖς καὶ Λευΐτας ἵνα ἐρωτήσωσιν αὐτόν, Σὺ τίς εἶ;
20 καὶ ὡμολόγησε, καὶ οὐκ ἠρνήσατο· καὶ ὡμολόγησεν ὅτι Οὐκ εἰμὶ ἐγὼ ὁ Χριστός.
21 καὶ ἠρώτησαν αὐτόν, Τί οὖν; Ἡλίας εἶ σύ; καὶ λέγει, Οὐκ εἰμί. Ὁ προφήτης εἶ σύ; καὶ ἀπεκρίθη, Οὔ.
22 εἶπον οὖν αὐτῷ, Τίς εἶ; ἵνα ἀπόκρισιν δῶμεν τοῖς πέμψασιν ἡμᾶς· τί λέγεις περὶ σεαυτοῦ;

13 Which were born, not of blood, nor of the will of the flesh, nor of the will of man, but of God.

14 And the Word was made flesh, and dwelt among us, (and we beheld his glory, the glory as of the only begotten of the Father,) full of grace and truth.

15 ¶John bare witness of him, and cried, saying, This was he of whom I spake, He that cometh after me is preferred before me: for he was before me.

16 And of his fulness have all we received, and grace for grace.

17 For the law was given by Moses, *but* grace and truth came by Jesus Christ.

18 No man hath seen God at any time; the only begotten Son, which is in the bosom of the Father, he hath declared *him*.

19 ¶And this is the record of John, when the Jews sent priests and Levites from Jerusalem to ask him, Who art thou?

20 And he confessed, and denied not; but confessed, I am not the Christ.

21 And they asked him, What then? Art thou Elias? And he saith, I am not. Art thou that prophet? And he answered, No.

22 Then said they unto him, Who art thou? that we may give an answer to them that sent us. What sayest thou of thyself?

23 ἔφη, Ἐγὼ φωνὴ βοῶντος ἐν τῇ ἐρήμῳ, Εὐθύνατε τὴν ὁδὸν Κυρίου, καθὼς εἶπεν Ἠσαΐας ὁ προφήτης.

24 καὶ οἱ ἀπεσταλμένοι ἦσαν ἐκ τῶν Φαρισαίων.

25 καὶ ἠρώτησαν αὐτόν, καὶ εἶπον αὐτῷ, Τί οὖν βαπτίζεις, εἰ σὺ οὐκ εἶ ὁ Χριστός, οὔτε Ἠλίας, οὔτε ὁ προφήτης;

26 ἀπεκρίθη αὐτοῖς ὁ Ἰωάννης, λέγων, Ἐγὼ βαπτίζω ἐν ὕδατι· μέσος δὲ ὑμῶν ἕστηκεν ὃν ὑμεῖς οὐκ οἴδατε·

27 αὐτός ἐστιν ὁ ὀπίσω μου ἐρχόμενος, ὃς ἔμπροσθέν μου γέγονεν· οὗ ἐγὼ οὐκ εἰμὶ ἄξιος ἵνα λύσω αὐτοῦ τὸν ἱμάντα τοῦ ὑποδήματος.

28 ταῦτα ἐν Βηθαβαρᾷ ἐγένετο πέραν τοῦ Ἰορδάνου, ὅπου ἦν Ἰωάννης βαπτίζων.

29 Τῇ ἐπαύριον βλέπει ὁ Ἰωάννης τὸν Ἰησοῦν ἐρχόμενον πρὸς αὐτόν, καὶ λέγει, Ἴδε ὁ ἀμνὸς τοῦ Θεοῦ, ὁ αἴρων τὴν ἁμαρτίαν τοῦ κόσμου.

30 οὗτός ἐστι περὶ οὗ ἐγὼ εἶπον, Ὀπίσω μου ἔρχεται ἀνήρ, ὃς ἔμπροσθέν μου γέγονεν, ὅτι πρῶτός μου ἦν.

31 κἀγὼ οὐκ ᾔδειν αὐτόν· ἀλλ' ἵνα φανερωθῇ τῷ Ἰσραήλ, διὰ τοῦτο ἦλθον ἐγὼ ἐν τῷ ὕδατι βαπτίζων.

32 καὶ ἐμαρτύρησεν Ἰωάννης, λέγων ὅτι Τεθέαμαι τὸ Πνεῦμα καταβαῖνον ὡσεὶ περιστερὰν ἐξ οὐρανοῦ, καὶ ἔμεινεν ἐπ' αὐτόν.

23 He said, I *am* the voice of one crying in the wilderness, Make straight the way of the Lord, as said the prophet Esaias.

24 And they which were sent were of the Pharisees.

25 And they asked him, and said unto him, Why baptizest thou then, if thou be not that Christ, nor Elias, neither that prophet?

26 John answered them, saying, I baptize with water: but there standeth one among you, whom ye know not;

27 He it is, who coming after me is preferred before me, whose shoe's latchet I am not worthy to unloose.

28 These things were done in Bethabara beyond Jordan, where John was baptizing.

29 ¶The next day John seeth Jesus coming unto him, and saith, Behold the Lamb of God, which taketh away the sin of the world.

30 This is he of whom I said, After me cometh a man which is preferred before me: for he was before me.

31 And I knew him not: but that he should be made manifest to Israel, therefore am I come baptizing with water.

32 And John bare record, saying, I saw the Spirit descending from heaven like a dove, and it abode upon him.

33 κἀγὼ οὐκ ᾔδειν αὐτόν· ἀλλ' ὁ πέμψας με βαπτίζειν ἐν ὕδατι, ἐκεῖνός μοι εἶπεν, Ἐφ' ὃν ἂν ἴδῃς τὸ Πνεῦμα καταβαῖνον καὶ μένον ἐπ' αὐτόν, οὗτός ἐστιν ὁ βαπτίζων ἐν Πνεύματι Ἁγίῳ.
34 κἀγὼ ἑώρακα, καὶ μεμαρτύρηκα ὅτι οὗτός ἐστιν ὁ υἱὸς τοῦ Θεοῦ.
35 Τῇ ἐπαύριον πάλιν εἱστήκει ὁ Ἰωάννης, καὶ ἐκ τῶν μαθητῶν αὐτοῦ δύο·
36 καὶ ἐμβλέψας τῷ Ἰησοῦ περιπατοῦντι, λέγει, Ἴδε ὁ ἀμνὸς τοῦ Θεοῦ.
37 καὶ ἤκουσαν αὐτοῦ οἱ δύο μαθηταὶ λαλοῦντος, καὶ ἠκολούθησαν τῷ Ἰησοῦ.
38 στραφεὶς δὲ ὁ Ἰησοῦς καὶ θεασάμενος αὐτοὺς ἀκολουθοῦντας, λέγει αὐτοῖς, Τί ζητεῖτε; οἱ δὲ εἶπον αὐτῷ, Ῥαββί (ὃ λέγεται ἑρμηνευόμενον, Διδάσκαλε), ποῦ μένεις;
39 λέγει αὐτοῖς, Ἔρχεσθε καὶ ἴδετε. ἦλθον καὶ εἶδον ποῦ μένει· καὶ παρ' αὐτῷ ἔμειναν τὴν ἡμέραν ἐκείνην· ὥρα δὲ ἦν ὡς δεκάτη.
40 ἦν Ἀνδρέας ὁ ἀδελφὸς Σίμωνος Πέτρου εἷς ἐκ τῶν δύο τῶν ἀκουσάντων παρὰ Ἰωάννου καὶ ἀκολουθησάντων αὐτῷ.
41 εὑρίσκει οὗτος πρῶτος τὸν ἀδελφὸν τὸν ἴδιον Σίμωνα, καὶ λέγει αὐτῷ, Εὑρήκαμεν τὸν Μεσσίαν, (ὅ ἐστι μεθερμηνευόμενον, ὁ Χριστός).
42 καὶ ἤγαγεν αὐτὸν πρὸς τὸν Ἰησοῦν. ἐμβλέψας δὲ αὐτῷ ὁ Ἰησοῦς εἶπε, Σὺ εἶ Σίμων ὁ υἱὸς Ἰωνᾶ· σὺ κληθήσῃ Κηφᾶς, (ὃ ἑρμηνεύεται Πέτρος).

33 And I knew him not: but he that sent me to baptize with water, the same said unto me, Upon whom thou shalt see the Spirit descending, and remaining on him, the same is he which baptizeth with the Holy Ghost.
34 And I saw, and bare record that this is the Son of God.
35 Again the next day after John stood, and two of his disciples;
36 And looking upon Jesus as he walked, he saith, Behold the Lamb of God!
37 ¶And the two disciples heard him speak, and they followed Jesus.
38 Then Jesus turned, and saw them following, and saith unto them, What seek ye? They said unto him, Rabbi, (which is to say, being interpreted, Master,) where dwellest thou?
39 He saith unto them, Come and see. They came and saw where he dwelt, and abode with him that day: for it was about the tenth hour.
40 One of the two which heard John *speak*, and followed him, was Andrew, Simon Peter's brother.
41 He first findeth his own brother Simon, and saith unto him, We have found the Messias, which is, being interpreted, the Christ.
42 And he brought him to Jesus. And when Jesus beheld him, he said, Thou art Simon the son of Jona: thou shalt be called Cephas, which is by interpretation, A stone.

43 Τῇ ἐπαύριον ἠθέλησεν ὁ Ἰησοῦς ἐξελθεῖν εἰς τὴν Γαλιλαίαν, καὶ εὑρίσκει Φίλιππον, καὶ λέγει αὐτῷ, Ἀκολούθει μοι.
44 ἦν δὲ ὁ Φίλιππος ἀπὸ Βηθσαϊδά, ἐκ τῆς πόλεως Ἀνδρέου καὶ Πέτρου.
45 εὑρίσκει Φίλιππος τὸν Ναθαναήλ, καὶ λέγει αὐτῷ, Ὃν ἔγραψε Μωσῆς ἐν τῷ νόμῳ καὶ οἱ προφῆται εὑρήκαμεν, Ἰησοῦν τὸν υἱὸν τοῦ Ἰωσὴφ τὸν ἀπὸ Ναζαρέθ.
46 καὶ εἶπεν αὐτῷ Ναθαναήλ, Ἐκ Ναζαρὲθ δύναταί τι ἀγαθὸν εἶναι; λέγει αὐτῷ Φίλιππος, Ἔρχου καὶ ἴδε.
47 εἶδεν ὁ Ἰησοῦς τὸν Ναθαναὴλ ἐρχόμενον πρὸς αὐτόν, καὶ λέγει περὶ αὐτοῦ, Ἴδε ἀληθῶς Ἰσραηλίτης, ἐν ᾧ δόλος οὐκ ἔστι.
48 λέγει αὐτῷ Ναθαναήλ, Πόθεν με γινώσκεις; ἀπεκρίθη ὁ Ἰησοῦς καὶ εἶπεν αὐτῷ, Πρὸ τοῦ σε Φίλιππον φωνῆσαι, ὄντα ὑπὸ τὴν συκῆν, εἶδόν σε.
49 ἀπεκρίθη Ναθαναὴλ καὶ λέγει αὐτῷ, Ῥαββί, σὺ εἶ ὁ υἱὸς τοῦ Θεοῦ, σὺ εἶ ὁ βασιλεὺς τοῦ Ἰσραήλ.
50 ἀπεκρίθη Ἰησοῦς καὶ εἶπεν αὐτῷ, Ὅτι εἶπόν σοι, εἶδόν σε ὑποκάτω τῆς συκῆς, πιστεύεις; μείζω τούτων ὄψει.
51 καὶ λέγει αὐτῷ, Ἀμὴν ἀμὴν λέγω ὑμῖν, ἀπ' ἄρτι ὄψεσθε τὸν οὐρανὸν ἀνεῳγότα, καὶ τοὺς ἀγγέλους τοῦ Θεοῦ ἀναβαίνοντας καὶ καταβαίνοντας ἐπὶ τὸν υἱὸν τοῦ ἀνθρώπου.

43 ¶The day following Jesus would go forth into Galilee, and findeth Philip, and saith unto him, Follow me.
44 Now Philip was of Bethsaida, the city of Andrew and Peter.
45 Philip findeth Nathanael, and saith unto him, We have found him, of whom Moses in the law, and the prophets, did write, Jesus of Nazareth, the son of Joseph.
46 And Nathanael said unto him, Can there any good thing come out of Nazareth? Philip saith unto him, Come and see.
47 Jesus saw Nathanael coming to him, and saith of him, Behold an Israelite indeed, in whom is no guile!
48 Nathanael saith unto him, Whence knowest thou me? Jesus answered and said unto him, Before that Philip called thee, when thou wast under the fig tree, I saw thee.
49 Nathanael answered and saith unto him, Rabbi, thou art the Son of God; thou art the King of Israel.
50 Jesus answered and said unto him, Because I said unto thee, I saw thee under the fig tree, believest thou? thou shalt see greater things than these.
51 And he saith unto him, Verily, verily, I say unto you, Hereafter ye shall see heaven open, and the angels of God ascending and descending upon the Son of man.

CHAPTER NINE
THE ARTICLE

John 1:1 - Ἐν ἀρχῇ ἦν **ὁ** λόγος, καὶ **ὁ** λόγος ἦν πρὸς **τὸν** Θεόν, καὶ Θεὸς ἦν **ὁ** λόγος.

John 1:1 - In the beginning was **the** Word, and **the** Word was with God, and **the** Word was God.

The Greek articles in John 1:1 are highlighted in the example above.

1. Greek has a *definite article*, corresponding to *the* in English. However, it has no *indefinite article*, which corresponds to *a* or *an* in English. *In general,* if the definite article is missing in Greek, the indefinite article is understood in the singular and may be inserted in the translation. However, in some languages, it may be necessary to insert a definite article when the target language grammar requires it, even though the Greek text does not have an article. It is proper to do so in such cases.

2. The article has case, gender, and number.

3. Case:

    There are five cases in Greek.

    Nominative Case: The *subject* of a sentence or a predicate nominative.

    Genitive: The case of *possession*. As such, it is often translated as a prepositional phrase starting with "of." However, it has several other uses, which will be explained later.

    Dative: The case of the *indirect object* and is often translated as a prepositional phrase starting with "to." The dative also has several other uses that will be explained later.

    Accusative: This is the case of the *direct object*, as well as other uses that will be learned.

    Vocative: This is the case of *direct address*.

4. Gender and number: Greek has three genders and two numbers.

Gender: masculine, feminine, and neuter.
Number: singular and plural.

5. The declension of the Greek article is below.

Case	Singular			Plural		
	Masc.	Fem.	Neut.	Masc.	Fem.	Neut.
Nom.	ὁ	ἡ	τό	οἱ	αἱ	τά
Gen.	τοῦ	τῆς	τοῦ	τῶν	τῶν	τῶν
Dat.	τῷ	τῇ	τῷ	τοῖς	ταῖς	τοῖς
Acc.	τόν	τήν	τό	τούς	τάς	τά

6. The article is used in a manner like its use in English. Λόγος means *a word*. Ὁ λόγος means *the word*. The article is also used as a pronoun. We will discuss that use later.

7. The article agrees in case, number, and gender with the noun it modifies.

8. **Exercise:**

   1) Practice reading the Greek of John 1 aloud.

   2) Go through John 1 and pick out as many definite articles as you can. For each article, name its case, gender, and number, a process that is called *parsing*. It is generally done by using codes. The code for the definite article is T. Codes for case are based on the first letter of each case name. The code for number is either S (for singular) or P (for plural) and finally gender is M, F, or N for masculine, feminine, or neuter. Nouns are parsed the same way. An example of parsing for an article is:

   T-NSM

   This means: **A**rticle-**N**ominative **S**ingular **M**asculine

9. **Important Grammar Point:** There are many different forms in Greek for various parts of speech. The student should become familiar and comfortable with the forms. The greatest value comes when you memorize all the forms. You must be able to fluently pronounce the words, understand how the words are built, know what the parts of speech mean and how they are translated. There are also many tools available that include the Greek text and will tell you what the part of speech each word is. Two of these that we

recommend are free downloadable software programs: e-sword.net and theWord.net. This grammar is based on using the e-sword system.

CHAPTER TEN
INTRODUCTION TO GREEK VERBS
The Imperfect Active Indicative
The Imperfect of εἰμί

John 1:1 Greek - Ἐν ἀρχῇ **ἦν** ὁ λόγος, καὶ ὁ λόγος **ἦν** πρὸς τὸν Θεόν, καὶ Θεὸς **ἦν** ὁ λόγος.

John 1:1 KJV - In the beginning was the Word, and the Word was with God, and the Word was God.

1. Vocabulary

Word	Meaning	Word	Meaning
εἰμί	am	ἦν, Imperf of εἰμί (I am)	was
Φαρισαῖος, ο	Pharisee	ἱερεύς, ο	priest
Ἡσαΐας, ο	Esaias, Isaiah	Λευΐτης, ο	levite
Ἰουδαῖος, ο	Jew	κύριος, ο	Lord
λύω	I loose	Ἰησοῦς, ο	Jesus
λέγω	I say	Χριστός, ο	Christ

The vocabulary includes both verbs and nouns. Nouns are listed with a definite article showing their gender. Nouns will be introduced in the next chapter.

2. **Introduction to Greek Verbs:** A Greek verb shows action or a state of being, just as in English. All Greek verbs have **tense** (present, imperfect, aorist, perfect, pluperfect, Future), **voice** (active, passive, or middle), **mood** (indicative, subjunctive, optative, imperative), **person**, and **number**.

These are indicated by various endings on the verb. For example, in the verb form *Imperfect Active Indicative* (explained below) the following imperfect active indicative first person singular for λέγω, *I say*, and how it is divided.

ἔλεγον (I was saying) { ἔ / λεγ / ον
                       augment/stem/ending

The part of the verb that stays the same (λεγ-) is called the *stem*.
The *augment* (prefix) is the special mark of the imperfect tense. (It is also used with the aorist tense).

The *ending* indicates tense, voice, mood, person, and number.

3. **Introduction to Tense:** Tense in English has to do with the time of action, when it took place, whether past time, present time, or future time. Greek tense has to with the same, but more important in Greek than time is the *kind of action*. There are two major kinds of action: *completed action* and *continuous action*. This can increase the difficulties of translation. The Greek present tense usually takes place in present time, but in other tenses the kind of action is more important than time. Translators must consider context when translating tense.

4. **Introduction to Voice:** Voice expresses the *type* of action being described by the verb. There are three voices in Greek: Active, passive, and middle. The model verb in the examples below is λύω, *I loose*.

> **Active Voice:**
>
> This shows that the subject of the sentence is doing the action rather than being acted upon. *I loose, or I am loosing.*
>
> **Passive Voice:**
>
> The subject is being acted upon. *He is loosed, or he is being loosed.*
>
> **Middle Voice:**
>
> The subject is acting for or on behalf of himself. *He is loosing for himself.*

5. **Introduction to Mood:** Mood has to do with a verb's relationship to reality. Does the verb make a statement of fact or issue a command or express a wish or express a possibility? These are the types of questions that mood answers. There are several moods in Greek.

6. **Introduction to Person and Number:** There are three persons in Greek: first, second, and third person. There are two numbers in Greek: singular and plural. The following chart illustrates this.

	Singular	Plural
First Person	I	We
Second Person	You (thou)	You (ye)
Third Person	He, she, It	They

7.   **Introduction to Parsing:** To parse a verb means to name its part of speech in detail. In this course, we will parse verbs by using codes. The codes for nouns have a minimum of two sections with four positions. The codes for verbs have a minimum of three sections with six positions. For example, a verb that is *imperfect active indicative third person singular* has the following code: **V-IAI-3S.**

This stands for: **V**erb-**I**mperfect **A**ctive **I**ndicative-**3** person **S**ingular

8.   **Introduction to the Imperfect Tense:** This verb form is the specific tense for *continuous or repeated action in past time*, with emphasis on type of action rather than time. Continuous or repeated action is the basic nature of the Imperfect Indicative. For example, John *was speaking* for a long time. However, it cannot always be translated as continuous in English. The example in John 1:1 is ἦν. This word is the imperfect tense of εἰμί (I am). It means "was being," But, it is awkward to translate it that way in English. It is best to translate it simply as "was."

9.   **Continuous or pointed action:** Some Greek verbs express contiuous action, such as the imperfect. Some verbs express pointed action. Pointed action is one-time simple action in past, present, or future. The aorist tense expresses pointed action. The present tense can express either. The future tense can be either pointed or continuous. This is called the *aspect* of the Greek verb.

10.   **Exploring the Uses of the Imperfect Tense:**

1) The Temporary Continuous Imperfect: The imperfect describes temporary continuous action in past time.

ἐδίδασκεν αὐτοὺς ἐν τῇ συναγωγῇ αὐτῶν
He taught them   in the synagogue of them
(Mat. 13:54)

The verb, ἐδίδασκεν, is **I**mperfect **A**ctive **I**ndicative **T**hird person **S**ingular (V-IAI-3S). It is translated as a simple past tense in English. In Greek, it indicates it was an activity that continued for a period of time. Whether that period was short or long is not given, but it continued for some period of time. Of course, this same fact is *implied* in English, but to say *he was teaching* would not be the ordinary way to express the thought in English. The ordinary expression in English would be the simple past tense, as the KJB has it.

ὁ Ἰησοῦς ... ἐθεώρει πῶς ὁ ὄχλος   βάλλει χαλκὸν εἰς
   Jesus   beheld how the people cast   money into
τὸ γαζοφυλάκιον   (Mk 12:41)
the treasury

The verb, ἐθεώρει, is also V-IAI-3S (-ει is a contracted ending, because the present tense of this verb ends in -αω. Contractions will be covered later.) The English word *beheld* means *saw*. So, Jesus saw them casting into the treasury, but it was more than a quick glance. The imperfect tells us that He was sitting there watching them for some while.

2) The Enduring Continuous Imperfect: Sometimes the imperfect is used for continuing action in the past without an indication that the action ended in the past.

ἐγὼ ἐφύτευσα,   Ἀπολλὼς ἐπότισεν, ἀλλ' ὁ Θεὸς ηὔξανεν
 I   have planted, Apollos   watered; but   God gave the increase
(1 Cor. 3:6)

The verb, ηὔξανεν, is V-IAI-3S. God *was giving the increase.* There is no indication of an ending point. God is continually, even until now, giving the increase.

3) The Repeated Imperfect: The imperfect is used for actions that are repeated from time to time. They may be repeated habitually or customarily.

Κατὰ δὲ ἑορτὴν   ἀπέλυεν   αὐτοῖς   ἕνα δέσμιον,
Now at *that* feast he released unto them one prisoner,
ὅνπερ   ἠτοῦντο.
whomsoever they desired. (Mark 15:6)

The verb, ἀπέλυεν, is also V-IAI-3S. The imperfect tense indicates that Pilate was accustomed to releasing a prisoner at this feast, as is also explained in Matthew 27:15.

11.   Knowing these uses of the Imperfect will help your understanding and sometimes it will affect your translating. However, a translator must be true to the customary ways the target language expresses meaning. Most often, in English, the imperfect will fit normal, customary, idiomatic English, when it is translated as a simple past tense verb. Other times, it can be translated using a helping verb, such as *was*. An example is the sentence, *He was often spending a lot of time at his friend's house*.

12.   **Introduction to the Indicative Mood:** The indicative mood is the mood of reality. It expresses that something is taking place or is real or is true. The indicative makes a statement of fact as opposed, for instance, to a command or a wish; as something real rather than supposed, wished for, hoped for, or urged.

13.   Our model verb for this lesson is λέγω, *I say*. This is the present tense form and is the form in which verbs are found in the dictionary (which is called a lexicon).

14.   The imperfect adds a prefix called an *augment* to the beginning of the stem of the verb.

15.   With verbs that begin with a consonant, the augment is ε-.

16.   With verbs that begin with a vowel, that vowel is lengthened (see chapter 6 section VII). However, α- is not lengthened to long α-, but to η-. For example, the imperfect indicative of ἐγείρω is ἤγειρον.

17.   The Imperfect Active Indicative conjugation of λέγω, I say, with parsing is as follows.

Singular

1	ἔλεγον V-IAI-1S	I was saying
2	ἔλεγες V-IAI-2S	You were saying
3	ἔλεγε (ν) V-IAI-3S	He, she, it was saying

Plural

1	ἐλέγομεν V-IAI-1P	We were saying
2	ἐλέγετε V-IAI-2P	You were saying
3	ἔλεγον V-IAI-3P	They were saying

18.   **The *Moveable* ν:** The third person singular may have -ν placed on the end when the verb precedes a word that begins with a vowel. This is called the *moveable ν*.

19. Since the first person singular and the third person plural are the same, only the context will enable the translator to determine which is meant.

The Imperfect Middle and Passive Indicative

20. **Introduction to the Middle Voice:** The middle voice is not used in English. It is used in Greek when the subject is acting on his own behalf or is acting upon something that belongs to himself. It is difficult to adequately describe and categorize the Greek middle voice. English does not have an equivalent part of speech. For example, βουλεύω means *I counsel*, but βουλεύομαι means *I take counsel* or *I counsel myself*. Another example is this: λούω means *I wash*, but λούομαι means *I wash myself*. The emphasis of the active voice is on the action, while the emphasis of the middle voice is on the agent of the action. The exact manner of the relation of the middle voice to the agent must be found in the context. The distinction most often cannot be expressed in English. Sometimes the middle requires a different verb in English. The verb, ἄρχω, means *I rule*, but the verb, ἄρχομαι, means *I begin*.

21. Examples of the meaning of the Middle Voice:

   1) John cleaned the garage for himself.

   This emphasizes doing something for a benefit or in self-interest. It is also used when the subject is voluntarily yielding itself to the results of an action.

   καὶ κειράσθω – 1 Cor. 11:6
   let her also be shorn

   2) *John slapped himself*. This is called reflexive and is rare in the New Testament.

   καὶ ἀπελθὼν ἀπήγξατο. – Mt. 27:5
   and hanged himself.

   3) *The participants congratulated each other*. This is called reciprocal and is also not frequent in the New Testament.

   συνετέθειντο οἱ Ἰουδαῖοι – Jn. 9:22
   the Jews had agreed (with one another)

22. **Introduction to the Passive Voice:** The passive voice is used when the subject is being acted upon. For example, *the book was written by John*. The subject, book, is receiving the action.

23. The conjugation of the Imperfect Middle and Passive Indicative are the same

24. The conjugation of the Imperfect Middle and Passive Indicative is as follows. V-IPI-1S means **V**erb-**I**mperfect **P**assive **I**ndicative-**1**st person **S**ingular. In the parsing for middle voice, an M is substituted for P.

Singular   Plural

1	ἐλεγόμην V-IPI-1S	I was being told	1	ἐλεγόμεθα V-IPI-1P	We were being told
2	ἐλέγου V-IPI-2S	You were being told	2	ἐλέγεσθε V-IPI-2P	You were being told
3	ἐλέγετο V-IPI-3S	He was being told	3	ἐλέγοντο V-IPI-3P	They were being told

25. **Deponent Verbs (dep.):** A deponent verb only has middle or passive forms, but active meaning. Many verbs ending in –ομαι are deponent and are conjugated like a middle voice verb.

26. The translator must look to the context to determine if a verb is being used in the sense of middle voice. Very often, a middle can be translated into English as active or passive without loss of meaning. In the lessons, it is recommended that the student use active or passive in the translations from Greek, unless it is clear from the context that middle voice must be translated.

The Imperfect of Εἰμί

27. The Imperfect Active Indicative of εἰμι, *I am,* is as follows.

1	ἤμην	I was	1	ἦμεν	We were
2	ἦς	You were	2	ἦτε	You (Ye) were
3	ἦν	He, she, it was	3	ἦσαν	They were

Parsing is the same as in paragraph 17 and 24 of this lesson.

28. The verb ειμι takes a **predicate nominative**, not a direct object. A predicate nominative is an object of the verb *to be* that restates the same person, place, thing, or idea that the subject expresses. Ἐν ἀρχῇ ἦν ὁ λόγος, καὶ ὁ λόγος ἦν πρὸς τὸν Θεόν, καὶ **Θεὸς ἦν ὁ λόγος**. "In the beginning was the Word, and the Word was with God, and **the Word was God**." The emphasized portion of John 1:1 contains this predicate nominative. The verb "ἦν" is

imperfect tense (3PS) of ειμι. The *word* and *God* are the same person. So, "God" is the predicate nominative of "Word."

29. **Exercises:**

1) Read through John 1 and pick out any verbs that look like imperfect active indicative. It will help you judge this if you look for an augment and endings like those in this chapter.

2) When you find the verbs **parse** each one.

3) Fill in the spaces with the correct *imperfect form* and English translation of one of the listed verbs, which are in present tense.

εἰμί (I am)   πυνθάνομαι (I demand-passive deponent)
ἔχω (I have, augment is εἴ)   δέω (I need)   αὐξάνω (I give increase)
ἀρέσκω (I please)

Matthew 2:4

	παρ'	αὐτῶν	ποῦ	ὁ	Χριστὸς	γεννᾶται
	of	them	where	the	Christ	should be born

John 1:2

οὗτος		ἐν	ἀρχῇ	πρὸς	τὸν	θεόν
The same		in	beginning	with	the	God

Acts 1:16

	πληρωθῆναι	τὴν	γραφὴν	ταύτην
	to be fulfilled	the	scripture	this

Romans 6:21

τίνα	οὖν	καρπὸν		τότε	ἐφ'	οἷς
What	therefore	fruit		then	in	those things

1 Corinthians 3:6

ἀλλ'	ὁ	Θεὸς	
but	the	God	

Galatians 1:10

εἰ	ἔτι	ἀνθρώποις	
if	yet	men	

CHAPTER ELEVEN
NOUNS: THE SECOND DECLENSION
Uses of the Nominative Case

John 1:1 Greek - Ἐν ἀρχῇ ἦν ὁ **λόγος**, καὶ ὁ **λόγος** ἦν πρὸς τὸν **Θεόν**, καὶ **Θεὸς** ἦν ὁ **λόγος**.

John 1:1 KJV - In the beginning was the Word, and the Word was with God, and the Word was God.

1. Vocabulary

Word	Meaning	Word	Meaning
λόγος, ὁ	word	οὐρανός, ὁ	heaven
Θεὸς, ὁ	God	ἀδελφός, ὁ	brother
ἄνθρωπος, ὁ	brother	υἱός, ὁ	son
κόσμος, ὁ	world	δόλος, ὁ	guile
πατρός, ὁ	father	ἄγγελος, ὁ	angel
νόμος, ὁ	law	ἀπόστολος, ὁ	apostle
κόλπος, ὁ	bosom	δοῦλος, ὁ	servant
αἴρω	I take up	θάνατος, ὁ	death
ἀναβαίνω	I go up	δῶρον, τὸ	gift
ἀμνὸς, ὁ	lamb	ἱερόν, τὸ	temple
κράζω	I cry out	ἐξηγέομαι, deponent	I declare
ἄρχω	I rule	πορεύομαι, depeponent	I go
πλήρωμα, τὸ	fullness	ἀληθινός, ὁ Adjective	True
χάρις, ἡ	grace	ἐξέρχομαι	I go out
διέρχομαι, deponent	I go through	ἀποθνήσκω	I die
ἔχω	I have	ἀποκτείνω	I Kill
ἐσθίω	I eat	οὐκέτι, adv.	no longer

2. Nouns in Greek name a person, place, thing, or idea. Greek has three noun declensions. We will start with the second declension, because John 1 has

many second declension nouns, and it is easier than the first and third declensions.

3. Nouns in Greek have *case, number*, and *gender*.

4. There are three genders: *masculine, feminine*, and *neuter*. When the student learns a noun, he should learn the singular article that goes with it so that he will know the noun's gender.

5. Nouns have two numbers: singular and plural.

6. **Introduction to Noun Cases**

   1) The Nominative Case (parsing code N): The nominative case is used for the subject of a sentence, for predicate nominatives, and for predicate adjectives.

   2) The Genitive (parsing code G): The genitive case is the case of possession and is often translated as a prepositional phrase starting with *of* or *from*.

   3) The Dative Case (parsing code D): The dative case is the case of the indirect object and is often translated as a prepositional phrase starting with *to, in, at, by,* or *with*.

   4) The Accusative Case (parsing code A): The accusative case is the case of the direct object.

   5) The Vocative Case (parsing code V): The vocative case is the case of direct address.

7. Subject nouns and their verbs agree in number.

8. The case of nouns is determined by the *endings*. The part of the noun that does not change is called the *stem*. For example, the stem of λόγος is λογ- and the ending is -ος.

9. The normal lexicon form of a second declension noun is the nominative singular. Most nouns of the second declension ending in -ος are masculine.

10. Nouns of the second declension ending in –ον are neuter.

11. The declension of the masculine noun, λόγος, word, is below. The first digit of the parsing code for a noun is N, and it is followed by the case, number (S, P), and gender (M, F, N), in that order, as seen in the chart below. **N-NSM** stands for **N**oun-**N**ominative **S**ingular **M**asculine.

Case	Singular	Plural	Translation (singular)	Parsing Sing/Plural
Nom.	λόγος	λόγοι	a Word	N-NSM/ N-NPM
Gen.	λόγου	λόγων	of/from a word	N-GSM/ N-GPM
Dat.	λόγῳ	λόγοις	to/in/with/by a word	N-DSM/ N-DPM
Acc.	λόγον	λόγους	a word	N-ASM/ N-APM
Voc.	λόγε	λόγοι	word	N-VSM/ N-VPM

12. The declension of the masculine noun, υἱός, son, is below.

Case	Singular	Plural	Translation (singular)	Parsing (Sing/Pl)
Nom.	υἱός	υἱοί	a son	N-NSM/ N-NPM
Gen.	υἱοῦ	υἱῶν	of/from a son	N-GSM/ N-GPM
Dat.	υἱῷ	υἱοῖς	to/in/with/by a son	N-DSM/ N-DPM
Acc.	υἱόν	υἱούς	a son	N-ASM/ N-APM
Voc.	υἱέ	υἱοί	son	N-VSM/ N-VPM

13. The declension of the neuter noun, δωρον, το, a gift is below.

Case	Singular	Plural	Translation (singular)	Parsing
Nom.	δῶρον	δῶρα	a gift	N-NSN/ N-NPN
Gen.	δώρου	δώρων	of/from a gift	N-GSN/ N-GPN
Dat.	δώρῳ	δώροις	to/in/with/by a gift	N-DSN/ N-DPN
Acc.	δῶρον	δῶρα	a gift	N-ASN/ N-APN
Voc.	δῶρον	δῶρα	gift	N-VSN/ N-VPN

14. Notice carefully the similarities of the endings in each declension example.

15. **More About the Uses of the Nominative Case:**

1) **The Subject Nominative:** The nominative case is used for the subject of the sentence or clause. The subject is the noun or pronoun performing the action, upon whom the action is performed, or that controls the action of the verb. An example is seen in John 1:1.

ὁ **λόγος** ἦν πρὸς τὸν Θεόν, *the word was with God*. The subject of the clause is λόγος, which is N-NSM (Noun-Nominative Singular Masculine).

A definite article without a noun can be used as the subject:
An example is: οἱ δὲ εἶπον, *and they said*, (Matthew 16:14). The article is T-NPM. Since it is plural masculine, it can be translated *they* or *the*

men, depending on the context. In this context, the best translation is *they*.

2) **The Predicate Nominative:** The nominative case is used for a predicate nominative. The predicative nominative is an object of the verse that renames the subject. It is the same as the subject. Again, John 1:1 has an example.

Θεὸς ἦν ὁ λόγος, *the word was God*. The New World Translation mistranslates this clause. It says, "the word was a god," because Θεὸς does not have an article. That is an error. The fact that both nouns are in the nominative case makes one of the nouns a predicate nominative. So, the subject and the object are the same. The noun that carries the article is the subject of the clause and if the subject has an article, the article also applies to the predicate nominative. The translation *a god* is incorrect.

3) **Nominative of Apposition:** This occurs when one nominative follows another with additional information. In Mark 2:7, the nominative εἷς (one) is followed by Θεός, explaining who the one is.

Mk 2:7 τίς δύναται ἀφιέναι ἁμαρτίας εἰ μὴ <u>εἷς</u> (NSM), ὁ <u>Θεός</u> (NSM);
       who can   forgive sins   but only   God?

Exercises

16. Answers to correct imperfect form exercises in Lesson Ten.

    1) Matthew 2:4, ἐπυνθάνετο, he demanded
    2) John 1:2, ἦν, was
    3) Acts 1:16, ἔδει, it needed
    4) Romans 6:21, εἴχετε, you have
    5) 1 Corinthians 3:6, ηὔξανεν, gave the increase
    6) Galatians 1:10, ἤρεσκον, I pleased

17. New Exercises:

    1) First, review each declension until you feel comfortable.

    2) Next, look at each verse in John 1 and try to pick out each second declension noun without looking at the list in paragraph 36.

    3) Translate the missing English word in the following verses and parse the Greek word. If you do not know the meaning of the Greek word, look it up in the lexicon at the back of the book.

Luke 20:4

Τὸ βάπτισμα	Ἰωάννου	ἐξ		οὐρανοῦ	ἦν,	ἢ	ἐξ		ἀνθρώπων;
The Baptism	------	out of	-------		was,	or	out of	-------	?

Acts 15:6

Συνήχθησάν	οἱ	**ἀπόστολοι**	καὶ	οἱ		**πρεσβύτεροι**
came together	the	------	and	the		------
ἰδεῖν	περὶ	τοῦ	**λόγου**	τούτου.		
to consider	concerning	the	------	this		

Romans 10:9

ὁμολογήσῃς	ἐν	τῷ	στόματί	σου		**Κύριον**	Ἰησοῦν
... confess	with	the	mouth	of you	-----		Jesus
ὁ	**Θεὸς**	αὐτὸν	ἤγειρεν	ἐκ		νεκρῶν	
... the	-----	him	raised	out of		dead	

CHAPTER TWELVE
NOUNS: THE FIRST DECLENSION;
Uses of the Dative Case

John 1:1 Greek - Ἐν **ἀρχῇ** ἦν ὁ λόγος, καὶ ὁ λόγος ἦν πρὸς τὸν Θεόν, καὶ Θεὸς ἦν ὁ λόγος.
John 1:1 KJV - In the beginning was the Word, and the Word was with God, and the Word was God.

1. Most nouns in the first declension are feminine.

2. All nouns in the first declension ending in -α or -η are feminine. Nouns ending in –ης are masculine.

3. Vocabulary.

Noun	Meaning	Noun	Meaning
ἀρχή, η	beginning	βασιλεία, η	Kingdom
ζωή, η	life	γραφή, η	writing, scripture
σκοτία, η	darkness	εἰρήνη, η	peace
ἐξουσία, η	power, authority	ἐκκλησία, η	assembly, church
δόξα, η	glory	ἐντολή, η	commandment
ἀλήθεια, η	truth	ἡμέρα, η	day
προφήτης, ο	prophet	καρδία, η	heart
φωνή, η	voice	παραβολή, η	parable
μαθητής, ο	disciple	ψυχή, η	soul
ὥρα, η	hour	ἀγάπη, η	love
συκῆ, η	Fig tree	ἁμαρτία, η	sin

4. The singular declensions of nouns vary depending on the ending of the noun. The declension of δόξα is below:

Case	Singular	Plural	Translation (singular)	Codes Sing/Plur
Nom.	δόξα	δόξαι	glory	N-NSF/N-NPF
Gen.	δόξης	δοξῶν	of/from glory	N-GSF/N-GPF
Dat.	δόξῃ	δόξαις	to/in/with/by glory	N-DSF/N-DPF
Acc.	δόξαν	δόξας	glory	N-ASF/N-APF
Voc.	δόξα	δόξαι	glory	N-VSF/N-VPF

5. The –α ending in the nominative singular changes to –η in the genitive and dative singular, except after ε or ι or ρ. An example of a noun ending in –α is the declension of ἀλήθεια, truth.

Case	Singular	Plural	Translation (singular)	Codes Sing/Plur
Nom.	ἀλήθεια	ἀλήθειαι	a truth	N-NSF/N-NPF
Gen.	ἀληθείας	ἀληθειῶν	of/ from a truth	N-GSF/N-GPF
Dat.	ἀληθείᾳ	ἀληθείαις	to/ in/ with/ by a truth	N-DSF/N-DPF
Acc.	ἀλήθειαν	ἀληθείας	a truth	N-ASF/N-APF
Voc.	ἀλήθεια	ἀλήθειαι	truth	N-VSF/N-VPF

6. The stem of ωρα, hour, is actually ωρα. It would be easier for the beginning student to think of the stem as ωρ-. The declension of ωρα is the same as ἀλήθεια.

Case	Singular	Plural	Translation (singular)	Codes Sing/Plur
Nom.	ὥρα	ὧραι	hour	N-NSF/N-NPF
Gen.	ὥρας	ὡρῶν	of/from an hour	N-GSF/N-GPF
Dat.	ὥρᾳ	ὥραις	to/in/with/by an hour	N-DSF/N-DPF
Acc.	ὥραν	ὥρας	an hour	N-ASF/N-APF
Voc.	ὥρα	ὧραι	hour	N-VSF/N-VPF

7. Some nouns of the first declension end in –η. When the noun ends this way in the nominative singular, the –η is kept throughout the singular part of the declension. The declension of γραφή, a writing, a scripture, is below.

Case	Singular	Plural	Translation (singular)	Codes Sing/Plur
Nom.	γραφή	γραφαί	a writing	N-NSF/N-NPF
Gen.	γραφῆς	γραφῶν	of/from a writing	N-GSF/N-GPF
Dat.	γραφῇ	γραφαῖς	to/in/with/by a writing	N-DSF/N-DPF
Acc.	γραφήν	γραφάς	a writing	N-ASF/N-APF
Voc.	γραφή	γραφαί	writing	N-VSF/N-VPF

8.   Nouns of the first declension that end in – ης are masculine. Below are the declensions of προφήτης, *prophet*, and μαθητής, *disciple*.

Case	Singular	Plural	Translation (singular)	Codes Sing/Plur
Nom.	προφήτης	προφῆται	a prophet	N-NSM/N-NPM
Gen.	προφήτου	προφητῶν	of/from a prophet	N-GSM/N-GPM
Dat.	προφήτῃ	προφήταις	to/in/with/by a prophet	N-DSM/N-DPM
Acc.	προπήτην	προφήτας	a prophet	N-ASM/N-APM
Voc.	προφῆτα	προφῆται	prophet	N-VSM/N-VPM

Case	Singular	Plural	Translation (singular)	Codes Sing/Plur
Nom.	μαθητής	μαθηταί	a disciple	N-NSM/N-NPM
Gen.	μαθητοῦ	μαυητῶν	of/from a disciple	N-GSM/N-GPM
Dat.	μαθητῇ	μαθηταῖς	to/in/with/by a disciple	N-DSM/N-DPM
Acc.	μαθητήν	μαθητάς	a disciple	N-ASM/N-APM
Voc.	μαθητά	μαθηταί	disciple	N-VSM/N-VPM

9.   If the stem ends in ς, λλ, ζ, ξ, or ψ, the noun is declined the same as δόξα. See paragraph 4.

The ***plural*** of all first declension nouns is the same.

10.   **Functions of the Dative Case:** The preposition, ἀρχή, η, is a noun in the dative case, N-DSF (Noun-Dative Singular Feminine). **The *basic function* of the dative case is as *the indirect object* of a sentence or a clause. As such, it is often translated as the object of a prepositional phrase starting with *to, unto,* or *for*. When working with the dative, the translator should think of this first**. However, there are other uses of the dative case, as you will see below. There are only five distinct noun forms in Greek. That is why this grammar teaches a five-case system. However, some grammars teach an eight-case system. To get eight cases, they divide the genitive form into genitive and ablative. Further, they divide the dative form into three cases: dative, locative, and instrumental. We consider all these to be only two cases, the genitive and dative, with various uses of each. We will see more information on the genitive later. Now we will look at various functions of the dative. In the list below, each function is labeled

when it falls into either the locative or the instrumental category. These labels are only for the student's knowledge and do not affect the translation.

1) **The Dative of Indirect Object:** An indirect object is the object that is indirectly affected by the verb or the object to whom or for whom the action of the verb is performed. As noted above this is the basic function of the dative case. Below are two examples.

Mat. 18:26 πάντα σοι ἀποδώσω, *all things to you I will give;* σοι is a personal pronoun, second person dative singular (P-2DS).

Mat. 13:3 καὶ ἐλάλησεν αὐτοῖς πολλὰ, and *he said to them many things*; αὐτοῖς is a pronoun dative plural masculine (P-DPM).

2) **Dative of Possession:** The dative case can be used in such a personal way that it indicates ownership. English does not have an equivalent expression, so a literal translation is sometimes difficult.

Luke 1:7 καὶ οὐκ ἦν   αὐτοῖς   τέκνον
Literal   and not was to them a child
KJB   And they had no child

John 1:6 ὄνομα αὐτῷ Ἰωάννης
Literal: Name to him John
KJV: whose name *was* John

3) **Dative of Advantage or Disadvantage:** This is an expression of personal interest, either to advantage or disadvantage. The meaning is either *for* or *against*.

Mat. 23:31 μαρτυρεῖτε ἑαυτοῖς, *ye be witnesses unto yourselves.* This is a dative of disadvantage. The idea here is that they are witnesses *against* themselves. The context makes this meaning clear. Note: some target languages may *require* that a translator translate the word ἑαυτοῖς as *against yourselves*. If that is the case, it is acceptable to do so, although it is accurately translated into English using the preposition *unto*.

1 Cor. 6:13 τὰ βρώματα τῇ κοιλίᾳ, *meats for the belly*. (dative of advantage)

4) **Dative of Place (Locative: location of place):** The dative sometimes expresses the place where the action took place.

John 21:8 οἱ δὲ ἄλλοι μαθηταὶ <u>τῷ πλοιαρίῳ</u> ἦλθον, *and the other disciples came <u>in a little ship</u>*. In this use, the dative is translated using the preposition *in* or *with*.

5) **Dative of Time (Locative: location in time):** The dative sometimes expresses the time when the action takes place. To express time, the translator may use the prepositions *on, in, by,* or not use a preposition at all. Sometimes, as in the following example, the preposition is supplied.

John 1:1 <u>Ἐν ἀρχῇ</u> ἦν ὁ λόγος, *in the beginning was the word*.

Mat. 20:19 καὶ <u>τῇ τρίτῃ ἡμέρᾳ</u> ἀναστήσεται, *and <u>the third day</u> he shall rise again*.

6) **Dative of Sphere (Locative: spiritual or metaphorical location):** This is similar to the dative of place, but it is less concrete and more metaphorical. The use of the preposition *in* is appropriate for this use.

Rom. 3:24 τῆς ἀπολυτρώσεως τῆς <u>ἐν Χριστῷ Ἰησοῦ</u>, *the redemption that is <u>in Christ Jesus.</u>*

7) **Dative of Means (Instrumental):** The dative form can express the means by which something is accomplished. Prepositions appropriate to translate this use are *by, of, by means of,* or *with*.

Eph. 2:8 <u>τῇ γὰρ χάριτί</u> ἐστε σεσωσμένοι διὰ τῆς πίστεως, *for <u>by grace</u> are ye saved through faith*. Χάριτί, grace, is translated using the preposition *by* to show that it is the means of salvation.

8) **Dative of Personal Agency (Instrumental):** This is very similar to the Dative of Means. It expresses the personal agent by which action is performed. It is often translated using the preposition *by* or *through*.

Rom. 8:14 ὅσοι γὰρ <u>Πνεύματι</u> Θεοῦ ἄγονται, For as many as are led <u>by the Spirit</u> of God ... The Spirit is the agent by whom we are led.

9) **Dative of Cause (Instrumental):** The dative can be used to express the cause of an action. It can be translated using prepositions, such as *through, because of,* or *on the basis of*.

Heb. 2:15 καὶ ἀπαλλάξῃ τούτους, ὅσοι <u>φόβῳ</u> θανάτου διὰ παντὸς τοῦ ζῆν ἔνοχοι ἦσαν δουλείας. *And deliver them who <u>through fear</u> of death were all their lifetime subject to bondage*. The cause of being subject to bondage was the fear of death, so the one dative word *fear* is translated *through fear* to express it as a cause.

10) Dative of Manner (Instrumental): This function expresses the method used in accomplishing the action.

1 Cor. 11:15 πᾶσα δὲ γυνὴ προσευχομένη ἢ προφητεύουσα <u>ἀκατακαλύπτῳ</u> τῇ κεφαλῇ, *But every woman that prayeth or prophesieth <u>with her head</u> uncovered* ... Uncovered is the manner in which this woman prays or prophecies, therefore it is translated *with her*.

11) Dative of Measure (Instrumental): The dative is sometimes used to express that two points in time or space are separated by some distance. In the New Testament, it is usually used to express distance in time. You can use *by, from, since*, or another fitting preposition.

Rom. 16:25 κατὰ ἀποκάλυψιν μυστηρίου <u>χρόνοις αἰωνίοις</u> σεσιγημένου ... *according to the revelation of the mystery, which was kept secret <u>since the world began</u>* ...

Exercises

11. Answers to Translation Exercises of Chapter 11.

    1) Luke 20:4, Ἰωάννου, N-GSM, of John
    2) Luke 20:4, οὐρανοῦ, N-GSM, of heaven
    3) Luke 20:4, ἀνθρώπων, N-GPM, of men
    4) Acts 15:6, ἀπόστολοι, N-NPM, Apostles
    5) Acts 15:6, πρεσβύτεροι, N-NPM, Elders
    6) Romans 10:9, Κύριον, N-ASM, Lord
    7) Romans 10:9, Θεὸς, N-NSM, God

12. New Exercises:

1) Look at each verse in John 1 and try to pick out each first declension noun without looking at the list in paragraph 3.

2) When you find them, parse them.

3) Translate the missing English translations in the following verses. Parse each Greek word you translate. Look up any words you do not know in the lexicon in the back of the book.

Romans 1:2

ὃ	προεπηγγείλατο	διὰ τῶν **προφητῶν** αὐτοῦ	
which he promised before		by the --------	of him
ἐν **γραφαῖς**	ἁγίαις,		
in --------	holy		

Romans 2:8

τοῖς δὲ	ἐξ **ἐριθείας**, καὶ ἀπειθοῦσι μὲν τῇ **ἀληθείᾳ**
but to them (who are) of ----- ,	and do not obey the ------
πειθομένοις δὲ τῇ **ἀδικίᾳ**, θυμὸς	καὶ **ὀργή**,
but obey the ------	indignation and -----

CHAPTER THIRTEEN
PREPOSITIONS AND CONJUNCTIONS
Uses of Prepositional Phrases
Conjunctions, and Main Clauses

John 1:1 Greek - Ἐν ἀρχῇ ἦν ὁ λόγος, **καὶ** ὁ λόγος ἦν **πρὸς** τὸν Θεόν, **καὶ** Θεὸς ἦν ὁ λόγος.

John 1:1 KJV - **In** the beginning was the Word, **and** the Word was **with** God, **and** the Word was God.

1. Vocabulary.

Word and Description	Basic Meanings
εν, prep. with dative	in, by, among, near
προς, prep. with genitive	for, concerning
with dative	at, by, near, on, by means of
with accusative	toward, to, against, with
δια, prep. with genitive	through, throughout, during, after, by means of
with accusative	through, by, by means of, on account of
και, conjunction	and, also
ου (ουκ before vowels; ουχ before rough breathing)	no, not
παρα, prep. with genitive	from, of, by, with
with dative	beside, with, in the presence
with accusative	at, more then, along side of
εις, prep. with accusative	into, to, toward, for, unto
ινα, conjunction	in order to/ that, that, to
αλλα, conjunction	but (stronger than δε)
δε, conjunction	but, and, now, then, yet
εκ, prep. (εξ before vowels) with genitive	out, out of
ως, adverb	as, like, even as, etc.
περι, prep. with genitive	concerning, about, to. of
with accusative	around
οτι, conjunction	that, because
αντι, prep. with genitive	for, instead of, over against, opposite to, before

ουν, conjunction	accordingly, therefore
επι, prep. with genitive	over, on, at the time of
with dative	on the basis of, at
with accusative.........................	on, to, against
περιστερα, η	dove
μενω	I remain, I abide
μέτα, prep. with genitive	with
with accusative.........................	after
κατα, prep. with genitive...........	down, from, against
with accusative.........................	according to, throughout, during
απο, prep. with genitive	from, of, by
οὐδέ	not, nor, not even

Prepositions

2. Prepositions are words that express relationships between two nouns or between a noun and a verb. The Parsing code for prepositions is PREP. The phrase ἐν αὐτῷ ζωὴ ἦν, *In him was life*, shows the relationship between *life* and *Him*. Life is located IN Him. Read the following verse that contains several prepositions:

οὗτος ἦλθεν **εἰς** μαρτυρίαν, ἵνα μαρτυρήσῃ **περὶ** τοῦ φωτός, ἵνα πάντες πιστεύσωσι **δι'** αὐτοῦ. (John 1:7)

The same came **for** a witness, to bear witness **of** the Light, that all *men* **through** him might believe.

The prepositions show the relationship of the subject to the verb. They describe the reason why he came.

3. A preposition stands in a "prepositional phrase." The prepositional phrase contains a *preposition* and the *object* of the preposition, which is a noun or pronoun. Often, between the two, there is an *article*. Thus, in the phrase, περὶ τοῦ φωτός, of the light, we have the preposition-article-object. φωτός is the object of the preposition and between that and the preposition, περὶ, stands the definite article, τοῦ.

4. In Greek, prepositions require their objects to be in certain cases. When the case changes, the meaning of the preposition changes. Some prepositions take their objects in three cases (genitive, dative, and accusative), some take objects in two cases, and some take objects in only one case. For prepositions that take more than one case, the meaning of the preposition can change when the case changes. Both the object of the preposition and the definite article must be in the appropriate case. As prepositions are learned,

their meaning should be learned along with the case or cases connected with that preposition.

5. Greek prepositions have a great deal of flexibility in how they are translated. The definition of prepositions that are given in the vocabulary are indications of the general meaning of the prepositions. They include some of the ways the words have been translated. However, the student should realize that the actual translation depends on the use of the preposition in the sentence and he should feel some freedom and latitude in choosing what word to use in the translation.

6. The rule for translation should be to translate a preposition in Greek into a preposition in the target language that is appropriate to the meaning of the context. What preposition is chosen for the target language should be guided by the general meaning of the Greek preposition in combination with the context.

7. An example of this is the preposition πρoς.

    1) It takes the genitive, dative, and accusative.
    2) Most of the time in the New Testament it takes the accusative.
    3) It is important to learn the words the vocabulary gives as the basic ways to translate the preposition.
    4) Those words for the accusative are: toward, to, against, and with.
    5) However, in actual translation, there is more flexibility, as this table will illustrate. The table shows many of the various ways the KJV translated this preposition.

Uses of πρoς in the New Testament:

Ref.	Greek Phrase	English Translation
Jn 1:1	πρὸς τὸν Θεόν	**with** God
Mt 4:6	πρὸς λίθον	**against** a stone
Mk 8:16	πρὸς ἀλλήλους	**among** themselves
Mk 11:1	πρὸς τὸ ὄρος	**at** the mount
Lk 24:29	πρὸς ἑσπέραν	**toward** evening
2 Co 5:10	πρὸς ἃ ἔπραξεν	**according to** that he hath done
Mt. 19:8	πρὸς τὴν σκληροκαρδίαν ὑμῶν	**because of** the hardness of your hearts
Rom. 4:2	πρὸς τὸν Θεόν	**before** God
Lk 23:12	πρὸς ἑαυτούς	**between** themselves
Mk 5:11	πρὸς τῳ ὄρη	**nigh** unto the mountains

8.   The student and prospective translators should be aware of this flexibility because it will be necessary to apply it when translating. However, G. Gresham Machen gives a warning in his book, *New Testament Greek for Beginners*, page 41.

> A further important principle is that of *precision* in learning the meaning of prepositions. It is true that no one English word or phrase is capable of translating in all cases a single Greek preposition. Sometimes, for example, ἐν with the dative cannot be translated by *in* in English. But the proper method is learn first the usual meaning before proceeding to the unusual. A reversal of this method will lead to hopeless confusion. [75]

9.   The importance of learning the prepositions cannot be overestimated. The New Testament is incomprehensible without them.

10.   When a preposition ends in a vowel and precedes a word that starts with a vowel, the final vowel of the preposition is often dropped and an apostrophe is added. For example, διά becomes δι'.

11.   **Compound Verbs**: Sometimes prepositions are attached to verbs. When this happens, the meaning of the verb is changed. For example, ἐκ means *out of*, so, ἐκπορεύομαι means *I go out*. However, it is not always so simple to determine the meaning of a compound word. An example of that is ἀπο. Ἀπο means *from* and κρίνω means *I judge*, but when you put them together, their compound, ἀποκρίνομαι, means *I answer*. It is best to learn the specific meaning of compound verbs as they occur, rather than depend on discerning the meaning from its component parts.

Uses of Prepositional Phrases

12.   Prepositional phrases can be used as adjectives, adverbs, and even nouns.

13.   Prepositional phrases may modify and describe a noun. By doing this, they function as an adjective.

> Example:
>
> John 1:1 And the word was with God (πρὸς τὸν Θεόν) - The prepositional phrase describes the *location* of the word.

14.   A preposition is sometimes used as an adverb. An adverb modifies a verb, adjective, or another adverb.

Example:

John 1:1 In the beginning (Ἐν ἀρχῇ) was the word - Here we have a description of the *time* of the word's existence, *when* the word *was*. It modifies the verb.

John 1:3 All things were made by him (δι' αὐτοῦ) - The prepositional phrase describes *how* all thing *were made*. It modifies the verb.

John 1:5 - And the light shineth in the darkness (ἐν τῇ σκοτίᾳ) - The prepositional phrase describes *where* the light *shines*. Again, it modifies the verb.

15.   Sometimes, prepositional phrases act as *attributive* adjectives. This happens when the preposition is immediately preceded by a definite article.

Example:

John 1:45 - Ἰησοῦν τὸν υἱὸν τοῦ Ἰωσὴφ **τὸν ἀπὸ Ναζαρέθ**. The prepositional phrase, "the from Nazareth," modifies "Jesus." The literal meaning is *the from Nazareth Jesus,* or, if these words occurred by themselves, they could be translated *Jesus who is from Nazareth*.

16.   When there is no noun or pronoun, prepositional phrases following an article can be used in place of a noun. The construction is equivalent of he who, she who, it which or simply as he, she, it.

Example:

Galatians 4:23 - ὁ δὲ ἐκ τῆς ἐλευθέρας / *but he of the freewoman.* In this example, the pronoun *he* is not specifically given. The prepositional phrase follows the article (the intervening δὲ is normally translated before the article). Since the phrase stands in this position without the explicit presence of a noun or pronoun, one can be supplied in the translation. The noun or pronoun is *implied* by the article, which is masculine. Therefore, the KJV translates it, "*But he of the freewoman.*" A similar construction at the beginning of the verse is translated, "But he *who was* of the bondwoman …"

Conjunctions

17. Conjunctions are connecting words, parsing code CONJ. They connect words, phrases, clauses, and sentences. The conjunction may also be more than a mere connecter, adding significant information with words such as ινα, *that, in order that*, and ωστε, *so that*. Conjunctions are used in Greek the same way they are used in English, except that they are more numerous in the Greek New Testament.

18. Some conjunctions are *postpositive*. That is, they never come first in a sentence or clause. Usually, they come second. Some of the most frequent postpositive conjunctions are: γάρ, *for*, δέ, *and, but*, and οὖν, *therefore, accordingly*.

19. Conjunctions have some of the same flexibility in translating that prepositions have. The same guidance given for prepositions applies.

20. **Uses of καί, οὐδέ, and οὔτε:** Καί, *and*, is a conjunction, but it is not limited to this meaning. It often means *also* and *even*. When it means *also*, the Greek word order is the opposite of the English word order. For example:

Greek order: ἦν δὲ καὶ Ἰωάννης βαπτίζων ἐν Αἰνὼν (And was also John baptizing in Aenon) (John 3:23-TR)
English order: And John also was baptizing in Aenon (John 3:23-KJV)

21. Often, οὐδέ simply means *and not* or *nor*. However, it also means *not even*.

Greek 1 Cor. 11:14 - ἢ **οὐδὲ** αὐτὴ ἡ φύσις διδάσκει ὑμᾶς
KJV - Doth **not even** nature itself teach you

22. Καί and οὐδέ and οὔτε (not) can also be used in combinations:
Καί ... Καί means both ... and
οὐδέ ... οὐδέ and οὔτε ... οὔτε mean neither ... nor

Exercises

23. Answers to exercises of chapter twelve.

Romans 1:2, προφητῶν, prophets, N-GPM
Romans 1:2, γραφαῖς, scriptures, N-DPF
Romans 2:8, ἐριθείας, contention, N-GSF
Romans 2:8, ἀδικίᾳ, unrighteousness, N-DSF

Romans 2:8, ἀληθείᾳ, truth, N-DSF
Romans 2:8, ὀργή, wrath, N-NSF

24. New Exercises.

1) Translate John 1:1

2) Translate and parse the following prepositional phrases. Look up words you do not know.

Romans 1:1

| ἀφωρισμένος εἰς εὐαγγέλιον Θεοῦ, |
| separated   ------------------------- |

Romans 1:3

| περὶ τοῦ υἱοῦ αὐτοῦ, τοῦ γενομένου |
| ------------------------- which was made |
| ἐκ σπέρματος Δαβὶδ   κατὰ σάρκα, |
| ------------------ of David   ---------------- |

Romans 1:18

| Ἀποκαλύπτεται γὰρ ὀργὴ Θεοῦ   ἀπ' οὐρανοῦ ἐπὶ πᾶσαν ἀσέβειαν |
| is revealed   for wrath of God -------------- -------------------- |
| καὶ ἀδικίαν   ἀνθρώπων τῶν τὴν ἀλήθειαν |
| and unrighteousness of men   who the truth |
| ἐν ἀδικίᾳ κατεχόντων· |
| ------------ hold |

CHAPTER FOURTEEN
VERBS: PRESENT ACTIVE INDICATIVE
PRESENT MIDDLE AND PASSIVE INDICATIVE
AND VOWEL CONTRACTIONS

John 1:5 καὶ τὸ φῶς ἐν τῇ σκοτίᾳ **φαίνει**, καὶ ἡ σκοτία αὐτὸ οὐ κατέλαβεν.
John 1:5 And the light shineth in darkness; and the darkness comprehended it not.

In this lesson, we will skip ahead to John 1:5 and focus on the word φαίνει and the Present Active Indicative verb system.

1. Vocabulary.

Word	Meaning	Word	Meaning	Word	Meaning
φαίνω	shine	πέμπω	send	ἀγαπάω	I love
ἀποστέλλω	send out	βοάω	cry out	γινομαι, dep.	become
μαρτυρέω	witness			ερχομαι, dep.	come
φωτίζω	light	βαπτίζω	baptize	τέκνον	child
λαμβανω	take, receive	εἴδω	perceive	γεννάω	born
καταλαμβάνω	comprehend	λύω	loose	μονογενής	only begotten
παραλαμβάνω	take, receive	βλέπω	see	θεάομαι, dep.	see-look at
ποιέω	I do	περιπατέω	walk	πρῶτος, adj.	first, chief
σκηνόω	dwell	στρέφω	turn	ἀποκρίνομαι. Dep.	answer
ὁράω	see	ζητέω	seek	πληρόω	I fill
λαλέω	I speak	μένω	remain	κἀγώ	and I, I also
ἐρωτάω	ask	εὑρίσκω	find	διδάσκαλος	teacher
ὁμολογέω	confess	ἐμβλέπω	look at	ἀκούω	hear
καλέω	call	γινώσκω	know	εἰσέρχομαι, dep.	enter, go in
θέλω	want	φωνέω	call	σώζω	save
ἀκολουθέω	follow	πιστεύω	believe	ἁμαρτωλός, ὁ	sinner
γράφω	write	καταβαίνω	go down	παρακαλέω	beseech

2.   Many of these verbs are used in John 1 in tenses other than the present active indicative. The following verses contain verbs in present active indicative form: 5, 9, 15, 19, 20, 21, 22, 25, 26, 27, 29, 30, 33, 34, 36, 38, 39, 41, 42, 43, 45, 46, 47, 48, 49, 50, and 51.

3.   **Parsing the present active indicative:** Follow this example. When parsing, the following designation can be used for present active indicative first person singular: V-PAI-1S. The beginning "V" means "verb." **PAI**=Present Active Indicative. 1S means first person singular. Second person, third person, and plural can be modified appropriately: 2S, 3S, 2P, and 3P.

4.   The Present active indicative expresses action in present time. The present tense may be translated either of two ways: as pointed action or as continuous action. So, ὁράω can be translated *I see* or *I am seeing*. There is absolutely no distinction between pointed and continuing action in the present tense.

5.   The basic conjugation of the present active indicative can be seen in the model verb φαίνω, I shine. PAI verbs do not have an augment. This is the general method of conjugation followed in the PAI.

Pers.	Singular		Plural	
1	φαίνω	I shine	φαίνομεν	We shine
2	φαίνεις	You shine	φαίνετε	You (ye) shine
3	φαίνει	He, she, it shines	φαίνουσι (ν)	They shine

6.   **Moveable Nu:** When the –ουσι of the third person plural is followed by a word that begins with a vowel the moveable nu, -ν, may be added to the end of the third person plural verb.

7.   In the vocabulary in paragraph 1, there are five categories of verbs. The *first* (1) is verbs whose stems end in a consonant. They are conjugated the same as the example in paragraph 5. The others are 2) stems ending in –ε, 3) stems ending in –α, 4) stems ending in –ο, and 5) the verb to be, ειμι. When a verb stem ends in a vowel and is followed by the PAI ending which starts with a vowel, the two vowels may be *contracted*.

8.   This is a general rule, so do not assume that two vowels are *always* contracted.

9. If two vowels are *not* to be contracted and are *not* to be pronounced as a diphthong, they will often be spelled with a diaresis (two döts) over one of the vowels showing they are to be pronounced separately, as in the following example: Πρωϊνός, *morning*.

10. The rules of contraction apply in general to words where two vowels or a vowel and a diphthong come together. The rules of contraction are as follows:

   1) Rules for Contracting Vowel with Vowel

      (1) The open vowels are α, ε, and o. The close vowels are ι and υ.
      (2) When an open vowel comes first, followed by a close vowel, the two are united in a diphthong composed of the two vowels. For example, ε-ι combines into ει.
      (3) But if the close vowel comes first, the two vowels make two syllables, never a diphthong.
      (4) Two like vowels form a common long vowel.
          For example: α-α makes α; ε-η makes η; o-ω = ω
      (5) The next rule is an exception to rule 4; ε-ε makes ει and o-o makes ου.
      (6) The vowels o and ω overcome α, ε, and η making ω. It does not matter whether the o and ω come first or second. Examples are α-o makes ω and ε-ω makes ω.
      (7) This rule is an exception to rule 6. An ε-o and o-ε makes ου.
      (8) When α and ε or η come together, what comes first overcomes the other and forms its own long vowel. For example: α-ε and α-η make α; ε-α makes η.

   2) Rules for contracting a vowel with a Diphthong

      (1) If a vowel comes before a diphthong and it is the same as the first vowel of the diphthong, it is absorbed by the diphthong. For example: ε-ει makes ει; o-ου makes ου.
      (2) If the vowel comes before a diphthong and it is different from the first vowel of the diphthong, it contracts with the first vowel and the second vowel of the diphthong disappears unless it is ι, which become iota-subscript.

Examples:

- α-ει becomes ᾳ: α is contracted with ε according to rule 1)-(8) and then ι becomes subscript according to rule 2)-(2).

- α-ου becomes ω: α is contracted with ο according to rule 1)-(6) and υ disappears).

(3) An exception is that ο-ει and ο-η makes οι.

11.   Now, let us apply these principles to some PAI verbs. The conjugations of μαρτυρέω, *I witness*, ὁράω, *I see*, and ἐρωτάω, *I ask*, are below.

Singular   Plural

1	μαρτυρῶ	μαρτυροῦμεν
2	μαρτυρεῖς	μαρτυρεῖτε
3	μαρτυρεῖ	μαρτυροῦσι (ν)

1	ὁράω	ορῶμεν
2	ορᾷς	ορᾶτε
3	ορᾷ	ορῶσι (ν)

1	ἐρωτω	ἐρωτῶμεν
2	ἐρωτᾷς	ἐρωτᾶτε
3	ἐρωτᾷ	ἐρωτῶσι (ν)

12.   The Present Active Indicative of εἰμί, *I am*, is as follows.

Singular   Plural

1	εἰμί	I am	1	ἐσμέν	We are
2	εἶ	You are	2	ἐστέ	You are
3	ἐστί (ν)	He, she, it is	3	εἰσί (ν)	They are

13.   The verb εἰμί takes a **predicate nominative**, not a direct object.

Present Middle and Passive Indicative

14. The present middle and passive indicative forms of φωτίζω, *I light*, are as follows:

Singular   Plural

1	φωτίζομαι	I hear, or I am hearing for myself	1	φωτιζόμεθα	We hear or are hearing for ourselves
2	φωτίζῃ	You hear or are hearing for yourself	2	φωτίζεσθε	You hear or are hearing for yourself
3	φωτίζεται	He, she, it hears or is hearing for himself, etc.	3	φωτίζονται	They hear or are hearing for themselves

15. The passive form and the middle form are the same in the present indicative but vary in other tenses. The difference between them in the present tense must be discerned by the context.

16. The present passive indicative of γινώσκω, *I know*, is follows:

1	γινώσκομαι	I am known	1	γινωσκόμεθα	We are known
2	γινώσκῃ	You are known	2	γινώσκεσθε	You are known
3	γινώσκεται	He, she, it is known	3	γινώσκονται	They are known

Example: καὶ γινώσκω τὰ ἐμὰ καὶ **γινώσκομαι** ὑπὸ τῶν ἐμῶν –
And know my (sheep) and **am known** of mine - Jn. 10:14

Exercises

17. Answers to the exercises of chapter thirteen.

   1) Translate John 1:1

   First, identify and translate each word.

Greek	Parsing	Translation	Greek	Parsing	Translation
Ἐν	Prep	In	πρὸς	Prep	with
ἀρχῇ	N-DSF	beginning	τὸν	T-ASM	the
ἦν	V-IAI-3S	was	Θεόν	N-ASM	God
ὁ	T-NSM	the	καὶ	Conj	and
λόγος	N-NSM	word	Θεὸς	N-NSM	God
καὶ	Conj	and	ἦν	V-IAI-3S	was
ὁ	T-NSM	the	ὁ	T-NSM	the
λόγος	N-NSM	word	λόγος	N-NSM	word
ἦν	V-IAI-3S	was			

KJV: "In the beginning was the Word, and the Word was with God, and the Word was God."

The bare literal translation is not good English grammar. It is close but needs to be adjusted slightly. The goal is not just to have an accurate translation. The goal is to make an accurate translation that is also good English. Note the following.

The first prepositional phrase needs a definite article. It should be translated "In the beginning."

The phrase "with the God" is improper with the article. Therefore, the article should be moved to the first prepositional phrase.

In the phrase "God was the word," One of the two nouns is the subject of the phrase and the other is a predicate nominative. A predicate nominative is a noun that means the same as the subject yet is still the object of the verb. The Predicate nominative is not a direct object because both nouns are in the nominative case. If there was a direct object, it would be in the accusative case. So, which one is the predicate nominative, and which one is the subject? Remember, Greek does not always follow the subject-verb-object sentence order. The noun that is preceded by a definite article is the subject. Therefore, the word order in the KJV is the correct word order for English. A smooth accurate English translation results in precisely the translation as it is in the KJV.

The main verb of John 1:1 is imperfect active indicative. The three phrases of the verse are simple statements of fact. Therefore, they are excellent examples of the indicative mood. The indicative basically means a straight forward statement of fact and of reality. It tells us what is real and what is actually happening or what will happen as a certain fact.

Note that the New World Translation has this phrase as "the word was a god." The "JW's" justify this heretical translation by stating the word Θεὸς does not have a definite article so we must supply the word "a." This is a failure to recon with the fact that Θεὸς is a predicate nominative. As such, the force of the article on λόγος also applies to the predicate nominative Θεὸς.

2) Romans 1:1, εἰς εὐαγγέλιον Θεοῦ, unto the gospel of God
Romans 1:3, περὶ τοῦ υἱοῦ αὐτοῦ, concerning the son of him
Romans 1:3, ἐκ σπέρματος, of (the) seed
Romans 1:3, κατὰ σάρκα, according to (the) flesh
Romans 1:18, ἀπ' οὐρανοῦ, from heaven
Romans 1:18, ἐπὶ πᾶσαν ἀσέβειαν, against all ungodliness
Romans 1:18, ἐν ἀδικίᾳ, in unrighteousness

3) εὐαγγέλιον, N-ASN
Θεοῦ, N-GSM
υἱοῦ, N-GSM
σπέρματος, N,GSM
σάρκα, N-ASF
οὐρανοῦ, N-GSM
ἀσέβειαν, N-ASF
ἀδικίᾳ, N-DSF

18. New Exercises:

Translate the following present active indicative verbs and parse them.

1. φωτίζει Jn 1:9
2. μαρτυρεῖ Jn. 1:19
3. ἐστὶν Jn. 1:19
4. εἰμὶ Jn. 1:20
5. εἶ Jn. 1:21
6. λέγεις Jn. 1:22
7. βαπτίζεις Jn. 1:25
8. βαπτίζω Jn. 1:26
9. βλέπει Jn. 1:29
10. λέγει Jn. 1:36
11. μένεις Jn. 1:38
12. ζητεῖτε Jn. 1:38
13. εὑρίσκει Jn. 1:45
14. γινώσκεις Jn. 1:48
15. πιστεύεις Jn. 1:50

CHAPTER FIFTEEN
PERSONAL PRONOUNS

John 1:2 **οὗτος** ἦν ἐν ἀρχῇ πρὸς τὸν Θεόν.
John 1:3 πάντα δι' **αὐτοῦ** ἐγένετο, καὶ χωρὶς **αὐτοῦ** ἐγένετο οὐδὲ ἕν ὃ γέγονεν.
John 1:2 **The same** was in the beginning with God.
John 1:3 All things were made by **him**; and without **him** was not any thing made that was made.

1. In John 1:2-3, **αὐτοῦ** is a personal pronoun, meaning *him*, and **οὗτος** is a demonstrative pronoun meaning *this one* or the *same one*. They bring up the whole subject of pronouns. In New Testament Greek, there are personal pronouns, demonstrative pronouns, Interogative pronouns, Indefinite pronouns, and relative pronouns. In this chapter, we will study personal pronouns and in the next chapter, the others.

2. Vocabulary

| αὐτός, ἡ, ὁ, pron. | he | εἰμί | I am |
| ἐγώ, pron. | I | σύ, pron. | you |

3. A pronoun in Greek is defined the same way a pronoun in English is defined and functions much the same way. A pronoun is a word that stands in the place of a noun. The noun for which a pronoun stands is called its *antecedent*.

4. The declension of the personal pronoun of the first person is as follows.

Singular   Plural

N	ἐγώ, I		N	ἡμεῖς, we
G	μου or ἐμοῦ, of me		G	ἡμῶν, of us
D	μοι or ἐμοί, to or for me		D	ἡμῖν, to or for us
A	με or ἐμέ, me		A	ἡμᾶς, us

The forms ἐμοῦ, ἐμοί, and ἐμέ are used for emphasis. The forms μου, μοι, and με are the unemphatic forms and are the forms usually employed. The unemphatic forms have no accent. When a word goes so closely with the word before it as to have no accent of its own, it is called *enclitic*. When a word goes so closely with a following word as to have no accent of its own, it is called *proclitic*.

5. Parsing Pronouns: The code for *personal pronoun* is P. Otherwise, the codes following P are the same as those for nouns. For example, P-GSM means **P**ersonal Pronoun-**G**enitive **S**ingular **M**asculine. However, there are two distinct methods of parsing. The above example is used for **third** person pronouns. The **first** person pronouns are parsed thus, ἐγώ, P-1NS (**P**ronoun-**F**irst person **N**ominative **S**ingular) and the second person thus, ὑμῶν, P-2GP (**P**ronoun-**S**econd person **G**enitive **P**lural).

6. The declension of the personal pronoun of the second person is as follows.

Singular   Plural

N	σύ, you, thou
G	σοῦ, of you, of thee
D	σοί, to or for you, thee
A	σέ, you, thee

N	ὑμεῖς, you, ye
G	ὑμῶν, of you
D	ὑμῖν, to or for you
A	ὑμᾶς, you

This chart shows the way these pronouns are translated in the KJV. In the Early Modern English language of the KJV, "you" is plural. The forms σοῦ, σοί, and σέ are enclitic. They are accented when they are emphatic and, in that case, you will see the forms shown here.

7. The third person pronoun, αὐτός, is specific to gender. The declension of the personal pronoun of the third person is as follows.

Singular

Masculine   Feminine   Neuter

N	αὐτός, he	αὐτή, she	αὐτό, it
G	αὐτοῦ, of him	αυτῆς, of her	αὐτοῦ, of it
D	αὐτῷ, to or for him	αὐτη, to or for her	αὐτῷ, to or for it
A	αὐτόν, him	αὐτήν, her	αὐτό, it

Plural

Masculine   Feminine   Neuter

N	αὐτόι, they	αὐταί, they	αὐτά, they
G	αὐτῶν, of them	αυτῶν, of them	αὐτῶν, of them
D	αὐτοῖς, to or for them	αὐταῖς, to or for them	αὐτοῖς, to or for them
A	αὐτούς, them	αὐτάς, them	αὐτά, them

8. The Uses of the Personal Pronoun

1) Pronouns, in general, agree in gender and number with their antecedents. The case of the pronoun will be according to the function of the pronoun in the sentence. If a pronoun has two or more antecedents, it will be plural while the antecedent may be singular.

2) Verbs imply a pronoun. For example, εἰμί means *I am*. A separate pronoun is not used in the nominative case, unless it is being emphasized. So, ἐγώ εἰμί also means *I am*.

3) The unemphatic forms of the personal pronouns are usually used when expressing possession. An example is John 5:24, ὁ τὸν **λόγον μου** ἀκούων, *The one (he) who hears **my word***.

4) The emphatic forms of the personal pronoun are often used as the objects of propositions. The final vowel of a preposition is usually omitted before a word that starts with a vowel.

   Examples: John. 10:9-δι' ἐμοῦ, *by me*
   John. 10:38-ἐν ἐμοί, *in me*

5) Pronouns function in every way a noun does. The genitive of personal pronouns are possessive pronouns.

6.) The personal pronoun may function as a reflexive pronoun. A reflexive pronoun is used when the action of the verb is referred back onto its own subject. This use is rare in the New Testament.

   Examples:

   Mt. 6:19 Μὴ θησαυρίζετε **ὑμῖν** θησαυροὺς ἐπὶ τῆς γῆς / Lay not up for **yourselves** treasures upon earth
   Mt. 6:20 θησαυρίζετε δὲ **ὑμῖν** θησαυροὺς ἐν οὐρανῷ / But lay up for **yourselves** treasures in heaven

9. Additional Uses of αὐτός:

1) Sometimes αὐτός means *the same*. The context usually makes it clear when this is the case. When used in this way, the pronoun usually (but not always) is immediately preceded by an article. This is called the attributive position, which will be further explained in chapter seventeen on Adjectives.

   Examples:
   Mt. 3:4 Αὐτὸς δὲ ὁ Ἰωάννης- *And the same John*
   Mt. 5:46 οἱ τελῶναι τὸ αὐτὸ / *the publicans the same*

Mt. 26:44 τὸν αὐτὸν λόγον / the same words
Lk. 2:8 ἐν τῇ χώρᾳ τῇ αὐτῇ / in the same country
Lk 10:7 ἐν αυτῃ δὲ τῇ οἰκίᾳ / And in the same house
Lk. 12:12 ἐν αὐτῇ τῇὥρᾳ / the same hour
John 5:36-αὐτὰ τὰ ἔργα / the same works
Acts 15:27 τὰ αὐτά / the same things
1 Cor. 15:39 ἡ αὐτὴ σάρξ / the same flesh

2) In other contexts, αὐτός has an intensive use and means *himself, herself, itself, yourself, themselves*, etc. When used in this way, the pronoun usually does *not* have an article in front of it. (This is called the Predicate position. See chapter seventeen on adjectives for more about the predicate position.)

Examples:
Mk. 12:36 αὐτὸς γὰρ Δαυῒδ εἶπεν / for David himself said
Mk. 12:37 αὐτὸς οὖν Δαυῒδ λέγει αὐτὸν Κύριον / David therefore himself calleth him Lord
Lk 23:7 Ἡρῴδην, ὄντα καὶ αὐτὸν ἐν Ἱεροσολύμοις / Herod, who himself also was at Jerusalem
Jn. 4:2 Ἰησοῦς αὐτὸς οὐκ ἐβάπτιζεν / Jesus himself baptized not
Jn. 4:44 αὐτὸς γὰρ ὁ Ἰησοῦς ἐμαρτύρησεν / For Jesus himself testified
Jn. 18:28 καὶ αὐτοὶ οὐκ εἰσῆλθον / and they themselves went not
Acts 20:30 καὶ ἐξ ὑμῶν αὐτῶν / Also of your own selves

3) Αὐτός is sometimes used in the nominative case as the subject of the clause. When this occurs, the KJV may translate it as *himself* or *thyself*, etc. This was accurate for the Early Modern English of the KJV. But, in current Modern English, we would simply use *he* (or another appropriate pronoun), as I will illustrate. In the following verses, the clause that shows this use of αὐτός is in bold.

Examples:
Mt. 8:17 λέγοντος, **Αὐτὸς** τὰς ἀσθενείας ἡμῶν **ἔλαβε** / saying, **Himself took** our infirmities
Although, the KJV accurately translated αὐτός as *himself*, it stands in the position of subject to the verb. Therefore, in current English, it would be *he*.
Mt. 8:24 αὐτὸς δὲ ἐκάθευδε / but he was asleep.
In this case, αὐτὸς is clearly the subject of the clause and is translated *he*.

Exercises

10. Answers to exercises in chapter 14

   1. φωτίζει Jn 1:9 — He lights V-PAI-3S
   2. μαρτυρεῖ Jn. 1:19 — He witnesses V-PAI-3S
   3. ἐστὶν Jn. 1:19 — It is V-PAI-3S
   4. εἰμὶ Jn. 1:20 — I am V-PAI-1S
   5. εἶ Jn. 1:21 — You are V-PAI-2S
   6. λέγεις Jn. 1:22 — You say V-PAI-2S
   7. βαπτίζεις Jn. 1:25 — You baptize V-PAI-2S
   8. βαπτίζω Jn. 1:26 — I baptize V-PAI-1S
   9. βλέπει Jn. 1:29 — he sees V-PAI-3S
   10. λέγει Jn. 1:36 — he says V-PAI-3S
   11. μένεις Jn. 1:38 — He abide, he remains V-PAI-3S
   12. ζητεῖτε Jn. 1:38 — You seek V-PAI-3P
   13. εὑρίσκει Jn. 1:45 — He finds V-PAI-3S
   14. γινώσκεις Jn. 1:48 — You know V-PAI-2S
   15. πιστεύεις Jn. 1:50 — You believe V-PAI-2S

11. New Exercises:

Read through John 1, starting at verse 4, and pick out ten uses of the personal pronoun. Show the KJV translation and parse them. Several examples of parsing codes and their explanations are below.

αὐτῷ - P-DSM (Pronoun-Dative Singular Masculine)
εἰμὶ - V-PAI-1S (Pronoun-Present Active Indicative-1 person Singular)
ἐγώ - P-1NS (Pronoun-1 person Nominative Singular)
ὑμῶν - P-2GP (Pronoun-2 person Genitive Singular)

Notice that the third person personal pronoun is parsed differently than the first and second persons. Also, the parsing of the present active indicative form of εἰμὶ is consistent with the parsing of present active indicative verbs.

CHAPTER SIXTEEN
PRONOUNS: DEMONSTRATIVE, INTERROGATIVE, INDEFINITE, REFLEXIVE, RECIPROCAL, AND RELATIVE

2 **οὗτος** ἦν ἐν ἀρχῇ πρὸς τὸν Θεόν.
3 πάντα δι' αὐτοῦ ἐγένετο, καὶ χωρὶς αὐτοῦ ἐγένετο οὐ δὲ ἕν ὃ γέγονεν.
33 ... ἀλλ' ὁ πέμψας με βαπτίζειν ἐν ὕδατι, **ἐκεῖνός** μοι εἶπεν

2 **The same** was in the beginning with God.
3 All things were made by him; and without him was not any thing made that was made.
33... but, he that sent me to baptize with water, **the same** said to me

1. Vocabulary

Word	Basic Meanings	Word	Basic Meanings
οὗτος, αὕτη, τοῦτο, Pron.	This	ἐμαυτοῦ, ῆς, reflexive pronoun	of myself
νῦν, adverb	now	σεαυτοῦ, ῆς, reflexive pronoun	of yourself (thyself)
οὕτως, adverb	thus, so	ἑαυτοῦ, ῆς, οῦ, relexive pronoun	of himself, of herself, of itself.
ἐκεῖνος, η, ο, pron.	that	ἀλλήλους, reciprocal pronoun	one another
ὅς, ἥ, ὅ relative pronoun	who, which	πõυ, adverb	where
ὅτε, adverb	when (relative)	πῶς, adverb	how
ἐγείρω	I raise up	τις, τι, indefinite pronoun	someone, something, a certain one, a certain thing
οἶνος, ὁ	wine	τίς, τί, interrogative pronoun	who, which, what

2. All the pronouns taught in this lesson agree with their antecedents in gender, number. Case is according to use in the sentence, with the exception that is explained in paragraph 25 of this lesson.

Demonstrative Pronouns

3.   **Οὗτος and ἐκεῖνός** in John 1:2, 33, are demonstrative pronouns. A demonstrative pronoun is a word that points to other persons or things. Both English and Greek have only two of them: this, οὗτος, and that, ἐκεῖνος. They are similar in meaning. As you will notice, they are translated alike in John 1:2, 33, but that is not always the case. The basic meaning of the pronoun in john 1:2 is *this one*, translated *the same*. The basic meaning of the pronoun in John 1:33 is *that one*, also translated *the same*.

4.   The declension of οὗτος, αὕτη, τοῦτο, *this,* is below.

	Singular			Plural		
	M	F	N	M	F	N
N	οὗτος	αὕτη	τοῦτο	οὗτοι	αὗται	ταῦτα
G	τούτου	ταύτης	τούτου	τούτων	τούτων	τούτων
D	τούτῳ	ταύτῃ	τούτῳ	τούτοις	τούταις	τούτοις
A	τοῦτον	ταύτην	τοῦτο	τούτους	ταύτας	ταῦτα

5.   The declension of ἐκεῖνος is below.

	Singular			Plural		
	M	F	N	M	F	N
N	ἐκεῖνος	ἐκείνη	ἐκεῖνο	ἐκεῖνοι	ἐκεῖναι	ἐκεῖνα
G	ἐκείνου	ἐκείνης	ἐκείνου	ἐκείνων	ἐκείνων	ἐκείνων
D	ἐκείνῳ	ἐκείνῃ	ἐκείνῳ	ἐκείνοις	ἐκείναις	ἐκείνοις
A	ἐκεῖνον	ἐκείνην	ἐκεῖνο	ἐκείνους	ἐκείνας	ἐκεῖνα

6.   Uses of οὗτος and ἐκεῖνος:

1) The demonstrative pronoun may be used with nouns. When used with a noun, the noun generally has the article.

Examples of οὗτος:

John 1:19 - αὕτη ἐστὶν ἡ μαρτυρία / this is the record
John 1:34 - οὗτός ἐστιν ὁ υἱὸς τοῦ Θεοῦ / this is the Son of God
John 2:20 - ὁ ναὸς οὗτος / this temple
John 3:19 - αὕτη δέ ἐστιν ἡ κρίσις / and this is the condemnation

Examples of ἐκεῖνος:

Luke 13:4 - ἢ ἐκεῖνοι οἱ δέκα / or those twelve
Luke 20:1 - ἐν μιᾷ τῶν ἡμερῶν ἐκείνων / in one of those days
Acts 2:18 - ἐν ταῖς ἡμέραις ἐκείναις / in those days

Acts 16:3 - ἐν τοῖς τόποις ἐκείνοις / in those quarters

2) The demonstrative pronoun may also be used by itself without a noun.

Examples of οὗτος:

John 6:5 - ἵνα φάγωσιν οὗτοι / that these may eat
John 17:11 - οὗτοι ἐν τῷ κόσμῳ εἰσί / these are in the world
John 17:25 - καὶ οὗτοι ἔγνωσαν ὅτι σύ με ἀπέστειλας/ and these have known that thou hast sent me

Examples of ἐκεῖνος:

Luke 18:14 – δεδικαιωμένος εἰς τὸν οἶκον αὐτοῦ ἢ ἐκεῖνος / down to his house justified rather than the other (that one)
John 5:11 - ἐκεῖνός μοι εἶπεν /the same (that one or he) said unto me
John 12:48 - ὁ λόγος ὃν ἐλάλησα, ἐκεῖνος κρινεῖ αὐτὸν / the word that I have spoken, the same (that one) shall judge him
2 Timothy 3:9 - ὡς καὶ ἡ ἐκείνων ἐγένετο / as theirs also was

The Interrogative Pronoun

7. The interrogative pronoun is τίς, τί, who? whom? what? which? *Who* is used for the subject and *whom* for the direct object. The declension of the interrogative pronoun is as follows.

Singular　　　　　　　　　　Plural

	M/F	N	M/F	N
N	τίς	τί	τίνες	τίνα
G	τίνος	τίνος	τίνων	τίνων
D	τίνι	τίνι	τίσι (ν)	τίσι (ν)
A	τίνα	τί	τίνας	τίνα

8. Examples of interrogative pronoun use:

John 1:19 - Σὺ τίς εἶ; / Who art thou?
John 1:21 - Τί οὖν; / What then?
John 1:25 – Τί οὖν βαπτίζεις …; / Why baptizest thou then … ?

The Indefinite Pronoun

9. The indefinite pronoun is τις, τι, *someone, something, a certain one, a certain thing*. It is the same as the interrogative pronoun, except for the accent.

The indefinite pronoun is declined the same as the interrogative pronoun, *except for the differences in the accent*. There is no accent in the nominative M/F/N singular and in the accusative neuter singular. In the remainder of the forms, the accent is on the second syllable (or no accent in certain instances), rather than the first, as in the interrogative pronoun. The declension of the indefinite pronoun is as follows.

	Singular		Plural	
	M/F	N	M/F	N
N	τις	τι	τινές	τινά
G	τινός	τινός	τινῶν	τινῶν
D	τινί	τινί	τισί (ν)	τισί (ν)
A	τινά	τι	τινάς	τινά

10. The indefinite pronouns can be used with or without a noun.

11. Examples of the indefinite pronoun.
    Acts 3:5 προσδοκῶν τι παρ' αὐτῶν λαβεῖν.
      expecting something from them to receive
    Phil. 3:15 καὶ εἴ τι ἑτέρως φρονεῖτε
      and if in anything ye be otherwise minded

12. The indefinite pronoun can function as an adjective:
    Luke 1:5 Ἐγένετο ... ἱερεύς τις / There was ... a certain priest

13. Some Greek idioms using the indefinite pronoun, τι:

    1) οὐ ... τι, nothing, literally: not ... something
       2Co 13.8 οὐ γὰρ δυνάμεθά τι / For we can do nothing
       Literally: for we can do not something

    2) ἄν τινων, whoever,
       Jn 20.23 ἄν τινων ἀφῆτε τὰς ἁμαρτίας / Whose soever sins ye remit

    3) ὃ ἐάν τι, whatever, literally: whatever
       Eph 6.8 εἰδότες ὅτι **ὃ ἐάν τι** ἕκαστος ποιήσῃ ἀγαθόν / Knowing that **whatsoever** good thing any man doeth

    4) **μὴ ... τι,** no, literally: not ... some
       Lu 11.36 **μὴ** ἔχον **τι** μέρος σκοτεινόν
         having **no** part dark/ Literally, **not** having **some** part dark

Reflexive Pronouns

14. A reflexive pronoun is a pronoun that refers back to the subject of a sentence or clause. An example is: *He accidentally cut himself.* Notice that this is different from the emphatic use of the personal pronoun, such as *He himself made the cut.* The reflexive pronouns are: ἐμαυτοῦ, of myself, σεαυτοῦ, of yourself (thyself), and ἑαυτοῦ, of himself, of herself, of itself.

15. The declension of ἐμαυτοῦ, of myself, first person reflexive pronoun, is as follows.

Singular   Plural

	M	F	M	F
G	ἐμαυτοῦ	ἐμαυτῆς	ἑαυτῶν	ἑαυτῶν
D	ἐμαυτῷ	ἐμαυτῇ	ἑαυτοῖς	ἑαυταῖς
A	ἐμαυτόν	ἐμαυτήν	ἑαυτούς	ἑαυτάς

16. The declension of σεαυτοῦ, of yourself (thyself), second person reflexive pronoun, is as follows.

Singular   Plural

	M	F	M	F
G	σεαυτοῦ	σεαυτῆς	ἑαυτῶν	ἑαυτῶν
D	σεαυτῷ	σεαυτῇ	ἑαυτοῖς	ἑαυταῖς
A	σεαυτόν	σεαυτήν	ἑαυτούς	ἑαυτάς

17. The declension of ἑαυτοῦ, of himself, of herself, of itself, third person reflexive pronoun, is as follows.

Singular   Plural

	M	F	N	M	F	N
G	ἑαυτοῦ	ἑαυτῆς	ἑαυτοῦ	ἑαυτῶν	ἑαυτῶν	ἑαυτῶν
D	ἑαυτῷ	ἑαυτῇ	ἑαυτῷ	ἑαυτοῖς	ἑαυταῖς	ἑαυτοῖς
A	ἑαυτόν	ἑαυτήν	ἑαυτό	ἑαυτούς	ἑαυτάς	ἑαυτά

18. Examples of the reflexive pronoun

Acts 5:36 λέγων εἶναί τινα **ἑαυτόν**
    boasting **himself** to be somebody
Acts 16:28 Μηδὲν πράξῃς **σεαυτῷ** κακόν
    Do **thyself** no harm
Romans 11:4 Κατέλιπον **ἐμαυτῷ** ἑπτακισχιλίους ἄνδρας
    I have reserved to **myself** seven thousand men

Reciprocal Pronouns

19. The reciprocal pronoun, *another*, occurs in the New Testament only in the following forms.

ἀλλήλων	of one another
ἀλλήλοις	to or for one another
ἀλλήλους	one another

20. Examples of the reciprocal pronoun:

John 13:34 - ἵνα καὶ ὑμεῖς ἀγαπᾶτε **ἀλλήλους**
   that ye also love **one another**
Romans 15:7 – προσλαμβάνεσθε **ἀλλήλους**
   receive **one another**
Galatians 5:13 – ἀλλὰ διὰ τῆς ἀγάπης δουλεύετε **ἀλλήλοις**
   but by love serve **one another**

Relative Pronouns

21. The relative pronoun, ὅς, ἥ, ὅ, expresses *who* and *which* as pronouns, rather than interrogatives.

22. The declension of the relative pronoun is as follows.

Singular   Plural

	M	F	N	M	F	N
N	ὅς	ἥ	ὅ	οἵ	αἵ	ἅ
G	οὗ	ἧς	οὗ	ὧν	ὧν	ὧν
D	ᾧ	ᾗ	ᾧ	οἷς	αἷς	οἷς
A	ὅν	ἥν	ὅ	οὕς	ἅς	ἅ

23. The relative pronoun agrees with its antecedent in gender and number, the same as other pronouns. It takes its case from its use in the sentence.

24. However, there is an exception to the rule in paragraph 20. When the antecedent of the relative pronoun is in the dative or genitive cases and the relative pronoun would normally be in the accusative case, the pronoun takes the case of the antecedent.

25. The antecedent of the relative pronoun is often left unexpressed. So, ὅς can mean *he who*, ἥ can mean *she who*, and ὅ can mean *it which*.

26.   Examples of the relative pronoun.

Rom. 2:5,6 ἀποκαλύψεως δικαιοκρισίας τοῦ Θεοῦ, **ὃς** ἀποδώσει
revelation of the righteousness of God, **who** will render
ἑκάστῳ /
to every man
Romans 4:16 Ἀβραάμ, **ὅς** ἐστι πατὴρ πάντων ἡμῶν
... Abraham; **who** is the father of us all
Romans 11:2 οὐκ ἀπώσατο ὁ Θεὸς τὸν λαὸν αὐτοῦ **ὃν** προέγνω.
God hat not cast away his people, **which** he foreknew

Exercises

27.   Answer to the exercises of chapter fifteen.

1) V. 4 - αὐτῷ - him - P-DSM
2) V. 5 - αὐτὸ - it - P-ASN
3) V. 6 - αὐτῷ - whose - P-DSM
4) V. 7 - αὐτοῦ - him - P-GSM
5) V.10 - αὐτοῦ - him - P-GSM
6) V. 10 - αὐτὸν - him - P-ASM
7) V. 11 - αὐτὸν - him - P-ASM
8) V. 12 - αὐτὸν - him - P-ASM
9) V. 12 - αὐτοῦ - his - P-GSM
10) V. 14 - ἡμῖν - us - P-1DP

28.   New Exercises:

1) Starting at John 1:15, find ten pronouns that are NOT personal pronouns. List the verse, list the pronoun, give the KJV translation, and parse them.

New parsing codes to use:

D- Demonstrative Pronoun
I - Interrogative pronouns
X - Indefinite Pronoun
F - Reflexive pronoun
C - Reciprocal pronoun
R- Relative pronoun

2)   Translate John 1:2. Parse each word.

CHAPTER SEVENTEEN
ADJECTIVES:
ADJECTIVES OF THE FIRST AND SECOND DECLENSION; Agreement of Adjectives; Attributive and Predicate Positions of Adjectives; Use of an Adjective as a Substantive; The Declension of πᾶς, πολύς, μέγας

Jn. 1:3 **πάντα** δι' αὐτοῦ ἐγένετο, καὶ χωρὶς αὐτοῦ ἐγένετο οὐ δὲ ἕν ὃ γέγονεν.
Jn. 1:4 ἐν αὐτῷ ζωὴ ἦν, καὶ ἡ ζωὴ ἦν τὸ φῶς τῶν ἀνθρώπων,

3 All things were made by him; and without him was not any thing made that was made.
4 In him was life; and the life was the light of men.

1. Vocabulary

Word	Basic Meanings	Word	Basic Meanings
πᾶς, α, ᾶν, adj	all, every	ἔσχατος, ἡ, ον, adj	last
ἀληθής, ης, ες, adj	true	κακός, ἡ, όν, adj	bad
ὅσος, η, ον adj	as many as	καλός, ἡ, όν. adj	good, beautiful
βάλλω	I cast	μικρός, ά, όν, adj	small
μέσος, adjective	middle (midst)	νεκρός, ά, όν, adj	dead
ἄξιος, α, ον adj	worthy	ὁδός, ἡ	way, road
ἀγαθός, ἡ, όν, adj	good	πιστός, ἡ, όν, adj	faithful
ἄλλος, ἡ, ο, adj	other	πρῶτος, ἡ, όν, adj	first
ἔρημος, ἡ,	wilderness, desert	δίκαιος, α, όν, adj	righteous
πολύς, ἡ, ύ, adj	much, many	ἄδικος, -ος, -ον, adj	unrighteous
μέγας, η, α, adj	great	ὀλίγος, η, ον, adj	few, little
καθαρός, ά, όν, adj	clean, pure	ἤ,	or
οὐδείς, οὐδεμία, οὐδέν	no one, nothing (in indicative)	τότε, adv.	when
μηδείς, μηδεμία, μηδέν	no one, nothing (not in indicative)	ἐλάσσων, -ων, -ον, adj	worse, less
	willing		

2. Greek adjectives modify and describe nouns and pronouns, just as they do in English.

3. You should learn the Greek adjectives with all three gender forms. That is why they are listed in this way: ἄλλος, -η, -ov. It shows that the nominative masculine, feminine, and neuter end in -ος, -ή, and -ov. In this chapter, we will look first at the general declension of adjectives of the first and second declension. Afterward, we will look at πᾶς, John 1:2.

4. There are three degrees of adjectives in both Greek and English: positive, comparative, and superlative.

>   Positive: A description of the noun or pronoun.
>   Comparative: A comparison of two individual nouns or pronouns.
>   Superlative: A comparison to a greater degree and used for emphasis.
>
>   The English Equivalent is:
>
>   Positive: Great
>   Comparative: Greater
>   Superlative: Greatest
>
>   In English there are irregular adjectives such as *bad, worse, worst* and *much, more, most* and *more important* rather than i*mportanter.* There are also irregular adjectives in New Testament Greek.

The Positive Degree of Adjectives

5. There are several systems of declension for Greek adjectives. It may seem confusing to beginning students, but each adjective should be learned with its feminine and neuter endings.

6. The declension of ἀγαθός, -ή, -όν, *good*, is below.

Singular   Plural

	Masc.	Fem.	Neut.	Masc.	Fem.	Neut.
N	ἀγαθός	ἀγαθή	ἀγαθόν	ἀγαθοί	ἀγαθαί	ἀγαθά
G	ἀγαθοῦ	ἀγαθῆς	ἀγαθοῦ	ἀγαθῶν	ἀγαθῶν	ἀγαθῶν
D	ἀγαθῷ	ἀγαθῇ	ἀγαθῷ	ἀγαθοῖς	ἀγαθαῖς	ἀγαθοῖς
A	ἀγαθόν	ἀγαθήν	ἀγαθόν	ἀγαθούς	ἀγαθάς	ἀγαθά
V	ἀγαθέ	ἀγαθή	ἀγαθόν	ἀγαθοί	ἀγαθαί	ἀγαθά

7. The declension of μικρός, -α, -ov, *small*, John 1:27, is as follows.

Singular   Plural

	Masc.	Fem.	Neut.	Masc.	Fem.	Neut.
N	μικρός	μικρά	μικρόν	μικροί	μικραί	μικρά
G	μικροῦ	μικρᾶς	μικροῦ	μικρῶν	μικρῶν	μικρῶν
D	μικρῷ	μικρᾷ	μικρῷ	μικροῖς	μικραῖς	μικροῖς
A	μικρόν	μικράν	μικρόν	μικρούς	μικράς	μικρά
V	μικρέ	μικρά	μικρόν	μικροί	μικραί	μικρά

8. The declension of ἄδικος, -ος, -ov, *unjust, unrighteous* is below.

Singular   Plural

	M / F	Neut.	M / F	Neut.
N	ἄδικος	ἄδικον	ἄδικοι	ἄδικα
G	ἀδίκου	ἀδίκου	ἀδίκων	ἀδίκων
D	ἀδίκῳ	ἀδίκῳ	ἀδίκοις	ἀδίκοις
A	ἄδικον	ἄδικον	ἀδίκους	ἄδικα
V	ἄδικε	ἄδικον	ἄδικοι	ἄδικα

9. **Agreement:** Adjectives agree with the nouns they modify in case, number, and gender.

10. **Atributive and Predicate Use of Adjectives:** Adjectives are used in these two ways. Both have to do with the presence or absence of the article and where it is placed. This is important and determines how the adjective is translated.

   1) **Attributive use** means that the article is placed immediately before the adjective. This can be done in two ways: 1) ο αγαθος λογος, *the good word.* or 2) ο λογος ο αγαθος, *the good word.*

   2) **Predicate use** means that the article does not come immediately before the adjective. This also is constructed in two ways: 1) ο λογος αγαθος, *the word is good*, 2) αγαθος ο λογος, *the word is good.*

   3) To summarize, the adjective directly modifies the noun when it is in the attributive position, *the good word.* When the adjective is in the predicate position, add "is" to the adjectival phrase, *the word is good.* The adjective is called a *predicate adjective.*

11. **The adjective used as a substantive:** A *substantive* is a noun. When an adjective is used alone without a noun, it could be acting as a noun. The adjective αγαθος by itself means *a good man* or *a good one*, αγαθη means *a good woman*, and αγαθον means *a good thing*. With an article, ο αγαθος means *the good man*, ο αγαθη means *the good woman*, and ο αγαθον means *the good thing*. A perfect example of this is in John 1:2. παντα means *all*. It is used without a noun or article and is, therefore, translated as *all things*.

The Declension and Use of πᾶς, πολύς, and μέγας

12. The declension of πᾶς, -α, -ᾶν, adj., *all, every*, (see John 1:3) is as follows.

	Singular			Plural		
	Masc.	Fem.	Neut.	Masc.	Fem.	Neut.
N	πᾶς	πᾶσα	πᾶν	πάντες	πᾶσαι	πάντα
G	παντός	πάσης	παντός	πάντων	πασῶν	πάντων
D	παντί	πάσῃ	παντί	πᾶσι (ν)	πάσαις	πάσι (ν)
A	πάντα	πᾶσαν	πᾶν	πάντας	πάσας	πάντα

13. The Uses of πᾶς:

1) πᾶς can be used in the predicate position with a noun that has the article, but do not add the verb "is." The meaning is *all inclusive*. For example, πᾶσα ἡ τόλις means *all the city*.

2) πᾶς can also be used in the attributive position. An example would be ἡ πᾶσα πόλις, *the whole city* or *the entire city*.

3) πᾶς sometimes means *every* when used with a singular noun. For example, πᾶν ὄρος, every mountain.

14. The declension of πολύς, -ή, -ύ, *much, many*, is as follows.

	Singular			Plural		
	Masc.	Fem.	Neut.	Masc.	Fem.	Neut.
N	πολύς	πολλή	πολύ	πολλοί	πολλαί	πολλά
G	πολλοῦ	πολλῆς	πολλοῦ	πολλῶν	πολλῶν	πολλῶν
D	πολλῷ	πολλῇ	πολλῷ	πολλοῖς	πολλαῖς	πολλοῖς
A	πολύν	πολλήν	πολύ	πολλούς	πολλάς	πολλά

15. The declension of μέγας, -η, -α, *great*, is as follows.

	Masc.	Fem.	Neut.	Masc.	Fem.	Neut.
N	μέγας	μεγάλη	μέγα	μεγάλοι	μεγάλαι	μεγάλα
G	μεγάλου	μεγάλης	μεγάλου	μεγάλων	μεγαλῶν	μεγάλων
D	μεγάλῳ	μεγάλη	μεγάλῳ	μεγάλοις	μεγάλαις	μεγάλοις
A	μέγαν	μεγάλην	μέγα	μεγάλους	μεγάλας	μεγάλα

Exercises

16. Answers to exercises of chapter sixteen:

    1) Pronouns:

        (1) V. 15 - ὄν - he of whom - R-ASM
        (2) V. 21 - τί - what - I-NSN
        (3) V. 22 - τίς - who - I-NSM
        (4) V. 22 - τί - what - I-NSN
        (5) V. 25 - τί - why - I-NSN
        (6) V. 26 - ὄν - whom - R-ASM
        (7) V. 27 - ὅς - who - R-NSM
        (8) V. 27 - οὗ - whose - R-GSM
        (9) V. 28 - ταῦτα - these - D-NPN
        (10) V. 30 - οὗτός - this - D-NSM

    2) Translate John 1:2

οὗτος	ἦν	ἐν	ἀρχῇ	πρὸς	τὸν	Θεόν.
D-NSM	V-IAI-3S	PREP	N-DSF	PREP	T-ASM	N-ASM
This one was		in the beginning		with	the	God

KJV: The same was in the beginning with God.

οὗτος was accurately translated *the same*. It could also have been accurately translated *he* or *this one*. Sometimes more than one word can be accurately used in translating a Greek word. It is the job of a translator to prayerfully choose which is best.

17. New Exercises:

Translate the following and parse the adjective:

Example of parsing an adjective

ἀγαθόν - A-ASM (Adjective-Accusative Singular Masculine)

1) John 1:46 τι ἀγαθὸν
2) John 10:11 ἐγώ εἰμι ὁ ποιμὴν ὁ καλός
3) John 1:27 ἐγὼ οὐκ εἰμὶ ἄξιος ἵνα λύσω
4) 1 Timothy 1:5 ἐκ καθαρᾶς καρδίας
5) John 10:16 καὶ ἄλλα πρόβατα ἔχω
6) John. 1:3 πάντα δι' αὐτοῦ ἐγένετο (was made)
7) John 17:25 πάτερ δίκαιε
8) Acts 26:22 μαρτυρούμενος (witnessing) μικρῷτε (both) καὶ μεγάλῳ

CHAPTER EIGHTEEN
COMPARISON ADJECTIVES, ADVERBS, AND GENITIVES; POSSESSIVE ADJECTIVES; USE OF ἤ

John 1:50 ἀπεκρίθη Ἰησοῦς καὶ εἶπεν αὐτῷ, Ὅτι εἶπόν σοι, εἶδόν σε ὑποκάτω τῆς συκῆς, πιστεύεις; **μείζω τούτων ὄψει.**
John 1:50 Jesus answered and said unto him, Because I said unto thee, I saw thee under the fig tree, believest thou? **thou shalt see greater things than these**.

1. Vocabulary

Word	Basic Meanings	Word	Basic Meanings
μείζων, ων, ον, adj	greater, comparative of μέγας, great	καλῶς, adv.	well
ἴδιος, α, ον adj	belonging to one's self; one's own	κρείσσων, ον	better, comparative of ἀγαθός
ἐμός, ή, όν, poss. adj.	belonging to me, my	μή, conj. and adv.	lest, so that not, (μή also = not)
ἔμπροσθεν, adv. with genitive	in front of, in the presence of	μήποτε	lest, perchance
ἐνώπιον, adv. with Genitive	before, in the sight of, in the presence of	ὅπως	in order that- used similar to ἵνα
ἔξω, adv.	outside, outside of	πάλιν, adv.	again
ἐχθρός, ὁ	enemy	πλείων, ον	more comp. of πολύς
ἡμέτερος, α, ον, poss. adjective	belonging to us, our	μᾶλλον, adv.	more, rather
ἱκανός, ή, όν	sufficient, worthy, considerable	σός, ή, όν, poss. adj.	belonging to you (thee), your (thy)
ἰσχυρότερος, α, ον	stronger, comp. of ἰσχυρός, α, ον, strong	ὑμέτερος, α, ον, poss, adj.	belonging to you, your
ἤ, conj.	than, or	ὅταν, Conj	when, whenever
ἐκεῖ, adv.	there		

The Comparison of Adjectives

2.   *Regular* adjectives that end in -ος can form the comparative by adding the ending -τερος, -α, -ον and are declined like regular first and second declension adjectives (see chapter seventeen). Sometimes they end in -ων and -ον, being declined as μείζων in paragraph 4 below.

   Example: Luke 15:12

   καὶ εἶπεν ὁ **νεώτερος** αὐτῶν τῳ πατρί
   and said the **younger** of them to (his) father

3.   There are also *irregular* adjectives that do not conform to these rules. These must be learned as they occur.

4.   The declension of μείζων, -ων, -ον, *greater*, comparative of μέγας, *great*, is as follows.

	Singular		Plural	
	M/F	N	M/F	N
N	μείζων	μεῖζον	μείζονες or μείζους	μείζονα or μείξω
G	μείζονος	μείζονος	μειζόνων	μειζόνων
D	μείζονι	μείζονι	μείζοσι (v)	μείζοσι (v)
A	μείζονα or μείξω	μεῖζον	μείζονας or μείζους	μείζονα or μείξω

5.   In the accusative singular masculine and feminine and in the nominative and accusative neuter plural, you may see either μείζονα or μείξω. Also, you may see either μείζονες (Nom), μείζονας (Acc) or μείζους in the nominative and accusative masculine and feminine plural.

The Superlative of Adjectives

6.   Regular adjectives in the superlative degree end in -τατος, -η, -ον or -ιστος, -η, -ον. However, the regular superlative degree is rare in the New Testament.

   Example: Jude 1:20 -
   Ὑμεῖς δέ, ἀγαπητοί, τῃ **ἁγιωτάτῃ** ὑμῶν **πίστει** ἐποικοδομοῦντες ἑαυτοὺς
   But ye, beloved, on your **most holy** faith buiilding up yourselves

7. Often the comparative degree is substituted for the superlative in the New Testament.

> Example: 1 Cor. 13:13
> νυνὶ δὲ μένει πίστις, ἐλπίς, ἀγάπη, τὰ τρία ταῦτα·
> and now abideth faith, hope, charity, the three these;
> **μείζων** δὲ τούτων ἡ ἀγάπη.
> but the **greatest** of these *is* charity.

The English idiom requires that the superlative degree must be used in 1 Corinthians 13:13, because three things are being compared. The comparative degree only compares two things. More than two must use the superlative. Nevertheless, in Greek, the comparative degree is used, not the superlative. This is acceptable in Greek idiom.

Genitive of Comparisons and Uses of ἤ

8. English has the ability to use the word *than* following a comparison word, such as *John is taller than Jim*. Greek has two ways to do the same. 1) the *Genitive of Comparison* and 2) ἤ followed by a noun or pronoun in the same case as the other noun or pronoun in the comparison.

> 1) Example of Genitive of Comparison:
> John 1:50 - μείζω **τούτων** ὄψει
>   greater things **than these** thou shalt see
> μείζω is accusative singular neuter and τούτων is *genitive* plural neuter. This construction is comparative.
>
> 2) Example of using ἤ to mean *than*.
> John 3:19 - καὶ ἠγάπησαν οἱ ἄνθρωποι μᾶλλον τὸ σκότος **ἤ** τὸ φῶς
>   and loved men rather darkness **than** light
> Both σκότος and φῶς are accusative singular neuter. ἤ = than.

9. ἤ may be found repeated in the manner ἤ ... ἤ, in which case it means either ... or.

> Example: Matt. 6:24

ἤ γὰρ τὸν ἕνα μισήσει καὶ τὸν ἕτερον ἀγαπήσει,
for **either** the one he will hate and the other he will love
ἤ ἑνὸς ἀνθέξεται καὶ τοῦ ἑτέρου καταφρονήσει
or to the one he will hold and the other he will despise

10.   Combining the words ἀλλά, but and ἤ into ἀλλ'ἤ means *but rather, except, unless.*

> Example: Luke 12:51
> οὐχί,   λέγω ὑμῖν,   **ἀλλ'ἤ**   διαμερισμόν.
> not   I say to you,   **but rather**   division

11.   The combination ἤ καὶ means *or also, or even, yes and,* and sometimes simply *or.*

> Example: Luke 18:11
> **ἤ καὶ**   ὡς οὗτος   ὁ τελώνης
> **or even**   as this   the publican

At times, this combination is translated simply as *or* without a separate word for καὶ . This works well in English and the KJV translators decided it was necessary. However, that may not work in other languages and καὶ may have to be separately translated.

> Example: Luke 11:12
> **ἤ καὶ** ἐὰν αἰτήσῃ   ὠόν
> **or**   if   he shall ask   an egg

Adverbs

12.   Adverbs are descriptive words. In Greek, they describe verbs, adjectives, and other adverbs, and occasionally even nouns. In addition, many times prepositional phrases, participles, and other constructions can function as both adjectives and adverbs. Adverbs answer and express the questions: when, how, where, how much, and why.

> *Time*: Adverbs tell *when* the action took place, e. g. νῦν, *now.*
> *Manner:* Adverbs tell *how,* e. g. καλῶς, *well.*
> *Place:* Adverbs tell *where* the action took place, e. g. ἐκεῖ, *there.*
> *Quantity:* Adverbs tell or ask how much, e. g. πόσον, *how much.*
> *Reason:* Adverbs tell or ask why, e. g. διατί, *why.*

13.   Adjectives can be changed into adverbs by using ς in place of ν in the genitive plural masculine and neuter.

> Example: καλός, good;
>   genitive plural, καλῶν
>   adverb, καλῶς, *well.*

14. The comparative degree of the adverb is like the accusative singular neuter of the corresponding adjective. The superlative degree of the adverb corresponds to the accusative plural neuter.

15. Once again, there are irregular forms of the adverb that may be learned as they are encountered.

16. **Adverbs of place** take the genitive. If the adverb takes an object, it is in the genitive case. For example, the term ἔξω means outside, as in ἔξω τῆς πόλεως, "without the city" (Rev. 14:20). τῆς πόλεως is in the genitive case.

Possessive Adjectives

17. There are possessive adjectives that are used for emphasis. This use is not frequent, but the student should be aware of it. Normally, the genitive form of the personal pronoun is used. The possessive adjectives are declined like regular adjectives of the first and second declensions. They are:

Singular: ἐμός, my   σός, your (thy)
Plural: ἡμέτερος, our   ὑμέτερος, your

Exercises

18. Answers to the exercises of chapter seventeen.

    1)   John 1:46 τι <u>ἀγαθὸν</u>
        Ans: any <u>good</u> thing - A-NSN
    2)   John 10:11 ἐγώ εἰμι ὁ ποιμὴν ὁ <u>καλός</u>
        Ans: I am the <u>good</u> shepherd - A-NSM
    3)   John 1:27 ἐγὼ οὐ κεὶμὶ <u>ἄξιος</u> ἵνα λύσω
        Ans: I am not <u>worthy</u> to unloose - A-NSM
    4)   1 Timothy 1:5 ἐκ <u>καθαρᾶς</u> καρδίας
        Ans: out of a <u>clean</u> heart - A-GSF
    5)   John 10:16 καὶ <u>ἄλλα</u> πρόβατα ἔχω
        Ans: and <u>other</u> sheep I have - A-APN
    6)   John. 1:3 <u>πάντα</u> δι' αὐτοῦ ἐγένετο
        Ans: <u>All</u> things were made through him - A-NPN
    7)   John 17:25 πάτερ <u>δίκαιε</u>
        Ans: <u>righteous</u> father - A-VSM
    8)   Acts 26:22 μαρτυρούμενος <u>μικρῷ</u> τε καὶ <u>μεγάλῳ</u>
        Ans: witnessing to both <u>small</u> and <u>great</u> - both are A-DSM

19. New Exercises:

Translate the following phrases and parse all adjectives and identify adverbs.

1) John 2:10 - καὶ λέγει αὐτῷ, Πᾶς ἄνθρωπος πρῶτον τὸν καλὸν οἶνον τίθησι (set forth), καὶ ὅταν μεθυσθῶσι (men have drunk well), τότε τὸν ἐλάσσω
2) John 2:12 - καὶ ἐκεῖ ἔμειναν (continued) οὐ πολλὰς ἡμέρας
3) Mark 9:43 - καλόν σοι ἐστὶ κυλλὸν (maimed) εἰς τὴν ζωὴν εἰσελθεῖν (to enter)
4) John 4:41 - καὶ πολλῷ πλείους ἐπίστευσαν (believed) διὰ τὸν λόγον αὐτοῦ,
5) 1 Tim. 5:1 - ἀλλὰ παρακάλει (entreat) ὡς πατέρα· νεωτέρους, ὡς ἀδελφούς·

CHAPTER NINETEEN
VERB: FIRST AND SECOND AORIST ACTIVE, MIDDLE, AND PASSIVE

First Aorist Endings on Second Aorist Stems; Constructions with πιστευω; Use of the Aorist Tense; The Aorist of Εἰμί

Jn. 1:3 πάντα δι' αὐτοῦ **ἐγένετο**, καὶ χωρὶς αὐτοῦ **ἐγένετο** οὐ δὲ ἕν ὃ γέγονεν.
Jn. 1:4 ἐν αὐτῷ ζωὴ ἦν, καὶ ἡ ζωὴ ἦν τὸ φῶς τῶν ἀνθρώπων,
Jn. 1:5 καὶ τὸ φῶς ἐν τῇ σκοτίᾳ φαίνει, καὶ ἡ σκοτία αὐτὸ οὐ **κατέλαβεν**.

3 All things **were made** by him; and without him **was not** any thing **made** that was made.
4 In him was life; and the life was the light of men.
5 And the light shineth in darkness; and the darkness **comprehended** it not.

1. Vocabulary:

Word	Meaning	Word	Meaning
ἀπολύω	release	θεραπεύω	heal
πλήρης, adj	full, filled up	ἱμάς, ὁ	shoe latchet
ὀπίσω, adv	back, behind, after	πείθω	pursuade
κηπύσσω	preach	ἐπαύριον, adv	the next day
θαυμάζω	wonder, marvel, wonder at	ἔμπροσθεν, prep with genitive	in front, before
ἑτοιμάζω	prepare	ἑρμηνεύω	I explain, I interpret
γῆ, γῆς, ἡ	earth, land	ὑποκάτω, adv	under, underneath
ἤδη, adv.	already	ἀνοίγω	open
γάρ, conj. postpositive	for	φέρω	bear, bring
ἄγω	lead	προσφέρω	bring to

2. The simplest way to think understand the aorist tense is that it represents *pointed action in the past*. It is the simple past tense, but it is more than that as we will see.

3. The aorist is *pointed action* as opposed to *continuous action*. Pointed action is the primary nature of the aorist tense. Time is secondary and sometimes the aorist can be translated in something other than past time. The tenses we have encountered so far are these:

>Present Tense: I speak, or I am speaking
>Imperfect Tense: I was speaking
>Aorist Tense: I spoke, or, I have spoken

4. The aorist can be translated in the English simple past, *I spoke*, or the English perfect tense, *I have spoken*. The context can determine which is appropriate.

5. There are two forms of the aorist tense: the *first aorist* and the *second aorist*. The only difference between them is how they are formed. There is NO difference in their meaning or in how they are translated.

6. **The First Aorist Active Indicative** conjugation of λύω, I loose:

Singular   Plural

1	ἔλυσα	I loosed	1	ἐλύσαμεν	We loosed
2	ἔλυσας	You loosed	2	ἐλύσατε	You loosed
3	ἔλυσε(ν)	He, she, it loosed	3	ἔλυσαν	They loosed

7. The Aorist, just as the imperfect, has an augment. The Aorist augment is the same as the imperfect augment.

8. The -σα- in these verb forms is a tense suffix, which is added to the stem of the verb in the first aorist. The ending of the first person singular is -ν, but it is dropped in the first aorist.

9. There is no ending on the third person singular and the tense suffix -σα- is changed to -σε-. The third person singular may also have the moveable -ν.

10. As an example, the word ἐλύσαμεν can be broken down this way: ἐ / λύ / σα / μεν. In order, these segments are identified as ἐ-augment/ λύ-stem/ σα-sign of the first aorist/ μεν-personal ending of first-person plural.

11. The conjugation of the first aorist middle Indicative:

	Singular			Plural	
1	ἐλυσάμην	I loosed for myself	1	ἐλυσάμεθα	We loosed for ourselves
2	ἐλύσω	You loosed for yourself	2	ἐλύσασθα	You loosed for yourselves
3	ἐλύσατο	He loosed for himself	3	ἐλύσαντο	They loosed for themselves

12. The middle form of the both the first and second aorist is different from the passive form. The middle also has the first aorist sign -σα-. It is the same as the active except in the second person singular, which is shortened to -σ-. The passive form of both the first and second aorist is the same with the difference explained in paragraph 23.

13. **The Second Aorist Active**: The second aorist is not just a second way to form the aorist tense. Many verbs in Greek require the second aorist. Very few Greek words have both first and second aorist forms. This is exemplified by English. Some verbs form their past tense by adding -ed and some verbs form their past tense other ways. The past tense of *live* is *lived*, but the past tense of *rise* is *rose*.

14. It cannot be known beforehand whether a Greek verb will have a first aorist or a second aorist form. It also cannot be known what the exact second aorist form will be. It will require a lexicon to settle this question. In many lexicons, you will find the principal parts of each of the verbs listed. In Greek, there are six principal parts that may change the verb stem. The six principal parts are:

    1)   Present (This form is the dictionary form of the verb)
    2)   Future
    3)   Aorist Active
    4)   Perfect Active
    5)   Perfect Middle and Passive
    6)   Aorist Passive

15. The student should make use of the lexicon in the back of the book, because the lexicon includes all the words of John 1 in all their various forms.

16. The conjugation of the second aorist active of λείπω, *I leave*, is below. Notice the change in the stem of the second aorist.

Singular			Plural		
1	ἔλιπον	I left	1	ἐλίπομεν	We left
2	ἔλιπες	You left	2	ἐλίπετε	You left
3	ἔλιπε (ν)	He, she, it left	3	ἔλιπον	They left

17. The conjugation of the second aorist middle of λείπω is below:

Singular		Plural	
1	ἐλιπόμην	1	ἐλιπόμεθα
2	ἐλίπου	2	ἐλίπεσθε
3	ἐλίπετο	3	ἐλίποντο

18. **The Aorist Passive Indicative:** The aorist passive indicative is built on the aorist passive stem. The aorist passive stem is formed by adding -θε- to the verb stem, not -σα-. However, in the indicative, the stem is lengthened to θη. So, the aorist passive stem of λύω is λυθη-.

19. The augment is prefixed to the stem and the personal endings are added. The endings in the aorist passive are of the *active* form. The endings are suffixed directly to the verb stem without any intervening variable vowels.

20. Aorist passive indicative is the same for both the first and second aorist.

21. The conjugation of the aorist passive indicative of λύω is below:

Singular			Plural		
1	ἐλύθην	I was loosed	1	ἐλύθημεν	We were loosed
2	ἐλύθης	You were loosed	2	ἐλύθητε	You were loosed
3	ἐλύθη	He, she, it was loosed	3	ἐλύθησαν	They were loosed

22. Changes may take place in the verb stem when it ends in a consonant before the θ.

    1) A final π or β it changes to φ.
    2) A final κ or γ is changed to χ.
    3) A final τ or δ or θ is changed to σ.

Examples:

πέμπω becomes ἐπέμφθην
ἄγω becomes ἤχθην
πείθω becomes ἐπείσθην

23. **Second Aorist Passive:** A few verbs have a different second aorist passive. These verbs are conjugated exactly as paragraph 21, but they do not have a θ in the tense stem.

24. Some deponent verbs have passive, not middle, forms. Other deponent verbs have both middle and passive forms.

25. There are irregular forms that are exceptions to the general rules. Each verb must be examined on its own.

Constructions with πιστευω

26. The verb, **πιστεύω,** takes its object in the dative. Therefore, οὐκ ἐπιστεύσατε αὐτῷ means "you did not believe in him." It is an example of verbs that require their objects to be in certain cases. It is necessary to learn them as they occur.

27. Sometimes πιστεύω is followed by εἰς or ἐπί with the accusative. In that case it is to be translated as *I believe in* or *on*. So, πίστευσον ἐπὶ τὸν Κύριον Ἰησοῦν Χριστὸν means *"believe on the Lord Jesus Christ."*

Use of the Aorist Tense

28. As stated in paragraph 3, the primary emphasis is pointed action. It is also the simple past tense. However, it is not *limited* to the past in its use. The example in paragraph 27 shows πιστεύω used as an imperative or command in the aorist tense. It comes from Acts 16:31. Although it is in the aorist tense, the Philippian jailer was not commanded in the past. In the context, it was a present command. Therefore, it can only be translated into English in the present tense.

The Aorist of Εἰμί

29. There is no Aorist Indicative form of the verb εἰμί. The imperfect supplies the past tense.

Exercises

30. Answers to the exercises of chapter eighteen.

   1) John 2:10

   -καὶ λέγει αὐτῷ, Πᾶς ἄνθρωπος πρῶτον τὸν καλὸν οἶνον τίθησι (set forth), καὶ ὅταν μεθυσθῶσι (men have well drunk), τότε τὸν ἐλάσσω
   -and he says to him, every man the good wine sets forth, and when men have drank well, then the worse

   πρῶτον - Adverb
   Πᾶς - A-NSM
   καλὸν - A-ASM
   τότε - Adverb
   ἐλάσσω - A-ASM

   2) John 2:12

   -καὶ ἐκεῖ ἔμειναν (continued) οὐ πολλὰς ἡμέρας
   -and there he continued not many days

   ἐκεῖ - Adverb
   πολλὰς - A-APF

   3) Mark 9:43

   -καλόν σοι ἐστὶ κυλλὸν (maimed) εἰς τὴν ζωὴν εἰσ ελθεῖν (to enter)
   -good (better) to you is maimed into life to enter (it is better for thee to enter into life maimed)

   καλόν - A-NSN
   κυλλὸν - A-ASM

   4) John 4:41

   -καὶ πολλῷ πλείους ἐπίστευσαν (believed) διὰ τὸν λόγον αὐτοῦ,
   -and many more believed through his own word

   πολλῷ - A-DSM
   πλείους - A-NPM

   5) 1 Tim. 5:1

   -ἀλλὰ παρακάλει (intreat) ὡς πατέρα· νεωτέρους, ὡς ἀδελφούς·
   -but intreat as a father younger men as brothers

ὡς - Adverb
νεωτέρους - A-APM

31. New Exercises.

1) Translate John 1:4-5 and parse each word.

2) Translate the following from Romans 1:9
μάρτυς γάρ μού ἐστιν ὁ θεός, ᾧ λατρεύω ἐν τῷ πνεύματί μου ἐν τῷ εὐαγγελίῳ τοῦ υἱοῦ αὐτοῦ

3) Translate the following from Romans 1:16
οὐ γὰρ ἐπαισχύνομαι τὸ εὐαγγέλιον τοῦ Χριστοῦ·

CHAPTER TWENTY
THE FUTURE ACTIVE, MIDDLE, AND PASSIVE INDICATIVE TENSE

John 1:50 ἀπεκρίθη Ἰησοῦς καὶ εἶπεν αὐτῷ, Ὅτι εἶπόν σοι, εἶδόν σε ὑποκάτω τῆς συκῆς, πιστεύεις; μείζω τούτων **ὄψει**.
John 1:51 καὶ λέγει αὐτῷ, Ἀμὴν ἀμὴν λέγω ὑμῖν, ἀπ' ἄρτι **ὄψεσθε** τὸν οὐρανὸν ἀνεῳγότα, καὶ τοὺς ἀγγέλους τοῦ Θεοῦ ἀναβαίνοντας καὶ καταβαίνοντας ἐπὶ τὸν υἱὸν τοῦ ἀνθρώπου.

John 1:50 Jesus answered and said unto him, Because I said unto thee, I saw thee under the fig tree, believest thou? **thou shalt see** greater things than these.
John 1:51 And he saith unto him, Verily, verily, I say unto you, Hereafter **ye shall see** heaven open, and the angels of God ascending and descending upon the Son of man.

1. Vocabularies

Word	Meaning	Word	Meaning
ἀναβλέπω	I look up	εἰ	if
βαίνω	I go	οἶδα	I know
διδάσκω	I teach	ὑπό, prep. gen.	by, of
διώκω	I pursue, persecute	ὑπό, prep. acc.	under
δοξάζω	I glorify	ἁμαρτία, ἡ	sin
προσεύχομαι	I pray	ὅστις, ἥτις, ὅτι	whoever, whichever, whatever
τυφλός, ὁ	blind man	δύναμαι	be able
ἀναλαμβάνω	I take up	ὄχλος, ὁ	crowd, multitude
πορεύομαι	I go	καθώς, adv.	as, even as
ἅγιος, α, ον, adj.	holy, saint	ὑπέρ, prep. gen.	in behalf of
μεθύω	over drink	ὑπέρ, prep. acc.	above
κύλλος, adj.	maimed	ἕως, prep. gen.	until, as far as
ἐάν	if	ζάω	I live

2. The future tense is built on the future stem, which is the second principal part of the Greek verb. The future stem is built by adding the tense suffix -σ to the stem of the verb. So, the present tense stem of the verb λύω is

λυ-. The future stem of λύω is λυσ- making the first-person singular verb λύσω. There is no augment with the future stem.

3.   In the present and imperfect tenses, the middle and passive forms are the same. However, the future tense middle and passive are different.

4.   The conjugation of the future active indicative of λύω, λύσω, is as follows. Notice the similarity to the present active indicative.

Singular   Plural

1	λύσω	I will loose	1	λύσομεν	we will loose
2	λύσεις	You will loose	2	λύσετε	you (ye) will loose
3	λύσει	he, she, it will loose	3	λύσουσι (ν)	they will loose

5.   The conjugation of the future middle indicative of λύσω, λύσομαι, is as follows.

Singular   Plural

1	λύσομαι	I will loose for myself	1	λυσόμεθα	we will loose for ourselves
2	λύση	You will loose for yourself	2	λύσεσθε	you (ye) will loose for yourself
3	λύσεται	he, she, it will loose for himself	3	λύσονται	they will loose for themselves

6.   If the future active and middle stems end in a consonant, the addition of the tense suffix -σ causes two consonants to come together. This causes changes in the stem. There are five combinations.

1) If the stem ends in κ, γ, or χ adding σ = ξ

   Example: ἔχω = ἕξω   I will have

2) If the stem ends in π, β, or φ adding σ = ψ

   Examples: βλέπω = βλέψω I will see
   γράφω = γράψω I will write

3) If the stem ends in τ, δ, θ, σ, ζ, add σ = these drop out and leave σ

   Examples: πείθω + σ = πείσω   I will persuade
   σώζω + σ = σώσω   I will save

4) If the stem ends in λ, μ, ν, or ρ adding σ = drop the σ and the accent changes to a circumflex on the final -ω. The only difference is the change in accent.

    Example: μένω = μενῶ   I will remain

If the stem ends in a double consonant, it is changed to a single consonant. Other changes take place, when the -σ is dropped and the following letter is an -ο or an -ε. The -ο is changed to -ου and the -ε is changed to -ει. See the following examples.

    ἀποστέλλω = ἀποστελῶ   I will send
    ἀποστελλ + σ + ομεθα = ἀποστελ<u>ού</u>μεθα   We will send
    μέν + σ + ετε = μεν<u>εῖ</u>τε   You will remain

7.   A future verb is formed on the future stem, which is used for the future active and middle. The formation of the future stem is not subject to consistent rules. Therefore, the student will have to rely on a good Lexicon or other guidebook. Starting from the present tense stem, the formation of the other five principal part stems is very irregular.

8.   The irregularity of the formation of the future stem can be seen from several examples of the future active indicative first person singular.

    The future stem of κηρύσσω is not κηρυσσ-, but rather κηρυκ-.
    The future stem of βαπτίζω is not βαπτιζ-, but rather βαπτιδ-.
    The future stem of ἔρχομαι is not ερχ- but rather ελευ-.

9.   **Deponent Future Verbs:** Some verbs are deponent in the future tense, but not in the present tense. For example, the future of βαίνω is βήσομαι.

Future Passive Indicative

10.   The future passive indicative is built on the aorist passive stem, which is in sixth place among the principal parts.

11.   The future passive stem has -θε- added to the stem. Throughout the indicative the -θε- is lengthened to -θη-. So, the future passive indicative stem of λύω is λυθη-.

12.   Just as the future active and middle have the future identifier -σ-, the future passive identifier is -σο- or -σε-. From there, the endings are added,

which are the same as the future middle indicative. So, the conjugation of the future passive is as follows.

1	λυθήσομαι	I will be loosed	1	λυθησόμεθα	we will be loosed
2	λυθήση	You will be loosed	2	λυθήσεσθε	you (ye) will be loosed
3	λυθήσεται	he, she, it will be loosed	3	λυθήσονται	they will be loosed

Exercises

13.   Answers to the exercise of chapter nineteen.

Translate John 1:4, 5 and parse each word, are below.

4. ἐν	αὐτῷ	ζωὴ	ἦν,	καὶ	ἡ
Prep	P-DSM	N-NSF	V-IAI-3S	CONJ	T-NSF
In	him	life	was	and	the
ζωὴ	ἦν	τὸ	φῶς	τῶν	ἀνθρώπων,
N-NSF	V-IAI-3S	T-NSN	N-NSN	T-GPM	N-GPM
life	was	the	light	of the	men
5. καὶ	τὸ	φῶς	ἐν	τῇ	σκοτία
Conj	T-NSN	N-NSN	Prep	T-DSF	N-DSF
and	the	light	in	the	darkness
φαίνει,	καὶ	ἡ	σκοτία	αὐτὸ	οὐ
V-PAI-3S	Conj	T-NSF	N-NSF	P-ASN	PRT-N
shines	and	the	darkness	it	not
κατέλαβεν.					
V-2AAI-3S					
comprehended					

14.   Notes on the translation of John 1:4-5.

1) The literal word order of the Greek NT will not always make a good English translation. The order of the words must be arranged in a way that fits good English grammar and usage. For example, "In him life was," must become "In him was life" or it would be just as accurate to say, "Life was in him." The KJV puts it this way:

In him was life; and the life was the light of men. And the light shineth in darkness; and the darkness comprehended it not.

2) The word, κατέλαβεν, is an example of a second aorist active indicative verb. The primary sense of the aorist is pointed action instead of continuous action. The light came into the world at a specific point in history. At that moment, this light began to shine. When that happened, spiritual darkness had a reaction. It could not comprehend the light. The emphasis is on how darkness reacts to the shining of the light.

3) Modern versions tend to translate the word, κατέλαβεν, different than the King James. Note the following examples:

> NIV: "the darkness has not overcome it."
> Modern English Version: "the darkness has not overcome it."
> ESV: "the darkness has not overcome it."
> CEV: "darkness has never put it out."

And so on. Which is the best translation: comprehend or overcome? There are two things needed to answer this question. First, you must know the *definitions* of the Greek word. Often, Greek words have *more than one meaning* and we must choose between them. This is called the *Principle of Polysemy*. Second, you must know the *greater context* of the Bible, that is, what other places in Scripture have to say about it. *Cross-references* often clear up the questions. The Bible tends to explain itself. Being a good Bible student (reading, studying, and memorizing the Bible) will help you become a better translator. So, what do we learn from these sources?

> (1) Greek Definitions from *The Complete Word Study Dictionary* in e-sword.net are as follows (you should also check other lexicons):
>
> -To lay hold of, seize, with eagerness, suddenness.
> -To obtain the prize.
> -To seize with the mind, comprehend.
>
> From this, we can conclude there is a basis for both the translations in the KJV and the one in the NIV. However, to lay hold or seize does not necessarily imply "overcoming." You may have to overcome an opponent to obtain a prize, but there is no conflict implied like there is between light and darkness. Also, there is no prize named in John 1.

(2) The greater context:

John 3:19-20, Ephesians 4:18, and Proverbs 4:19 have information about the attitudes of the children of darkness toward the light.

Jn. 3:19-20 And this is the condemnation, that light is come into the world, and men loved darkness rather than light, because their deeds were evil. For every one that doeth evil hateth the light, neither cometh to the light, lest his deeds should be reproved.

Eph. 4:18 Having the understanding darkened, being alienated from the life of God through the ignorance that is in them, because of the blindness of their heart:

Prov. 4:19 The way of the wicked is as darkness: they know not at what they stumble.

Darkness fears the light. It has no desire to come to the light. It runs from the light. Darkness cannot thrive unless there is an absence of light. Among the chief characteristics of darkness is ignorance, blindness of heart, and darkened understanding. Therefore, the correct translation in John 1:5 is *comprehended*.

4) Translate the following from Romans 1:9

μάρτυς γάρ μού ἐστιν ὁ θεός, ᾧ λατρεύω
ἐν τῷ πνεύματί μου ἐν τῷ εὐαγγελίῳ τοῦ
υἱοῦ αὐτοῦ

For my witness is God, whom I serve with my spirit in the gospel of His Son

KJV For God is my witness, whom I serve with my spirit in the gospel of his Son

5) Translate the following from Romans 1:16

οὐ γὰρ ἐπαισχύνομαι τὸ εὐαγγέλιον τοῦ
Χριστοῦ·

For I am not ashamed of the gospel of Christ;
KJV For I am not ashamed of the gospel of Christ:

15. New Exercises.

1) Parse each word in John 1:50-51.

2) Translate and parse the following phrases. You will need to use the lexicon in the back of the book.

- ὅτε οἱ νεκροὶ ἀκούσονται τῆς φωνῆς τοῦ υἱοῦ τοῦ Θεοῦ, καὶ οἱ ἀκούσαντες (they that hear-do not parse) ζήσονται (John 5:25)
- καὶ ἐκπορεύσονται (John 5:29)
- Πόθεν ἀγοράσομεν ἄρτους (John 6:5)
- ἀλλὰ ἀναστήσω αὐτὸ ἐν τῇ ἐσχάτῃ ἡμέρᾳ (John 6:39)

CHAPTER TWENTY-ONE
NOUNS OF THE THIRD DECLENSION
ADJECTIVES OF THE THIRD DECLENSION

John 1:3 πάντα δι' αὐτοῦ ἐγένετο, καὶ χωρὶς αὐτοῦ ἐγένετο οὐδὲ ἕν ὃ γέγονεν.
6 ἐγένετο ἄνθρωπος ἀπεσταλμένος παρὰ Θεοῦ, **ὄνομα** αὐτῷ Ἰωάννης
7 οὗτος ἦλθεν εἰς μαρτυρίαν, ἵνα μαρτυρήσῃ περὶ τοῦ **φωτός**, ἵνα πάντες πιστεύσωσι δι' αὐτοῦ.
8 οὐκ ἦν ἐκεῖνος τὸ **φῶς**, ἀλλ' ἵνα μαρτυρήσῃ περὶ τοῦ **φωτός**.

1. This set of verses, John 1:3, 6-8, introduces a wealth of new topics: the perfect tense, participles, the subjunctive mood, and third declension nouns. We will look into these things in this and the next five chapters. The highlighted words in the above verses are third declension nouns. In this chapter we will study the third declension.

2. Vocabulary

Word	Meaning	Word	Meaning
ὄνομα ονοματος,το	name	πνεῦμα, πνεύματος,το	Spirit, spirit
φῶς, φωτός, το	light	σῶμα, σώματος, το	body
θέλημα, θελήματος,το	wish, will, want	αἴων, αἴωνος, ο	age
αἷμα, αἵματος, το	blood	ἐλπίς, ἐλπίδος, η	hope
σάρξ, σαρκός, η	flesh	ῥῆμα, ῥήματος, το	word, speech
ἄρχων, ἄρχοντος, ο	ruler	γράμμα, γράμματος,το	letter
νύξ, νυκτός, η	night	ἀνήρ, ἀνδρός, ο	a man (a male)
ὕδωρ, ὕδατος, το	water	ἑκών, -α, -ον, adj	willing
ταχύς, -α, -ύ, adj	swift	σώφρων, -ων, -ον, adj	sober, discreet, temperate
ἀληθής, -ης, -ες, adj	true	ἑκών, -α, -ον,	willing
ἰχθύς, ἰχθύος, ὁ	fish	γένος, γένους, τό	kind, offspring
νοῦς, νοῦ, ὁ	mind		

3. The third declension covers all remaining nouns not included in the first and second declensions. Many of them have stems which end in a consonant. The final consonant of the nominative singular may change in cases other than nominative.

4.   The stem of first and second declension nouns is *not* determined by the nominative singular. The stem of third declension nouns is determined from the *genitive* singular. Therefore, in the vocabulary, both the nominative and genitive spellings are given. The genitive singular ending is –ος. To find the stem of a third declension noun, remove the –ος from the end.

5.   The nominative singular is formed in different ways, so it is best not to attempt to categorize them.

6.   The declensions of 1) ἐλπίς, ἐλπίδος, ἡ, a hope, 2) νύξ, νυκτός, ἡ, a night and 3) ἄρχων, ἄρχοντος, ὁ, ruler are below.

Sing.	Nom.	ἐλπίς	νύξ	ἄρχων
	Gen.	ἐλπίδος	νυκτός	ἄρχοντος
	Dat.	ἐλπίδι	νυκτί	ἄρχοντι
	Acc.	ἐλπίδα	νύκτα	ἄρχοντα
	Voc.	ἐλπί	νύξ	ἄρχων

Plur.	Nom.	ἐλπίδες	νύκτες	ἄρχοντες
	Gen.	ἐλπίδων	νυκτῶν	ἀρχόντων
	Dat.	ἐλπίσι (ν)	νυξί (ν)	ἄρχουσι (ν)
	Acc.	ἐλπίδας	νύκτας	ἄρχοντας
	Voc.	ἐλπίδες	νύκτες	ἄρχοντες

7.   The declensions of 1) ὄνομα, ὀνόματος, ὁ, a name, 2) ἀνήρ, ἀνδρός, ὁ, a man, and 3) σῶμα, σώματος, τό, body, are as follows.

Sing.	Nom.	ὄνομα	ἀνήρ	σῶμα
	Gen.	ὀνόματος	ἀνδρός	σώματος
	Dat.	ὀνόματι	ἀνδρί	σώματι
	Acc.	ὄνομα	ἄνδρα	σῶμα
	Voc.	ὄνομα	ἄνερ	σῶμα

Plur.	Nom.	ὀνόματα	ἄνδρες	σώματα
	Gen.	ὀνομάτων	ἀνδρῶν	σωμάτων
	Dat.	ὀνόμασι (ν)	ἀνδράσι (ν)	σώμασι (ν)
	Acc.	ὀνόματα	ἄνδρας	σώματα
	Voc.	ὀνόματα	ἄνδρες	σώματα

8.   The declensions of 1) ἰχθύς, ἰχθύος, ὁ, a fish, 2) γένος, γένους, τό, kind, offspring, and 3) the irregular noun, νοῦς, νοῦ, ὁ, mind, are as follows.

Sing.	Nom.	ἰχθύς	γένος	νοῦς
	Gen.	ἰχθύος	γένους	νοῦ
	Dat.	ἰχθύι	γένει	νῷ
	Acc.	ἰχθύν	γένος	νοῦν
	Voc.	ἰχθύ	γένος	νοῦ

Plur.	Nom.	ἰχθύες	γένη	νοῖ
	Gen.	ἰθύων	γενῶν	νῶν
	Dat.	ἰχθύσι (ν)	γένεσι	νοῖς
	Acc.	ιχθύας, ἰχθύς	γένη	νοῦς
	Voc.	ἰχθύες	γένη	νοῖ

9.   The vocative is very often the same as the nominative, but not always.

10.   Bear in mind that the Third Declension also contains irregular forms, which may need to be learned as they are encountered.

11.   The Third Declension includes all three genders. So, the gender must be learned with each noun.

12.   The dative plural may have a change in the stem when it ends in a consonant, as in ἄρχοντος. The stem is αρχοντ- and the dative plural ending is –σι. When the –σ is added to the final consonants of the stem –ντ, the -ντ is dropped and the –ο- is changed to –ου, ἄρχουσι.

13.   The general rules for these changes in the dative plural, when the stem ends in these listed consonants, are as follows:

> 1) Ending consonants π, β, φ combine with the –σ to become ψ
> 2) Ending consonants κ, γ, χ combine with the –σ to become ξ
> 3) Ending consonants τ, δ, θ drop out before the -σ
> 4) A double consonant, such as the ντ in αρχοντ-, drops out before the –σ and the preceding vowel becomes lengthened. So, in the example of paragraph 12, the –ο- is changed to -ου.
> 5) In the case of ἀνδρός in paragraph 7, with the stem ἀνδρ-, shows another way to add the final ending -σι in the dative plural. The double consonant, -δρ is retained and an -α- is added after the double consonant making ἀνδράσι.

14.   **Moveable Nu:** When the –σι of the dative plural comes before a word that begins with a vowel, a moveable –ν may be added to the –σι.

15. Important Expressions:

Memorize these Greek idioms.

εις τον αιωνα (literal-into the ages)=forever

εις τους αιωνας των αιωνων (lit. into the ages of the ages) = forever and ever.

Adjectives of the Third Declension

16. Below are the declensions of some third declension adjectives. In general, third declension adjectives follow the declension of third declension nouns.

1) The declension of ταχυς, *swift*, is as follows.

		Masc.	Fem.	Neut.
Sing.	Nom.	ταχύς	ταχεῖα	ταχύ
	Gen.	ταχέος	ταχείας	ταχέος
	Dat.	ταχεῖ	ταχείᾳ	ταχεῖ
	Acc.	ταχύν	ταχεῖαν	ταχύ
	Voc.	ταχύ	ταχεία	ταχύ

		Masc.	Fem.	Neut.
Plur.	Nom.	ταχεῖς	ταχεῖαι	ταχέα
	Gen.	ταχέων	ταχειῶν	ταχέων
	Dat.	ταχέσι	ταχείαις	ταχέσι
	Acc.	ταχεῖς	ταχείας	ταχέα
	Voc.	ταχεῖς	ταχεῖαι	ταχέα

2) The declension of σώφρων, *discreet, sober, temperate*, is as follows.

		Masc./ Fem.	Neut.
Sing.	Nom.	σώφρων	σῶφρον
	Gen.	σώφρονος	σώφρονος
	Dat.	σώφρονι	σώφρονι
	Acc.	σώφρονα	σῶφρον
	Voc.	σῶφρον	σῶφρον

		Masc./ Fem.	Neut.
Plur.	Nom.	σώφρονες	σώφρονα
	Gen.	σωφρόνων	σωφρόνων
	Dat.	σώφροσι	σώφροσι
	Acc.	σώφρονας	σώφρονα
	Voc.	σώφρονες	σώφρονα

3) The declension of ἀληθής, *true*, is as follows.

		Masc. Fem.	Neut.
Sing.	Nom.	ἀληθής	ἀληθές
	Gen.	ἀληθοῦς	ἀληθοῦς
	Dat.	ἀληθεῖ	ἀληθεῖ
	Acc.	ἀληθῆ	ἀληθές
	Voc.	ἀληθές	ἀληθές

		Masc. Fem.	Neut.
Plur.	Nom.	ἀληθεῖς	ἀληθῆ
	Gen.	ἀληθῶν	ἀληθῶν
	Dat.	αληθέσι (v)	αληθέσι (v)
	Acc.	ἀληθεῖς	ἀληθῆ
	Voc.	ἀληθεῖς	ἀληθῆ

4) The declension of ἑκών, *willing*, is as follows.

Singular   Plural

	Masc.	Fem.	Neut.	Masc.	Fem.	Neut.
N	ἑκών	ἑκοῦσα	ἑκόν	ἑκόντες	ἑκοῦσαι	ἑκόντα
G	ἑκόντος	ἑκούσης	ἑκόντος	ἑκόντων	ἑκουσῶν	ἑκόντων
D	ἑκόντι	ἑκούσῃ	ἑκόντι	ἑκοῦσι (v)	ἑκούσαις	ἑκοῦσι(v)
A	ἑκόντα	ἑκοῦσαν	ἑκόν	ἑκόντας	ἑκούσας	ἑκόντα
V	ἑκών	ἑκοῦσα	ἑκόν	ἑκόντες	ἑκοῦσαι	ἑκόντα

Exercises

17. Answers to the exercises of chapter twenty:

1) Parse each word in John 1:50-51.

50 ἀπεκρίθη Ἰησοῦς καὶ εἶπεν αὐτῷ, Ὅτι εἶπόν σοι,
V-ADI-3S N-NSM CONJ V-2AAI-3S P-DSM CONJ V-2AAI-1S P-2DS
εἶδόν σε ὑποκάτω τῆς συκῆς, πιστεύεις; μείζω τούτων ὄψει.
V-2AAI-1S P-2AS ADV   T-GSF N-GSF V-PAI-2S A-APN D-GPN V-FDI-2S
51 καὶ λέγει αὐτῷ, Ἀμὴν ἀμὴν λέγω ὑμῖν, ἀπ' ἄρτι ὄψεσθε
CONJ V-PAI-3S P-DSM HEB HEB V-PAI-1S P-2DP PREP ADV V-FDI-2P
τὸν οὐρανὸν ἀνεῳγότα, καὶ τοὺς ἀγγέλους τοῦ Θεοῦ
T-ASM N-ASM V-2RAP-ASM CONJ T-APM N-APM T-GSM N-GSM
ἀναβαίνοντας καὶ καταβαίνοντας ἐπὶ τὸν υἱὸν τοῦ ἀνθρώπου
V-PAP-APM CONJ V-PAP-APM   PREP T-ASM N-ASM T-GSM N-GSM

HEB=Hebrew

2) Translating phrases:

John 5:25

ὅτε	οἱ	νεκροὶ	ἀκούσονται	τῆς	φωνῆς	τοῦ	υἱοῦ	τοῦ
ADV	T-NPM	A-NPM	V-FDI-3P	T-GSF	N-GSF	T-GSM	N-GSM	T-GSM
When	the	dead	will hear	the	voice	of the	son	of

Θεοῦ,	καὶ	οἱ	ἀκούσαντες	ζήσονται
N-GSM	CONJ	T-NPM	V-AAP-NPM	V-FDI-3P
God	and		they that hear	shall live

John 5:29

καὶ	ἐκπορεύσονται
CONJ	V-FDI-3P
And	shall come forth

John 6:5

Πόθεν	ἀγοράσομεν	ἄρτους
ADV-I	V-FAI-1P	N-APM
From where (whence)	shall we buy	bread

John 6:39

ἀλλὰ ἀναστήσω	αὐτὸ	ἐν	τῇ	ἐσχάτῃ	ἡμέρᾳ
CONJ V-FAI-1S	P-ASN	PREP	T-DSF	A-DSF-S	N-DSF
But shall raise	it	in	the	last	day

Note on John 6:39:

The KJV translation of ἀναστήσω αὐτὸ is "should raise it up again." The KJV uses *should* instead of *shall* because *should* had a definition in 1611 that it no longer carries. This definition is found in Webster's 1828 dictionary: " 'We think it strange that stones should fall from the aerial regions.' In this use, should implies that stones do fall. In all similar phrases, should implies the actual existence of the fact, without a condition of supposition." This use of *should* is equivalent to *shall*. It expresses that the resurrection will truly take place in reality. Note the same use in John 3:16. In the subjunctive mood *should* is often equivalent to *would*.

18. New Exercises.

Translate and parse the following phrases.

1) πολλοὶ ἐπίστευσαν εἰς τὸ ὄνομα αὐτοῦ (John 2:23)

2) οἳ οὐκ ἐξ αἱμάτων, οὐδὲ ἐκ θελήματος σαρκός, οὐδὲ ἐκ θελήματος ἀνδρός, ἀλλ' ἐκ Θεοῦ ἐγεννήθησαν. (John 1:13)

3) ἐλπίδα ἔχων εἰς τὸν Θεόν (Acts 24:15)

>ἔχων is a participle (which we will study later). Here it is translated simply as *have*.

4) Ἦν δὲ ἄνθρωπος ἐκ τῶν Φαρισαίων, Νικόδημος ὄνομα αὐτῷ, ἄρχων τῶν Ἰουδαίων (John 3:1)

6) οὗτος ἦλθε πρὸς τὸν Ἰησοῦν νυκτός (John 3:2)

CHAPTER TWENTY-TWO
PRESENT PARTICIPLES

The Nominative of Appellation; Uses of the Genitive

John 1:3 πάντα δι' αὐτοῦ ἐγένετο, καὶ χωρὶς αὐτοῦ ἐγένετο οὐδὲ ἕν ὃ γέγονεν.
6 ἐγένετο ἄνθρωπος **ἀπεσταλμένος** παρὰ Θεοῦ, ὄνομα αὐτῷ Ἰωάννης
7 οὗτος ἦλθεν εἰς μαρτυρίαν, ἵνα μαρτυρήσῃ περὶ τοῦ φωτός, ἵνα πάντες πιστεύσωσι δι' αὐτοῦ.

John 1:3 All things were made by him; and without him was not any thing made that was made.
6 There was a man sent from God, whose name was John.
7 The same came for a witness, to bear witness of the Light, that all men through him might believe.

1. The word, **ἀπεσταλμένος,** is a perfect passive participle (V-RPP-NSM). This chapter will introduce participles with the present participle.

2. Vocabulary

Word	Meaning	Word	Meaning
ὅπου, Adv.	Where (ever), whereas	βαπτίζων, V-PAP-NSM of βαπτίζω	baptizing
ὤν, οὖσα, ὄν present active participle V-PAP-NSM of εἰμί	being	αἴρων, V-PAP-NSM of αἴρω	raising up
ἐρχόμενον, Pres. Deponent Part. V-PNP-ASM of ἔρχομαι	coming	καταβαῖνον, V-PAP-ASN of καταβαίνω	going down
πιστεύουσιν, V-PAP-DPM of πιστεύω	believing	περιπατοῦντι, V-PAP-DSM of περιπατέω	walking
λέγων, V-PAP-NSM of λέγω	saying	λαλοῦντος, V-PAP-GSM of λαλέω	speaking
βοῶντος, V-PAP-GSM of βοάω	crying out	ἀκολουθοῦντας, V-PAP-APM of ἀκολουθέω	following

3.	The participle is one of the most frequently used constructions in Greek grammar. It exists in the present, aorist, and perfect tenses. It is also found in the active, middle, and passive voices. It is one of the most versatile verbal constructions, and because of this, it is sometimes difficult to translate. The code for participle, P, stands in the *mood* position in the coding. A participle is a verb, thus a Present Active Participle is coded V-PAP. To this is added case number and gender, as explained below. So, V-PAP-NSM stands for **V**erb-**P**resent **A**ctive **P**articiple-**N**ominative **S**ingular **M**asculine.

4.	The participle is a verbal adjective, but it can also be used as an adverb. As a verb, it has tense, and voice. Also, as a verb, it 1) takes adverbial modifiers and 2) if it is a participle of a transitive verb, it can take a direct object. As an adjective, it has case, number, and gender. Also, as an adjective, it agrees in case, number, and gender with the noun it modifies. As an adverb, it modifies verbs.

5.	The declension of the present active participle of λύω is as follows. The present participle is formed on the present principal part stem. The masculine and neuter are declined like the third declension and the feminine like the first declension.

Singular: Masc.		Fem.		Neut.

N. V.	λύων	λύουσα	λῦον
G.	λύοντος	λυούσης	λύοντος
D.	λύοντι	λυούσῃ	λύοντι
A.	λύοντα	λύουσαν	λῦον

Plural: Masc.		Fem.		Neut.

N. V.	λύοντες	λύουσαι	λύοντα
G.	λυόντων	λυουσῶν	λυόντων
D.	λύουσι (ν)	λυούσαις	λύουσι (ν)
A.	λύοντας	λυούσας	λύοντα

6.	The declension of the present *middle* and *passive* participle of λύω is as follows. The middle and passive are the same. This declension is like that of first and second declension adjectives.

Singular: Masc.		Fem.		Neut.

N. V.	λυόμενος	λυομένη	λυόμενον
G.	λυομένου	λυομένης	λυομένου
D.	λυομένῳ	λυομένῃ	λυομένῳ
A.	λυόμενον	λυομένην	λυόμενον

Plural:	Masc.	Fem.	Neut.
N. V.	λυόμενοι	λυόμεναι	λυόμενα
G.	λυομένων	λυομένων	λυομένων
D.	λυομένοις	λυομέναις	λυομένοις
A.	λυομένους	λυομένας	λυόμενα

The Use and Translation of Participles

7. In English, the participle is sometimes written as a verb with an -ing ending, such as "being." This is also sometimes the proper translation of a Greek participle. Often it is not. The participle can be translated in a variety of ways and *it often cannot be translated literally*. This is an important point to remember. Because of this, the translator must not feel obligated to translate the participle literally.

8. **The Tense of the Participle.** *The tense of the participle is relative to the main verb of the sentence.* If it is a present participle, the action of the participle is taking place at the same time as the main verb. That is, for example, if the main verb is aorist (past) tense, then the present participle is also past tense, taking place at the same time as the main verb. If the main verb is present tense, the tense of the present participle is present time. We will study aorist participles later, but at this point note that the action of an aorist participle takes place before the main verb.

Example-John 2:6

<u>ἦσαν</u> δὲ ἐκεῖ ὑδρίαι λίθιναι ἓξ **κείμεναι** κατὰ τὸν
<u>There was</u> and there water pots stone six **set** after the
καθαρισμὸν τῶν Ἰουδαίων, **χωροῦσαι** ἀνὰ μετρητὰς δύο ἢ
purifying of the Jews **containing** apiece firkins two or
τρεῖς.
three

The two highlighted words are present participles. The main verb is the underlined word. It is an imperfect active indicative. Since the main verb is past tense and the participles are present, the two participles take on the tense of the main verb, acting at the same time as the main verb.

The Participle as an Adjective

9. As an adjective, a participle describes and modifies nouns or pronouns. It may attribute some fact, quality, or characteristic directly to a noun or

pronoun. It can be used in both the attributive position and the predicate position, just as a regular adjective.

10.   **The Attributive Use of a Participle.** The participle may follow a definite article. When it does this, it is in the attributive position. The student may remember that the phrase ὁ ἀγαθὸς ἀπόστολος means *the good apostle*. In the same way, ὁ λέγων ταῦτα ἀπόστολος means *the saying-these-things apostle*. It can also be written ὁ ἀπόστολος ὁ λέγων ταῦτα. However, the translation, *the saying-these-things apostle*, is not good English. Normally, it would be translated *the apostle who is saying these things*.

Example, John 3:16:

ἵνα	πᾶς	ὁ	πιστεύων	εἰς αὐτὸν	μὴ ἀπόληται
that	all	the	believing-ones	on him	not should perish

KJV: that **whosoever believeth** in him should not perish

All the believing-ones is not good English, so the KJV translators made it *whosoever believeth*.

11.   **The Predicate Use of a Participle.** The participle may also be used in the predicate position. In this use, the participle is not preceded by a definite article and can have a different meaning. If the sentence, ὁ λέγων ταῦτα ἀπόστολος, the apostle who is saying these things, is written differently, it will change its meaning. The sentence, ὁ ἀπόστολος λέγων ταῦτα, puts the participle in the predicate position and it means, *the apostle, saying these things*.

Example John 1:6

ἐγένετο	ἄνθρωπος	**ἀπεσταλμένος**	παρὰ Θεοῦ	
There was	a man	sent	from God	

The participle in this sentence is in the predicate position. In this position it not only adds information to the subject, but also the main verb.

Example Galatians 1:22

ἤμην δὲ	**ἀγνοούμενος**	τῷ προσώπῳ	ταῖς ἐκκλησίαις
I was and	unknown	by face	to the churches

The participle is a present passive participle-NSM in the predicate position. In the attributive position, the participle functions as a pure adjective, modifying the noun or pronoun. When it is in the predicate position, it also has an adjectival function, but it is as much predicate as adjective. It modifies both the pronoun (I) and the verb (was).

12. General Example-Two Simple Sentences:

The following examples come from G. Gresham Machen in his grammar, pages 106 and 107 (see the acknowledgements).

Attributive position:

ὁ ἀπόστολος **ὁ λέγων** ταῦτα ἐν τῷ ἱερῷ βλέπει τὸν κύριον
The apostle, **who is saying** these things in the temple, sees the Lord.
Here the participle modifies the apostle. It does not modify the verb in any way. It tells us which apostle is being pointed out.

Predicate position:

Removing the definite article in front of λέγων changes the meaning of the sentence.

ὁ ἀπόστολος **λέγων** ταῦτα ἐν τῷ ἱερῷ βλέπει τὸν κύριον
The apostle, **while saying** these things in the temple, sees the Lord.
Here the participle is primarily modifying the verb "sees." The participle emphasizes what the apostle is doing when he sees the Lord.

13. **The Substantive Use of the Participle.** A substantive is a noun or pronoun. So, sometimes a participle is used as the equivalent of a noun or pronoun. This is also the same way adjectives are used. The adjectives, ὁ ἀγαθός and ἡ ἀγαθή, can mean *the good man* and *the good woman*.

Example John 1:12:

τέκνα Θεοῦ	γενέσθαι,	τοῖς	**πιστεύουσιν**	εἰς τὸ ὄνομα αὐτοῦ
sons of God	to become,	to the	**believing ones**	on the name of him

The participle is both an attributive participle and a substantive participle. In the attributive position, it is DPM and modifies αὐτοῖς (them) earlier in the verse. As a substantive it refers to specific persons who believe. Therefore, in the example, it is translated believing ones, but, once again, that is not good idiomatic English. So, the KJV translated it into idiomatic English by using the words them that, and the verse reads to become the sons of God, even to them that believe on his name.

14. At this point, the student should notice that the participle is not often translated with words that end in -ing. Rather, the translation frequently uses words like *who, when, which, that, while, etc*. Sometimes, a participle must be translated as an indicative verb and used as the main verb of the sentence. The requirements of the target language grammar will determine how it is best translated.

15.   **A Greek Expression: "He Who."** The expression *he who* or *he that* or the like is frequently found in the New Testament. However, the Greek language does not have an explicit way of expressing *he* in such a construction. So, how is it done? A good example of this is found in 1 John 4:21.

ἵνα **ὁ ἀγαπῶν**	τὸν Θεὸν, ἀγαπᾷ καὶ τὸν ἀδελφὸν αὐτοῦ
that **the loving-man**	the God, loves also the brother of him

KJV: That **he who loveth** God love his brother also.

The phrase *he who* is expressed in Greek by the definite article followed by a participle, which, in this case, says *the loving man*. This idiom does not always have to be translated *he who*, but in other contexts may be *they that* or *those who*, etc., depending on whether it is singular or plural, masculine or neuter, and so on.

The Present Participle of Εἰμί

16.   The declension of the present participle of εἰμί, *I am*, is as follows.

Singular: Masc.   Fem.   Neut.

N. V.	ὤν	οὖσα	ὄν
G.	ὄντος	οὔσης	ὄντος
D.	ὄντι	οὔσῃ	ὄντι
A.	ὄντα	οὖσαν	ὄν

Plural: Masc.   Fem.   Neut.

N. V.	ὄντες	οὖσαι	ὄντα
G.	ὄντων	οὐσῶν	ὄντων
D.	οὖσι (ν)	οὔσαις	οὖσι (ν)
A.	ὄντας	οὔσας	ὄντα

17.   **Negating a Participle:** Indicative verb forms use οὐ for negation. Since participles are not considered indicatives, therefore participles are negated using μή.

18.   For the Nominative of Appellation and the Genitive of Time: See the explanations in the exercises below.

Exercises

19.   Answers to the exercises of chapter twenty-one.
        Translate and parse the following phrases.

1) John 2:23

θεωροῦντες	αὐτοῦ	τὰ	σημεῖα	ἃ	ἐποίει
V-PAP-NPM	P-GSM	T-APN	N-APN	R-APN	V-IAI-3S
When they saw	of him	the	miracles	which	he did

KJV: when they saw the miracles which he did

Note on John 2:23: the literal Greek says, "when they saw the miracles **of him**, which **he did**." The KJV does not say *of him*. It is, rather translated *idiomatically*. In other words, it is translated into the correct English idiom. To say both *his miracles* and the miracles *he did* is redundant. It is awkward, as well as both 201idomatically and grammatically incorrect in English. A translation must be expressed in the target language the way it would be expressed if the target language was the original language.

2) John 1:13

οἳ	οὐκ	ἐξ	αἱμάτων,	οὐδὲ	ἐκ	θελήματος	σαρκός,
R-NPM	PRT-N	PREP	N-GPN	CONJ-N	PREP	N-GSN	N-GSF
Which	not	out of	blood,	nor	of	will	of flesh

οὐδὲ	ἐκ	θελήματος	ἀνδρός,	ἀλλ'	ἐκ	Θεοῦ	ἐγεννήθησαν
CONJ-N	PREP	N-GSN	N-GSM	CONJ	PREP	N-GSM	V-API-3P
nor	of	will	of man	but	of	God	were born

3) Acts 24:15

ἐλπίδα	ἔχων	εἰς	τὸν	Θεόν
N-ASF	V-PAP-NSM	PREP	T-ASM	N-ASM
hope	have	toward	the	God

4) John 3:1

Ἦν	δὲ	ἄνθρωπος	ἐκ	τῶν	Φαρισαίων,	Νικόδημος
V-IAI-3S	CONJ	N-NSM	PREP	T-GPM	N-GPM	N-NSM
(there) was	and	a man	of	the	Pharisees	Nicodemus

ὄνομα	αὐτῷ,	ἄρχων	τῶν	Ἰουδαίων
N-NSN	P-DSM	N-NSM	T-GPM	A-GPM
name	his	a ruler	of the	Jews

Note on John 3:1- The Nominative of Appellation

In John 3:1, Νικόδημος is in the nominative case, but it is not the subject of the sentence. However, the nominative case is naturally the *naming* case. Often, a name will be in the nominative case regardless of how it fits into the sentence grammatically. Sometimes this causes awkward grammar in the sentence and can cause confusion as to how a verse should be translated. Bearing this rule in mind can help clear up some translation difficulties.

5) John 3:2

οὗτος	ἦλθε	πρὸς	τὸν	Ἰησοῦν	νυκτός
D-NSM	V-2AAI-3S	PREP	T-ASM	N-ASM	N-GSF
the same	came	to	the	Jesus	by night

Note on John 3:2 – The Genitive of Time

The genitive case is sometimes used to express the time of action. However, it describes a specific time rather than a point of time (expressed by the dative) or duration of time (expressed by the accusative). It speaks of this time rather than that time. Such is the use of νυκτός in this verse: night time as opposed to daytime.

20. New Exercises: Translate and parse the following phrases.

1) ὃ φωτίζει πάντα ἄνθρωπον ἐρχόμενον εἰς τὸν κόσμον (John 1:9)
2) τοῖς πιστεύουσιν εἰς τὸ ὄνομα αὐτοῦ (John 1:12)
3) Ἐγὼ φωνὴ βοῶντος ἐν τῇ ἐρήμῳ (John 1:23)
4) αὐτός ἐστιν ὁ ὀπίσω μου ἐρχόμενος (John 1:27)

CHAPTER TWENTY-THREE
AORIST ACTIVE, MIDDLE, AND PASSIVE PARTICIPLES;
Additional General Uses of Participles; Genitive Absolute; More Uses of the Genitive Case

John 1:3 πάντα δι' αὐτοῦ ἐγένετο, καὶ χωρὶς αὐτοῦ ἐγένετο οὐδὲ ἕν ὃ γέγονεν.
6 ἐγένετο ἄνθρωπος **ἀπεσταλμένος** παρὰ Θεοῦ, ὄνομα αὐτῷ Ἰωάννης
7 οὗτος ἦλθεν εἰς μαρτυρίαν, ἵνα μαρτυρήσῃ περὶ τοῦ φωτός, ἵνα πάντες πιστεύσωσι δι' αὐτοῦ.
8 οὐκ ἦν ἐκεῖνος τὸ φῶς, ἀλλ' ἵνα μαρτυρήσῃ περὶ τοῦ φωτός.

John 1:3 ll things were made by him; and without him was not any thing made that was made.
6 There was a man sent from God, whose name was John.
7 The same came for a witness, to bear witness of the Light, that all men through him might believe.
8 He was not that Light, but was sent to bear witness of that Light.

1. Vocabulary

Word	Meaning	Word	Meaning
ἐμβλέψας, V-AAP-NSM of ἐμβλέπω	having beheld, looked at	ἐρχόμενος, V-PNP-NSM of ἔρχομαι	coming
θεασάμενος, V-ADP-NSM of θεάομαι	having seen, looked upon	ἀναβαίνοντας, V-PAP-APM of ἀναβαίνω	going up
ἑρμηνευόμενον, V-PPP-NSN of ἑρμηνεύω	explaining, expounding	εἰπών, 2AAP of λέγω	having said
στραφείς, V-2APP-NSM of στρέφω	having turned around	ἰδών, 2V-AAP of βλέπω (or ὁράω)	having seen
ἀκολουθησάντων, V-AAP-GPM of ἀκολουθέω	having followed	ἀγαγων, 2 AAP of ἄγω	having led
μεθερμηνευόμενον, V-PPP-NSN of μεθερμηνεύω	interpreting, translating	ἐλθών, V-2AAP of ἔρχομαι	having come

2. The first aorist active participle of λύω is below. It is declined like the third declension in the masculine and neuter and the first declension in the feminine. All aorist participles, except passive, are formed on the aorist stem.

Singular: Masc. Fem. Neut.

	Masc.	Fem.	Neut.
N. V.	λύσας	λύσασα	λῦσαν
G.	λύσαντος	λυσάσης	λύσαντος
D.	λύσαντι	λυσάσῃ	λύσαντι
A.	λύσαντα	λύσασαν	λῦσαν

Plural: Masc. Fem. Neut.

	Masc.	Fem.	Neut.
N. V.	λύσαντες	λύσασαι	λύσαντα
G.	λυσάντων	λυσασῶν	λυσάντων
D.	λύσασι (ν)	λυσάσαις	λύσασι (ν)
A.	λύσαντας	λυσάσας	λύσαντα

3. The aorist augment only appears in the indicative mood.

4. The declension of the first aorist middle participle of λύω is below. The first aorist participle is declined like a regular adjective of the first and second declensions.

Singular: Masc. Fem. Neut.

	Masc.	Fem.	Neut.
N. V.	λυσάμενος	λυσαμένη	λυσάμενον
G.	λυσαμένου	λυσαμένης	λυσαμένου
D.	λυσαμένῳ	λυσαμένῃ	λυσαμένῳ
A.	λυσάμενον	λυσαμένην	λυσάμενον

Plural: Masc. Fem. Neut.

	Masc.	Fem.	Neut.
N. V.	λυσάμενοι	λυσάμεναι	λυσάμενα
G.	λυσαμένων	λυσαμένων	λυσαμένων
D.	λυσαμένοις	λυσαμέναις	λυσαμένοις
A.	λυσαμένους	λυσαμένας	λυσάμενα

5. The *second aorist active participle* of ἰδών, *having seen,* is below. Ἰδών is the participle of the verbs, ὁράω and βλέπω, *I see.*

Singular: Masc. Fem. Neut.

	Masc.	Fem.	Neut.
N. V.	ἰδών	ἰδοῦσα	ἰδόν
G.	ἰδόντος	ἰδούσης	ἰδόντος
D.	ἰδόντι	ἰδούσῃ	ἰδόντι
A.	ἰδόντα	ἰδοῦσαν	ἰδόν

Plural:	Masc.	Fem.	Neut.
N. V.	ἰδόντες	ἰδοῦσαι	ἰδόντα
G.	ἰδόντων	ἰδουσῶν	ἰδόντων
D.	ἰδοῦσι (ν)	ἰδούσαις	ἰδοῦσι (ν)
A.	ἰδόντας	ἰδούσας	ἰδόντα

6. The second aorist middle participle is declined like the present middle participle. The difference is that the accent is irregular. Remember also, there is no augment on an aorist verb outside the indicative.

7. The aorist participle is parsed in the same manner as the present participle, except the first digit in the second section is A for aorist. So, **V-AAP-NSM** stands for **V**erb-**A**orist **A**ctive **P**articiple-**N**ominative **S**ingular **M**asculine.

8. The declension of the first aorist passive participle of λύω is as follows. The second aorist passive participle is built on the aorist passive stem, the sixth principal part.

Singular:	Masc.	Fem.	Neut.
N. V.	λυθείς	λυθεῖσα	λυθέν
G.	λυθέντος	λυθείσης	λυθέντος
D.	λυθέντι	λυθείσῃ	λυθέντι
A.	λυθέντα	λυθεῖσαν	λυθέν
Plural:	Masc.	Fem.	Neut.
N. V.	λυθέντες	λυθεῖσαι	λυθέντα
G.	λυθέντων	λυθεισῶν	λυθέντων
D.	λυθεῖσι (ν)	λυθείσαις	λυθεῖσι (ν)
A.	λυθέντας	λυθείσας	λυθέντα

Use of the Aorist Participle

9. **The Tense or Time of the Aorist Participle**: As in the present participle, the tense of the aorist participle is relative to the main verb of the sentence. It describes action that takes place *before* the action of the main verb, no matter whether the main verb is past, present, or future.

Example 1: Acts 7:36

οὗτος	ἐξήγαγεν	αὐτούς, **ποιήσας**	τέρατα
This man	brought out	them, **having done**	wonders
καὶ	σημεῖα ἐν γῇ	Αἰγύπτου	
and	signs in	land of Egypt	

The word, ποιήσας, is an aorist active participle. It stands in relation to the main verb of the sentence, ἐξήγαγεν, which is a second aorist active indicative verb meaning *brought out* (past tense). Since the main verb is past tense, the participle took place before the main verb. In the example the participle is given a literal translation of *having done* (it generally means done, worked, performed, and such like). *Having done* indicates that the wonders were done before the people were brought out of Egypt but *having done* is a somewhat awkward way to translate it. The King James uses the word, *after*. *He brought them out, **after that he had shewed** wonders and signs in the land of Egypt ...* Using the word, *after*, is one of the possible ways to translate an aorist participle.

Example 2: Acts 15:30

καὶ **συναγαγόντες**	τὸ πλῆθος,
and having gathered together	the crowd
ἐπέδωκαν	τὴν ἐπιστολήν
they delivered	the letter

The aorist participle, συναγαγόντες, having gathered together, takes place before the main verb, ἐπέδωκαν, they delivered. This participle could be translated using the word, after. However, the KJV translators used a second valid method: the English past perfect. The KJV translation is as follows:

*and **when they had gathered** the multitude together, they delivered the epistle.*

The KJV sentence describes two events. The most recent event was the delivery of the epistle. However, before that, they gathered the church together. The English past perfect describes an action that takes place in the past prior to another defined point in the past. An example is the sentence, "John had purchased the ring three days before he asked Jane to marry him" or "When John had purchased the ring, he planned a romantic dinner together."

Example 3: John 13:30

λαβὼν	οὖν	τὸ ψωμίον ἐκεῖνος,	εὐθέως
having received	therefore	the sop that one	immediately
ἐξῆλθεν			
went out			

KJV: He then **having received** the sop went immediately out

This verse illustrates a third translation method that works sometimes, but not always. The Aorist participle is λαβὼν, *having received*. The main verb is ἐξῆλθεν, an aorist verb meaning *went out*. So, before Judas went out, he received the sop. This participle was translated literally.

10. Once again, the aorist participle can be used attributively, predicatively, or as a substantive. See chapter twenty-two, paragraphs 9-14.

Additional General Uses of Participles

11. The participle may be more directed to modifying the main verb than it is a noun or pronoun. When it does this, it is acting as an adverb. It tells when, how, why, or in what circumstances the action of the verb takes place.

Example 1: Matt. 2:10

ἰδόντες	δὲ	τὸν ἀστέρα	ἐχάρησαν
having seen	and	the star	they rejoiced

In this case, the participle, ἰδόντες, having seen, describes <u>the time</u> (when) they rejoiced. Therefore, the KJV translates it thusly:

When they saw the star, they rejoiced

This is not simultaneous action. They saw the star *first*, *then* they rejoiced.

12. Conditional Phrases   Example 2: Acts 15:29

ἐξ	ὧν	**διατηροῦντες**	ἑαυτούς,	εὖ	πράξετε.
out of (from)	which	**keeping**	yourselves	well	you will do

The word, διατηροῦντες, *keeping,* is a present participle, which is part of a *conditional phrase*. It explains the condition upon which they would all *do well*. Due to the fact that it is conditional, the KJV translators used the word *if* with it. The entire KJV verse is below.

*That ye abstain from meats offered to idols, and from blood, and from things strangled, and from fornication: from which **if ye keep yourselves**, ye shall do well. Fare ye well.*

13. Means Statements

Example 3: Acts 16:16

ἥτις	ἐργασίαν	πολλὴν	παρεῖχε	τοῖς κυρίοις	αὐτῆς,	**μαντευομένη**.
which	gain	much	brought	the masters	of her	**by sooth saying**

Sometimes, a participle explains how or the means by which the action of the main verb is performed. The participle in this sentence, μαντευομένη, *sooth saying*, is a present participle. It tells us the means by which the demon possessed girl brought profit to their masters. In a construction like this, the use of the preposition *by* is appropriate.

KJV: And it came to pass, as we went to prayer, a certain damsel possessed with a spirit of divination met us, which brought her masters much gain by soothsaying:

14.   What Manner Statements

Example 4: Matt. 3:1

παραγίνεται Ἰωάννης ὁ βαπτιστὴς,	**κηρύσσων**
came John the Baptist,	**preaching**

The present participle, κηρύσσων, *preaching*, tells us in <u>what manner</u> John came. He came preaching.

KJV: In those days came John the Baptist, **preaching** in the wilderness of Judaea

The Participle Translated as a Main Verb and an Imperative

15.   A participle may also be used as the main verb of a sentence or as one of the verbs in a compound sentence.

Example: Mark 16:20

ἐκεῖνοι δὲ	**ἐξελθόντες**	**ἐκήρυξαν** πανταχοῦ	τοῦ Κυρίου
They	and **going out**	**preaching** everywhere	the Lord
συνεργοῦντος,	καὶ τὸν λόγον	**βεβαιοῦντος** διὰ	
working with them,	and the word	**confirming** through	
τῶν ἐπακολουθούντων σημείων.			
the **following**	signs		

There are five participles in this sentence. If they are all translated as participles in the manner of the previous examples, there would not be any main verb in the sentence. As the student, no doubt, knows, that would be poor English grammar. Therefore, one or more of the participles must be translated as main verbs. The KJV translators chose to do so with the first two participles. The result is a smooth correctly translated verse with correct English grammar.

KJV: And they **went forth, and preached** every where, the Lord <u>working</u> with them, and <u>confirming</u> the word with signs <u>following</u>. Amen.

16.   The participle may also be used as an imperative (a command) if the context calls for it.

Example: 1 Peter 3:1

Ὁμοίως, αἱ γυναῖκες **ὑποτασσόμεναι**	τοῖς	ἰδίοις ἀνδράσιν
Likewise, the wives **being in subjection**	to the	own husbands

This is a Greek idom only found a few times in the New Testament. The participle, ὑποτασσόμεναι, *being in subjection*, is translated as a command to wives.

KJV: Likewise, ye wives, **be in subjection** to your own husbands; that, if any obey not the word, they also may without the word be won by the conversation of the wives;

Genitive Absolute

17.   The genitive absolute refers to a participial construction in which the participle is connected to a noun/ pronoun, which is in the genitive case and only loosely connected with the rest of the sentence. The term *absolute* comes from the Latin "absolutus,' which means *separated*. The subject of the sentence is not the subject of this participial phrase. The genitive noun or pronoun in the phrase is the subject of the participle.

Example: Matt. 25:5

χρονίζοντος ...	τοῦ	νυμφίου,
tarrying	the	bridegroom
ἐνύσταξαν	πᾶσαι καὶ	ἐκάθευδον.
they slumbered	all	and slept

The phrase, χρονίζοντος τοῦ νυμφίου, is a genitive absolute. The participial phrase is loosely related to the main part of the sentence. The main subject is "they," while the subject of the participle is "bridegroom." It is a predicate participle, and the tense is present, making the action simultaneous with the main verb. Therefore, it is translated using the word *while*.

KJV: While the bridegroom tarried, they all slumbered and slept.

More Uses of the Genitive Case

18.   Most often the genitive is used in ways that are like expressions in English and can be translated with a prepositional phrase that begins with "of." However, the genitive is used in ways that require the use of a different preposition in the translation. Some examples of additional uses of the genitive case are below:

1) **Genitive of Place:** The genitive sometimes identifies a specific place where the action focuses.

Example: Luke 16:24

ἵνα βάψῃ	τὸ ἄκρον τοῦ	δακτύλου αὐτοῦ	**ὕδατος**
that he may dip the tip	of the finger	of him	**of? water**

The word, ὕδατος, is N-GSN. The first thing we would think of is possession and to use the preposition "of." However, it is clear this does not work in this sentence. The water is clearly the place where the finger is dipped, expressed as a genitive. Therefore, the correct way to translate the genitive is "in water."

2) **Genitive of Separation (sometimes called Ablative):** Two elements in a sentence which are separate can be expressed by a genitive and translated using the preposition *from*.

Example Eph. 2:12

ἀπηλλοτριωμένοι **τῆς**	**πολιτείας**	τοῦ Ἰσραὴλ
being aliens	**from the commonwealth** of	Israel

3) **Genitive of Content:** A genitive can modify a noun to show its contents and be translated using the preposition *with*.

Example John 21:8

σύροντες τὸ	δίκτυον **τῶν ἰχθύων**
dragging the net	**with fish**

Exercises

19. Answers to exercises of chapter twenty-two.
    Translate and parse the following phrases.

1) John 1:9

ὃ	φωτίζει	πάντα	ἄνθρωπον	ἐρχόμενον	εἰς	τὸν	κόσμον
R-NSN	V-PAI-3S	A-ASM	N-ASM	V-PNP-NSN	PREP	T-ASM	N-ASM
which lights		every	man	who comes	into	the	world

2) John 1:12

τοῖς	πιστεύουσιν	εἰς	τὸ	ὄνομα	αὐτοῦ
T-DPM	V-PAP-DPM	PREP	T-ASN	N-ASN	P-GSM
to them	that believe	on	the	name	of him

3) John 1:23

Ἐγὼ	φωνὴ	βοῶντος	ἐν	τῇ	ἐρήμῳ
P-1NS	N-NSF	V-PAP-GSM	PREP	T-DSF	A-DSF
I am	a voice	crying	in	the	wilderness

4) John 1:27

αὐτός	ἐστιν	ὁ	ὀπίσω	μου	ἐρχόμενος
P-NSM	V-PAI-3S	T-NSM	ADV	P-1GS	V-PNP-NSM
He	it is	the (one)	after	me	who is coming

20. New Exercises:
Translate and parse the following.

1) ἀλλὰ τὸ θέλημα τοῦ πέμψαντός με πατρός (John 5:30)
2) ὁ ἐκ τοῦ οὐρανοῦ καταβάς, ὁ υἱὸς τοῦ ἀνθρώπου (John 3:13)
3) ὁ λαβὼν αὐτοῦ τὴν μαρτυρίαν (John 3:33)
4) ἐλθὼν ἐκ τῆς Ἰουδαίας εἰς τὴν Γαλιλαίαν. (John 4:54)
5) ὁ οὖν πρῶτος ἐμβὰς μετὰ τὴν ταραχὴν τοῦ ὕδατος, ὑγιὴς ἐγίνετο, ᾧ δήποτε κατείχετο νοσήματι. (John 5:4)

CHAPTER TWENTY-FOUR
VERBS: THE PERFECT AND PLUPERFECT TENSES
WITH THE PERFECT PARTICIPLE

John 1:3 πάντα δι' αὐτοῦ ἐγένετο, καὶ χωρὶς αὐτοῦ ἐγένετο οὐδὲ ἕν ὃ **γέγονεν**.
6 ἐγένετο ἄνθρωπος ἀπεσταλμένος παρὰ Θεοῦ, ὄνομα αὐτῷ Ἰωάννης
7 οὗτος ἦλθεν εἰς μαρτυρίαν, ἵνα μαρτυρήσῃ περὶ τοῦ φωτός, ἵνα πάντες πιστεύσωσι δι' αὐτοῦ.
8 οὐκ ἦν ἐκεῖνος τὸ φῶς, ἀλλ' ἵνα μαρτυρήσῃ περὶ τοῦ φωτός.

1.   The word, **γέγονεν**, is in the perfect tense. In this chapter we will study the perfect tense and its related tense, the pluperfect.

2.   The parsing code for the perfect tense is R and the code for pluperfect is L. So, a **V**erb-**P**erfect **A**ctive **I**ndicative **T**hird **P**erson **P**lural is **V-RAI-3P**. With pluperfect, L would be substituted for R.

3.   Vocabulary

Word	Meaning	Word	Meaning
γέγονεν, perfect V-2RAI-3S of γίνομαι	he, she, it become	μεμαρτύρηκα, V-RAI-1S to μαρτυρέω	I witness
κέκραγε, perf. V-2RAI-3S of κράζω	he, she, it cries out	εἱστήκει, pluperfect, V-LAI-3S of ἵστημι	he, she, it causes to stand
ἑώρακε, perf. V-RAI-3S of ὁράω	he, she, it sees	εὑρήκαμεν, V-RAI-1S of εὑρίσκω	I find
ἀπεσταλμένοι, V-RPP-NPM of ἀποστέλλω	I send	ἀνεῳγότα, V-RAP-ASM of ἀνοίγω	I open
ἕστηκεν, perf. V-RAI-3S of ἵστημι	he, she, it causes to stand	ἀκήκοα, V-RAI-1S of ἀκούω	I hear
οἴδατε, perf. V-RAI-2P of εἴδω	you see	ἔγνωκα, V-RAI-1S of γινώσκω	I know
τεθέαμαι, perf. V-RNI-1S of θεάομαι	I behold, look upon	ἐλήλυθα, V-RAI-1S of ἔρχομαι	I come

4. There is no English equivalent to the perfect tense. English has a tense that it calls the perfect, but it is not the same as the Greek perfect. The Greek perfect is often translated as a simple past tense or a simple present tense in the KJV. For example, in Galatians 2:20, "I am crucified with Christ," is in the perfect tense. In John 1:3, the word, **γέγονεν,** is translated "was made." In both cases, there are elements of both past and present implied, but both are not stated. "I am crucified," being in present tense, *implies* that I *was* crucified sometime in the past, and I *still am* crucified. In John 1:3, we are to understand that everything was created in the past, and, as we look around, we see that the creation is still here.

5. The perfect tense focuses on the current condition that is the result of a past action. One may also say, it describes a past action that has a present result. For example, "the bed is made" implies that sometime, in the past, someone made the bed, and it is still made. In that case, the perfect tense would be used in Greek. The reason for this is that the focus is on the resulting condition of a made bed. However, if one would say, "I have made the bed three times in the last three days," the aorist tense would be used rather than the perfect. In this example, the focus is on the past action without considering the result of that action. The perfect keeps both the past action and the present result in view and may emphasize either.

6. The **perfect active indicative** of λύω is as follows. The *perfect system* stem is formed on the fourth of the principal parts.

	Singular		Plural
1	λέλυκα	1	λελύκαμεν
2	λέλυκας	2	λελύκατε
3	λέλυκε (ν)	3	λελύκασι (ν) (or λέλυκαν)

7. Forming the Perfect stem:

   1) In the indicative add -κα. In other moods add -κ.

   2) Prefix the *reduplication*. The reduplication is the first consonant of the stem followed by -ε-. To λύω is added λε-, so that the stem becomes λελυκα.

3) If the stem begins with a vowel or diphthong, the reduplication lengthens that vowel or diphthong. See the chart in chapter six. For example, ἀγαπάω becomes ἠγάπηκα.

4) If the stem ends with a vowel, it is lengthened before the κ of the perfect active.

5) If the stem begins with two consonants, in many cases (but not all) the reduplication is to prefix ἐ like an augment. However, this is also the case with certain verbs that do not begin with two consonants. So, the perfect of γράφω is γέγραφα, but the perfect of γινώσκω is ἔγνωκα. In the course of studying the Greek New Testament, you will get used to this.

6) If the stem begins with φ, θ, or χ, they are reduplicated with π, τ, and κ respectively. For example, the perfect of φιλέω, *I love*, is πεφίληκα.

7) If the verb stem ends with τ, δ, or θ, they are dropped before the κ of the perfect active.

8. **The Second Perfect**: some verbs have a second perfect active form, which is conjugated like the first perfect, but without the κ.

9. The conjugation of the **perfect middle and passive** is below.

Singular		Plural	
1	λέλυμαι	1	λελύμεθα
2	λέλυσαι	2	λέλυσθε
3	λέλυται	3	λέλυνται

10. The forms above are the *perfect middle system*, which is formed on the fifth of the principal parts of the Greek verb, the perfect passive part. The reduplication is the same as the perfect active.

11. The conjugation of the **perfect active participle** is as follows.

Singular:
	Masc.	Fem.	Neut.
N.	λελυκώς	λελυκυῖα	λελυκός
G.	λελυκότος	λελυκυίας	λελυκότος
D.	λελυκότι	λελυκυίᾳ	λελυκότι
A.	λελυκότα	λελυκυῖαν	λελυκός

Plural:

	Masc.	Fem.	Neut.
N.	λελυκότες	λελυκυῖαι	λελυκότα
G.	λελυκότων	λελυκυιῶν	λελυκότων
D.	λελυκόσι (ν)	λελυκυίαις	λελυκόσι (ν)
A.	λελυκότας	λελυκυίας	λελυκότα

12. The declension of the perfect passive and middle participle is:

Singular: Masc.   Fem.   Neut.

	Masc.	Fem.	Neut.
N.	λελυμένος	λελυμένη	λελυμένον
G.	λελυμένου	λελυμένης	λελυμένου
D.	λελυμένῳ	λελυμένῃ	λελυμένῳ
A.	λελυμένον	λελυμένην	λελυμένον

Plural: Masc.   Fem.   Neut.

	Masc.	Fem.	Neut.
N.	λελυμένοι	λελυμέναι	λελυμένα
G.	λελυμένων	λελυμένων	λελυμένων
D.	λελυμένοις	λελυμέναις	λελυμένοις
A.	λελυμένους	λελυμένας	λελυμένα

13. **The Pluperfect Tense:** The pluperfect tense is used little in the New Testament. It is related to the perfect tense in meaning, but the difference should be understood. The perfect tense refers to an action in the past with present results. The pluperfect is also a past action that has lasting result, but the result only lasted until a specific point in the past, not until the present.

Example, John 1:31

κἀγὼ οὐκ **ᾔδειν**	αὐτόν· ἀλλ' ἵνα φανερωθῇ	τῷ Ἰσραήλ
And I did not **know** him;	but that he may be made manifest to Israel	

The pluperfect (in bold) indicates John did not know him. However, since it is in the pluperfect, that was a past condition that only lasted until another point in the past. The context makes it clear that that point was the decent of the Spirit like a dove onto Jesus at his baptism. When John made the statement in John 1:31, the baptism was past and in the present, he knew who Jesus is.

14. The conjugation of the pluperfect active indicative of λύω is as follows.

Singular   Plural

1	ἐλελύκειν	1	ἐλελύκειμεν
2	ἐλελύκεις	2	ἐλελύκειτε
3	ἐλελύκει	3	ἐλελύκεισαν

15. The pluperfect middle and passive indicative of is λύω below.

Singular   Plural

1	ἐλελύμην	1	ἐλελύμεθα
2	ἐλέλυσο	2	ἐλέλυσθε
3	ἐλέλυτο	3	ἐλέλυντο

16. The pluperfect has the reduplication and an ε- prefix.

Exercises

17. Answers to the exercises of chapter twenty-three.

1) John 5:30

ἀλλὰ	τὸ	θέλημα	τοῦ	πέμψαντός	με	πατρός
CONJ	T-ASN	N-ASN	T-GSM	V- AAP-GSM	P-1AS	N-GSM
but	the	will	of the	who sent	me	father

2) John 3:13

ὁ	ἐκ	τοῦ	οὐρανοῦ	καταβάς,	ὁ	υἱὸς	τοῦ
T-NSM	PREP	T-GSM	N-GSM	V-2AAP-NSM	T-NSM	N-NSM	TGSM
the (man)	out of	the	heaven	who came down	the	son	of the
ἀνθρώπου							
N-GSM							
man							

3) John 3:33

ὁ	λαβὼν	αὐτοῦ	τὴν	μαρτυρίαν
T-NSM	V-2AAP-NSM	P-GSM	T-ASF	N-ASF
the man (he)	who has received	his	the	witness

4) John 4:54

ἐλθὼν	ἐκ	τῆς	Ἰουδαίας	εἰς	τὴν
V-2AAP-NSM	PREP	T-GSF	N-GSF	PREP	T-ASF
when he came	out of	the	Judea	into	the
Γαλιλαίαν					
N-ASF					
Galilee					

5) John 5:4

ὁ	οὖν	πρῶτος	ἐμβὰς	μετὰ τὴν	ταραχὴν	τοῦ
T-NSM	CONJ	A-NSM	V-2AAP-NSM	PREP T-ASF	N-ASF	T-GSN
the (one)	then	first	stepping in	after the	troubling	of the

ὕδατος,	ὑγιὴς	ἐγίνετο,	ᾧ	δήποτε	κατείχετο	νοσήματι.
N-GSN	A-NSM	V-INI-3S	R-DSN	PRT	V-IPI-3S	N-DSN
water	whole	was made	what	ever	he had	disease

19. New Exercises:

Translate and parse John 1:6-7.

CHAPTER TWENTY-FIVE
THE SUBJUNCTIVE MOOD;

Conditional Clauses; Μη Used as a Conjunction; the Subjunctive and ινα; Subjunctive of -εἰμί; Review Jn. 1:6-7; Dative of Possession; Purpose Clauses; Inserted Word

Jn. 1:8 οὐκ ἦν ἐκεῖνος τὸ φῶς, ἀλλ' ἵνα **μαρτυρήσῃ** περὶ τοῦ φωτός.
Jn. 1:8 He was not that Light, but was sent to bear witness of that Light.

1. This chapter will introduce you to the **subjunctive mood**. The verb μαρτυρήσῃ is *Aorist Active Subjunctive Third person Singular,* V-AAS-3S.

2. Vocabulary

Word	Meaning	Word	Meaning
μαρτυρήσῃ, subj. of μαρτυρέω	bear witness	μεθυσθῶσι, V-APS-3S of μεθύω	drink wine or strong drink, be drunk
λύσω, V-AAS-1S of λύω	loose, release	ἁμαρτάνω,	to sin
φανερωθῇ, V-APS-3S of φανερόω	make manifest	εὐαγγελίζομαι, dep.	to preach the gospel
ἴδῃς, V-AAS-2S of ὁράω	see, perceive	μηδέ	and not, nor, not even μηδέ...μηδέ - neither ... nor
λέγῃ, V-PAS-3S of λέγω	say	μηκέτι	no longer
δικαιοσύνη, ἡ	righteousness	μακάριος, α, ον adj.	blessed

3. In the New Testament, you will only find the subjunctive mood in the present and aorist tenses (and in rare occurrences of the perfect). The declension of the present active subjunctive (V-PAS) of λύω, *I loose,* is below.

Singular		Plural	
1	λύω	1	λύωμεν
2	λύῃς	2	λύητε
3	λύῃ	3	λύωσι (ν)

4. The conjugation of the present middle and passive subjunctive (V-PMS and V-PPS) is as follows.

Singular		Plural	
1	λύωμαι	1	λυώμεθα
2	λύῃ	2	λύησθε
3	λυήται	3	λύωνται

5. The present subjunctive forms are similar to the present tense forms, except that a long vowel is used after the stem on several of them.

6. The conjugation of the aorist active subjunctive of λύω, *I loosed*, is as follows.

Singular		Plural	
1	λύσω	1	λύσωμεν
2	λύσῃς	2	λύσητε
3	λύσῃ	3	λύσωσι (ν)

7. The conjugation of aorist middle subjunctive is below.

Singular		Plural	
1	λύσωμαι	1	λυσώμεθα
2	λύσῃ	2	λύσησθε
3	λυσήται	3	λύσωνται

8. The conjugation of the aorist passive subjunctive is as follows.

Singular		Plural	
1	λυθῶ	1	λυθῶμεν
2	λυθῇς	2	λύθῆτε
3	λυθῇ	3	λυθῶσι (ν)

9. The second aorist subjunctive conjugation of λείπω, *I leave*, in the active and middle, and γραφω, *I write*, in the passive, is as follows.

		Active	Middle	Passive
Singular	1	λίπω	λίπωμαι	γράφω
	2	λίπῃς	λίπῃ	γράφῃς
	3	λίπῃ	λίπηται	γράφῃ
Plural	1	λίπωμεν	λιπώμεθα	γραφώμεν
	2	λίπητε	λίπησθε	γράφητε
	3	λίπωσι(ν)	λίπωνται	γράφωσι(ν)

Uses of the Subjunctive

10.   The subjunctive mood is the mood of possibility and purpose. It does not express something that is actually happening. Actual events are expressed by the indicative mood. The subjunctive expresses an event that is possible, planned, or purposed. It is not actually happening, but it is definitely possible.

11.   In the subjunctive mood, there is absolutely *no distinction in time* between the present and aorist subjunctive or any other tense. The present subjunctive does not refer to present time and the aorist subjunctive does not refer to past time. The difference between the two is in the manner of action. The present subjunctive refers to the action as continuing or being repeated, while the aorist subjunction says nothing about whether it is continuing action or whether it is one-time pointed action. So, ἵνα λύσω means *that I might loose*, and ἵνα λύω means *that I might be loosing*. However, this distinction is most often impossible to bring out in an English translation. The aorist and present will ordinarily be translated exactly alike.

12.   Subjunctive clauses are often introduced by the following words:

   1) ἵνα in order that (used most often)
   2) ἐάν if
   3) ὅς ἄν whoever
   4) ἕως until

13.   **The Simple Subjunctive:** The simple subjunctive can be translated by the use of the words "may" or "might," "could," "would," and the KJV often uses the word "should."

   Example, John 5:34

ἀλλὰ ταῦτα	λέγω ἵνα ὑμεῖς **σωθῆτε.**
but these things I say that you	**might be saved**

   The word, **σωθῆτε,** is V-APS-2P. The word expresses the fact that the people the Lord was speaking to were not actually getting saved at that moment, but that they *could* get saved and His sayings were for the purpose of getting them saved.

14.   **The Hortatory Subjunctive:** The first person singular and plural (usually the plural) of the subjunctive is used for exhortations. It is usually at the

beginning of a clause and translated "let us ..." It has been characterized as a "first person plural imperative." [76]

Example, John 11:7

λέγει	τοῖς	μαθηταῖς,	Ἄγωμεν	εἰς	τὴν	Ἰουδαίαν	πάλιν
he said	to the	disciples	**Let us go**	into	the	Judea	again

15. **The Deliberative Subjunctive:** The subjunctive is used to ask a question when the audience is expected to think about the question. It may be a rhetorical question or a real question, but it does not expect an answer.

Example, 1 Cor. 11:22

τί	ὑμῖν	**εἴπω;**
What	to you	**shall I say?**

16. **The Prohibitive or Negative subjunctive:** The subjunctive with the particle, μη, is used for a negative command or entreaty.

Example, Rev. 22:10

Μὴ σφραγίσῃς	τοὺς	λόγους	τῆς	προφητείας	τοῦ	βιβλίου	τούτο
do not seal	the	sayings	of the	prophecy		of the book	this

KJV: Seal not the sayings of the prophecy of this book

17. **The Emphatic Negation Subjunctive:** A double negative (ου μη) may be used with a subjunctive to *emphasize* the negative nature of the statement. It can be translated "never" or "by no means."

Example, Heb. 13:5

αὐτὸς	γὰρ εἴρηκεν,	**Οὐ μή**	σε	**ἀνῶ,**	οὐδ'	**οὐ μή**	σε	**ἐγκαταλίπω**
he	for has said,	**Never**	you	**leave,**	nor	**never**	you	**forsake**

KJV: for he hath said, I will never leave thee, nor forsake thee.

Ἀνῶ and ἐγκαταλίπω are the subjunctives in this sentence, V-2AAS-1S. There is no doubt about whether the Lord will be with us forever and never forsake us. The emphasized negatives are there to assure us of that fact. So, why is there a subjunctive in the sentence? It is there because the Lord has not yet fully fulfilled this promise. He is busy fulfilling it daily, but it is not yet complete.

Οὐ μή: the double negation is used twice in this sentence. The second time it is used along with οὐδέ, *not, nor*. This increased the strength of the negative. However, in the KJV οὐ μή is translated only once. The reason for this is the English grammar rule of negatives: in any clause, you cannot have a *double negative*. In Greek you can have a double negative, but not in English. Therefore, in the final clause of the English sentence, only one negative could be translated. The KJV translates οὐδέ. Nevertheless, *never* is implied in the clause, because it is explicitly stated in the preceding clause.

18. **The Subjunctive Showing Purpose:** Purpose clauses are one of the most frequent uses of the subjunctive. They are expressed using ἵνα with the subjunctive. ἵνα carries the idea of *in order that* and is sometimes translated simply as *that*. However, do not confuse it with ὅτι used with the indicative. ὅτι means *that*, but it is not used to introduce a purpose clause. The subjunctive in a purpose clause can be translated using the word *might* or as a statement. In the KJV, it is often translated using the word *should,* which in the past, was often used to express the English subjunctive mood. ἵνα, in a purpose clause, may be translated *that, so that, to, for, in order to (or that),* and so on.

Example, John 1:7

οὗτος ἦλθεν εἰς μαρτυρίαν, ἵνα **μαρτυρήσῃ** περὶ
the same came to be a witness that **he might witness** concerning
τοῦ φωτός, ἵνα πάντες **πιστεύσωσι** δι' αὐτοῦ
the light that all men **might believe** through him

The highlighted word, **μαρτυρήσῃ,** is V-AAS-3S.

The highlighted word, **πιστεύσωσι,** is V-AAS-3P.

The KJV translation is "The same came for a witness, to bear witness of the Light, that all men through him might believe."

Μαρτυρήσῃ could be translated "might witness." However, it seems a bit awkward in English. The subjunctive is quite flexible in how it can be translated, so the KJV simply chose to translate the phrase "ἵνα μαρτυρήσῃ" as "to bear witness." This translation is accurate. The Greek phrase is a purpose statement, and the English translation also translates it as a purpose statement. The same type of subjunctive in the same sentence, **πιστεύσωσι,** V-AAS-3P, is accurately translated "might believe." Both ways of translating the subjunctive are accurate.

Example, John 3:16

ἵνα πᾶς ὁ	πιστεύων εἰς αὐτὸν μὴ ἀπόληται,	ἀλλ' ἔχῃ ζωὴν
that all who	believe on him **not would perish**	but have life
αἰώνιον.		
everlasting.		

KJV: that whosoever believeth in him **should not perish**, but have everlasting life.

We have two things regarding the subjunctive in this portion of John 3:16. First, we have a negation of the subjunctive with the use of the word, μή. As you know, Μὴ has the negative meaning *not* and *no* and is used with moods other than the indicative. The second thing we have is the subjunctive ἀπόληται used with the word ἵνα placed earlier in the clause. This makes the subjunctive a purpose statement. Some have suggested that eternal life is uncertain, even if you believe, because the subjunction makes it a *possibility only*. This is absolutely untrue. The subjunctive tells us that the purpose of God is to save those who believe. This makes salvation certain when one believes.

NOTE on the KJV use of the word *should*: The stage of the development of the English language in 1611 is called *Early Modern English*. The word *should* in 1611 carried meanings that it no longer carries in our current form of Modern English. In 1611, one of its meanings was 1) something will certainly take place when certain conditions are fulfilled, and 2) it implies that the fact actually exists without condition. Today, we think of *should* as a conditional word and most often as equivalent to *ought*, but at that time it also meant something would definitely happen. In current Modern English, we are more likely to use the word, *would*, instead of *should*.

Conditional Clauses and the Subjunctive

19.   Conditional clauses are "if ... then" statements. They contain a condition (the "if") and a fulfillment (the "then"). The condition is called the *protasis* and the fulfillment is the *apodosis*.

1) **Future Conditions in the Subjunctive**: Where the condition or protasis is clearly future it is expressed by ἐάν with the subjunctive mood. The fulfillment can be any tense or mood.

Example, John 3:12

πῶς,	ἐὰν εἴπω	ὑμῖν	τὰ	ἐπουράνια,	πιστεύσετε;
how	if I tell	you	the	heavenly things	shall you believe?

KJV: how shall ye believe, if I tell you *of* heavenly things?

The *condition* is to tell Nicodemus about heavenly things. it is clearly something Jesus might do at any time in the *future*. The *fulfillment* is to believe.

2) Conditional Relative Clauses: Indefinite relative clauses in English have the suffix -ever attached to a relative pronoun e. g., whoever, whatever, whichever, whenever, wherever, etc. In Greek, the condition is expressed by the particle ἄν or ἐάν with the subjunctive and the fulfillment is in any mood or tense.

Example, Luke 9:24

ὃς γὰρ ἂν	θέλῃ	τὴν ψυχὴν αὐτοῦ σῶσαι,	ἀπολέσει αὐτήν
For **whoever**	**will**	the life of him save	shall loose it

θέλῃ is V-PAS-3S.

3) Other Conditions: Present conditions can be expressed with εἰ and the indicative mood. The fulfillment can be any tense or mood.

Example, Gal. 5:18

εἰ δὲ Πνεύματι ἄγεσθε,	οὐκ ἐστὲ ὑπὸ νόμον.
but if by Spirit you are led,	not ye are under law

KJV: But if ye be led of the Spirit, ye are not under the law.

The condition and the fulfillment are both happening in present time. In this conditional statement, εἰ can be translated *if* or *since*, depending on which best fits the context.

Example, John 11:32

εἰ ἦς	ὧδε, οὐκ ἂν ἀπέθανέ μου ὁ ἀδελφός.
if you had been	here not have died of me the brother

This condition is a past, but impossible, condition with a present fulfillment. "If thou hadst been here ..." Obviously, Jesus wasn't there. Therefore, the fulfillment part of the condition was impossible. It was too late for such a thing to happen.

In addition to the use of εἰ with the indicative, it also uses the particle ἄν with the indicative in the fulfillment. The particle ἄν has no specific English translation.

KJV: if thou hadst been here, my brother had not died.

The Subjunctive with ἕως and ἄν and ὅτου

20. ἕως is used with the subjunctive, along with ἄν or ὅτου to mean *until*, unless the verb which it introduces refers to an actual event in past time. The ἄν is sometimes omitted.

Example, Luke 22:18

ἕως ὅτου ἡ	βασιλεία τοῦ	Θεοῦ **ἔλθῃ (V-2AAS-3S)**.
until	the kingdom of the God	**shall come**

Example, Acts 2:35

ἕως ἄν θῶ	τοὺς ἐχθρούς σου	ὑποπόδιον τῶν ποδῶν σου.
until **I make**	the foes of you	stool of the feet of you

θῶ is V-2AAS-1S

Μή as a Conjunction

20. Μή can be used as a conjunction and, in that case, it does not mean "not." Words that indicate fear may be followed by μή (meaning *lest*) with the subjunctive.

Example, John 3:20

ἵνα μὴ ἐλεγχθῇ	τὰ ἔργα αὐτοῦ.
lest would be reproved	the deeds of him

KJV: lest his deeds should be reproved.

21. Negative purpose clauses may be introduced by μή alone, rather than ἵνα μή.

22. The normal way this construction is translated in the KJV is by the word *lest*. Translators may find that some languages cannot use *lest*. In these cases, it is acceptable to translate the clause using *that not* or *so that not*. For example, in John 3:20, one could say, *so that his deeds would not be reproved* or another way is, *that his deeds may not be reproved*.

ἵνα with the Subjunctive in Various Uses

23.   In addition to its use in purpose statements, ἵνα with the subjunctive is also used with exhortations, wishes, striving, and in various other ways that are not easily categorized.

Example, Matthew 4:3

εἰπὲ	ἵνα οἱ λίθοι οὗτοι ἄρτοι **γένωνται** (V-2ADS-3P)
command	that the stones these bread be made

KJV: command that these stones be made bread.

The Optative Mood

24.   The optative mood was used in Classical Greek. It is rarely seen in the New Testament. It is used to express a wish. Since it is so rare, we will not study its forms.

Example, Romans 3:3-4

μὴ ἡ ἀπιστία αὐτῶν τὴν πίστιν τοῦ Θεοῦ καταργήσει;
not the unbelief of them the faith of God make ineffectual?
μὴ γένοιτο·
May it never be

KJV: shall their unbelief make the faith of God without effect? God forbid:

μὴ γένοιτο is an aorist deponent optative verb and is a Greek idiom literally meaning *may it never be*, "God forbid" is an English idiom that means *may it never be*.

25.   **The Subjunctive of εἰμί:** The Conjugation of εἰμί in the subjunctive mood is as follows.

	Singular		Plural
1	ὦ	1	ὦμεν
2	ᾖς	2	ἦτε
3	ᾖ	3	ὦσι (ν)

Exercises

26. **Review of John 1:6-7**

6 ἐγένετο	ἄνθρωπος	ἀπεσταλμένος	παρὰ	Θεοῦ,
V-2ADI-3S	N-NSM	V-RPP-NSM	PREP	N-GSM
(There) was	a man	who came	from	God
ὄνομα αὐτῷ Ἰωάννης				
N-NSN P-DSM N-NSM				
name to him John				

7 οὗτος	ἦλθεν	εἰς	μαρτυρίαν,	ἵνα	μαρτυρήσῃ	περὶ
D-NSM	V-2AAI-3S	PREP	N-ASF	CONJ	V-AAS-3S	PREP
The same	came	for	a witness	in order to	witness	of
τοῦ	φωτός,	ἵνα	πάντες	πιστεύσωσι	δι'	αὐτοῦ.
T-GSN	N-GSN	CONJ	A-NPM	V-AAS-3P	PREP	P-GSM
the	light	that	all	might believe	through	him

27. **The Dative of Possession:** Verse six contains a Greek idiom. The words, ὄνομα αὐτῷ, in the context of the verse, expresses the fact that the name, John, belongs to the one who was sent. The dative case is sometimes used to express possession. Therefore, it is not necessary to translate it literally as is done above. The KJV translated αὐτῷ as *whose*: "whose name was John." There is no equivalent to this idiom in English, so it may be translated as a normal possessive pronoun.

28. **Inserted word:** πάντες, in verse 7, is translated in the example simply as *all*. The KJV inserts the word *men* and translates it *all men*. The reason for this is that πάντες is masculine and adding *men* is a valid translation. The KJV was honest in showing by italics that *men* is an inserted word not in the Greek text. One should note, however, that in 1611 the masculine was used regularly, when the reference was to everyone regardless of gender. This is also often done today.

29. New Exercises:

Translate John 1:8-10 and parse each word.

CHAPTER TWENTY-SIX
IMPERATIVES AND INFINITIVES

Direct and Indirect Discourse; Review Jn. 1:8-10; Word Order in Translation; Use of Italics in Translation; Διά with the Genitive and the Expression of Agency

John 1:33 ἀλλ' ὁ πέμψας με **βαπτίζειν** ἐν ὕδατι,
John 1:33 but he that sent me **to baptize** with water,
John 1:39 λέγει αὐτοῖς,"**Ἔρχεσθε καὶ ἴδετε**.
John 1:39 He saith unto them, **Come and see.**

John 1:43 Τῇ ἐπαύριον ἠθέλησεν ὁ Ἰησοῦς **ἐξελθεῖν** εἰς τὴν Γαλιλαίαν
John 1:43 The day following Jesus would **go forth** into Galilee

1. **Ἔρχεσθε** is Present Middle *Imperative* Second person Plural, **V-PMM-2P**. **ἴδετε** is Aorist Active Imperative Second person Plural, **V-AAM-2P**. The code for imperative is **M** in the third position of the second section of the code.

2. **ἐξελθεῖν** is Aorist Active *Infinitive*, V-AAN. The code for infinitive is **N**, in the third position of the second section.

3. Vocabulary

Word	Meaning	Word	Meaning
Ἔρχεσθε, V-PMM-2P of ἔρχομαι	to come	ἠθέλησεν, V-AAI-3S of θέλω	to want, to will
ἴδετε, V-AAM-2P of ὀράωen	to see	ὅσος, η, ον, adj.	as great as, as much as, as many as
ἐξελθεῖν, V-AAN of ἐξέρχομαι	to go out	ὅστις, ἥτις, ὅτι, pron.	whoever, wich ever, what ever
Ἀκολούθει, V-PAM-2S of ἀκολουθέω	to follow	ἁγιάζω,	to hallow, to sanctify
ποιήσατε, V-AAP-2P of ποιέω	to do, make	ἐγγύς, adv.	near
γεμίσατε, V-AAP-2P of γεμίζω	to fill entirely	ἐλεέω,	to have mercy on, to pity

4. **The Imperative Mood:** The imperative mood expresses commands, requests or entreaties, and prohibitions. It is found in the New Testament almost exclusively in the present and aorist tenses.

5. The present imperative is formed on the present stem and the aorist active and middle imperatives are formed on the aorist stem. The aorist passive imperative is formed on the aorist passive stem. In the aorist imperative, there is no augment.

6. The imperative mood has only second and third persons.

7. The conjugation of the **present active imperative** is as follows.

Singular			Plural	
2	λῦ	loose	2	λύετε	you (ye) loose
3	λυέτω	let him loose	3	λυέτωσαν	let them loose

8. The conjugation of the **present middle and passive imperative** is as follow.

Singular | | Plural |
---|---|---|---
2 | λύου | 2 | λύεσθε
3 | λυέσθω | 3 | λυέσθωσαν

9. The conjugation of the **aorist active imperative** is as follows.

Singular			Plural	
2	λῦσον	loose (thou)	2	λύσατε	loose (ye)
3	λυσάτω	let him loose	3	λυσάτωσαν	let them loose

10. The conjugation of the **aorist middle imperative** is as follows.

Singular | | Plural |
---|---|---|---
2 | λῦσαι | 2 | λύσασθε
3 | λυσάσθω | 3 | λυσάσθωσαν

11. The conjugation of the **aorist passive imperative** is as follows.

Singular | | Plural |
---|---|---|---
2 | λύθητι | 2 | λύθητε
3 | λυθήτω | 3 | λυθήτωσαν

12. The conjugation of the **second aorist active imperative** of λείπω, *I leave*, is as follows.

	Singular		Plural
2	λίπε	2	λίπετε
3	λιπέτω	3	λιπέτωσαν

13. The conjugation of the **second aorist middle imperative** is as follows.

	Singular		Plural
2	λιποῦ	2	λίπεσθε
3	λιπέσθω	3	λιπέσθωσαν

14. The second aorist active and middle imperative are formed on the second aorist stem. The endings are the same as the present imperative. The aorist passive imperative forms serve both the first and second aorists.

15. **Tenses in the imperative:** There is no difference in time between the present and the aorist in the imperative mood. The present imperative refers to a one-time action or the action as being repeated or continuing. The aorist imperative says nothing about whether the action continues or not. It is often impossible to bring out this difference in an English translation.

16. **Prohibitions:** A prohibition is a negative command, that is, a command to *not* do something. This is expressed using μὴ with the present imperative or μὴ with the aorist subjunctive. Thus, μὴ λῦε means *do not loose*.

17. The conjugation of the **present imperative of εἰμί** is as follows.

	Singular			Plural	
2	ἴσθι	be	2	ἔστε	be (ye)
3	ἔστω	let him be	3	ἔστωσαν	let them be

Infinitives

18. The infinitive is a verbal noun. Its use in Greek is very much like its use in English, in many cases. For example, the infinitive, ἀκούειν, can be translated *to hear* or simply *hear*, depending on the context.

19. As a noun, the infinitive is treated as an *indeclinable neuter* noun. When it has the article, the article is in the neuter gender, always singular. As a verb, the infinitive is found in the New Testament in the present, aorist, and

perfect tenses. Once again, tense in the infinitive has nothing to do with time. Tense indicates aspect or type of action. The present tense indicates continuing or repeated action. The aorist indicates completed action without regard to when it was completed. The perfect indicates a state of being. The following examples may help understand this.

1) Present: continue to call
2) Aorist: to call
3) Perfect: to have called -or- to be called

20. The infinitive can have adverbial modifiers, a direct object, and a subject. The subject of an infinitive is in the accusative case.

21. The infinitive is negated by μὴ.

22. **Infinitive Forms of λύω and second aorist for λείπω:**

	Active	Middle	Passive
Present	λύειν	λύεσθαι	λύεσθαι
	to loose	to loose for yourself	to be loosed
Aorist	λῦσαι	λύσασθαι	λυθῆναι
Second Aorist- λείπω (to leave)	λιπεῖν	λιπέσθαι	λειφθῆναι
Perfect	λελυκέναι	λελύσθαι	λελύσθαι

23. **The present infinitive of εἰμί:** εἶναι, *to be*

The Uses of the Infintive

24. **The Articular Infinitive**: The infinitive with an article can stand in most of the constructions, in which other nouns can stand. The infinitive can be used with or without an article. When used with an article, it is a neuter article, and it is called the *articular infinitive*.

25. The articular infinitive is often translated into English as a phrase that is introduced by a conjunction. Although, this is accurate translating, it is not precisely literal translating. It is the total idea of the Greek phrase translated into English in a somewhat different idiom that means the same. Please note the examples below.

26.   **The Infinitive as a Verb:** The infinitive can function exactly like a verb in an independent or dependent clause.

1) *Purpose*: the infinitive may express purpose.

Example, Mt. 2:2

καὶ ἤλθομεν	**προσκυνῆσαι**	αὐτῷ.
and (we) are come	**to worship**	him

This same meaning can also be expressed with an articular infinitive using πρός or with the Genitive, thus:

πρός + article + infinitive (ὥστε, ὡς, or εἰς may also be used)

Example, Mt. 6:1

Προσέχετε τὴν ἐλεημοσύνην ὑμῶν	μὴ	ποιεῖν	ἔμπροσθεν
Take heed the alms	of you not to do		before
τῶν ἀνθρώπων **πρὸς τὸ θεαθῆναι** αὐτοῖς			
the men **to be seen** of them			

Genitive + the articular infinitive

Example, Mt. 3:13

Τότε παραγίνεται	ὁ Ἰησοῦς	ἀπὸ τῆς
Then cometh	Jesus	from the
Γαλιλαίας ἐπὶ τὸν Ἰορδάνην	πρὸς τὸν	
Gallilee to Jordan	to	
Ἰωάννην, **τοῦ βαπτισθῆναι**	ὑπ' αὐτοῦ.	
John **to be baptized**	of him	

2) *Result*: an infinitive can also be used to show the result of an action.

Example, Rom. 1:10

εὐοδωθήσομαι ...	**ἐλθεῖν**	πρὸς ὑμᾶς.
have a prosperous journey ...	**to come**	to you

The result of a prosperous journey is that Paul would come to them. Express the same meaning with the prepositions εἰς or ὥστε.

εἰς + article + infinitive/ or ὥστε + infinitive

Example, Romans 7:4

ὑμεῖς ἐθανατώθητε τῷ νόμῳ	διὰ	τοῦ σώματος
Ye ... are dead to the law	through	the body
τοῦ Χριστοῦ, **εἰς τὸ γενέσθαι**	ὑμᾶς ἑτέρῳ	
of Christ **to become** (be married) ye	to another	

Being dead to the law results in being free to be married to Christ.

Example, Luke 12:1

ἐπισυναχθεισῶν	τῶν μυριάδων
when there were gathered together	an innumerable multitude
τοῦ ὄχλου, ὥστε	καταπατεῖν ἀλλήλους
of people, **insomuch that**	they trode one upon another

A large multitude results in some getting trampled.

3) **Time**: The infinitive can be part of a temporal clause when used with a preposition. This tells us when the action takes place. It can describe time in three ways.

(1) πρίν + article + infinitive expresses time *before*, or *antecedent* time.

Example, Mark 14:30

πρὶν ἢ δὶς ἀλέκτορα **φωνῆσαι**,
before the twice cock **crow**

(2) ἐν +article + infinitive denotes *contemporaneous* time.

Example, Mt. 13:4

καὶ **ἐν τῷ σπείρειν** αὐτὸν, ἃ μὲν	ἔπεσε
and **when sowed** he	some (seeds) fell

The infinitive, σπείρειν, is taking place at the same time as the main verb, ἔπεσε.

(3) μετά + article +infinitive expresses time *after* or *subsequent* time.

Example, Mt. 26:32

μετὰ ... τὸ ἐγερθῆναί με,
after am risen me

4) **Cause**: διά with an accusative infinitive expresses cause.

Example, Mt. 13:5

καὶ εὐθέως ἐξανέτειλε,	**διὰ**	**τὸ μὴ ἔχειν**
and forthwith they sprung up,	**because**	**they had no**
βάθος γῆς		
deepness of earth		

5) **Command:** This is a rare construction in the New Testament. It is often called the *imperative infinitive*.

Example, Phil. 3:16

εἰς ὃ	ἐφθάσαμεν,	τῷ αὐτῷ στοιχεῖν
whereto	we have already attained	**let us walk**

6) The Infinitive with a subject: As a verb the infinitive can have a subject.

Example, John 1:33

ἀλλ' ὁ πέμψας με **βαπτίζειν** ἐν ὕδατι,
but he that sent me **to baptize** in water

The word, πέμψας, is V-AAP-NSM and με being in the accusative case is the object of the participle. However, με is *also* the *subject* of the the infinitive, βαπτίζειν, to baptize. The one who is doing the baptizing is *me*, με. *The subject of an infinitive is always in the accusative case.*

Example, Luke 9:34

ἐφοβήθησαν δὲ	ἐν τῷ ἐκείνους εἰσελθεῖν εἰς	τὴν νεφέλην
and they feared	**as they entered**	into the cloud

KJV and they feared as they entered into the cloud.

ἐν τῷ ἐκείνους εἰσελθεῖν is an articular infinitive phrase meaning *as they entered*. ἐν τῷ ἐκείνους would normally look like a prepositional phrase, but ἐν, as a preposition takes it's object in the dative and ἐκείνους is accusative. Since ἐκείνους is accusative following a neuter article, τῷ, and preceding an infinitive, it is the subject of the infinitive. It is *they* who entered the cloud.

Example, Luke 18:35

Ἐγένετο δὲ	ἐν τῷ ἐγγίζειν αὐτὸν	εἰς Ἰεριχώ,
and it came to pass,	**that as he was come nigh**	unto Jericho

This is a similar construction Luke 9:34 above. He, αὐτὸν, is in the accusative case and is the subject of the infinitive, ἐγγίζειν.

Example, Matthew 6:8

οἶδε γὰρ ὁ πατὴρ ὑμῶν ὧν		χρείαν ἔχετε,
for knows the father of you what things of need you have		
πρὸ	τοῦ **ὑμᾶς αἰτῆσαι** αὐτόν.	
before	**You ask** him	

The subject of the infinitive, αἰτῆσαι, is ὑμᾶς, you. Notice that ὑμᾶς is in the accusative case.

27. **The Infinitive as a Noun, Adjective, and Adverb:** The infinitive functions as a noun in many ways: subject, direct object, indirect object, etc. It can also modify a noun, like an adjective. It can even modify another adjective, like an adverb.

1) *Subject*: The infinitive can function as the subject of a verb. We have the same construction in English, for example, *to finish well was his goal*.

Example, Rom. 7:18

τὸ γὰρ **θέλειν**	παράκειταί	μοι
for **to will**	is present	with me

2) *Direct Object*: An infinitive may also be used as the direct object of a verb.

Example, Mark 12:12

καὶ ἐζήτουν	αὐτὸν	**κρατῆσαι**
and they sought	on him	**to lay hold**

The primary objective of the main verb is to make an arrest, *lay hold*.

3) *Indirect object*: An infinitive may function as the indirect object of a verb, the same as a noun in the dative case.

Example, Luke 10:40

ἡ ἀδελφή μου	μόνην με	κατέλιπε **διακονεῖν**
the sister of me	alone me	has left **to serve**

KJV: my sister hath left me to serve alone.
The direct object is *me*, με, and the indirect object is *to serve*.

4) *Apposition*: In grammar, an apposition refers to two equivalent nouns or noun phrases standing in relation to one another so that one is an explanation of the other.

Example, 1 Thess. 4:3

τοῦτο γὰρ ἐστι θέλημα τοῦ	Θεοῦ, ὁ ἁγιασμὸς	ὑμῶν,
this for is will	of the God the sanctification	of you
ἀπέχεσθαι ὑμᾶς ἀπὸ τῆς πορνείας·		
to abstain you from the fornication		

Sanctification is explained by *to abstain from fornication*.

5) *Instrument*: The infinitive can explain the means by which an action takes place (adverbial use).

Example, Acts 15:10

νῦν οὖν	τί	πειράζετε τὸν Θεόν,	**ἐπιθεῖναι**	ζυγὸν
now therefore	why	tempt ye the God	to put (by putting)	a yoke
ἐπὶ τὸν τράχηλον τῶν		μαθητῶν		
upon the necks		of the disciples		

KJV: Now therefore why tempt ye God, to put a yoke upon the neck of the disciples

The disciples were in a conference to determine whether to put Gentile Christians under the law. The sentence indicates that they would tempt God by trying to put that yoke on the neck of the disciples.

6) *Modifier*: The infinitive can act as an adjective or adverb modifying a noun or an adjective.

(1) An Infinitive as an adjective modifying a noun:
Example, John 1:12

ἔδωκεν αὐτοῖς	ἐξουσίαν τέκνα Θεοῦ	**γενέσθαι**
he gave to them	power sons of God	to become

The infinitive describes what kind of power it is.

(2) An Infinitive as an adverb modifying an adjective:
Example, Mark 1:7

οὐκ εἰμὶ ἱκανὸς κύψας	**λῦσαι**	τὸν ἱμάντα
not I am worthy stooping down	to unloose	the latchet

The infinitive here modifies the adjective "worthy."

28. The Infinitive can Function as Imperative and Greeting:

1) An infinitive can be used as a command.
Example, Romans 12:15

χαίρειν μετὰ χαιρόντων,	καὶ **κλαίειν** μετὰ κλαιόντων.
Rejoice with them that do rejoice,	and **weep** with them that weep.

2) The infinitive can function to insert a greeting. This is sometimes called the *infinitive absolute*.

Example, James 1:1

ταῖς δώδεκα φυλαῖς ταῖς ἐν τῇ διασπορᾷ,	**χαίρειν**.
to the twelve tribes which are scattered abroad,	**greeting**.

Direct and Indirect Discourse

29. Direct discourse is a direct quote. Usually, direct discourse follows a verb of speaking, such as, λέγει αὐτῷ ὁ Ἰησοῦς, Jesus saith unto him (John 14:9). Frequently, direct discourse is introduced by ὅτι. When the translator finds this construction, he should leave the ὅτι untranslated. In these cases, the ὅτι takes the place of quotation marks.

Example, Mark 1:37

λέγουσιν αὐτῷ,	ὅτι Πάντες ζητοῦσί σε.
they said unto him,	-- All men seek for thee

30. **Indirect discourse** is a report of what a person said without an exact quote. Usually, indirect discourse is also expressed in Greek by ὅτι followed by a verb in the indicative. In addition to this, generally the same tense and mood that was in the original direct discourse are retained.

Example of ὅτι with the indicative, John 11:20

ἡ οὖν Μάρθα, ὡς	ἤκουσεν	ὅτι	ὁ Ἰησοῦς ἔρχεται,
Then Martha, as soon as	she heard	that	Jesus was coming,

31. Indirect discourse is also sometimes expressed in Greek by the infinitive with the accusative.

Example, Luke 24:23

ἦλθον	λέγουσαι	καὶ ὀπτασίαν ἀγγέλων	**ἑωρακέναι**, (V-RAN)
they came, saying,	**that** also a vision	of angels	**they had seen**,
οἳ λέγουσιν	**αὐτὸν ζῆν.** (V-PAN)		
which said	that he was alive.		

KJV they came, saying, that they had also seen a vision of angels,

32. Indirect discourse may also be expressed by a participle.

Example, 2 Thessalonians 3:11

ἀκούομεν γάρ		τινας **περιπατοῦντας** ἐν ὑμῖν	ἀτάκτως,
For we hear	**that** there are some **who walk**	among you disorderly	

KJV For we hear that there are some which walk among you disorderly

Exercises

33. Review John 1:8-10.

8 οὐκ ἦν		ἐκεῖνος τὸ		φῶς,	ἀλλ'	ἵνα	μαρτυρήσῃ	περὶ
PRT-N	V-IAI-3S	D-NSM	T-NSN	N-NSN	CONJ	CONJ	V-AAS-3S	PREP
8 not	he was	that	the	light	but	that	he might witness	of
τοῦ	φωτός							
T-GSN	N-GSN							
the	light							

KJV: (Joh 1:8) He was not that Light, but *was sent* to bear witness of that Light.

9 ἦν	τὸ	φῶς	τὸ	ἀληθινόν,	ὃ	φωτίζει	πάντα
V-IAI-3S	T-NSN	N-NSN	T-NSN	A-NSN	R-NSN	V-PAI-3S	A-ASM
it was	the	light	the	true	that	lights	every
ἄνθρωπον	ἐρχόμενον	εἰς	τὸν	κόσμον.			
N-ASM	V-PNP-ASM	PREP	T-ASM	N-ASM			
man	who comes	into	the	world			

KJV: *That* was the true Light, which lighteth every man that cometh into the world.

10 ἐν	τῷ	κόσμῳ	ἦν,	καὶ	ὁ	κόσμος	δι'	αὐτοῦ
PREP	T-DSM	N-DSM	V-IAI-3S	CONJ	T-NSM	N-NSM	PREP	P-GSM
10 in	the	world	he was	and	the	world	by	him
ἐγένετο,	καὶ	ὁ	κόσμος	αὐτὸν	οὐκ	ἔγνω.		
V-2ADI-3S	CONJ	T-NSM	N-NSM	P-ASM	PRT-N	V-2AAI-3S		
was made	and	the	world	him	not	knew		

KJV: He was in the world, and the world was made by him, and the world knew him not.

34. Points About Translation:

1) **Language differences in Translation (Verse 8):** The Greek word order does not match the requirements of English grammar. Therefore, the translator must rearrange some of the words. For example, instead of *not he was*, it should be *he was not*.

2) **Use of Italics in Translation (Verse 8):** Notice that the translation given above of ἀλλ' ἵνα μαρτυρήσῃ περὶ is *but that he might witness of*. However, the KJV translated it *but was sent to bear witness of*. The KJV is an accurate translation. Notice, it adds *was sent*. The words are in italics to show that they are not in the Greek text. The words are taken from the context, which states that God sent John, and they accurately complete the thought of the verse. Sometimes, added words are necessary so that the target language will read with a natural and normal flow in the target language. Added words should be put in italics.

3) **A further language difference (Verse 9):** The phrase, ἦν τὸ φῶς τὸ ἀληθινόν, would be very awkward if the final translation was: *that was the light the true*. Only one article is needed, so the translation should leave out one of the articles and translate it as the KJB did, *that was the true light*. Remember God is the author of all such differences in language. Your goal as a translator is to translate the words of God into the target language, *in the same form they would have been, if the original were inspired in the target language*.

4) **Διά with the Genitive and the Expression of Agency (Verse 10):** Διά is used with both the accusative and the Genitive. In verse 10, it is used with the genitive, ὁ κόσμος δι' αὐτοῦ ἐγένετο, *the world by him was made*. Διά is often used in the sense of *movement through something*. An example of this is Matthew 12:1, ἐπορεύθη ὁ Ἰησοῦς τοῖς σάββασι διὰ τῶν σπορίμων, *Jesus went on the sabbath day through the corn*. Διά with the genitive is also used in the sense of by means of or the agency by which something is done. Another example of this is Matthew 1:22, ἵνα πληρωθῇ τὸ ῥηθὲν ὑπὸ τοῦ Κυρίου **διὰ τοῦ προφήτου**, *that it might be fulfilled which was spoken of the Lord* **by the prophet**. While it is clear that the prophet was inspired by the Lord and the Lord spoke *through* the prophet, it is also clear that the prophet himself spoke. John 1:10 is another example of this and tells us that all things were made **by the Lord Jesus**. However, it appears that some would declare that Jesus was a mere agent *through whom*

God made all things. Dana and Mantey have this to say about διά with the genitive in relation to creation.

> Although διά is occasionally used to express agency, it does not approximate the full strength of ὑπό. This distinction throws light on Jesus' relation to the creation, implying that Jesus was not the absolute, independent creator, but rather the intermediate agent in creation. [77]

In this statement, Dana and Mantey betray their bias. This is a statement of their opinion, not a grammatical rule. At the best, this statement fails to recognize the nature of the Trinity. At the worst, it denies that nature. Jesus said he does "what he seeth the Father do: for what things soever he doeth, these also doeth the Son likewise" (John 5:19). Later, He prayed, "that they may be one, even as we are one" (John 17:22). The Lord God is only one person (Deut. 6:4). We must not forget that. He is three parts,[78] but one person. The greatest illustration of that is man, whom He created in His own image and who is also a trinity. He tells us that a human being is one person with three parts: body, soul, and spirit (1 Thess. 5:23). If I conceive in my mind that I wish to go somewhere and then do it, can I say that my soul (where I conceived the idea) was the doer of the action and my body was merely the agent *through which* it was done? Was it not both my soul and my body (and my spirit) that did the action? Was it not my whole person? Therefore, the creation of the universe was accomplished by the whole person of God (Father, Word, and Spirit-1 John 5:7-8). Did he not say, "Let **us** make man in **our** image"? Is not Elohim (Hebrew for God) in Genesis 1:1 a *plural noun*? So, Jesus was more than the intermediate means by which God the Father created. Jesus is the Creator. Therefore, διά frequently means *by*, just as it was translated in the KJB. Be careful when the experts give you *opinion* rather than Biblical truth.

35. New Exercises:

Translate John 1:11-13 and parse each word. For verse 13, do not use your translation and parsing from the assignment in chapter twenty-two. Translate and parse the verse afresh.

CHAPTER TWENTY-SEVEN
GENERAL POINTS OF GRAMMAR I:

ὑπό with the genitive, The Dative of Means, The Negatives οὐ and μή, Various Cases with Verbs, Proper Names;

Review Jn. 1:11-13; Pronoun Showing Possession, ἴδιος; Polysemy and the Meaning of Words

1. Vocabulary

Word	Meaning	Word	Meaning
πόλις, πόλεως, ἡ	City	ἐκβάλλω	I cast out
Ὁ Ἰησοῦς, Ἰησοῦ	Jesus	δαιμονίζομαι	I have a devil
Ὁ Σίμων, Σίμωνος	Simon	προσφέρω	I lead to
Ὁ Ἰωάννης, Ἰωάννου	John	διαπορεύομαι	I travel through
πέδη, ἡ	Fetter, shackle	σπόριμος, ὁ	A planted field
ἅλυσις, ἡ	Chain, bond	τίλλω	I pull off
Δέω	I bind, tie, fasten	στάχυς, ὁ	A head of grain
Δεασπάω	I break asunder	χείρ, ἡ	Hand

ὑπό with the Genitive

2. The preposition ὑπό takes the genitive or the accusative case. When this preposition takes the genitive case, it emphasizes the agent by which an action takes place. To express this usage the preposition is translated *by, with,* and *of*. This usage occurs primarily in the passive voice. Below you will find some examples of this construction and how it was translated in the KJV:

Mt. 1:22 - be fulfilled which was spoken **of** the Lord (ὑπὸ τοῦ Κυρίου) by the prophet

Mt. 2:16, 17 - when he saw that he was mocked **of** the wise men (ὑπὸ τῶν μάγων) ... which was spoken **by** Jeremy the prophet (ὑπὸ Ἰερεμίου τοῦ προφήτου)

Mt. 8:24 - the ship was covered **with** the waves (ὑπὸ τῶν κυμάτων)

Mark 1:13 -forty days, tempted **of** Satan (ὑπὸ τοῦ Σατανᾶ)

Mark 5:4 - the chains had been plucked asunder **by** him (ὑπ' αὐτοῦ)

Luke 6:18 - vexed **with** unclean spirits (ὑπό πνευμάτων)

John 8:9 - convicted **by** *their own* conscience (ὑπὸ τῆς συνειδήσεως)
Acts 15:3 - And being brought on their way **by** the church (ὑπὸ τῆς ἐκκλησίας)
Acts 24:26 - He hoped also that money should have been given him **of** Paul (ὑπὸ τοῦ Παύλου)
Eph. 5:12 - things which are done **of** them (ὑπ' αὐτῶν) in secret

The Dative of Means

3. As stated in chapter twelve, the simple dative is sometimes used to express *by means of* without using a Greek preposition. It can be translated *by, with,* and sometimes *in* (which still carries the idea of with). This should be distinguished from μετα, which can also be translated *with*. Μετα means *with* in the sense of accompaniment, as in, *I am going with you*. The dative of means is similar to ὑπό in that it expresses the agent of action. It expresses that something is done *by means of* something else. Some examples are below:

Examples:

Mark 5:4

διὰ	τὸ αὐτὸν πολλάκις **πέδαις**	καὶ **ἁλύσεσι** δεδέσθαι
because	he often **with fetters** and **chains**	was bound

Mt. 8:16

ἐξέβαλε	τὰ πνεύματα **λόγῳ**
he cast out the spirits	**with** *his* word

Luke 6:1

ἤσθιον ψώχοντες	**ταῖς χερσί**
did eat, rubbing *them*	**in** *their* hands

John 19:34

εἷς τῶν στρατιωτῶν **λόγχῃ**	αὐτοῦ τὴν πλευρὰν ἔνυξε
one of the soldiers **with a spear**	of him the side pierced

The Negatives οὐ and μή and Their Uses

4. The primary words for *no* and *not* are οὐ and μή. Οὐ is the negative for the indicative mood. It is very strong and denies things that are said to be facts. It is the stronger of the two negatives.

5. Μή is the negative of the other moods, including the participle and the infinitive.

6.	The negatives are not always restricted to specific moods. Paragraphs 4 and 5 are general rules. There are exceptions.

7.	The Position of οὐ. The negative οὐ comes before the word that it negates. Most of the time it negates a verb, so normally it will precede the verb.

8.	The negative οὐ changes to οὐκ when it comes before vowels and diphthongs that have a *smooth* breathing. It changes to οὐχ when it comes before vowels and diphthongs that have a *rough* breathing.

9.	When οὐ is used in a question, the expected answer is yes. An example of that is found in Mt. 13:55, οὐχ οὗτός ἐστιν ὁ τοῦ τέκτονος υἱός, *Is not this the carpenter's son?*

10.	Μή is a negative that has some uncertainty about it. It leaves room for more information or discussion. It has been described as a qualified negation. It is not a hard set negative.

11.	When μή is used in questions, the implied answer is no and is usually used with the indicative.

Various Cases with Verbs

12.	English Sentences generally require a direct object. The same is true of Greek sentences. The usual Greek case for a direct object is the accusative case. However, some verbs can take a different case to complete the thought. Some verbs take the dative case and others take the genitive case. For example, the verb, πιστεύω, believe, takes its object in the dative case.

Proper Names

13.	Proper names are names spelled with a capital. They often have the article, similar to the Spanish method, e.g., El Senior Clark, *the Mr. Clark*. However, in an English translation, the article cannot be translated.

14.	The declension of Ὁ Ἰησοῦς, Jesus.

    Nom. Ἰησοῦς
    Gen.   Ἰησοῦ
    Dat.   Ἰησοῦν
    Acc.   Ἰησοῦ
    Voc.   Ἰησοῦ

15. **Review of John 1:11-13**

11 εἰς	τὰ	ἴδια	ἦλθε,	καὶ	οἱ	ἴδιοι	αὐτὸν	οὐ
PREP	T-APN	A-APN	V-2AAI-3S	CONJ	T-NPM	A-NPM	P-ASM	PRT-N
to	the	own	he came	and	the	own	him	not

παρέλαβον.
V-2AAI-3P
they received

KJV: He came unto his own, and his own received him not.

12 ὅσοι	δὲ	ἔλαβον	αὐτόν,	ἔδωκεν	αὐτοῖς	ἐξουσίαν	τέκνα
K-NPM	CONJ	V-2AAI-3P	P-ASM	V-AAI-3S	P-DPM	N-ASF	N-NPN
As many as	but	received	him,	he gave	to them	power	sons

Θεοῦ	γενέσθαι,	τοῖς	πιστεύουσιν	εἰς	τὸ	ὄνομα	αὐτοῦ
N-GSM	V-2ADN	T-DPM	V-PAP-DPM	PREP	T-ASN	N-ASN	P-GSM
of God	to become	to	those who believe	on	the	name	of him

KJV: But as many as received him, to them gave he power to become the sons of God, *even* to them that believe on his name:

13 οἵ	οὐκ	ἐξ	αἱμάτων,	οὐδὲ	ἐκ	θελήματος	σαρκός,	οὐδὲ
R-NPM	PRT-N	PREP	N-GPN	CONJ-N	PREP	N-GSN	N-GSF	CONJ
who	not	out of	blood	not	out of	will	of flesh	not

ἐκ	θελήματος	ἀνδρός,	ἀλλ'	ἐκ	Θεοῦ	ἐγεννήθησαν
PREP	N-GSN	N-GSM	CONJ	PREP	N-GSM	V-API-3P
out of	will	man	but	out of	God	were born

KJV: Which were born, not of blood, nor of the will of the flesh, nor of the will of man, but of God.

Points About Translation:

16. **Pronoun Showing Possession, ἴδιος (Verse 11):** One method of showing possession in Greek, as you have learned, is by using the pronoun ἴδιος, *one's own*. The translation above simply says *the own*, but the proper final translation would be *his own*, because it refers to that which belongs to the Lord Jesus in the context. The KJV translated it *his own*. The pronoun, ἴδιος, is often used when the writer wished to *emphasize* the possession.

17.   **Polysemy and the Meaning of Words (Verse 12):** *Polysemy* is the principle that some words have several definitions. For example, in Isaiah 7:14, the word, *Almah*, was translated virgin. However, in Hebrew, it also means *young woman.* Over the years the right translation has been repeatedly debated.   Liberals favor young woman, while conservatives and fundamentalists prefer virgin. Regardless, when Isaiah 7:14 was quoted in the New Testament, the issue was settled by the inspired word, παρθένος, used in Matthew 1:23 and translated *virgin*. The Greek word can *only* be translated *virgin*.

The same issue arises around the word, τέκνον. The word τέκνον means several things. The primary meaning is *a child,* and this is often the translation. The KJV has been severely criticized for translating the word in various ways: child, children, son, sons, daughters. However, the fuller meaning of τέκνον is "to bring forth, bear children. A child, male or female, son or daughter ... a child ... Specifically a son." [79]   The word can be translated child, children, son, or daughter.

18.   New Exercises.

Translate John 1:14-16 and parse each word.

CHAPTER TWENTY-EIGHT
MI VERBS

Review Jn. 1:14-16; The Meaning of Μονογενῆ, Only-begotten;
Flexibility of the word γίνομαι

1. Vocabulary

Word	Meaning	Word	Meaning
Ἀποδίδωμι	give back, pay	παραδίδωμι	deliver over
πώποτε, Adv.	at any time	ἐπιτίθημι	lay upon
ἀπόλλυμι	destroy, perish	μόνος, η, ον, Adj.	only, alone
Ἀφίημι	let go, permit	ἰδού, particle	behold, lo
Δείκνυμι	show	πειράζω	tempt
δίδωμι,	give	γήνη, γυναικός, η	woman
ἵστημι	stand	μυστήριον, το	mystery
Τίθημι	place, put	χρόνος, ο	time

2. The verbs we have studied so far all belong to the same conjugation system (except for εἰμί). We call this the ω conjugation. However, there is a second conjugation system in Greek for verbs that end in -μι. It is called the μι *conjugation,* because the present active indication first person singular ends in -μι. These include δίδωμι, *I give,* τίθημι, *I place, I put,* αφίημι, *I let go, I permit, I forgive,* δείκνυμι, *I show,* ἀπόλλυμι, *I destroy, I perish,* ἵστημι, *I stand, I cause to stand,* and others.

3. Μι verbs differ from ω verbs only in the present and second aorist tenses.

4. Μι conjugations in the **active indicative** of δίδωμι are as follows.

	Present	Imperfect	Future	Aorist	Perfect
Singular					
1	δίδωμι	ἐδίδουν	δώσω	ἔδωκα	δέδωκα
2	δίδως	ἐδίδους	δώσεις	ἔδωκας	δέδωκας
3	δίδωσι(ν)	ἐδίδου	δώσει	ἔδωκε(ν)	δέδωκε(ν)
Plural					
1	δίδομεν	ἐδίδομεν	δώσομεν	ἐδώκαμεν	δεδώκαμεν
2	δίδοτε	ἐδίδοτε	δώσετε	ἐδώκατε	δεδώκατε
3	διδόασι(ν)	ἐδίδοσαν	δώσουσι(ν)	ἔδωκαν	δέδωκαν

5. The **Active Middle and Passive Indicative** conjugations of δίδωμι are as follows.

	Present Mid/Pas	Imperfect Mid/Pas	Future Middle	Aorist Middle	Perfect Mid/Pas
	Singular				
1	δίδομαι	εδιδόμην	δώσομαι	ἐδόμην	δέδομαι
2	δίδοσαι	εδίδοσο	δώσῃ	ἔδου	δέδοσαι
3	δίδοται	εδίδοτο	δώσεται	ἔδοτο	δέδοται
	Plural				
1	διδόμεθα	ἐδιδόμεθα	δωσόμεθα	ἐδόμεθα	δεδόμεθα
2	δίδοσθε	ἐδίδοσθε	δώσεσθε	ἔδοσθε,	δέδοσθε
3	δίδονται	ἐδίδοντο	δώσονται	ἔδοντο	δέδονται

6. Future and Aorist Passive conjugations of δίδωμι are as follows.

	Future Passive	Aorist Passive
	Singular	
1	δοθήσομαι	ἐδόθην
2	δοθήσῃ	ἐδόθης
3	δοθήσεται	ἐδόθη
	Plural	
1	δοθησόμεθα	ἐδόθημεν
2	δοθήσεσθε	ἐδόθητε
3	δοθήσονται	ἐδόθησαν

7. Μι conjugations in **other Active moods** of δίδωμι are as follows.

	Present Subjunctive	Aorist Subjunctive	Present Imperative	Aorist Imperative
	Singular			
1	διδῶ	δῶ	—	—
2	διδῷς	δῷς	δίδου	δός
3	διδῷ	δῷ	διδότω	δότω
	Plural			
1	διδῶμεν	δῶμεν	—	—
2	διδῶτε	δῶτε	δίδοτε	δότε
3	διδῶσι(ν)	δῶσι(ν)	διδότωσαν	δότωσαν

8. Infinitives occur in the New Testement in the present and aorist tenses.

	Present	Aorist
Active	διδόναι	δοῦναι
Middle	δίδοσθαι	δόσθαι
Passive	δίδοσθαι	δοθῆναι

Μι Participles

9. The conjugation of the participles of δίδωμι is as follows. Only the nominative forms are shown here, because μι participles are regularly declined.

Present   Masc.   Fem.   Neut.

Active	διδούς	διδοῦσα	διδόν
Middle/Passive	διδόμενος	διδομένη	διδόμενον

Aorist   Masc.   Fem.   Neut.

Active	δούς	δοῦσα	δόν
Middle	δόμενος	δομένη	δόμενον
Passive	δοθείς	δοθεῖσα	δοθέν

Perfect   Masc.   Fem.   Neut.

Active	δεδωκώς	δεδωκυῖα	δεδωκός
Middle/Passive	δεδόμενος	δεδομένη	δεδόμενον

10. **The conjugation of τίθημι:** Following are some distinctives of the conjugation of τίθημι.

    1) The present system of τίθημι is like δίδωμι.
    2) The aorist is regular (that is, it is like the ω verbs) except it has -κ- instead of -σ-.
    3) The future is regular.
    4) The perfect active and the perfect middle are regular, except θε- is lengthened to θει- rather than θη-.
    5) The aorist passive is regular with two exceptions: 1) the final vowel on the stem is not lengthened and 2) the θε- of the stem is changed to τε-.

11. **Conjugation of ἀπόλλυμι, δείκνυμι, etc.:** There are some distinctives in the conjugations of these verbs. With the information in the above paragraphs, you can recognize most of their occurrences. Since the μι verbs are

far less common than the ω verbs, there are resources that help you recognize them when they occur. Two of these resources are: 1) the free Bible program at www.e-sword.net, for both Mac and PC, and 2) *The Translator's Concise Lexicon of the Textus Receptus,* by Steve Combs, which is available from The Old Paths Publications in print and PDF. There are also other online resources.

12. **Review of John 1:14-16**

14 καὶ ὁ		λόγος	σὰρξ	ἐγένετο,	καὶ	ἐσκήνωσεν ἐν ἡμῖν,		
CONJ T-NSM		N-NSM	N-NSF	V-2ADI-3S	CONJ	V-AAI-3S PREP P-1DP		
and the		word	flesh	was made	and	dwelled among us		
καὶ ἐθεασάμεθα τὴν			δόξαν αὐτοῦ,		δόξαν ὡς	μονογενοῦς		
Conj V-ADI-1P		T-ASF	N-ASF P-GSM		N-ASF ADV	A-GSM		
and we saw		the	glory his		glory as	of only-begotten		
παρὰ πατρός),		πλήρης χάριτος καὶ				ἀληθείας		
PREP N-GSM		A-NSF	N-GSF CONJ			N-GSF		
of father		full	of grace and			of truth		

KJV: And the Word was made flesh, and dwelt among us, (and we beheld his glory, the glory as of the only begotten of the Father,) full of grace and truth.

15 Ἰωάννης	μαρτυρεῖ	περὶ αὐτοῦ,	καὶ	κέκραγε	λέγων,
N-NSM	V-PAI-3S	PREP P-GSM	CONJ	V-2RAI-3S	V-PAP-NSM
John	bore witness	of him	and	cried	saying
Οὗτος ἦν	ὃν	εἶπον,	Ὁ	ὀπίσω μου	ἐρχόμενος
D-NSM V-IAI-3S	R-ASM	V-2AAI-1S	T-NSM	ADV P-1GS	V-PNP-NSM
This was	he (of) whom	I spoke	the	after me	he who comes
ἔμπροσθέν μου	γέγονεν·	ὅτι	πρῶτός μου		ἦν.
PREP P-1GS	V-2RAI-3S	CONJ	A-NSM-S P-1GS		V-IAI-3S
before me	becomes	because	before me		he was

KJV: John bare witness of him, and cried, saying, This was he of whom I spake, He that cometh after me is preferred before me: for he was before me.

16 καὶ ἐκ	τοῦ	πληρώματος αὐτοῦ	ἡμεῖς
CONJ PREP	T-GSN	N-GSN	P-GSM P-1NP
and of	the	fulness	of him we
πάντες ἐλάβομεν,	καὶ	χάριν ἀντὶ	χάριτος.
A-NPM V-2AAI-1P	CONJ	N-ASF PREP	N-GSF
all have received	and	grace for	grace

KJV: And of his fulness have all we received, and grace for grace.

Points on Translation

13. Is Jesus the only begotten? What does μονογενής really mean? (Verse 14, 16)

The NIV translates the word, μονογενής, "one and only." Others translate it similarly. Nathan Lawrence, in *"Is Yeshua the Only begotten...?"* says this.

> Why is this latter translation a better though not a perfect one? This is because Greek scholars originally thought that *monogenes* was derived from two Greek words: *mono* (only) and *genao* (to beget, to bear). Greek scholars have now discovered that *monogenes* actually derives not from *gennao*, but from *genos* meaning 'one of a kind or class' and therefore means 'unique, the one and only, the one and only of a family' " (*The Unseen Realm*, pp. 36–37, by Michael S. Heiser; see also *The Complete Word Study Dictionary* pp. 995–996, by Spiros Zodhiates). [80]

He is wrong in this. The word γενος (genos) means *family, offspring, race, nation, and kind, sort, or class* (A Manual Greek Lexicon of the New Testament, by G. Abbott-Smith). [81] The full definition from the Word Study Dictionary is as follows.

> génos; gen. génous, neut. noun from gínomai (G1096), to become. Offspring, posterity (Act 17:28-29; Rev 22:16; Sept.: Jer 36:31). Family, lineage, stock (Act 4:6 where some translate it as "sect" or "order"; Sept.: Jer 41:1; Act 7:13; Act 13:26; Php 3:5); nation, people (Mar 7:26; Act 4:36; Act 7:19; Act 18:2, Act 18:24; 2Co 11:26; Gal 1:4; 1Pe 2:9; Sept.: Gen 11:6; Est 2:10); kind, sort, species (Mat 13:47; Mat 17:21; Mar 9:29; 1Co 12:10, 1Co 12:28; 1Co 14:10; Sept.: Gen 6:20; Gen 7:14; 2Ch 4:13). [82]

Γενος is a noun that comes from γινομαι, a very versatile verb. Regarding persons, things, or circumstances, Γινομαι means to *come into being, be born, arise, come on* (G. Abbott-Smith). Since γενός is referring to a person, when it applies to Jesus Christ, this definition applies. Therefore, μονογενής, referring to Jesus Christ, means the Son of God entered this world as a human being by the process of begetting and birth. Γινος definitely carries the idea of birth.

Uses of Γενος:

Kindred-Acts 7:14
Born-Acts 18:2, 24
Offspring-Rev. 22:16
Nation-Gal. 1:14 (an ethnic people)

Stock-Phil. 3:5 (still an ethnic people)
Country-Acts 4:36 (may refer to the people)
Countrymen-2 Cor 11:26 (Paul's countrymen-the Jews)
Diversities-1 Cor 12:28 (kinds of tongues)
Generation-1 Peter 2:9

Although in some contexts the word carries the idea of a *kind* (as in Mt. 13:47; 17:21; Mk. 9:29; and 1 Cor. 14:10), this is not the case when it applies to a creature entering the world. In the context of entering the world, it means a birth and a begetting.

Doctrinal significance of "only begotten":

The begetting prophesied:

"I will declare the decree: the LORD hath said unto me, Thou art my Son; this day have I begotten thee." (Ps. 2:7)

The begetting was on a day. Since there were no days in eternity past, the begetting must have occurred during time and history. It would be impossible to have the begetting prophesied, but not at all mentioned in the New Testament, as might be the case if every use of monogenes is to be translated as "only," "unique," or "one and only" rather than "only begotten."

The Begetting Described:

Then said Mary unto the angel, How shall this be, seeing I know not a man? And the angel answered and said unto her, The Holy Ghost shall come upon thee, and the power of the Highest shall overshadow thee: **therefore** also that holy thing which shall be born of thee shall be called the Son of God. (Luke 1:34-35)

Jesus is the only human being ever to enter the world through having been begotten by God the Father. He was certainly unique and one of a kind, but He was far more than that. He was begotten by the almighty power of God the Father, creating a fertilized egg in a woman's womb. That is the *reason* He is called the Son of God.

The Importance of the Begetting

Behold, a virgin shall be with child, and shall bring forth a son, and they shall call his name Emmanuel, which being interpreted is, God with us. (Matt. 1:23)

The next day John seeth Jesus coming unto him, and saith, Behold the Lamb of God, which taketh away the sin of the world. (John 1:29).

He was the Son of God, God manifest in the flesh, born of a virgin, a lamb without spot or blemish, fit to be the eternal offering for sin.

14.   **Flexibility of the word γίνομαι (Verse 15).** In verse 15, the word γέγονεν is used. It comes from γίνομαι. The basic meaning of this word is *to come into existence or to happen.* However, in connection with ἔμπροσθέν the KJV translated it *is preferred*. Why? First, you must understand more about the word γίνομαι and how it is used. This is perhaps the most versatile word in the New Testament. It is a word that the translator must get to know thoroughly. One of the best treatments of this word can be found in *The Complete Word Study Dictionary*. A shorter definition found in *Thayer's Greek Definitions* is below.

> 1) to become, i.e. to come into existence, begin to be, receive being
> 2) to become, i.e. to come to pass, happen
>   2a) of events
> 3) to arise, appear in history, come upon the stage
>   3a) of men appearing in public
> 4) to be made, finished
>   4a) of miracles, to be performed, wrought
> 5) to become, be made [83]

As said above and defined by Thayer, the basic idea of γίνομαι is *to come into existence* or *to happen.* However, it is used in many varied contexts and the translation must be adjusted to fit the context. The following is a list of how the KJV translated this word.

> Arise, be assembled, be (come, -fall, -have self), be brought (to pass), (be) come (to pass), continue, be divided, be done, draw, be ended, fall, be finished, follow, be found, be fulfilled, God forbid, grow, happen, have, be kept, be made, be married, be ordained, to be, partake, pass, be performed, be published, require, seem, be showed, soon as it was, sound, be taken, be turned, use, wax, will, would, be wrought. [84]

An example, in Romans 7, shows how varied the translation of γινομαι can be. Romans 7:3 says, "So then if, while her husband liveth, she **be married** to another man, she shall be called an adulteress …" The word for *be married* is γινομαι. We could translate it, "So then if, while her husband liveth, she

became to another man ..." However, this makes no sense in English. What did she become? In the context, she became a wife or she became married. Therefore, the KJV correctly translates it "be married." To be, to become, was, etc. are good translations of this word if they fit with the context. Otherwise consider being creative, but still within the basic meaning of the word. For a discussion of why the KJV gave the translation "is preferred" see chapter thirty-one.

15.   **The Preposition, ἀντί:** There is some possibility of confusion about the preposition, ἀντί, in the phrase, χάριν ἀντὶ χάριτος, grace for grace. Ἀντί was translated *for* in the KJV. The student should understand the uses of ἀντί. The following is the definition found in *The Word Study Dictionary*.

> antí; prep. with the general meaning of over against, in the presence of, in lieu of. Spoken metaphorically either in a hostile sense, meaning against, or by way of comparison, where it implies something of equivalent value, and denotes substitution, exchange, requital. In the NT used in the following:
>
> **(I)** By way of substitution, in place of, instead of (Luk_11:11; 1Co_11:15; Jas_4:15). As implying succession (Mat_2:22, the one kind succeeding the other). In Joh_1:16, trans. with "for" in the phrase "and grace for grace," meaning grace upon grace, most abundant grace, one favor in place of or after another. God's grace is not given once-and-for-all, but there is a renewal of it that is constant.
>
> **(II)** By way of exchange, requital, equivalent, meaning in consideration of, on account of, spoken: [85]

The word has several meanings and is used numerous times in the New Testament. In John 1:16, ἀντί means *instead of* or *in place of*. It is consistent with the modern definition of *for*. One of the many definitions of *for* is: "In place of." [86]

Grace does much more than save us. Grace is needed much more often than many of us think. We are saved by grace (Eph. 2:8-9). We come to God to get grace in every need (Heb. 4:16). We need grace today, and tomorrow we will need it for something else. Yesterday, I received grace that helped me and today I need new grace in place of (for) the grace I had yesterday.

16.   New Exercises.

   Translate John 1:17-20 and parse each word.

CHAPTER TWENTY-NINE
GENERAL POINTS OF GRAMMAR II:

The Second Aorist of γινώσκω; The Article Before μέν and δέ; Aorist Participle and Leading Verb; First Aorist on Second Aorist Stems; ἕως and ἄν with Subjunctive

Review of John 1:17-20; Abstract Nouns; The Preposition εἰς; Attributive and Predicate Positions of Adjectives; Consistency in Bible Translation; Uses of ὅτι

1. Vocabulary.

Word	Meaning	Word	Meaning
ἀρνέομαι, dep.	deny, refuse	ἀπόκρισις, η	answer, decision
ἐπαγγελία, η	promise	εὐθύνω	make straight, steer
αἰτέω	ask for	Ἡσαίας	Isaiah
αἰώνιος, ον	eternal	φανερόω	make manifest
βασιλεύς, βασιλέως, ο	king	φημί	say
βιβλίον, το	book	φιλέω	love
Γαλιλαία, η	Galilee	φοβέομαι	fear
γραμματεύς, γραμματεώς, ο	scribe	φυλακή, η	guard, prison

2. The declension of the **second aorist of γινώσκω**, I know, is below. This is a verb of the ω conjugation. However, it has a second aorist conjugation in the μι form.

Indicative	Singular	1	ἔγνων
		2	ἔγνως
		3	ἔγνω
	Plural	1	ἔγνωμεν
		2	ἔγνωτε
		3	ἔγνωσαν
Subjunctive	Singular	1	γνῶ
		2	γνῷς
		3	γνῷ (γνοῖ)
	Plural	1	γνῶμεν
		2	γνῶτε

		3	γνῶσι (ν)
Imperative	Singular	2	γνῶθι
		3	γνῶτω
	Plural	2	γνῶτε
		3	γνῶτωσαν
Infinitive			γνῶναι
Participle			γνούς, γνοῦσα, γνόν

3. **The Article Before μέν and δέ:** The article is often placed before these two particles to mean *he, she* or *it*.

4. **The Aorist or Present Participle and the Leading Verb:** The aorist or present participles are sometimes used to indicate the same act as the leading verb.

Example – John 10:33

ἀπεκρίθησαν αὐτῷ	οἱ	Ἰουδαῖοι	λέγοντες,
V-ADI-3P	P-DSM T-NPM	A-NPM	V-PAP-NPM
answered	to him the	Jews	saying

5. **First aorist Endings on Second Aorist Stems:** In the New testament, you will sometimes find first aorist endings used on second aorist stems.

6. **ἕως and ἄν with the Subjunctive:** Here is some additional information about the words, ἕως and ἄν.

   1) When ἕως means *until*, it takes the subjunctive with ἄν.
   2) The exception to the above is when the verb that ἕως introduces is an actual occurrence in past time. In this case, ἄν may be omitted.
   3) When ἕως means *while*, it is used with the indicative.
   4) In the phrase, ἕως οὗ, ἕως is a preposition and οὗ is the genitive singular neuter of the relative pronoun. The phrase means the same as ἕως alone means, when it is a conjunction.

7. Review John 1:17-20

17 ὅτι ὁ	νόμος	διὰ	Μωσέως ἐδόθη,	ἡ	χάρις
CONJ T-NSM	N-NSM	PREP	N-GSM V-API-3S	T-NSF	N-NSF
that the	law	by	Moses was given	the	grace
καὶ ἡ	ἀλήθεια διὰ	Ἰησοῦ	Χριστοῦ ἐγένετο.		
CONJ T-NSF N-NSF	PREP	N-GSM	N-GSM V-2ADI-3S		
and the	truth by	Jesus	Christ came		

KJV: For the law was given by Moses, *but* grace and truth came by Jesus Christ.

18 Θεὸν	οὐδεὶς	ἑώρακε	πώποτε·	ὁ	μονογενὴς υἱός,
N-ASM	A-NSM-N	V-RAI-3S	ADV	T-NSM A-NSM	N-NSM
God	no man	has seen	at any time	the	only begotten son

ὁ	ὢν	εἰς	τὸν	κόλπον τοῦ	πατρός
T-NSM	V-PAP-NSM	PREP	T-ASM	N-ASM T-GSM	N-GSM
the	which being	in	the	bosom of	the father

ἐκεῖνος	ἐξηγήσατο.
D-NSM	V-ADI-3S
that one (he)	has declared

KJV: No man hath seen God at any time; the only begotten Son, which is in the bosom of the Father, he hath declared *him*.

19 Καὶ	αὕτη	ἐστὶν	ἡ	μαρτυρία τοῦ	Ἰωάννου,	ὅτε
CONJ	D-NSF	V-PAI-3S	T-NSF	N-NSF T-GSM	N-GSM	ADV
and	this	is	the	record of	John	when

ἀπέστειλαν οἱ	Ἰουδαῖοι ἐξ	Ἱεροσολύμων	ἱερεῖς	καὶ
V-AAI-3P T-NPM	A-NPM PREP	N-GPN	N-APM	CONJ
sent the	Jews of	Jerusalem	priests	and

Λευΐτας	ἵνα	ἐρωτήσωσιν αὐτόν,	Σὺ	τίς	εἶ;
N-APM	CONJ	V-AAS-3P P-ASM	P-2NS	I-NSM	V-PAI-2S
Levites	to	ask him	you	who	are

KJV: And this is the record of John, when the Jews sent priests and Levites from Jerusalem to ask him, Who art thou?

20 καὶ	ὡμολόγησε,	καὶ	οὐκ	ἠρνήσατο·
CONJ	V-AAI-3S	CONJ	PRT-N	V-ADI-3S
and	he confessed	and	not	denied

καὶ	ὡμολόγησεν ὅτι	Οὐκ	εἰμὶ	ἐγὼ	ὁ	Χριστός.
CONJ	V-AAI-3S CONJ	PRT-N	V-PAI-1S	P-1NS	T-NSM	N-NSM
and	confessed that	not	am	I	the	Christ

KJV: And he confessed, and denied not; but confessed, I am not the Christ.

Pointers on Translation

8.   **Abstract Nouns (Verse 17):** In verse 17, νόμος, *the law*, is a concrete noun. It refers to a specific law that you can touch and read, the law of Moses.

The nouns, χάρις and ἀλήθεια, *grace and truth*, are abstract nouns. Abstract nouns can be difficult to translate in some languages. English and most European languages are full of easy-to-understand abstract nouns. That is not so in some languages. When these two words were combined with "came" in Trique (Mexico) they were understood to be the names of two angels. This only occurred because of the combination with "came." [87] How should a translator react to such a situation? It depends on the verse and the words involved. First, a translator might find an accurate way to translate the difficult word that conveys the proper meaning while avoiding the misunderstanding. Second, if this is not possible, the translator must avoid paraphrasing the verse. If there is no way to avoid a misunderstanding without inaccurate or paraphrased translation, then the verse must be clarified in teaching.

9. **The Preposition εἰς (Verse 18):** The basic meaning of εἰς is often given as *into*. However, it can be translated several ways. According to Dana and Mantey, the root meaning is *within* or *in*. [88] It may be used with verbs of place (into, to, toward, upon), time (to, up to, until), or purpose (in, unto, for).

10. **Further Information Regarding the Attributive and Predicate Positions of Adjectives (Verse 18):** An adjective in the attributive position, such as ὁ ἄδικος κριτής, *the unjust judge*, describes a quality of the noun it modifies. An adjective in the predicate position makes an assertion about the noun it modifies. ὁ κριτής ἄδικος means *the judge is unjust*. While it is typical that the article appears in front of the adjective in the attributive and the predicate does not have an article in front of the adjective, there are exceptions as we can see from verse 18. In the phrase, ὁ μονογενὴς υἱός, μονογενὴς is a typical attributive adjective and the phrase means *the only begotten son*. However, in the phrase Θεὸν οὐδεὶς, οὐδεὶς looks like a predicate adjective, but it is not. The phrase certainly does not mean *no man is God*. While that statement is true, it is nonsense in the context. The translator will have to look at the context carefully to determine which rule applies with each adjective. The article is not always the final determiner.

In the phrase, Θεὸν οὐδεὶς, the adjective is fulfilling three functions. It is an attributive adjective, but without the article. Οὐδεὶς means *not one, not at all, no one,* etc. However, it is masculine and means *no man* in this sentence, with the force of *not any man at all*. Due to this, the adjective is used as both an adjective and a noun. Finally, the adjective is in the nominative case and is used as the subject of its clause. Θεὸν is accusative and, so, is the direct object of the clause. Therefore, the phrase, Θεὸν οὐδεὶς ἑώρακε, means *No man has seen God*.

11.   **Note on Consistency in Bible Translation (Verse 19):** In verse 19, the KJV translated the word, μαρτυρία, as *record*. In verse 7, the same word was translated *witness*. This is only one small example showing that the translators did not hold themselves to a standard that required translating the same Greek word by the same English word every time. Translators should have flexibility in this regard. Since Greek words most often have several meanings (see the discussion on polysemy in chapter twenty-seven, paragraph 17), translators must use the definition that is most appropriate for the context in which the word is found. A single target language word does not necessarily fit in every context. On the other hand, if two contexts are the same, one target language word could be used in the first and the same or a synonym in the second. Let's allow the KJV translators to explain why they translated the *same* Greek word by *different* English words from the original preface to the KJV.

> Another thing we think good to admonish thee of, gentle reader, that we have not tied ourselves to an uniformity of phrasing, or to an identity of words, as some peradventure would wish that we had done, because they observe that some learned men somewhere have been as exact as they could that way. Truly, that we might not vary from the sense of that which we had translated before, if the word signified the same thing in both places (for there be some words that be not of the same sense everywhere) we were especially careful, and made a conscience, according to our duty. But that we should express the same notion in the same particular word; as, for example, if we translate the *Hebrew* or *Greek* word once by *purpose*, never to call it *intent*; if one where *journeying*, never *travelling*; if one where *think*, never *suppose*; if one where *pain*, never *ache*; if one where *joy*, never *gladness*, &c.; thus to mince the matter, we thought to savour more of curiosity than wisdom, and that rather it would breed scorn in the atheist than bring profit to the godly reader. For is the kingdom of God become words or syllables? Why should we be in bondage to them, if we may be free? use one precisely when we may use another no less fit as commodiously?

As a result of this approach, one may examine how the KJV translated the same Greek word in different contexts and, by doing so, obtain a fuller understanding of the meaning of the Greek word. The KJV translators used different translations of words in different contexts, but they always translated in agreement with the correct definitions of the Greek word.

12. **The Conjunction ὅτι (Verse 20):** The form of this conjunction is the relative pronoun ὅ τι. There are several ways in which ὅτι is used.

> 1. It is used as a causal particle meaning *because* or *for* (See Jn. 1:30).
> 2. It is commonly used as a conjunction to introduce a clause.
> 3. It can be translated as *why* in some instances (e.g. Mk. 9:11, 28).
> 4. Finally, it introduces direct quotes. In this use, it is equivalent to our quotation marks. There are no such marks in Koine Greek. When it is used in this way, ὅτι does not need to be translated. This is the case in John 1:20. The KJV does not translate the word in the latter half of the verse, "but confessed, I am not the Christ."

13. **New Exercises.**

> Translate and parse John 1:21-24.

CHAPTER THIRTY
NUMBERS
Review of John 1:21-24
Implied Information; The Article as a Pronoun

1. Vocabulary:

Word	Meaning	Word	Meaning
ἄν	untranslatable – makes statements contingent	πόλις, πόλεως, η	city
ἀρχιερεύς, ἀρχιερέως, ο	King	χείρ, χειρός, η	hand
μηδείς, μηδεμία, μηδέν	no one, nothing	τε	particle, and often not translated
ἔθνος, το	nation	σύν, Pron Dat.	With
εἷς, μία, ἕν	one	ἀπέρχομαι	Depart
ἔργον, το	work	δεῖ	It is necessary
λαός, ο	people	δύναμις, δυνάμεως, η	power
πίστις, πίστεως, η	faith, belief, trust	κρίνω	Judge, decide

2. **Numerals:** Numbers are also declined in Greek. The declension of εἷς, μία, ἕν, one, is below. There is, of course, no plural form of one.

    Masculine   Feminine   Neuter

N.	εἷς	μία	ἕν
G.	ἑνός	μιᾶς	ἑνός
D.	ἑνί	μιᾷ	ἑνί
A.	ἕνα	μίαν	ἕν

3. The declension of οὐδείς, οὐδενία, οὐδέν, *no one, nothing,* and μηδείς, μηδεμία, μηδέν, *no one, nothing,* is like εἷς.

4. δύο, two, is not declinable, except that it has a dative form, δύσι (ν).

5.   The declension of τρεῖς, three, is below.

   Masc./ Fem.   Neuter

N.	τρεῖς	τρία
G.	τριῶν	τριῶν
D.	τρισί (ν)	τρισι (ν)
A.	τρεῖς	τρία

6.   The declension of τέσσαρες, four, is as follows.

   Masc./ Fem.   Neuter

N.	τέσσαρες	τέσσαρα
G.	τεσσάρων	τεσσάρων
D.	τέσσαρσι (ν)	τέσσαρσι (ν)
A.	τέσσαρας	τέσσαρα

7.   Greek numbers are divided into cardinal numbers and ordinal numbers, as in English. Cardinal numbers are for counting, such as, one, two, three, four, etc. Ordinal number are for rank or order, such as, first, second, third, etc. Other cardinal numbers up to διακόσιοι, two hundred, are indeclinable. Numbers over two hundred are declined as regular first and second declension adjectives. A list of cardinal numbers follows.

πέντε	5	εἴκοσι (ν)	20	ἑξακόσιοι	600
ἕξ	6	εἴκοσιτέσσαρες	24	ἑπτακόσιοι	700
ἑπτά	7	τριάκοντα	30	ὀκτακόσιοι	800
ὀκτώ	8	τεσσαράκοντα	40	ἐνακόσιοι	900
ἐννέα	9	πεντήκοντα	50	χίλιοι	1000
δέκα	10	ἑξήκοντα	60	δισχίλιοι	2000
ἕνδεκα	11	ἑβδομήκοντα	70	τρισχίλιοι	3000
δώδεκα	12	ὀγδοήκοντα	80	τετρακισχίλιοι	4000
τρεισκαίδεκα	13	ἐνενήκοντα	90	πεντακισχίλιοι	5000
δεκατέσσαρες	14	ἐνενηκονταεννέα	99	ἑπτακισχίλιοι	7000
δεκαπέντε	15	ἑκατόν	100	μύριοι	10000
ἑκκαίδεκα	16	διακόσιοι	200	δώδεκα χιλιάδες	12000
ἑπτακαίδεκα	17	τριακόσιοι	300		
ὀκτωκαίδεκα	18	τετρακόσιοι	400		
ἐννεακαίδεκα	19	πεντακόσιοι	500		

8. Examples:

John 1:37 καὶ ἤκουσαν αὐτοῦ **οἱ δύο μαθηταὶ** λαλοῦντος, καὶ ἠκολούθησαν τῷ Ἰησοῦ.

John 2:6 **ἦσαν δὲ ἐκεῖ ὑδρίαι λίθιναι ἕξ** κείμεναι κατὰ τὸν καθαρισμὸν τῶν Ἰουδαίων, χωροῦσαι ἀνὰ **μετρητὰς δύο ἢ τρεῖς**.

9. Some numbers are made up of two or more numbers combined.

Examples:

Luke 13:4 - (eighteen) - ἢ ἐκεῖνοι οἱ **δέκα καὶ οκτώ**, ἐφ' οὓς ἔπεσεν ὁ πύργος ἐν τῷ Σιλωὰμ καὶ ἀπέκτεινεν αὐτούς,

Acts 1:15 - (120) - (ἦν τε ὄχλος ὀνομάτων ἐπὶ τὸ αὐτὸ ὡς **ἑκατὸν εἴκοσιν**),

Revelation 9:16 – 200,000,000 - καὶ ὁ ἀριθμὸς στρατευμάτων τοῦ ἱππικοῦ, **δύο μυριάδες μυριάδων**· καὶ ἤκουσα τὸν ἀριθμὸν αὐτῶν.

Literally, this reads *two 10,000 of 10,000*. It means 10,000 times 10,000 times 2, or a total of 200,000,000.

10. Some numbers can be abbreviated and in some places the abbreviation is used.

Examples:

Revelation 7:4 – (144,000) - καὶ ἤκουσα τὸν ἀριθμὸν τῶν ἐσφραγισμένων, **ρμδ' χιλιάδες**, ἐσφραγισμένοι ἐκ πάσης φυλῆς υἱῶν Ἰσραήλ.

ρμδ' is the abbreviation for one hundred forty-four and χιλιάδες is the number for 1000.

Revelation 7:5 – (12,000) Ἐκ φυλῆς Ἰούδα, **ιβ' χιλιάδες** ἐσφραγισμένοι· Ἐκ φυλῆς Ῥουβήν, **ιβ' χιλιάδες** ἐσφραγισμένοι·

ιβ' is the abbreviation for twelve.

11. **The Ordinal Numbers:** Below is a list of some of the ordinals that are used in the New Testament. The ordinals are declined like regular first and second declension adjectives.

πρῶτος, η, ον	first	ὄγδοος, η, ον	eighth
δεύτερος, α, ον	second	ἔνατος, η, ον	nineth
τρίτος, η, ον	third	δέκατος, η, ον	tenth

τέταρτος, η,ον	fourth	σένδέκατος, η, ο	eleventh
πέμπτος, η, ον	fifth	δωδέκατος, η, ον	twelfth
ἕκτος, η, ον	sixth	τεσσαρεσκαιδέκατος,η	fourteenth
ἕβδομος, η,ον	seventh	πεντεκαιδέκατος, η, ον	fifteenth

12. **Adverbs indicating numerical values:** Below are some Greek adverbs that have numerical value. Only those marked with an asterisk are used in the New Testament.

ἅπαξ*	once	ὀκτάκις	Eight times
δίς*	twice	ἐνάκις	nine times
τρίς*	three times	δεκάκις	ten times
τετράκις	four times	ἑνδεκάκις	eleven times
πεντάκις *	five times	δωδεκάκις	twelve times
ἑξάκις	six times	ποσάκις *	how many times
ἑπτάκις *	seven times		

13. **Review of John 1:21-24**

21 καὶ	ἠρώτησαν	αὐτόν,	Τί	οὖν;	Ἡλίας	εἶ
CONJ	V-AAI-3P	P-ASM	I-NSN	CONJ	N-NSM	V-PAI-2S
And	they asked	him	What	then?	Isaiah	are
σύ;	καὶ	λέγει,	Οὐκ	εἰμί.	Ὁ	προφήτης εἶ
P-2NS	CONJ	V-PAI-3S	PRT-N	V-PAI-1S	T-NSM	N-NSM V-PAI-2S
you?	And	he said	not	I am	the	prophet are
σύ;	καὶ	ἀπεκρίθη,	Οὔ.			
P-2NS	CONJ	V-ADI-3S	PRT-N			
you?	And	he answered	No.			

KJV: And they asked him, What then? Art thou Elias? And he saith, I am not. Art thou that prophet? And he answered, No.

22 εἶπον	οὖν	αὐτῷ,	Τίς	εἶ;	ἵνα	ἀπόκρισιν	δῶμεν
V-2AAI-3P	CONJ	P-DSM	I-NSM	V-PAI-2S	CONJ	N-ASF	V-2AAS-1P
they said	therefore	to him	who	are you	that	an answer	we may give
τοῖς	πέμψασιν	ἡμᾶς	τί	λέγεις	περὶ	σεαυτοῦ;	
T-DPM	V-AAP-DPM	P-1AP	I-NSN	V-PAI-2S	PREP	F-2GSM	
to	those who sent	us	what	say you	for	yourself?	

KJV: Then said they unto him, Who art thou? that we may give an answer to them that sent us. What sayest thou of thyself?

23 ἔφη,	Ἐγὼ	φωνὴ βοῶντος	ἐν	τῇ	ἐρήμῳ,	Εὐθύνατε
V-IAI-3S	P-1NS	N-NSF V-PAP-GSM	PREP	T-DSF	A-DSF	V-AAM-2P
He said,	I am	a voice crying	in	the	wilderness	make straight
τὴν	ὁδὸν	Κυρίου,	καθὼς εἶπεν	Ἡσαΐας	ὁ	προφήτης.
T-ASF	N-ASF	N-GSM	ADV V-2AAI-3S	N-NSM	T-NSM	N-NSM
the	way	of Lord	as said	Isaiah	the	prophet

KJV: He said, I *am* the voice of one crying in the wilderness, Make straight the way of the Lord, as said the prophet Esaias.

24 καὶ	οἱ	ἀπεσταλμένοι ἦσαν	ἐκ	τῶν	Φαρισαίων.
CONJ	T-NPM	V-RPP-NPM V-IAI-3P	PREP	T-GPM	N-GPM
and	those who	were sent were	of	the	Pharisees

KJV: And they which were sent were of the Pharisees.

Pointers on Translation

14. **Implied Information (Verse 21):** The question, Ὁ προφήτης εἶ σύ (Are you that prophet?), carries a lot of *implied information*. Implied information is information the original readers or speakers of the Bible would likely have known beforehand but is not in the immediate context. This goes beyond simply adding a word or two to make the translation clear. In our text, who is being referred to as "that prophet"? The question, "Are you that prophet," assumes John knew of whom they are asking. The prophet referred to in the verse was foretold in Deuteronomy 18:15, "The LORD thy God will raise up unto thee a Prophet from the midst of thee, of thy brethren, like unto me; unto him ye shall hearken." Modern readers in many countries where the gospel is well known and readers among unreached people may not know this information. Should a translator provide the implied information in the translation? One suggestion for this verse is to translate it, "Are you that prophet *who was promised*?" Although the KJV translators did sometimes include implied information, most of the time, they did not. They did not include it in John 1:21, thereby leaving the reader to discover it for himself or for teachers to inform believers. *The general principle of Bible translation is that the translator is to translate, not interpret or explain*. So, generally implied information should not be inserted into the text. However, the translator will have to prayerfully decide this issue each time it comes up. There are some general guidelines as to when implied information may be inserted.

1) It may be required by the grammar or the word structure of the target language.

2) Consistent misunderstanding caused by the structure of the target language may require it. For example, Acts 2:15 says, "For these are not drunken, as ye suppose …" In English, it is implied that Peter also is not drunk. In some languages, the word "these" may be understood to exclude Peter, implying that Peter was drunk.

One notable example of the KJV translators inserting implied information is in Matthew 1:6. The Greek text literally says, "David the king begat Solomon of her of the Urias." English grammar requires more. Therefore, the KJV translators gave us, "David the king begat Solomon of her *that had been the wife* of Urias."

15. **The Article Translated as a Pronoun (Verse 21):** Sometimes, in English, we will use the definite article to indicate something unique or special. An example of this is in the following conversation. "Who are you?" "I am George Bush." "Do you mean, you are *the* George Bush" (former President of the US)? In verse 21, we have a similar use of the article in Greek. "Ὁ προφήτης εἶ σύ?" "Are you *the* prophet?" In Greek "Ὁ προφήτης" is first in the sentence indicating the writer is emphasizing it. The question is about a special prophet foretold by Moses (Deut. 18:15). Therefore, the article was translated as a pronoun (that) so that the English translation would also indicate the fact that a unique prophet was in view, *that prophet.*

16. **New Exercises.**

Translate and Parse John 1:25-30.

From this point on, you will continue to translate the verses literally in the same word order as Greek, just as we have done so far. But now, you will also produce a finished translation into standard current modern English. (In the review, the book will provide an example translation into current Modern English.) You will do this without looking at the KJV or any other translation. When you are finished, you will compare your translation to the KJV.

CHAPTER THIRTY-ONE
REVIEW OF JOHN 1:25-30

εἰ verses εἶ, the Importance of Accent; Personal Pronouns Used for Emphasis; Word Analysis-Preferred or Made; Historical Present; Figures of Speech in Historical Context; Collocational Clash

1. Vocabulary

Word	Meaning	Word	Meaning
μέλλω	about to	πούς, ποδός, ὁ	foot
οἶκος, ὁ	house	τόπος, ὁ	place
οἰκία, ἡ	house	ὀφθαλμός, ὁ	eye
ὅλος, η, ον, Adj	whole	ἐκβάλλω	cast out
ἕτερος, α, ον, Adj	other, another	ἔτι	yet, still, even
θάλασσα, ἡ	Sea	κάθημαι	sit
οὔτε	not	καιρός, ὁ	time
οὔτε … οὔτε	neither … nor	μήτηρ, μητρός, ἡ	mother

2. Review of John 1:25-30 and Answers to the Exercise of chapter thirty-one.

25 καὶ	ἠρώτησαν	αὐτόν, καὶ	εἶπον	αὐτῷ,	Τί
CONJ	V-AAI-3P	P-ASM CONJ	V-2AAI-3P	P-DSM	I-NSN
and	they asked	him and	said	to him	Why

οὖν βαπτίζεις,	εἰ	σὺ	οὐκ	εἶ	ὁ	Χριστός, οὔτε
CONJ V-PAI-2S	COND	P-2NS	PRT-N	V-PAI-2S	T-NSM	N-NSM CONJ-N
then baptize you	if	you	not	are	the	Christ nor

Ἡλίας, οὔτε	ὁ	προφήτης;
N-NSM CONJ-N	T-NSM	N-NSM
Elias nor	the	prophet

Example Translation: And they asked him, and said to him, Why do you Baptize, then, if you are not the Christ, nor Elias, nor that prophet?

KJV: And they asked him, and said unto him, Why baptizest thou then, if thou be not that Christ, nor Elias, neither that prophet?

26 ἀπεκρίθη αὐτοῖς ὁ			Ἰωάννης, λέγων,		Ἐγὼ	βαπτίζω	
V-ADI-3S	P-DPM	T-NSM	N-NSM	V-PAP-NSM	P-1NS	V-PAI-1S	
answered	to them	the	John	saying	I	baptize	
ἐν	ὕδατι·	μέσος δὲ	ὑμῶν	ἕστηκεν	ὃν	ὑμεῖς οὐκ	οἴδατε
Prep	N-DSN	A-NSM Conj	P-2GP	V-RAI-3S	R-ASM	P-2NP PR-N	V-RAI-2P
in	water	(one) among but	you	stands	whom	you not	know

Example Translation: John answered them, saying, I baptize in water, but one stands among you, whom you do not know.

KJV: John answered them, saying, I baptize with water: but there standeth one among you, whom ye know not

27 αὐτός ἐστιν	ὁ	ὀπίσω μου	ἐρχόμενος,	ὃς	ἔμπροσθέν	
P-NSM V-PAI-3S	T-NSM	ADV P-1GS	V-PNP-NSM	R-NSM	PREP	
he is	the	(one) after me	coming	who	before	
μου	γέγονεν·	οὗ	ἐγὼ	οὐκ	εἰμὶ	ἄξιος	ἵνα
P-1GS	V-2RAI-3S	R-GSM	P-1NS	PRT-N	V-PAI-1S	A-NSM	CONJ
me	is preferred	who	I	not	am	worthy	that
λύσω	αὐτοῦ	τὸν	ἱμάντα	τοῦ	ὑποδήματος.		
V-AAS-1S	P-GSM	T-ASM	N-ASM	T-GSN	N-GSN		
I loose	of him	the	latchet	of the	shoes		

Example Translation: He it is who, coming after me, is preferred before me, whose shoe's latchet I am not worthy to loose.

KJV: He it is, who coming after me is preferred before me, whose shoe's latchet I am not worthy to unloose.

28 ταῦτα	ἐν	Βηθαβαρᾶ	ἐγένετο	πέραν	τοῦ
D-NPN	PREP	N-DSF	V-2ADI-3S	ADV	T-GSM
These	in	Bethabara	were done	beyond	the
Ἰορδάνου,	ὅπου	ἦν	Ἰωάννης	βαπτίζων.	
N-GSM	ADV	V-IAI-3S	N-NSM	V-PAP-NSM	
Jordan,	where	was	John	Baptizing	

Example Translation: These things were done in Bethabara, beyond Jordan where John was baptizing.

KJV: These things were done in Bethabara beyond Jordan, where John was baptizing.

29 Τῇ	ἐπαύριον	βλέπει	ὁ		Ἰωάννης τὸν		Ἰησοῦν	ἐρχόμενον
T-DSF	ADV	V-PAI-3S	T-NSM		N-NSM	T-ASM	N-ASM	V-PNP-ASM
	on the next day	sees	the		John	the	Jesus	coming
πρὸς αὐτόν,	καὶ	λέγει,	Ἴδε		ὁ		ἀμνὸς	τοῦ
PREP P-ASM	CONJ	V-PAI-3S	V-AAM-2S		T-NSM		N-NSM	T-GSM
to him	and	says	Behold		the		lamb	of the
Θεοῦ,	ὁ	αἴρων		τὴν	ἁμαρτίαν	τοῦ		κόσμου.
N-GSM	T-NSM	V-PAP-NSM		T-ASF	N-ASF	T-GSM		N-GSM
God	the	who takes away		the	sin	of the		world

Example Translation: The next day, John saw Jesus coming to him, and said, Behold, the lamb of God, who takes away the sin of the world!

KJV: The next day John seeth Jesus coming unto him, and saith, Behold the Lamb of God, which taketh away the sin of the world.

30 οὗτός	ἐστι	περὶ	οὗ	ἐγὼ	εἶπον,	Ὀπίσω	μου	ἔρχεται
D-NSM	V-PAI-3S	PREP	R-GSM	P-1NS	V-2AAI-1S	ADV	P-1GS	V-PNI3S
This	he is	about	whom	I	said	After	me	comes
ἀνὴρ,	ὃς	ἔμπροσθέν	μου	γέγονεν,	ὅτι	πρῶτός	μου	ἦν.
N-NSM	R-NSM	PREP	P-1GS	V-2RAI-3S	CONJ	A-NSM-S	P-1GS	V-IAI-3S
a man	who	preferred	before me	was	because	before	me	he was

Example Translation: This is he of whom I said, A man comes after me, who is preferred before me, because he was before me.

KJV: This is he of whom I said, After me cometh a man which is preferred before me: for he was before me.

Pointers for Translation

3.   **εἰ Verses εἶ, the Importance of Accent (Verse 25):** These words have the same letters, but they mean very different things. εἰ is a particle meaning *if*. εἶ is a verb, present active indicative second person singular of εἰμί, I am. The only difference between the spelling of these two words is the accent. The first has no accent and only a smooth breathing. The second has the smooth breathing and a circumflex accent. Some words are distinguished only by their accent. It is important to notice the accent on words.

4.   **Personal Pronouns Used for Emphasis (Verse 25):** In the phrase, εἰ σὺ οὐκ εἶ ὁ Χριστός, the word εἶ, being second person, implies the word *you* and

means *you are*. Nevertheless, the Biblical writer included the personal pronoun, σὺ. By contrast, the word βαπτίζεις is a second person verb and includes *you* in its meaning, but the personal pronoun, *you*, is not written separately in Greek. When the personal pronoun is written separately, it is very often done for emphasis. When the verb is used without a separate personal pronoun, the translation can often be made without a personal pronoun. However, when the personal pronoun is there, look carefully to see if it needs to be expressed in the translation.

5. **Preferred or was made? (Verse 27):** Why is "is preferred before" a good translation in verse 27. In this verse, the word ἔμπροσθέν is used closely with γίνομαι. According to Strong, one of the meanings of ἔμπροσθέν is *placed in front of*. According to the 1828 edition of Webster's Dictionary, the definition of *preferred* is "Regarded above others; elevated in station." [89] In other words, *preferred before* is a perfect translation of ἔμπροσθέν. In verse 27, γίνομαι was translated simply as *is*. This construction is also found in verses 15 and 30.

6. **Historical Present (Verse 29):** The historical present is a Greek idiom that views a past event with the intensity of a present event. The events and statements made in verse 29 were past events when they were written. Yet, John writes them in present tense, "John sees Jesus coming unto him" "and says." In verse 29, John also prophecies a future event in present tense, "which taketh away the sin of the world." John frequently uses present tense and often mixes present tense and past tense in one sentence.

7. **Figures of Speech in Historical Context (Verse 29):** There are figures of speech in the Bible that are so deeply embedded in Biblical history and truth, they cannot be changed. One of those figures of speech is the "Lamb of God." Some have tried to change the "lamb" to some other animal, because the lamb is unknown in the culture. In many tribes of Papua New Guinea, the main food animal is the pig. However, we cannot translate the Bible to say, "Behold! The pig of God!" without doing violence to the entire Bible and destroying a great picture of Christ's sacrifice on the cross. The idea of blood sacrifice for sin goes back to Genesis 3 and the idea of a lamb as that sacrifice goes back to at least Genesis 4. Therefore, these must be kept intact and translated literally, even if the translator must create a new word or use a word that is unknown to the national people.

8. **New Exercises.**

Translate and Parse and give a final translation of John 1:31-35.

CHAPTER THIRTY-TWO
REVIEW OF JOHN 1:31-35

Flexibility in Translation; Uses of ἐν with the Dative;

1. Vocabulary

Word	Meaning	Word	Meaning
ἀγαπητός, η ον	beloved	πονηρος, α, ον	evil
δαιμόνιον, το	demon	πίπτω	fall
δοκέω	think	πρόσωπον, το	face
εὐαγγέλιον, το	gospel	προσέρχομαι	come to
ἱμάτιον, το	garment	πῦρ, πυρός, το	fire
κεφαλή	head	στόμα, στόματος, το	mouth
ὅπου	where, whither	τηρέω	keep
πίνω	drink	ὥστε	so that

2. Review of John 1:31-35

31 κἀγὼ	οὐκ	ᾔδειν	αὐτόν·	ἀλλ'	ἵνα	φανερωθῇ	τῷ	Ἰσραὴλ
P-1NS	PRT-N	V-LAI-1S	P-ASM	CONJ	CONJ	V-APS-3S	T-DSM	N-PRI
And I	not	know	him	but	that	he might be known	to	Israel
διὰ	τοῦτο	ἦλθον	ἐγὼ	ἐν	τῷ	ὕδατι	βαπτίζων.	
PREP	D-ASN	V-2AAI-1S	P-1NS	PREP	T-DSN	N-DSN	V-PAP-NSM	
on account	of this	came	I	in	the	water	baptizing	

Example Translation: And I did not know him, but that he might be made known to Israel, therefore, I came baptizing in water.

KJV: And I knew him not: but that he should be made manifest to Israel, therefore am I come baptizing with water.

32 καὶ	ἐμαρτύρησεν	Ἰωάννης,	λέγων	ὅτι	Τεθέαμαι
CONJ	V-AAI-3S	N-NSM	V-PAP-NSM	CONJ	V-RNI-1S
And	testified	John	saying	that	I saw
τὸ	Πνεῦμα	καταβαῖνον	ὡσεὶ	περιστερὰν	
T-ASN	N-ASN	V-PAP-ASN	ADV	N-ASF	
the	Spirit	coming down	as	a dove	
ἐξ	οὐρανοῦ,	καὶ	ἔμεινεν	ἐπ'	αὐτόν.
PREP	N-GSM	CONJ	V-AAI-3S	PREP	P-ASM
out of	heaven	and	remained	on	him.

Example Translation: And, John testified saying that "I saw the Spirit coming down from heaven like a dove out of heaven and it remained on Him."

KJV: And John bare record, saying, I saw the Spirit descending from heaven like a dove, and it abode upon him.

33 κἀγὼ	οὐκ	ᾔδειν	αὐτόν·	ἀλλ'	ὁ	πέμψας	με
P-1NS	PRT-N	V-LAI-1S	P-ASM	CONJ	T-NSM	V-AAP-NSM	P-1AS
And I	not	know	him	but		the one who sent	me
βαπτίζειν	ἐν	ὕδατι,	ἐκεῖνός	μοι	εἶπεν,	Ἐφ'	ὃν	ἂν
V-PAN	PREP	N-DSN	D-NSM	P-1DS	V-2AAI-3S	PREP	R-ASM	PRT
to baptize	with	water	the same	to me	said		Upon whom	
ἴδῃς	τὸ	Πνεῦμα	καταβαῖνον	καὶ	μένον	ἐπ'	αὐτόν,
V-2AAS-2S	T-ASN	N-ASN	V-PAP-ASN	CONJ	V-PAP-ASN	PREP	P-ASM
you see	the	Spirit	decend	and	remain	on	him
οὗτός	ἐστιν	ὁ	βαπτίζων	ἐν	Πνεύματι	Ἁγίῳ.
D-NSM	V-PAI-3S	T-NSM	V-PAP-NSM	PREP	N-DSN	A-DSN
this	is		the one who baptizes	with	Spirit	Holy

Example Translation: And, I did not know Him, but he who sent me to baptize with water, he said to me, Upon whom you see the Spirit descend and remain on him, this is the one who baptizes with the Holy Spirit.

KJV: And I knew him not: but he that sent me to baptize with water, the same said unto me, Upon whom thou shalt see the Spirit descending, and remaining on him, the same is he which baptizeth with the Holy Ghost.

34 κἀγὼ	ἑώρακα,	καὶ	μεμαρτύρηκα	ὅτι	οὗτός	ἐστιν	ὁ
P-1NS	V-RAI-1S	CONJ	V-RAI-1S	CONJ	D-NSM	V-PAI-3S	T-NSM
And I	I saw	and	bore record	that	this	is	the
υἱὸς	τοῦ	Θεοῦ
N-NSM	T-GSM	N-GSM
son	of the	God.

Example Translation: And, I saw and bore record that this is the Son of God.

KJV: And I saw, and bare record that this is the Son of God.

35 Τῇ	ἐπαύριον πάλιν εἱστήκει ὁ		Ἰωάννης, καὶ	
T-DSF ADV	ADV V-LAI-3S	T-NSM	N-NSM	CONJ
the next day	again stood	the	John	and
ἐκ	τῶν	μαθητῶν αὐτοῦ δύο·		
PREP	T-GPM N-GPM	P-GSM A-NUI (**NU**meral Indeclinable)		
of	the	disciples of him two		

Translation: Again the next day, John and two of his disciples stood

KJV: Again the next day after John stood, and two of his disciples;

3. **Flexibility in Translation (Verse 32):** I would like to emphasize once more that there is some flexibility in how Greek can be translated into English. Other languages may be more rigid, and it is the responsibility of the translator to know how he should handle his target language. Three phrases of John 1:32 above are each different when the example is compared to the KJV. Yet, all are accurate translations of the Greek words.

    1) Example translation: "And John **testified**"
       KJV: "And John **bare record**"

    2) Example translation: "**coming down** from heaven"
       KJV: "**descending** from heaven"

    3) Example translation: "and it **remained** on him"
       KJV: "and it **abode** on him"

The words are different, but each came from the same set of Greek words, and all are accurate translations of those words. Take, for example, the Greek word, ἐμαρτύρησεν, which is V-AAI-3S of μαρτυρέω. As noted before, μαρτυρέω can be translated several ways accurately. It can be translated witness, bare witness, give witness, bare record, give testimony, testify, report, etc. All of these are accurate, if they fit the context. The KJV translates the word in this verse *bare record,* but it also translates it in many other ways in other verses. I am not suggesting that the KJV is anything other than the best translation, but, as a translator, you may find that you cannot translate the word *record* (v. 32) into your target language. You may have to substitute one of the other words instead. You, as a translator, need to feel free to do so. Find the best word available in the target language.

4. **Uses of ἐν with the Dative (Verse 33):** In verse 33, the preposition ἐν is translated *with* two times. Ἐν always takes its object in the dative case. The root meaning is *within.* When ἐν refers to location it means *in, into, on, at, within, among us, etc.* It is sometimes used with elevated objects, such as mountains, and means *in, on, and upon.* It sometimes refers to an instrument

or means by which something is accomplished. In that case, it means *with, through,* and *by means of.* It may imply contact or close proximity and, therefore, means *near, with, at, on*, and *by*. It may refer to time with similar meanings. Some other ways it is translated are *throughout, because of, toward, under, about, after, against, besides, and between.* Many of these last meanings are used only once in the New Testament. The exact word you use in your target language depends on being consistent (even loosely) with the basic meanings in the context of the verse, your knowledge of the target language vocabulary, and your creativity. This is generally true with other prepositions.

5. In verse 34, ἑώρακα and μεμαρτύρηκα are perfect active indicative, translated in past tense, *saw* and *bare record*. These words describe past events for John. Why, then, are they in the perfect tense? As you will recall, the perfect tense indicates a past action with present results. The past action is that John "saw" the baptism. The result is that he gained the knowledge of the Messiah's identity, and when he "bare record," others gained that knowledge.

6. **New Exercises.**

Translate and Parse John 1:36-40 and provide finished translations.

CHAPTER THIRTY-THREE
REVIEW JOHN 1:36-40

Uses of the Conjunction δὲ; Grammatical Structure and Meaning; Word Order; παρὰ with the Genitive of Person

1. Vocabulary

Word	Meaning	Word	Meaning
ἀσπάζομαι	salute, greet	προσκυνέω	worship
δέχομαι	receive	σάββατον, το	sabbath
ἐπερωτάω	ask, question	συνάγω	gather
θρόνος, ὁ	throne	συναγωγή, η	synagogue
καρπός, ὁ	fruit	τοιοῦτος, η, ον, adj	such
λοιπός, η, ον, adj	remaining, (noun=rest, adv=for the rest, henceforth)	ὑπάγω	depart
ὄρος, το	mountain	ὑπαρχω	exist
οὐχί	not, a strong form of οὐ	χαίρω	rejoice
πλοῖον, το	ship, boat	χαρά, η	joy, delight
πρεσβύτερος, α, ον, adj	elder	ὧδε	hither, here

2. Review of John 1:36-40.

36 καὶ	ἐμβλέψας	τῷ	Ἰησοῦ	περιπατοῦντι,	λέγει,	Ἴδε	ὁ
CONJ	V-AAP-NSM	T-DSM	N-DSM	V-PAP-DSM	V-PAI-3S	V-AAM-2S	T-NSM
And	looking upon	the	Jesus	while he walked	he says	behold	the

ἀμνὸς	τοῦ	Θεοῦ.
N-NSM	T-GSM	N-GSM
lamb	of	God

Example Translation: And, looking upon Jesus while He walked, he said, Behold the lamb of God!

274

KJV: And looking upon Jesus as he walked, he saith, Behold the Lamb of God!

37 καὶ	ἤκουσαν	αὐτοῦ	οἱ	δύο	μαθηταὶ	λαλοῦντος,
CONJ	V-AAI-3P	P-GSM	T-NPM	A-NUI	N-NPM	V-PAP-GSM
And	heard	him	the	two	disciples	speaking
καὶ	ἠκολούθησαν	τῷ	Ἰησοῦ.			
CONJ	V-AAI-3P	T-DSM	N-DSM			
and	followed	the	Jesus			

Example Translation: And, the two disciples heard him speak and followed Jesus.

KJV: And the two disciples heard him speak, and they followed Jesus.

38 στραφεὶς	δὲ	ὁ	Ἰησοῦς	καὶ	θεασάμενος	αὐτοὺς
V-2APP-NSM	CONJ	T-NSM	N-NSM	CONJ	V-ADP-NSM	P-APM
was turned	but	the	Jesus	and	having seen	them
ἀκολουθοῦντας,	λέγει	αὐτοῖς,	Τί	ζητεῖτε;	οἱ	δὲ	εἶπον
V-PAP-APM	V-PAI-3S	P-DPM	I-ASN	V-PAI-2P	T-NPM	CONJ	V-2AAI-3P
following	he says	to them	what	seek you	the	but	they said
αὐτῷ,	Ῥαββί	(ὃ	λέγεται	ἑρμηνευόμενον,	Διδάσκαλε),	ποῦ	μένεις;
P-DSM	HEB	R-NSN	V-PPI-3S	V-PPP-NSN	N-VSM	ADV	V-PAI-2S
to him	Rabbi	Which	says	being interpreted	Teacher	where	abide you

Example Translation: Then Jesus turned around and saw them following, he said to them. What do you seek? And, they said, Rabbi, (which is to say, being translated, Teacher) where are you staying?

KJV: Then Jesus turned, and saw them following, and saith unto them, What seek ye? They said unto him, Rabbi, (which is to say, being interpreted, Master,) where dwellest thou?

39 λέγει	αὐτοῖς,	Ἔρχεσθε	καὶ	ἴδετε.	ἦλθον	καὶ	εἶδον
V-PAI-3S	P-DPM	V-PNM-2P	CONJ	V-2AAM-2P	V-2AAI-3P	CONJ	V-2AAI-3P
He said	to them	Come	and	see	They came	and	saw
ποῦ	μένει·	καὶ	παρ' αὐτῷ	ἔμειναν	τὴν	ἡμέραν	ἐκείνην·	ὥρα
PRT	V-PAI-3S	CONJ	PREP P-DSM	V-AAI-3P	T-ASF	N-ASF	D-ASF	N-NSF
where	he stayed	and	with him	they remained	the	day	that	hour
δὲ	ἦν	ὡς	δεκάτη.					
CONJ	V-IAI-3S	ADV	A-NSF					
and	was	about	tenth					

Example translation: He said to them, Come and see. They came and saw where he was staying and remained with him that day, and it was about the tenth hour.

KJV: He saith unto them, Come and see. They came and saw where he dwelt, and abode with him that day: for it was about the tenth hour.

40 ἦν		Ἀνδρέας ὁ		ἀδελφὸς	Σίμωνος	Πέτρου	εἷς	ἐκ	τῶν
V-IAI-3S		N-NSM	T-NSM	N-NSM	N-GSM	N-GSM	A-NSM	PREP	T-GPM
was		Andrew	the	brother	of Simon	Peter	one	of	the
δύο	τῶν	ἀκουσάντων	παρὰ	Ἰωάννου	καὶ	ἀκολουθησάντων		αὐτῷ.	
A-NUI	T-GPM	V-AAP-GPM	PREP	N-GSM	CONJ	V-AAP-GPM		P-DSM	
two	who	heard	from	John	and	followed		him	

Example translation: One of the two, who heard John and followed him, was Andrew, the brother of Simon Peter.

KJV: One of the two which heard John *speak*, and followed him, was Andrew, Simon Peter's brother.

Pointers on Translation

3. **Uses of the Conjunction δὲ (Verse 38):** στραφεὶς δὲ ὁ Ἰησοῦς is translated in the KJV as, *"Then Jesus turned ..."* The conjunction δὲ is translated *then* in verse 38. δὲ has several functions.

    1) It is used as a conjunction that expresses *opposition* or *antithesis*. As such it can be translated *but, howbeit, however, yet, on the other hand*, and such like.

        John 2:21 ἐκεῖνος **δὲ** ἔλεγε περὶ τοῦ ναοῦ τοῦ σώματος αὐτοῦ.
        KJV: **But** he spake of the temple of his body.

        John 3:18 ὁ πιστεύων εἰς αὐτὸν οὐ κρίνεται· ὁ **δὲ** μὴ πιστεύων ἤδη κέκριται
        KJV: He that believeth on him is not condemned: **but** he that believeth not is condemned already,

        John 6:23 ἄλλα **δὲ** ἦλθε πλοιάρια
        KJV: **Howbeit** there came other boats

    2) Δὲ is also used as a *continuative* or *transitional* conjunction and can be translated *and, moreover, then, now*, etc. When δὲ is translated *now*, it often is used to introduce an *explanation*.

        John 4:6 ἦν **δὲ** ἐκεῖ πηγὴ τοῦ Ἰακὼβ

KJV: **Now** Jacob's well was there.

Acts 11:12 ἦλθον **δὲ** σὺν ἐμοὶ καὶ οἱ ἐξ ἀδελφοὶ οὗτοι,
KJV: **Moreover** these six brethren accompanied me,

3) At times it is used *emphatically* or *intensively*. In those instances, it can be translated *indeed, yea, really, in fact, etc.*

Acts 3:24 καὶ πάντες **δὲ** οἱ προφῆται ... προκατήγγειλαν τὰς ἡμέρας ταύτας.
KJV: **Yea**, and all the prophets ... have likewise foretold of these days.

4. **Grammar and Meaning (Verse 38):** The word, στραφείς, is passive participle that is translated as active voice in the KJV, "Jesus turned." The passive voice indicates that the subject (Jesus) is receiving the action not performing the action. So, the literal meaning of the Greek seems to be that Jesus was turned by something outside of Himself. However, that is not what it means and to translate it as *Then Jesus was turned and saw them* is awkward and incorrect English. It is also historically wrong. In the context, it was Jesus who was doing the turning. No one turned Him. So, the context shows the action to be active rather than passive.

This goes to illustrate a major point that a translator must keep in mind while translating: *A meaning in the source language that is expressed in a certain grammatical form may have to be translated into a different grammatical form in the target language to retain the same meaning.*

5. **Word Order Rearranged (Verse 40):** Sometimes it is necessary to rearrange words to make the translation have the same meaning as the Greek text. We have seen various examples of this throughout John 1.

Greek: was Andrew the brother of Simon Peter one of the two who heard from John and followed him

KJV: One of the two which heard John *speak*, and followed him, was Andrew, Simon Peter's brother.

As you can see, the words were rearranged. In Greek, the arrangement of words in a sentence is very flexible. Greek is an inflectional language, that is, the meaning of sentences depends on the various endings and prefixes of words, not word order. Many languages, such as English, are not inflectional and meaning depends on words being arranged in the proper order. The word order of the Greek text in verse forty is confusing in English. It must be rearranged to have the same meaning in English.

6. **Παρὰ with the Genitive of Person (Verse 40):** Another issue in verse 40, is that the word παρὰ seems to not be translated in the KJV. The object of the preposition, παρὰ, in verse 40 is Ἰωάννου. The preposition basically carries the idea of *with, beside, near*, but can be translated in a number of ways depending on the context. When παρὰ is used in the genitive case with persons, it carries the meaning of *going forth from* or *proceeding from the vicinity* of someone. Verse 40 speaks of the disciples hearing something that *proceeds from* John. The context reveals that what came from John was speech. Therefore, it was speech they heard. Since *from John* is awkward English in verse 40, the KJV translated παρὰ Ἰωάννου according to the actual *meaning* of the prepositional phrase, that *John spoke*. Therefore, ἀκουσάντων παρὰ Ἰωάννου was translated as *heard John speak*. The word, speak, was placed in italics to indicate to the reader that the Greek word for speak was not present. However, the meaning is present in παρὰ Ἰωάννου, so it was translated somewhat idiomatically.

7. **New Exercises**.

Translate and Parse John 1:41-45

CHAPTER THIRTY-FOUR
REVIEW OF JOHN 1: 41-45

The Foundational Method of Bible Translation; Basic Guidelines for Translating Idioms; Figures of Speech; Shifts in Verb Tense; The Word *Would*

1. Vocabulary

Word	Meaning	Word	Meaning
ἁμαπτάνω	sin	καθίζω	sit
ἀπαγγέλλω	announce, report	κρατέω	grasp
ἄρα	then, therefore	λίθος, ὁ	stone
ἄχρι, prep. with gen. or conj.	as far as, up to/ as conj. until	παιδίον, το	child, babe, infant
γλῶσσα, η	tongue, language	πρό, prep with gen.	before
δεξιός, α, ον	right	σοφία, η	wisdom
διό	wherefore	σπείπω	sow
ἔτος, το	year	σωτηρία, η	salvation
εὐαγγελίζω, η	preach the gospel	φόβος, ὁ	fear
εὐθύς	straightway, immediately	χπεία, η	need

2. Review of John 1:41-45.

41 εὑρίσκει	οὗτος	πρῶτος	τὸν	ἀδελφὸν	τὸν	ἴδιον	Σίμωνα,
V-PAI-3S	D-NSM	A-NSM	T-ASM	N-ASM	T-ASM	A-ASM	N-ASM
finds	he	first	the	brother	the	own	Simon
καὶ	λέγει	αὐτῷ,	Εὑρήκαμεν		τὸν	Μεσσίαν,	
CONJ	V-PAI-3S	P-DSM	V-RAI-1P		T-ASM	N-ASM	
and	he says	to him	We have found		the	Messiah	
(ὅ	ἐστι	μεθερμηνευόμενον,		ὁ		Χριστός).	
R-NSN	V-PAI-3S	V-PPP-NSN		oG3588		T-NSM	N-NSM
(which	is	being interpreted		the		Christ)	

Example translation: He first found his own brother, Simon, and said to him, We have found the Messiah (which is, being interpreted, the Christ).

KJV: He first findeth his own brother Simon, and saith unto him, We have found the Messias, which is, being interpreted, the Christ.

42 καὶ	ἤγαγεν	αὐτὸν	πρὸς	τὸν	Ἰησοῦν.	ἐμβλέψας	δὲ	αὐτῷ
CONJ	V-2AAI-3S	P-ASM	PREP	T-ASM	N-ASM	V-AAP-NSM	CONJ	P-DSM
And	he led	him	to	the	Jesus	looking	and	at him
ὁ	Ἰησοῦς εἶπε,	Σὺ	εἶ	Σίμων	ὁ	υἱὸς	Ἰωνᾶ·	σὺ
T-NSM	N-NSM V-2AAI-3S	P-2NS	V-PAI-2S	N-NSM	T-NSM	N-NSM	N-GSM	P2NS
the	Jesus said	You	are	Simon	the	son	of Jona	You
κληθήσῃ	Κηφᾶς, (ὃ		ἑρμηνεύεται			Πέτρος).		
V-FPI-2S	N-NSM R-NSN		V-PPI-3S			N-NSM		
shall be called	Cephas which		being interpreted			Peter		

Example translation: And, he led him to Jesus, and Jesus, looking at him, said, You are Simon, the son of Jona. You shall be called Cephas. (Which, being interpreted, is Peter.) (Note: Peter means a stone)

KJV: And he brought him to Jesus. And when Jesus beheld him, he said, Thou art Simon the son of Jona: thou shalt be called Cephas, which is by interpretation, A stone.

43 Τῇ	ἐπαύριον	ἠθέλησεν	ὁ	Ἰησοῦς	ἐξελθεῖν	εἰς	τὴν	Γαλιλαίαν,
T-DSF	ADV	V-AAI-3S	T-NSM	N-NSM	V-2AAN	PREP	T-ASF	N-ASF
The	next day	wanted	the	Jesus	to go	to	the	Galilee
καὶ	εὑρίσκει	Φίλιππον,	καὶ	λέγει	αὐτῷ,	Ἀκολούθει	μοι.	
CONJ	V-PAI-3S	N-ASM	CONJ	V-PAI-3S	P-DSM	V-PAM-2S	P-1DS	
and	finds	Philip	and	says	to him	Follow	me	

Example Translation: The next day, Jesus wanted to go to Galilee, and found Philip, and said to him, Follow me.

KJV: The day following Jesus would go forth into Galilee, and findeth Philip, and saith unto him, Follow me.

44 ἦν	δὲ	ὁ	Φίλιππος	ἀπὸ	Βηθσαϊδά,
V-IAI-3S	CONJ	T-NSM	N-NSM	PREP	N-PRI
was	and	the	Philip	from	Bethsaida,
ἐκ	τῆς	πόλεως	Ἀνδρέου	καὶ	Πέτρου.
PREP	T-GSF	N-GSF	N-GSM	CONJ	N-GSM
out of	the	city	of Andrew	and	of Peter

Example Translation: And Philip was from Bethsaida, the city of Andrew and Peter.

KJV: Now Philip was of Bethsaida, the city of Andrew and Peter.

45 εὑρίσκει Φίλιππος τὸν	Ναθαναήλ, καὶ	λέγει	αὐτῷ,
V-PAI-3S N-NSM T-ASM	N-PRI CONJ	V-PAI-3S	P-DSM
found Philip the	Nathaniel and	says	to him
Ὃν ἔγραψε Μωσῆς ἐν	τῷ νόμῳ καὶ	οἱ	προφῆται
R-ASM V-AAI-3S N-NSM PREP	T-DSM N-DSM CONJ	T-NPM	N-NPM
whom wrote of Moses in	the law and	the	prophets
εὑρήκαμεν, Ἰησοῦν τὸν	υἱὸν τοῦ	Ἰωσὴφ τὸν	ἀπὸ Ναζαρέθ.
V-RAI-1P N-ASM T-ASM	N-ASM T-GSM	N-PRI T-ASM	PREP N-PRI
we found Jesus the	son of the	Joseph the	from Nazareth

Example translation: Philip found Nathaniel and said to him, We have found him, of whom Moses, in the law, and the prophets wrote, Jesus, the son of Joseph from Nazareth.

KJV: Philip findeth Nathanael, and saith unto him, We have found him, of whom Moses in the law, and the prophets, did write, Jesus of Nazareth, the son of Joseph.

Pointers on Translation

3.   **The Foundational Method of Bible Translation (Verse 41):** In verse 41, the word, μεθερμηνευόμενον, present passive participle from μεθερμηνεύω, is translated *being interpreted.* One of the meanings of *interpret* is "To translate from one language into another." [90] There are several times Bible translation is mentioned in the Bible. Each of those places and some similar places are listed below.

> **Mark 7:34** And looking up to heaven, he sighed, and saith unto him, Ephphatha, that is, Be opened.
> **John 1:38** Then Jesus turned, and saw them following, and saith unto them, What seek ye? They said unto him, Rabbi, (which is to say, being interpreted, Master,) where dwellest thou?
> **John 1:41** He first findeth his own brother Simon, and saith unto him, We have found the Messias, which is, being interpreted, the Christ.
> **John 1:42** And he brought him to Jesus. And when Jesus beheld him, he said, Thou art Simon the son of Jona: thou shalt be called Cephas, which is by interpretation, A stone.

John 9:7 And said unto him, Go, wash in the pool of Siloam, (which is by interpretation, Sent.) He went his way therefore, and washed, and came seeing.
Acts 4:36 And Joses, who by the apostles was surnamed Barnabas, (which is, being interpreted, The son of consolation,) a Levite, and of the country of Cyprus,
Acts 9:36 ¶Now there was at Joppa a certain disciple named Tabitha, which by interpretation is called Dorcas: this woman was full of good works and almsdeeds which she did.
Acts 13:8 But Elymas the sorcerer (for so is his name by interpretation) withstood them, seeking to turn away the deputy from the faith.
Hebrews 7:1-2 For this Melchisedec, king of Salem, priest of the most high God, who met Abraham returning from the slaughter of the kings, and blessed him; To whom also Abraham gave a tenth part of all; first being by interpretation King of righteousness, and after that also King of Salem, which is, King of peace;
2 Peter 1:20 Knowing this first, that no prophecy of the scripture is of any private interpretation.

In each of the examples, the subject word is translated into a word in another language that has the same meaning. For example, in Hebrews 7:1-2, the name Melchisedec is interpreted. Melchisedec consists of two Hebrew words, Melek and Tsedek. Melek translates into *King* in English. Tsedek translates into *righteousness*. Since Melchisedec was a king, he was the king of Salem. Salem is a Hebrew word that translates to *peace*. Therefore, Melchisedec was the King of Peace and Righteousness. These translations are exactly correlated meanings between languages. Melchisedec was not a president or a governor. He was a Melek, a king. He was royal. That is what the word melek means and that is how it should be translated. Melchisedek was not a king of calm and good. He was King of peace and righteousness. The source words are words with specific meaning, so the target words must be specific words with matching meanings.

This type of translation is called *formal equivalent translation*. Sometimes, it is also called *word-for-word translating*. This kind of translating refers to a translation approach which attempts to retain the language forms of the original as much as possible in the translation. The Bible translation text must accurately translate all of the words of the source text into words of equivalent meaning in the clearest manner according to the grammar of the target language, and at the same time read and flow naturally as in the standard spoken target language. To accomplish this, the translator translates each **word** in the source language into a **word** with the **nearest equivalent** meaning in the target languages. **Grammar** in the target language should be translated into

grammar with the **nearest equivalent** meaning in the target language. Finally, **idioms** in the source language should be translated into **idioms** with the **nearest equivalent** meaning in the target language or be translated literally.

4.   **Word to the Nearest Equivalent Word:** Every word is important to God. Therefore, every word should be retained as much as possible, while also producing a target language translation that is grammatically accurate and has the same meaning. The usage and syntax of the target language must prevail. The target language translation must read clearly, smoothly, and naturally. When literal translating works well in the target language, its use should be primary.

Example: John 1:1

Greek John 1:1: εν αρχη ην ο λογος και ο λογος ην προς τον θεον και θεος ην ο λογος
Literal word-for word: In beginning was the word and the word was with the God and God was the word.
KJV John 1:1 In the beginning was the Word, and the Word was with God, and the Word was God.

The English and Greek are almost exact word-for-word translations. Notice that a definite article was inserted between "in" and "beginning" (εν αρχη). Notice also that a definite article was left out before the last "word" (λογος). These actions were necessary because of English grammar. Finally, word order was reversed in the last phrase. The final phrase contains a predicate nominative. The subject of the phrase has the article; therefore, it was placed first in the English translation.

5.   **Grammar to the Nearest Equivalent Grammar:** A grammatical structure in one language may require a different grammatical structure in another language to have the same meaning. Sometimes the same grammatical structure used in two languages cause a different meaning or creates an unnatural construction.

Example 1: John 1:1

The grammar in John 1:1 is the same in Greek and English with the changes mentioned above in the definite articles.

Example 2: Matthew 2:8

Matt. 2:8 Literal Translation from Greek: And **having sent** them to Bethlehem, he said, **When you have gone**, diligently search for the young child. And when you have found, bring word to me, that I also, **having come**, may worship him.

Matt. 2:8 KJV: And **he sent** them to Bethlehem, and said, **Go** and search diligently for the young child; and when ye have found him, bring me word again, **that I may come** and worship him also.

The Greek verse has three participles. To translate these with the same grammar in English is awkward, not good English. To produce a clear natural translation in English requires that the participles not be translated as participles. The first two were translated as English active verbs and the third was translated as an English subjunctive. The words used have the same meanings and the overall meaning of the verse is the same in Greek and English.

6.   **Idiom to the Nearest Equivalent Idioms:** Idioms are expressions that are of two types. The first type is how a language expresses ordinary everyday meaning or figurative language. For example, we may say, "What is your name?" However, Germans may say it differently, "How are you called?" The second type of idiom is such that the words used bear little relationship to the real meaning. For example, the meaning of *the cat is out of the bag* has nothing to do with cats or bags. It means *the secret is revealed*. Sometimes an idiom cannot be translated literally and retain its meaning. The goal should be to translate it in a way that makes it accurate and sound natural in the target language. The following are some general guidelines for translating idioms. For clarity, I will repeat some previous examples.

   1) Sometimes an Idiom is Translated by Modifying the Words or Grammar of the Source Language.

   Biblical Example: Matthew 1:23

   Mat 1:23 ιδου η παρθενος εν γαστρι εξει και τεξεται υιον...
   Literal Translation: Behold, the virgin in stomach shall have and shall produce a son...
   KJV Mat 1:23: Behold, a virgin shall be with child, and shall bring forth a son...

   The Greek idiom "in stomach" is translated in the KJV as "be with child." It means "to be pregnant."

   Biblical Example: Romans 3:4

   Rom 3:3-4 KJV For what if some did not believe? shall their unbelief make the faith of God without effect? **God forbid**
   Greek Rom. 3:4 μη γενοιτο

Literal Translation: May it not be! (the Greek does not use the word God. The KJV used an English idiom to translate the Greek idiom. The English idiom means the same as the Greek idiom.)
Meaning of English Expression: May it not be!

2) An idiom may be translated literally if the translator does not know the meaning of a particular idiom or when the literal translation is not seriously difficult to understand.

Biblical Example from the KJV: John 10:35

John 10:35 If he called them gods, unto whom the word of God came, and the scripture **cannot be broken** ...
"Cannot be broken" is a Jewish idiom that means "cannot be refuted." The phrase was often used by Jewish debaters to refer to any argument they believed to be irrefutable.

3) An idiom may be translated literally if it is explained in the Greater Context

Biblical Example: Philemon 1:7

Greek: χαρὰν γὰρ ἔχομεν πολλὴν καὶ παράκλησιν ἐπὶ τῇ ἀγάπῃ σου, ὅτι τὰ σπλάγχνα τῶν ἁγίων ἀναπέπαυται διὰ σοῦ, ἀδελφέ

Philemon 1:7 For we have great joy and consolation in thy love, because the **bowels** of the saints are refreshed by thee, brother.

The term "bowels" refers to the seat of the emotions and attitudes of a person. It is used in the sense we may use the word "heart." However, that is not clear from this verse.

It is clear, however, from Colossians 3:12

Colossians 3:12 Put on therefore, as the elect of God, holy and beloved, **bowels of** mercies, kindness, humbleness of mind, meekness, longsuffering;

4) An idiom may be translated literally by adding an explanation (even if that explanation is in the greater context)

Once again, the example is from Philemon 1:7

Philemon 1:7 For we have great joy and consolation in thy love, because the **bowels** of the saints are refreshed by thee, brother.

The added explanation is found in 1 John 3:17

Greek: ὅς δ' ἂν ἔχῃ τὸν βίον τοῦ κόσμου, καὶ θεωρῇ τὸν ἀδελφὸν αὐτοῦ χρείαν ἔχοντα, καὶ κλείσῃ τὰ σπλάγχνα αὐτοῦ ἀπ' αὐτοῦ, πῶς ἡ ἀγάπη τοῦ Θεοῦ μένει ἐν αὐτῷ;

1 John 3:17 But whoso hath this world's good, and seeth his brother have need, and shutteth up his **bowels *of compassion*** from him, how dwelleth the love of God in him?

The words "of compassion" are in italics in the KJV showing that they are not in the Greek text but were added by the translators to increase understanding.

5) Idioms are difficult.

Sometimes, it is especially difficult to translate idioms. Normally, an idiom has a specific and clear meaning. Sometimes they can have more than one meaning. It can be difficult to determine whether to translate an idiom literally or according to its meaning. Translate idioms with much prayer and study.

6) A Warning!

Idiomatic translating can become a trap. Some translators use an idiomatic translating style in all or most of the Scriptures. The meaning of any phrase, sentence, or verse becomes dependent on the understanding and, sometimes, the bias of the translator. This is the condition of the translation method known as *Dynamic Equivalence*. It leads toward paraphrase, that is the Scriptures are translated into the words of the translator. The *Message* translates "I charge you by the Lord that this epistle be read unto all the holy brethren" (KJV-1 Thess. 5:27) as "And make sure this letter gets read to all the brothers and sisters. Don't leave anyone out" (The Message-1 Th. 5:27). *This is NOT acceptable translating!*

The meaning of Scripture is set in the mind of God. The words God chose matter, and the translator must be faithful to render those words as closely and accurately as possible into the target language. True idioms normally have a *specific meaning*, not in any way dependent on the imagination of a translator. Idiomatic translating should be done *rarely*. The words of Scripture should only be translated idiomatically when it is *necessary* and when the translator *knows* the specific meaning of the idiom. God has called you to translate what is in the text, not your personal interpretation of what is in the text (2 Peter 1:20).

7. **Figures of Speech:** A type of idiom that uses words in a non-literal or unusual sense to express a specific meaning is a *figure of speech*. An example of this would be to say, "all the trees of the field shall clap their hands" (Is. 55:12). The trees do not have hands and do not clap, but the waving of the trees in a sudden strong breeze during a significant event may be characterized this way. Nevertheless, when God expresses it as the trees clapping of their hands, it should be translated as God said it.

1) **Biblical Examples**:

John 1:1 Behold the Lamb of God, which taketh away the sin of the world.
Lamb is a figure of speech, since Jesus was not literally a lamb. It expressed the fact that he became a sacrifice for our sins.

Matthew 11:18 For John came neither eating nor drinking, and they say, He hath a devil.
Of course, this verse does *not* say that John *never* ate or drank. It is a figurative way of pointing out the hypocrisy of the audience.

Mark 8:15 ... Take heed, beware of the leaven of the Pharisees, and of the leaven of Herod.
The word *leaven,* ζύμης, is used figuratively to refer to doctrine. However, translate the word ζύμης as *leaven*, not *doctrine*.

Luke 1:66 ... And the hand of the Lord was with him.
The phrase "hand of the Lord" stands in place of the Person who was with him, the Lord. Translate it literally.

Luke 13:32 And he said unto them, Go ye, and tell that fox,
The figure of speech is *fox*, referring to Herod, since the fox is a crafty animal. However, the word is fox, ἀλώπεκι, should be translated *fox*.

John 6:53 Then Jesus said unto them, Verily, verily, I say unto you, Except ye eat the flesh of the Son of man, and drink his blood, ye have no life in you.
Flesh and *blood* are used in a figurative sense here, but translate them literally.

John 10:9 I am the door
Jesus is not a literal physical door. the meaning is spiritual. However, the translation should say *door*.

Acts 4:30 By stretching forth thine hand to heal

This substitutes one thing for another. *Hand* is used in the place of the power of God. *Hand* is the word God chose, so it should be translated into the target language as *hand*.

Acts 13:36 For David, after he had served his own generation by the will of God, fell on sleep, and was laid unto his fathers, and saw corruption:
Death is called sleep and should be translated so.

Romans 8:22 For we know that the whole creation groaneth and travaileth in pain together until now.
In this verse, Paul attributes the human characteristics of childbirth to something that is not human. It should be translated literally.

Galatians 2:9 ... that we should go unto the heathen, and they unto the circumcision.
Circumcision is a real act, but here it is used figuratively to refer to the Jews. This is God's use of figurative language and, so, must be retained.

1 Corinthians 15:55 O death, where is thy sting? O grave, where is thy victory?
Here Paul is speaking to something that is not alive as though it was. it should be translated literally.

2 Corinthians 12:13 For what is it wherein ye were inferior to other churches, except it be that I myself was not burdensome to you? forgive me this wrong.
Paul was not admitting he was wrong. He was emphasizing how foolish their attitude was. It should be translated the same.

1 Timothy 4:8 For bodily exercise profiteth little: but godliness is profitable unto all things ...
This lowers one especially important thing (exercise) to emphasize something even more important (Godliness). It is a communication device that should be translated literally.

2) **Some of the Figures of Speech You Will Encounter:** [91]

Similes and Metaphors: These two figures of speech are used to compare two things. A simile clearly states what is being compared by using such *words* as like or *as*. A metaphor does not clearly state this (John 6:53 and 10:9 and Mark 8:15 above, also see 1 Peter 1:24; 1 Corinthians 3:1).

Euphemism: This is a less offensive word substituted for a more offensive word (see Acts 13:36 above and Luke 2:15; 7:37; Matthew 22:13; Acts 1:25; Acts 22:22).

Hyperbole: A hyperbole is an obvious and deliberate exaggeration (see Matthew 11:18 above and Mark 1:5; Luke 15:24; John 12:19; John 21:25; Acts 17:6; 1 Corinthians 1:17).

Litotes: A figure of speech consisting of an understatement in which an affirmative is expressed by negating its opposite, as in *This is no small problem* [92] (see 1 Timothy 4:8 above and Luke 17:9; Acts 20:12; Acts 21:39).

Metonymy: In a metonymy, an attribute of a thing is used to stand for the thing itself or a word is used to stand for something else, thereby describing the thing (see Acts 4:30 above and James 3:6; Mark 8:34; Acts 7:18; Acts 21:21).

Synecdoche: This is a figure of speech in which a part of something is used to describe the whole (see Luke 1:66 above and Matthew 15:37; Matthew 8:8; Romans 3:15; Mark 1:11).

Irony: Irony is to say one thing but mean the opposite (see 2 Corinthians 12:13 above and Mark 7:9; 2 Corinthians 11:4).

Apostrophe: This is a figure of speech in which the speaker is addressing something that is not present, is imaginary, or is spoken to something that is not alive (see 1 Corinthians 15:55 above and Matthew 2:6; Luke 13:34).

Personifications: A personification is when one speaks to something non-human as if it is human (see Romans 8:22 above and Revelation 11:8; 16:20; 20:14).

Chiasmus: A chiasmus is a series of related phrases or statements that are arranged in an order that emphasizes the relationship, rather than in logical or chronological sequence. The following example helps explain this.

> **Matthew 7:6** Give not that which is holy unto the dogs, neither cast ye your pearls before swine, lest they trample them under their feet, and turn again and rend you.

> The first two phrases are the first part that emphasize swine and dogs and the two phrases of the second part show the relationship. The third and fourth phrase could relate to both

the swine and dogs or each phrase could relate to one of the two. They are not arranged in logical order, but according to which one the author wants to emphasize. The dogs (A) come before the swine (B) in the first part. However, in the second part the relationship with the swine (B) comes first ("trample them under their feet"), followed by the relationship of the dogs (A) (rend you). It is arranged in an ABBA order. Dr. Turner give this paraphrase if you remove the chiasmus. "Do not give dogs what is holy, lest they turn and bite you, and do not throw your pearls before swine, lest they trample them under foot."

You should also notice that there is an ambiguity in this verse. Both dogs and swine may trample the pearls and the holy. Both dogs and pigs (which were probably wild boars) can tear (rend) you.

3) **How to Translate Figures of Speech:**

(1) The first choice is always to translate literally, no matter what kind of figure of speech it is. It will be the responsibility of teachers to make the people understand the meaning of the figurative language. "So they read in the book in the law of God distinctly, and gave the sense, and caused them to understand the reading" (Nehemiah 8:8).

(2) A figure of speech that is firmly rooted in the historical context of the Bible *must* be translated literally. This is the case with "lamb of God." It was these animals that were prescribed to be sacrificed for sin in the Old Testament. A translator can never translate this as some other animal familiar to the people who speak the target language. In the New Tribes film, Ee-Taow, the missionary to Papua New Guinea used a stuffed lamb to show the nationals what a lamb is.

(3) If the meaning of a figure of speech is tied to a major doctrine, the translator *must* translate literally.

8. **Shifts in Verb Tense (Verse 41):** There is a difference in verb tense in both the KJV and the Greek text. In verse 41, The present tense is used in the words "findeth" and "saith." This is followed in verse 42 with the past tense "brought" and then by another past tense, "said." This shift in verb tense is typical in the gospel of John and elsewhere in the NT. The inconsistency was acceptable in Greek (such as the historical present) and in the Early Modern

English of 1611. However, it is not always acceptable in other languages. If the KJV had been translated into current Modern English, the tense would have to be more consistent, especially in the narrative of a historical occurrence or story. Writers sometimes employ tense shifts for certain purposes, but the general rule in current English is: "Do not shift from one tense to another if the time frame for each action or state is the same." [93] This rule has *not* been presented here to encourage the student to translate a new version in English. The point is that any translation into any language must be careful about the grammatical rules of the target language.

9. **The Word *Would* (Verse 43):** The translation of the word, ἠθέλησεν in verse 43, aorist active indicative of θέλω, is *would*. The Greek word θέλω means *to will, desire, wish, etc.* [94] The English definition of the word *would* includes *intent, desire, wish.*[95] Therefore, *would* in the context of verse 43 expresses a desire and an intent. Jesus wished to go to Galilee and, therefore, intended to do just that.

10. **New Exercises.**

   Translate and Parse John 1:46-51

CHAPTER THIRTY-FIVE
REVIEW OF JOHN 1:46-51

Adding To or Taking Away From Scripture; Ambiguities; Cultural Substitutes; Anachronisms; Role of Teachers

1. Vocabulary

Word	Meaning	Word	Meaning
ἅπας, α, αν, adj.	all	ἐπιγινώσκω	come to know
βαστάζω	bear, carry	εὐλογέω	bless
βασιλεύω	reign	θηρίον, τό	wild beast
βάπτισμα, τό	baptism	θλῖψις,-εως, ἡ	tribulation
βλασφημυέω	blaspheme, revile	κατοικέω	inhabit, dwell
βούλομαι	wish, will, intend	ναός, ὁ	temple
βρῶμα, τό	meat, food	ὅμοιος, α, ον	like
γενεά, ἡ	generation	σπέρμα, -ατος,τό	seed
δέω	bind	σταυρόω	crucify
ἐγγίζω	come near	τιμή, ῆς, ἡ	honor, price

2. Review of John 1:46-51

46 καὶ	εἶπεν	αὐτῷ	Ναθαναήλ, Ἐκ	Ναζαρὲθ δύναταί τι		ἀγαθὸν
CONJ	V-2AAI-3S	P-DSM	N-PRI	PREP N-PRI	V-PNI-3S I-NSN	A-NSN
And	said	to him	Nathaniel, Out of	Nazareth can	anything	good
εἶναι;	λέγει	αὐτῷ	Φίλιππος,	Ἔρχου	καὶ	ἴδε.
V-PAN	V-PAI-3S	P-DSM	N-NSM	V-PNM-2S	CONJ	V-AAM-2S
be?	Says	to him	Philip,	Come	and	see.

Example Translation: And Nathaniel said to him, Can anything good come out of Nazareth? Philip said to him, Come and see.

KJV: And Nathanael said unto him, Can there any good thing come out of Nazareth? Philip saith unto him, Come and see.

47 εἶδεν	ὁ		Ἰησοῦς τὸν	Ναθαναὴλ ἐρχόμενον πρὸς αὐτόν, καὶ			
V-2AAI-3S	T-NSM		N-NSM T-ASM	N-PRI	V-PNP-ASM PREP P-ASM CONJ		
saw	the		Jesus the	Nathaniel	coming	to	him and
λέγει	περὶ	αὐτοῦ, Ἴδε		ἀληθῶς Ἰσραηλίτης, ἐν	ᾧ		δόλος
V-PAI-3S	PREP	P-GSM V-AAM-2S	ADV	N-NSM		PREP R-DSM	N-NSM
says	to	him Behold	truly	Israelite		in whom	guile
οὐκ	ἔστι.						
PRT-N	V-PAI-3S						

292

not/no	is

Example Translation: Jesus saw Nathaniel coming to Him and said to him, Behold! Truly an Israelite in whom is no guile!

KJV: Jesus saw Nathanael coming to him, and saith of him, Behold an Israelite indeed, in whom is no guile!

48 λέγει	αὐτῷ	Ναθαναήλ,	Πόθεν		με	γινώσκεις;	ἀπεκρίθη
V-PAI-3S	P-DSM	N-PRI	ADV		P-1AS	V-PAI-2S	V-ADI-3S
says	to him	Nathaniel,	From where		me	you know?	Answered
ὁ	Ἰησοῦς	καὶ	εἶπεν	αὐτῷ,	Πρὸ τοῦ	σε	Φίλιππον φωνῆσαι,
T-NSM	N-NSM	CONJ	V-2AAI-3S	P-DSM	PREP T-GSM	P-2AS	N-ASM V-AAN
the	Jesus	and	said	to him,	before the	you	Philip called
ὄντα	ὑπὸ	τὴν	συκῆν,	εἶδόν	σε.		
V-PAP-ASM	PREP	T-ASF	N-ASF	V-2AAI-1S	P-2AS		
being	under	the	fig tree	I saw	you.		

Example Translation: Nathaniel said to Him, From where do you know me? Jesus answered and said to him, Before Philip called you, when you were under the fig tree, I saw you.

KJV: Nathanael saith unto him, Whence knowest thou me? Jesus answered and said unto him, Before that Philip called thee, when thou wast under the fig tree, I saw thee.

49 ἀπεκρίθη	Ναθαναήλ	καὶ	λέγει	αὐτῷ,	Ῥαββί,	σὺ	εἶ	ὁ
V-ADI-3S	N-PRI	CONJ	V-PAI-3S	P-DSM	HEB	P-2NS	V-PAI-2S	T-NSM
Answered	Nathaniel	and	says	to him,	Rabbi,	You	are	the
υἱὸς	τοῦ	Θεοῦ,	σὺ	εἶ	ὁ	βασιλεὺς	τοῦ	Ἰσραήλ.
N-NSM	T-GSM	N-GSM	P-2NS	V-PAI-2S	T-NSM	N-NSM	T-GSM	N-PRI
Son	of the	God.	You	are	the	King	of the	Israel.

Example Translation: Nathaniel answered and said to Him, Rabbi, you are the Son of God. You are the King of Israel.

KJV: Nathanael answered and saith unto him, Rabbi, thou art the Son of God; thou art the King of Israel.

50 ἀπεκρίθη Ἰησοῦς καὶ	εἶπεν	αὐτῷ, Ὅτι	εἶπόν	σοι,	εἶδόν
V-ADI-3S N-NSM CONJ	V-2AAI-3S	P-DSM CONJ	V-2AAI-1S	P-2DS	V-2AAI-1S
Answered Jesus and	said	to him, that	I said	to you	I saw
σε ὑποκάτω τῆς συκῆς, πιστεύεις; μείζω				τούτων	ὄψει.
P-2AS ADV T-GSF N-GSF V-PAI-2S A-APN				D-GPN	V-FDI-2S
you under the fig tree you believe greater things				than these	you will see

Example Translation: Jesus answered and said to him, Do you believe, because I said I saw you under the fig tree? You will see greater things than these.

KJV: Jesus answered and said unto him, Because I said unto thee, I saw thee under the fig tree, believest thou? thou shalt see greater things than these.

51 καὶ	λέγει	αὐτῷ,	Ἀμὴν	ἀμὴν	λέγω	ὑμῖν,	ἀπ'	ἄρτι	ὄψεσθε
CONJ	V-PAI-3S	P-DSM	HEB	HEB	V-PAI-1S	P-2DP	PREP	ADV	V-FDI-2P
And	he says	to him	Amen	Amen	I say	to you,	after	this	you will see
τὸν	οὐρανὸν ἀνεῳγότα,	καὶ	τοὺς	ἀγγέλους	τοῦ			Θεοῦ	
T-ASM	N-ASM V-2RAP-ASM	CONJ	T-APM	N-APM	T-GSM			N-GSM	
the	heaven opened	and	the	angels	of the			God	
ἀναβαίνοντας καὶ	καταβαίνοντας	ἐπὶ	τὸν	υἱὸν	τοῦ			ἀνθρώπου.	
V-PAP-APM	CONJ V-PAP-APM	PREP	T-ASM	N-ASM	T-GSM			N-GSM	
ascending	and descending	upon	the	son	of the			man.	

Example Translation: And, He said to him, Truly, truly, I say to you, after this you will see heaven opened and the angels of God ascending and descending upon the Son of Man.

KJV: And he saith unto him, Verily, verily, I say unto you, Hereafter ye shall see heaven open, and the angels of God ascending and descending upon the Son of man.

Pointers for Translating

3.   **Adding To or Taking Away from Scripture:** The fear of taking away from Scripture or adding to it is a natural and healthy fear for a translator.

> Revelation 22:18, 19 For I testify unto every man that heareth the words of the prophecy of this book, If any man shall add unto these things, God shall add unto him the plagues that are written in this book: And if any man shall take away from the words of the book of this prophecy, God shall take away his

part out of the book of life, and out of the holy city, and from the things which are written in this book.

In several of the lessons we have talked about adding words to make the translation clear, to meet the needs of the target language grammar, or to include implied information. We have also found that definite articles need to be left out or added at times. It should also be clear by now that one word in the source language may require two or more words in the target language. The opposite is also true. Two or more words in the source language may be translated by only one word in the target language. Are these things in violation of Revelation 22:18-19?

The actions listed above do not violate the prohibitions of Revelation 22, because the grammar and syntax of the languages involved require them. No two languages can be translated exactly literally. So, if words must be added they should be printed in italics, or some other convention used to let people know they are not in the original Scriptures. Minor word omissions like direct articles are also necessary for the same reasons. God made languages and these matters are God-made characteristics of languages.

When does a translator take away from the words of God?

1) A translator takes away from God's words when he fails to translate source language words that are necessary to convey the meaning of the Biblical text.

2) A translator takes away from the words of God when he translates the words of Scripture with target language words that inadequately communicate the meaning. In other words, he uses the wrong target language words. However, note this. When a translator does his best, the review and checking process may find better words. So, when a translator prayerfully studies to determine the best word, he is doing well.

3) A translator may be taking away from God's word when he ignores how the words he has used and the grammar he has employed are understood by the native speakers. If he uses target language words that are not the usual words that convey the Biblical meaning and if he does not use grammar that is natural and appropriate to the meaning, he will likely take away from the word of God.

4) A translator can take away from God's word when he creates a confusing translation. Examples of poor translation have often come to light. In an airport in India, a sign boldly proclaimed, "Eating carpet

strictly prohibited." In an Arab country, a marketplace was selling "Syrian Paralysis Cheese." In Asia, a handicap pathway was marked, "Deformed Man Passage." This is one of the reasons that a translation must go through a rigorous checking process with native speakers of the language. The translator's job is to do all he can to avoid confusion.

5) A scholar might be taking away from the word of God by producing or promoting a Greek text that removes words from the Textus Receptus.

When does a translator add to the Word of God?

1) A translator *can* add to the Words of God by adding words that are not warranted by the source text, whether those words change the meaning or not. However, this is not *necessarily* adding to the Scriptures. Sometimes added words of explanation are necessary on rare occasions, as we have seen.

2) A translator can add to the Words of God by adding words that change the meaning of the source text.

3) A translator could add to the Word by adding words that reflect his own bias or translating according to his own ideas or private interpretation of Scripture. In this way the meaning of the source text can be twisted according to personal interpretation. Some of the KJV translators were Calvinists and some were Arminians. Nevertheless, they all translated honestly, letting the Scriptures speak for themselves.

4) A translator can add to the Word of God if he tries to translate in such a way that explains the meaning of Scripture. The translator is not writing a commentary. He is translating what God said. Commentaries and explanations are the job of teachers, not translators.

5) A scholar can add to the word of God by producing or promoting a Greek text that adds to the words of the Textus Receptus.

There are four things a translator needs if he is to do an accurate job.

1) The translator must understand the meaning of the source language words as well as he can.

2) The translator must know what words in the target language convey the same meaning as the words in the source language and how to use

target language grammar and syntax to precisely convey the Biblical meaning.

3) The translator must choose the target language words that are closest in meaning to the biblical words and arrange them in a final translation, translating as literally as possible.

4) That translation must convey to the target language speakers and readers the exact same meaning that is in the source language.

Being a Bible translator is an extremely serious thing. So, care must be taken not to add to or take from God's Word. In *Biblical Bible Translating*, Charles Turner has some encouragement to give translators.

> What is a translator to do then? Many missionaries have faced this dilemma, and rather than taking the risk of adding to or taking away from the Bible, they do not translate any Scripture at all. These missionaries take away more of God's Word from the people than anyone else! They do not give them any portion of God's Word ... A translator who has done his best to study the meaning of the Bible and learn the native language and culture will not be adding to Scripture or taking away from it. [96]

4. **Ambiguities:** Ambiguity means "the possibility of interpreting an expression in two or more distinct ways" [97] The Scriptures contain several ambiguities. Below are some examples offered by Dr. Turner.

> 1) Matthew 9:13 *But go ye and learn what that meaneth, I will have mercy, and not sacrifice: for I am not come to call the righteous, but sinners to repentance.*

Does this mean that God wants us to show mercy or that God would rather give us mercy than to have us come to Him through sacrifices?

> 2) Romans 6:3 *Know ye not, that so many of us as were baptized into Jesus Christ were baptized into his death?*

Does this mean water baptism or the Baptism of the Spirit? Arguments have been made both ways. Paul did not specify which it was.

> 3) 2 Corinthians 5:14 *For the love of Christ constraineth us; because we thus judge, that if one died for all, then were all dead:*

Does this mean the love Christ has for us or the love we have for Christ?

4) Ephesians 5:25 *Husbands, love your wives, even as Christ also loved the church, and gave himself for it;*

Does the word *church* mean the local church or all Christians as a whole?

These are not ambiguities because of the meaning of the Greek words. They are ambiguities in interpretation. Nevertheless, they can affect the translation. The translator may be tempted to add explanatory words, such as the word *water* or the word *spirit* in Romans 6:3. However, it should not be done. If God inspired a portion of the Scriptures so that the interpretation was ambiguous, it is because He wanted it that way. Therefore, the translator should allow the ambiguity to remain, if it is possible given the grammar and structure of the target language. The same advice given previously about implied information also applies with this subject. Also, do not add words to clear up ambiguities when those words are based on nothing more than the interpretation of the translators.

In some cases, a literal translation will create an ambiguity in the target language. Beekman and Callow in their book, *Translating the Word of God*, gives us the following example of that difficulty. [98]

Mark 10:38 *can ye drink of the cup that I drink of?*

In one culture of West Africa, this statement is what a drunkard says to his fellows to challenge them to drink as much and as strong liquor as he does. The translator may determine that this question must be translated idiomatically. A translator should translate as literally as possible, but in some cases, he may find that he has no choice except to translate idiomatically (see Matthew 1:23 for reference). One solution to this problem might be to add information that is implied by the verse: "can you drink of the cup *of suffering* that I drink of?" However, "this would be adding to the text something not necessary for understanding. The responsibility falls on the reader to study, not the translator to clarify." [99] The phrase can also be clarified by teaching.

5. **Cultural Substitutes:** A cultural substitute is an item in one culture that is substituted for an item in another culture, when both have the same *function*. Both items do not necessarily have the same meaning. An extreme, example is to substitute *pig* for *lamb* in Papua New Guinea for a tribe which knows nothing about lambs. There are other examples of more minor items, however. A few Examples of items that could potentially give rise to cultural substitutes are below.

1) The following examples are some places that may tempt one to do a cultural substitute: [100]

> Example 1: Luke 11:11 If a son shall ask bread of any of you that is a father, will he give him a stone? or if he ask a fish, will he for a fish give him a serpent?

It has been suggested that in some cultures one might wish to do a cultural substitute for the serpent, because in some areas of the world snake flesh is considered more delicious than fish flesh. Therefore, the people would say that the father would give the son a snake, even though he asked for a fish. For this reason, the translator should substitute some equivalent item for the serpent; something undesirable to the people of the target culture. However, this allows the culture to determine what you make God say in the translation, it misses the point of the lesson, and it ignores the first question. In the first question, the answer is obviously that the father would give the son what he asks for. That he would be certain not to give the son a stone would be obvious in any culture. So, the second question would be answered the same way. The father would give the Son what he asks for. That is the main point to the lesson. God listens to and answers our requests.

Example 2: Luke 18:13 And the publican, standing afar off, would not lift up so much as his eyes unto heaven, but smote upon his breast, saying, God be merciful to me a sinner.

In some cultures, beating the breast indicates anger or a show of strength. Therefore, some suggest that we substitute an act in the target culture that signifies repentance. That would help the target people to easily see the meaning of the act. However, the act is explained in the verse itself. When the publican says, "God be merciful to me a sinner," the act of beating the breast can be understood to express repentance.

Example 3: Acts 14:14 Which when the apostles, Barnabas and Paul, heard of, they rent their clothes, and ran in among the people, crying out,

In some cultures, this would seem extremely strange, because the target people would never consider tearing their clothes. Clothing is much too expensive to tear. Yet, we understand the significance of tearing the clothing in first century Jewish culture. Also, historically rending the clothing in distress goes all the way back to Genesis 37:29. All of this can be understood by reading and study and teaching.

2) The KJV does occasionally employ cultural substitutes, mainly in matters of weights, measures, and money. Some examples of that are listed below.

John 2:6 And there were set there six waterpots of stone, after the manner of the purifying of the Jews, containing **two or three firkins** apiece.

The Greek word translated firkin is μετρητής. This is the only place in the New Testament it is used. The Greek, μετρητής, contains about 8 3/8 gallons. It was translated into the closest British measure available. The firkin is a real British liquid measure containing 9 English gallons according to the Webster 1828 and Collins English dictionaries. On the other hand, Martin Luther translated it with a German word, *Maß*, which simply means *measure*.

John 6:19 So when they had rowed about **five and twenty or thirty furlongs**, they see Jesus walking on the sea, and drawing nigh unto the ship: and they were afraid.

The Greek word translated **furlong** is στάδιον. It is a Greek measure of length that is 600 Greek feet, but that measurement varied over time and by location. The Roman Stadion was 625 Roman feet or 606.9 English feet or 185 meters. There is a good chance the Roman measure is in view here, since it was a Roman controlled world. So, once again, the KJV translation is the nearest British measure to the Greek or Roman stadion, the furlong. The English Furlong is 660 feet, 220 yards, and 201 meters.

Matthew 20:2 And when he had agreed with the labourers for a **penny** a day, he sent them into his vineyard.

A penny is the Roman δηνάριον, equivalent to the Greek Drachma. It is translated penny and pence. There is not any real equivalence between the denarius and the English penny. However, the denarius was the standard gold coin of the Roman Empire in the first century, just as the penny is the basic coin of the English and American monetary systems.

Matthew 5:26 Verily I say unto thee, Thou shalt by no means come out thence, till thou hast paid the uttermost **farthing**.

A farthing is the translation of two Greek words ἀσσάριον (Matthew 10:29; Luke 12:6) and κοδράντης (Matthew 5:26; Mark 12:42). The first is the Roman coin As, valued at 1/10 of a denarius or 1.5 cents. The second is the Roman coin quadrans, valued at 1/4 of the As or about .375 cents. According to the 1828 Webster dictionary, a farthing was ¼ of an English penny. None of these are an exact match, but each of the Roman coins is a fraction of the denarius and in that way match the farthing, which is a fraction of the penny.

Mark 12:42 And there came a certain poor widow, and she threw in two **mites**, which make a farthing.

Mite is a translation of the Greek word λεπτόν, the smallest Roman copper coin. Two leptons make a Quadrans. Therefore, a lepton is equal to about 0.1875 cents. A mite is something that is very small or tiny. The lepton is the smallest Roman coin, so the word mite is an apt description of it. In addition, the mite was also a coin in 1611 and apparently dated back to the time of Chaucer. It was the smallest copper coin, so it matches the lepton in that way also.

Luke 19:13 And he called his ten servants, and delivered them ten **pounds**, and said unto them, Occupy till I come.

This is a money measure. The Greek word μνᾶ (pound) refers to a silver coin that consists of one hundred δραχμή and is 1/60 of a talent. Its weight was 12 ounces. The closest functional match was the British Pound, which was equal to 240 pence. Now, the Pound is worth 100 pence.

John 19:39 And there came also Nicodemus, which at the first came to Jesus by night, and brought a mixture of myrrh and aloes, about an hundred **pound** weight.

This pound is a measure of weight. The Greek word is λίτρα. The Roman pound was about twelve ounces, a close match to the British pound (16 ounces).

3) How to translate cultural substitutions:

(1) Avoid cultural substitutions if it is possible. Most substitutions are not true translating. They are an accommodation to the target

culture. They also deny the effectiveness of the teaching ministry, which is designed to clear up the confusion that cultural differences can cause. After all, the Scriptures are primarily written for the edification and training of believers, not evangelism. Cultural substitutions also downplay the ability of believers in every culture to understand that the Scriptures describe a culture different from their own. There are many cultural items in the Bible that are foreign to current western culture, but they can be understood with study and teaching.

(2) Regarding the terms referring to money, length, and weight above, there are no terms in English that are an exact translation. The same is true for many other languages. The translator's choices are limited to 1) choose a term in the target language that has the same or a similar function, or 2) transliterate the Greek words, that is, put the Greek names into target language letters. For example, this would make a translation use lepton, denarius, assarion, quadrans, etc.

(3) When a term is imbedded in the historical context of the Bible or history, leave it alone. When a term is necessary for doctrinal truth, leave it alone. No substitute is acceptable in these cases.

(4) It is important that readers of the Bible recognize the Bible is embedded in the Jewish and Graeco-Roman cultures of the day. It is important to understand that Christianity arose out of Judaism. To preserve this important connection a translation must remain faithful to that culture. Doing this will not compromise truth and the doctrinal truth of the Bible will still be clear.

(5) The conclusion is that any cultural substitution should be rare and only be done in extreme circumstances. The goal of the translator should be to refrain from cultural substitutions.

6. **Anachronisms:** An anachronism is something that is outside its proper time. That is, it is when something that did not exist in Biblical times is introduced into the Bible text. As a general rule, this should be avoided. Three examples of what this means and what should be avoided are below.[101]

> **Luke 12:3** Therefore whatsoever ye have spoken in darkness shall be heard in the light; and that which ye have spoken in the ear in closets shall be proclaimed upon the housetops.

"Proclaimed upon the housetops" should not be translated as "announced on the radio." There were no radios in the first century.

Acts 2:25 For David speaketh concerning him, I foresaw the Lord always before my face, for he is on my right hand, that I should not be moved:

"I foresaw the Lord always before my face" should not be translated "I foresaw the Lord *Jesus* before my face." The statement is a quote from the Old Testament. The name *Jesus*, referring to the Lord, had not been clearly revealed in the Old Testament, so should not be included in a quote from the OT.

Revelation 12:14 And to the woman were given two wings of a great eagle, that she might fly into the wilderness, into her place, where she is nourished for a time, and times, and half a time, from the face of the serpent.

"Two wings of a great eagle" should not be translated "airplane."

7. **The Role of the Teacher:** While it is important for a translator to know and understand as much of the Scriptures as he can, he is not to turn his translation into a running commentary. It is not the job of a translator to teach through his translation. It is his job to understand the words of God and then transfer those words into a new language as carefully and accurately as he can; no more and no less. If the translator goes beyond this, he may be injecting something into the Word that should not be there, or he may be hiding a profound truth from God's people.

God is a God of great wisdom. "O the depth of the riches both of the wisdom and knowledge of God! how unsearchable are his judgments, and his ways past finding out!" (Rom. 11:33). It is impossible for a translator to bring out all the many applications of God's wisdom. That is why he needs to stick to God's Words and not to change them. God has inspired the words that can bring out all the wisdom that He wants mankind to know. God is unlimited. He has unlimited depth in His understanding and wisdom and He has embedded that kind of depth into His Word. No man, be he translator or teacher, can reach the bottom of God's wisdom, knowledge, and understanding.

It is the calling of teachers, not translators, to explain God's Words. *"For Ezra had prepared his heart to seek the law of the LORD, and to do it, and to teach in Israel statutes and judgments"* (Ezra 7:10). *"And Ezra opened the book in the sight of all the people ... So they read in the book in the law of God distinctly, and gave the sense, and caused them to understand the reading"* (Neh. 8:4, 8).

THE TRANSLATOR'S GRAMMAR OF THE TEXTUS RECEPTUS

Is there anything hard to understand in the Book of God? Then translate the words and leave it hard to understand. God will give the teacher the ability to "give the sense."

CHAPTER THIRTY-SIX
SUMMARY OF GREEK GRAMMAR

Word Order:

Normal word order in Greek is subject-verb-object, the same as English. However, the grammatical structure of a sentence is created by case designations placed on the end of words. This is called *inflection*. Because of this, Greek word order is much more flexible than English and can be changed depending on what the writer wants to emphasize. For example, a normal sentence in Greek may read *the apostle speaks a word*. However, it would also be correct to read *A word the apostle speaks* or *speaks a word the apostle*. If this is done it is because the writer is emphasizing a different thing each time. Subjects, verbs, and objects are easily known by the endings on each word.

The Article:

There is no indefinite article, a or an. The definite article is ο (masculine), η (feminine), and το (neuter). They take case, gender, and number.

Noun:

As in English, a Greek noun is a word that names a person, place, thing, or idea. Greek nouns have case, gender, and number (either singular or plural.)

Case:

There are five cases in Greek.

> **Nominative Case:** The subject of a sentence or a predicate nominative.
> **Genitive:** The case of possession. As such, it is often translated as a prepositional phrase starting with "of." However, it also has several other uses.
> **Dative:** The case of the indirect object and is often translated as a prepositional phrase starting with "to." The dative also has several other uses.
> **Accusative:** This is the case of the direct object.
> **Vocative:** This is the case of commands or direct address.

Gender:

There are three genders in Greek: masculine, feminine, and neuter.

Number:

There are two numbers: singular and plural.

Declensions:

Greek has several different methods for constructing these cases. They are called "declensions."

Verbs:

A Greek verb shows action or a state of being, just as in English.

All Greek verbs have:

1) **tense** (present, imperfect, aorist, perfect, pluperfect, Future),
2) **voice** (active, middle, or passive),
3) **mood** (indicative, subjunctive, optative, imperative),
4) **person**, and
5) **number**.

All of these are indicated by various suffixes and prefixes on the verb. For example, in the verb form *Present Active Indicative* the following are the forms (that is the conjugation) for the verb λυω, *I loose*:

Singular: λυω (I loose), λυεις (you loose), λυει (he, she, or it looses).

Plural: λυομεν (we loose), λυετε (you loose), and λυουσι (they loose).

The part of the verb that stays the same (λυ-) is called the *stem*.

Tense:

Tense in English has to do with the time of action, whether past time, present time, or future time. Greek tense has to do with the same, but more important in Greek than time is *aspect*, or the *kind of action*. There are two major kinds of action: completed action and continuous action. This can increase the difficulties of translation. The Greek present tense usually takes place in present time, but in other tenses the kind of action is more important than time. Translators must consider context when translating tense.

Present Tense:

In most cases, the present tense speaks of present time. The kind of action can be *either* completed, pointed action, *or* it can be continuous, progressive, or repeated action. In this respect, it is very much like English present tense. The translator must be careful not to over emphasize the possibility of continuous action, as some do. In some languages, such as English, present tense is not normally expressed as progressive action, but simply as present time action, whether progressive or a one-time event. Sometimes the present represents action attempted, but not accomplished. It may express customary actions or general truths. It may express a past event in which a speaker pictures himself taking part. Other times it describes a future action (see Mark 9:31). For example, the present tense (in the active voice and indicative mood-see below) can be translated *I am going* or *I go*.

Imperfect Tense:

Basically, the imperfect tense expresses continuous, customary, or repeated action in past time, as in *I was going*. However, it cannot always be expressed as continuous in English. Often, there is no way to translate it as continuous action and must be translated as a simple past tense, *I went*.

Aorist Tense:

The aorist tense is simple pointed action in past time. However, it does not *always* mean past time, but it always means a single pointed event. That is the most basic emphasis of this tense. It does not look at the result of the action or whether it continues or not. It simply focuses on the event or action itself. There are two different ways to form the aorist tense called the first aorist and the second aorist. They are the same tense. They are merely two different ways to form the same tense. The aorist tense should be translated *I went* or *I had gone*.

Perfect Tense:

There is no English equivalent to the Greek perfect tense. The Greek perfect tense refers to an action that was performed and completed in the past, but it still has present effects. In Galatians 2:20, the KJV translates a Greek perfect into English present tense, "I am crucified with Christ," indicating *I was crucified in the past and am now dead to sin* (see Romans 6 for the explanation). A Greek perfect can be translated into the present or past tenses in English. If I say, "I am alive," it means I was born in the past and I'm still alive. If I say, "The bed is made," it means that someone made the bed in the past and it is still made. However, if I say, "The bed was made," it is clear someone made the bed, but it may not still be made. Be careful with how you translate the perfect tense.

Pluperfect Tense:

The pluperfect tense is similar to the prefect tense. It represents the verb as happening in past time with an effect that lasted until some point in the past, but not until the present. The point in the past where the effect is seen is indicated by the context. The emphasis is on the past effect. An example is in John 9:22, "These words spake his parents, because they feared the Jews: **for the Jews had agreed already**, that if any man did confess that he was Christ, he should be put out of the synagogue." The pluperfect is not often found in the New Testament.

Voice:

Active Voice:

This shows that the subject of the sentence is doing the action rather than being acted upon. *He is loosing.*

Passive Voice:

The subject is being acted upon. *He is being loosed.*

Middle Voice:

The subject is acting for or on behalf of himself. *He is loosing for himself.* This translation is merely an accommodation to Greek grammar to explain the middle voice. English has nothing like it. The middle voice expresses a subtle meaning of the Greek verb that is impossible to translate into English in most cases.

Mood:

Indicative Mood

This mood expresses a simple statement, an assertion, as opposed to a command or a question. It denotes actual activity as opposed to possible or probable activity.

Subjunctive Mood

The subjunctive is the mood of purpose, probability, or mild contingency. The translation into English often uses words like "should," "would," "might," or "may."

Optative Mood

The optative is the mood of possibility. It is not necessarily probably. It is merely possible. It is a sort of weaker subjunctive. "What will this babbler say?" (Acts 17:18)

Imperative Mood:

The imperative is the mood of command, giving orders.

Person

There are three persons in Greek.

	Singular	Plural
First Person:	I	We
Second Person:	You	You
Third Person:	He, she, It	They

Principle Parts of Verbs

The stem of a verb is the part that does not change when it is conjugated. Prefixes and suffixes are added to the stem to create the various types of verbs listed above. These changes are called *inflection*. Most inflections have been lost in English. In Early Modern English, we had things like adding -eth of -est to the end of verbs and conjugating the word *you* with thee, thou, thy, thine, you, and ye. We still have some inflection in English. The word *saying* is a participle. It consists of the verb stem *say* plus the ending *-ing*. We sometimes add prefixes to change the meaning of a word. The word *sensitive* is negated by adding *in-* to get *insensitive*.

There are six principle parts to Greek verbs when the stem itself changes. Occasionally, the stem changes so much as to not be recognizable as the same verb. The student will get used to this as he gets more and more experience with the Greek text. The six principle parts are:

1) The Present Tense stem
2) The Future Tense stem
3) The Aorist Tense stem
4) The Perfect Active stem
5) The Perfect Middle and Passive stem
6) The Aorist Passive Tense stem

Deponent

A deponent is a verb that takes the middle or passive voice endings, but in the context is clearly used as an active verb.

Infinitive

An infinitive is a verbal noun. An infinitive takes tense and voice. It can take an object and be modified by adverbs. It is widely used in the New Testament. It is translated very much like an English infinitive. "For **to will** is present with me" (Rom. 7:18). It is translated here as "to will" and the preposition "to" is used to express the infinitive, just as it is in English. Also, in Romans 7:18, it is an action, and it is the subject of the sentence. So, it is a verbal noun.

Participle

The participle is abundantly used in the New Testament, and it is used in a variety of ways. While the infinitive is a verbal noun, the participle is a verbal adjective. It takes case, voice, gender, and number. It also agrees with the noun it modifies in gender, number, and case. It can take an object and be modified by an adverb. The tense is relative to the time of the leading verb of the sentence or clause. So, a present participle takes place at the same time as the leading verb. An aorist participle takes place before the time of the leading verb. In English a participle is sometimes expressed by a verb ending in –ing. It is not always possible to translate a Greek participle that way. Most often one cannot translate a Greek participle literally. Most often it is translated with a phrase beginning with the following words when, while, who, which, or after.

Adjectives

Just as in English, Greek adjectives modify a noun or pronoun. They agree in case, number, and gender with the noun or pronoun they modify. Adjectives are used in three ways.

1) Attributively: When an adjective is used with a definite article, it is being used attributively. Ο αγαθος λογος or ο λογος ο αγαθος means *the good word*.

2) Predicate Use: An adjective is a predicate adjective if it is used without an article. Αγαθος ο λογος and ο λογος αγαθος mean *the word is good*. The article is used with the noun but not with the adjective.

3) As a Noun: the adjective can be used to express a noun. Αγαθος can mean *a good man*, αγαθη means *a good woman*, and αγαθον means *a good thing*. If it has the article, translate it with "the" rather than "a."

Adverb

Adverbs modify verbs, adjectives, and other adverbs.

Pronouns

A pronoun is a word that takes the place of a noun. There are several types of pronouns in the New Testament. Pronouns have case, gender, and number. They agree in all three with the noun for which they stand.

Personal Pronouns

The singular personal pronouns are I, you, he, she, and it. The plural personal pronouns are we, you, and they.

Relative Pronouns

These are who, which, whom, whoever, etc.

Interrogative pronouns: Who? What? Etc.

Indefinite Pronouns

The pronouns someone, something etc. are built the same as the interrogative pronouns except for a difference in accent.

Demonstrative pronouns: This and that, etc.

Reflexive pronoun

This type pronoun is basically a reference back onto the subject: myself, yourself, himself, etc.

Reciprocal pronoun

When the subject is affected by an interchange it is expressed as "one another" etc.

Possessive Pronouns

These are pronouns expressing possession: mine, yours, his, etc.

The Article

Sometimes the definite article is used as a pronoun.

Prepositions

Prepositions are designed to show relationships between words.

Parsing

To *parse* a Greek word is to identify the case, number, gender and the tense, voice, mood, number and person of Greek verbs. Codes are used to do this.

Target Language

One of the greatest reasons to learn New Testament Greek is for the purpose of translating God's word into the languages of the world. The target of the translation, or the language into which you are translating, is called the *target language*. The resulting translation is called the *target text*.

Source Language

The language you are using as the source of the translation is the *source language* and the text in that language is called the *source text*.

ABBREVIATIONS

Acc=Accusative
Act=active
Adj=Adjective
Adv=Adverb
Aram=Aramaic
Aro=Aorist
cf=compare with
Cond=conditional
Dat=Dative
Dep=deponent
Fem=Feminine
fig=figuratively
fr=from
Gen=Genitive
i.e.=that is
Inf=infinitive
Imp = Imperative
Interj = interjection
Masc = Masculine
Met = metaphorically
Mid = Middle
Neut = Neuter
Nom = Nominative
Perf = perfect
Pass = Passive
Pers = personal
Pl = plural
Poss = possessive
Prep = Preposition
Pres = present
Pron = Pronoun
PRT = Particle

tr = translated as
TR = Textus Receptus or Received Greek Text
UBS = United Bible Socieites
Voc = Vocative
Vs = Verse
w/ = with

GREEK TO ENGLISH LEXICON

Α, α, Ἄλφα

Αββᾶ	father (personal address)
Ἄβυσσος, ἡ	bottomless pit
ἀγαγων, V-AAP	See ἄγω
Αγαθοποιέω	do good, well doing
αγαθον A-NSN	See ἀγαθός
ἀγαθός, -ή, -όν, adj	good, well, beneficial
Ἀγαλλιάω	rejoice, am glad, have joy
Ἄγᾰμος, ὁ	unmarried
Ἀγανακτέω	pained, angry, vexed
ἀγαπάω	love
ἀγάπη, η	love
ἀγαπητός, -η, -ον, adj.	beloved
ἄγγελος, ο	angel
αγγελους N-APM	See ἄγγελος
ἁγιάζω	sanctify, hallow
ἁγιασμός, ο	sanctification
ἅγιος, -α, -ον, adj.	holy, saint
αγιω A-DSN	See ἅγιος
Ἁγνίζω	purify
Ἁγνισμός, ο	purification, abstinence
ἀγνοέω	know not; ignorant
Ἀγνόημα, ατος, τό,	error, sin of ignorance
Ἁγνότης, τητος, ἡ	purity
Ἄγνωστος, -ή, -ον, adj.	unknown
ἀγορά, η	market place
ἀγοράζω	buy
ἀγοράσομεν, V-FAI-1P	See ἀγοράζω
Ἄγρα, ἡ	draught of fishes, catching
Ἀγράμμᾰτος, -ή, -ον, adj.	unlearned, illiterate
ἀγρός, ο	field, country, land
ἄγω	to lead
ἀδελφή, η	sister
αδελφον N-ASM	See ἀδελφός
ἀδελφός, ο N-NSM	brother
ἄδης, ο	Hell

ἀδικέω	wrong, do wrong
ἀδικία, -η	unrighteousness
ἀδικία	See ἀδικία
ἄδικος, -η, -ον, adj.	unjust, unrighteous
ἀδύνατος, -η, -ον, adj.	incapable, impossible
ἀθετέω	reject
αιμα, αιματος, το	blood
αιματων N-GPN	See αιμα
αἴρω	take up, take away
αἴρων, V-PAP-NSM	See αἴρω
αἰτέω	ask for
αἰτία, η	cause, accusation
αἰών, αἰώνος, ο	age
ἀκαθαρσία, -η	uncleanness
ακάθαρτος, -η, -ον, adj.	unclean
ἄκανθα, η	thorn, thorn bush
ἀκήκοα, V-RAI-1S	See ἀκούω
ἀκοή, η	hearing, report
Ἀκολούθει, V-PAM-2S	See ἀκολουθέω
ἀκολουθέω	follow
ἀκολουθησάντων, V-AAP-GPM	See ἀκολουθέω
ἀκολουθοῦντας, V-PAP-APM	See ἀκολουθέω
ἀκούσαντες, V-AAP-NPM	See ἀκούω
ακουσαντων V-AAP-GPM	See ἀκούω
ἀκούσονται, V-FDI-3P	See ἀκούω
ἀκούω	hear
ἀκροβυστία, η	uncircumcision
ἀλέκτωρ, -ορος, ο	cock, rooster
ἀλήθεια, η, N-NSF	truth
ἀληθεία	See ἀλήθεια
αληθειας N-GSF	See ἀλήθεια
ἀληθής, -ες, adj. (syn. of ἀληθινός	true
αληθινον A-NSN	See ἀληθινός
ἀληθινός, -η, -ον, adj.	true
ἀληθῶς, adv.	truly
αλλα, conjunction	but (stronger than δε)
ἀλλήλους, reciprocal pronoun	one another
ἄλλος, ή, -ον, adj	other

ἀλλότριος, -α, -ον, adj.	strange, another's
ἅλυσις, -εως, η	chain
ἅμα, adv.	at the same time, together with
ἁμαρτάνω	sin
ἁμαρτία, ἡ	sin
αμαρτιαν N-ASF	See ἁμαρτία
ἁμαρτωλός, ο	sinner
ἀμὴν, Hebrew	Verily, Amen, Truly
ἀμνὸς, ο N-NSM	lamb
ἀμπελών, ο	vineyard
ἀμφότερος, -α, -ον, adj.	both
ἄν	untranslatable – makes statements contingent
ἀνά μέσον	into the midst, among
ἀνά, prep with acc.	up, upwards
ἀνά, with numerals	each
ἀναβαίνοντας, V-PAP-APM	See ἀναβαίνω
αναβαινω	I go up
ἀναβλέπω	I look up
ἀναγγέλλω	report, announce
ἀναγινώσω	read
ἀνάγκη, η	necessity
ἀνάγω	bring, launch forth
ἀναιρέω	take up, kill
ἀνάκειμαι	recline
ἀνακρίνω	examine
ἀναλαμβάνω	take up
ἀναπαύω	refresh, middle-take rest
ἀναπίπτω	recline
ἀνάστασιν, N-ASF	See ἀνάστασις
ἀνάστασις, η	raising from the dead, rise
ἀναστήσω V-FAI-1S	See ἀνίστημι
ἀναστρέφω	return
ἀναστροφή, η	conduct
ἀνατολή, η	east, dawn
ἀναφέρω	bring up, offer
ἀναχωρέω	depart
Ἀνδρέας, ὁ, N-NSM	Andrew
ανδρεου N-GSM	See Ἀνδρέας

ανδρος N-GSM	See Ἀνδρέας
ἄνεμος, ο	wind
ἀνέχομαι	endure
ἀνεῳγότα, V-RAP-ASM of ἀνοίγω	See ἀνοίγω
ανηρ, ανδρος, ο, N-NSM	a man (a male)
ἀνθίστημι	resist
ανθρωπον N-ASM	See ἄνθρωπος
ἄνθρωπος,ο, N-NSM	brother
ανθρωπου N-GSM	See ἄνθρωπος
ανθρωπων N-GPM	See ἄνθρωπος
ἀνίστημι	raise up
ἀνοίγω	open
ἀνομία, η	lawlessness
ἄνομος, -η, -ον	lawless
αντι, prep. with genitive	for, instead of, over against, opposite to, before
ἄνω, adv.	above, on high
ἄνωθεν, adv.	again, from above, (from) top
ἄξιος, -α, -ον, A-NSM	of equal value, worthy
ἀπαγγέλλω	announce, report
ἀπάγω	lead away
ἅπαξ	once, once for all
ἀπαρνέομαι	deny, refuse
ἅπας, -α, -ον, adj.	all
ἀπειθέω	disbelieve
ἀπεκρίθη, V-ADI-3S	See ἀποκρίνομαι
ἀπέρχομαι	Depart
ἀπεσταλμένοι, V-RPP-NPM	See ἀποστέλλω
ἀπεσταλμένος, V-RPP-NSM	See ἀποστέλλω
απεστειλαν V-AAI-3P	See ἀποστέλλω
ἀπέχω	received, hold back, keep off
ἀπιστία, η	unbelief
ἄπιστος, -η, -ον, adj.	unbelieving
ἀπο, prep. with genitive	from, of, by
ἀποδίδωμι	give back, pay
ἀποθνήσκω	I die
ἀποκαλύπτω	reveal
ἀποκάλυψις, -εως, η	revelation

ἀποκρίνομαι. Dep.	answer
αποκρισιν N-ASF	See ἀπόκρισις
ἀπόκρισις, η	answer, decision
ἀποκτείνω	I Kill
ἀπόλλυμι	destroy, perish
ἀπολογέομαι	defend myself
ἀπολύτρωσις, -εως, η	redermption
ἀπολύω	release
ἀποστέλλω	send out
ἀπόστολοι, N-NPM	see ἀπόστολος
ἀπόστολος, ο	apostle
ἅπτομαι (middle or deponent)	touch
ἀπώλεια, η	destruction
ἄρα	then, therefore
ἀργύριον, το	silver
Ἀρέσκω	please; to be pleasing
ἀριθμός, ο	number
ἀρνέομαι, dep.	deny, refuse
ἀρνίον, το	lamb
ἁρπάζω	seize
ἄρτι, adv.	Hereafter, henceforth, now, at this time, after this, hither to, present
ἄρτος, ο	bread
ἄρτους, N-APM	See ἄρτος
ἀρχαῖος, -α, -ον, adj.	old, ancient
ἀρχή, η, N-NSF	beginning
ἀρχή N-DSF	See ἀρχή
ἀρχιερεύς, ο,	high or chief priest
ἀρχιερέως, ο,	high or chief priest
ἄρχω	I rule
αρχων, αρχοντος, ο	ruler
ἀσέβεια, η	ungodliness
ἀσέβειαν	See ἀσέβεια
ἀσέλγεια, η	licentiousness
ἀσθενέω	weak, I am
ασθενής, -ης, -ες, adj.	weak
ἀσθένεια, -η	weakness, sickness
ἀσκός, ο	bottle, wine skin
ἀσπάζομαι	salute, greet

ἀσπασμός	greeting
ἀστήρ, -ερος, ο	star
ἀτενίζω	look intently, gaze upon
αὐλή, η	court
αὐξάνω	cause to grow, increase
αὔριον, Adv.	tomorrow
αὕτη D-NSF	See οὗτος /οὗτοι /αὕτη /αὗται
αυτο P-ASN	See αὐτός
αυτοις P-DPM	See αὐτός
αυτον P-ASM	See αὐτός
αὐτός, ή, ὁ, pron., P-NSM	he, she, it
αυτος P-NSM	See αὐτός
αυτου P-GSM	See αὐτός
αυτους P-APM	See αὐτός
αυτω P-DSM	See αὐτός
ἀφαιρέω	take away
ἄφεσις, -εως, η	remission, a sending away
αφίημι	let go, permit
ἀφίστημι	withdraw, depart
ἀφορίζω	separate
ἄφρων, -ων, -ον, adj.	foolish
ἄχρι, prep. with gen. or conj.	as far as, up to/ as conj. until

Β, β, Βῆτα

Βαθύς, -εῖα, adj.	deep
βαίνω	I go
βάλλω	I cast
βαπτιζειν V-PAN	See βαπτίζω
βαπτιζεις V-PAI-2S	See βαπτίζω
βαπτίζω V-PAI-1S	baptize
βαπτίζων, V-PAP-NSM	See βαπτίζω
βάπτισμα, το	baptism
Βαπτιστής, ὁ	Baptist, baptizer
Βάπτω	dip, dye
Βάρβᾰρος, ὁ	barabarian
Βαρέω	oppress, burden, lay heavy on
Βάρος, -εος, τό, adj.	grievous, hard to bear

βασανίζω	torment, I
Βασανισμός, ὁ	torment, torture
βασιλεία, η	Kingdom
βασιλεύς, βασιλέως, ο, N-NSM	king
Βασίλισσα, ης, ἡ	queen
βαστάζω	bear, carry
Βδέλυγμα, ατος, τό	abomination
Βέβαιος, -α, -ον	stedfast, established
Βεβαιόω	confirm, establish
Βέλος, εος, τό	dart, arrow
Βηθαβαρᾶ, η	Bethabara
βηθσαιδα	Bethsaida
βῆμα, -ατος, το	judgement seat
βιβλίον, το	book
Βίβλος, ἡ	book
Βίος, ὁ	life, means of living
Βλαστάνω	spring up, sprout
βλασφημέω	blaspheme, revile
βλασφημία, η	blasphemy, reproach
βλεπει V-PAI-3S	See βλέπω
βλέπω	see
βοάω	cry out
Βοηθέω	help those who cry out
Βόθῡνος, ὁ	well, pit
Βόσκω	feed, pasture
Βουλευτής, ου, ὁ	counsellor
Βουλεύω	counsel, I give
βουλή, η	counsel, purpose
βούλομαι	wish, will, intend
βοῶντος, V-PAP-GSM	See βοάω
βρέφος, -εος, τό	child, unborn
βρέχω	rain, cause or send
βροντή, ἡ	thunder
βρυγμός, οῦ, ὁ	gnash the teeth
βρῶμα, -ατος, το	meat, food
βρῶσις, -εως, ἡ	eating, the act of

Γ, γ, Γάμμα

Γαλιλαία, η	Galilee
γαμέω	marry
γάμος, ο	wedding, marriage
γάρ, conj. postpositive	for
γε	indeed, at least, really, even
γέγονεν, perf. V-2RAI-3S	See γίνομαι
γέεννα, η	Gehenna
γεμίσατε, V-AAP-2P	See γεμίζω
γέμω	fill
γενεά, η	generation
γενέσθαι, V-2ADN	See γίνομαι
γεννάω	beget
γένος, το	birth, race, kind
γεύομαι	taste
γεωργός, ο	farmer
γῆ, γῆς, ἡ	earth, land
γινομαι, dep.	become
γινωσκεις V-PAI-2S	See γινώσκω
γινώσκω	know, learn, realize
γλῶσσα, η	tongue, language
γνωρίζω	manifest, make known
γνῶσις, -εως, η	wisdom, knowledge
γνωστός, -ας, -η, adj.	known
γονεύς, -έως, ο	parent
γόνυ, -ατος, το	knee
γραμμα, -ατος, το	letter, (plural) writings
γραμματεύς, γραμματεώς, ο	scribe
γραφή, η	writing, scripture
γραφαῖς	See γραφή
γράφω	write
γρηγορέω	watch
γυμνός, -η, -ον, adj.	naked
γυνή, γυναικός, η	woman

Δ, δ, Δέλτα

δαιμονίζομαι	possessed by a devil, I am
δαιμόνιον, το	demon
δάκρυ, -υος, το or δάκρυον, το	tear

δε, conjunction	but, and, now, then, yet, yea
δέησις, η	entreaty
δεῖ	necessary, it is
δείκνυμι (or δεικνύω)	show
δεῖπνον, το	supper
δέκα	10
δεκαπέντε	15
δεκατέσσαρες	14
δεκατη A-NSF	See δέκατος
δέκατος, -η, -ον, adj.	tenth
δένδρον, το	tree
δεξιός, -α, -ον, adj.	right
δέομαι	beseech
δέρω	beat
δεσμιος, ο	prisoner
δεσμός, ο	bond, fetter
δεσπότης, ο	master, Lord
δεῦτε!	come!
Δεύτερος, -α, -ον, adj.	second
δέχομαι	receive
δέω	bind
δηνάριον, το	penney, denarius
δήποτε, PRT	at any time in general
δια, prep with accusative	through, by, by means of, on account of
δια, prep. with genitive	through, throughout, by, during, after, by means of
διάβολος, ο	devil
διαθήκη, η	testament, covenant
διακονέω	serve
διακονία, η	servant
διάκονος, ο	deacon, servant
διακόσιοι	200
διακρίνω	judge, discriminate
διαλέγομαι	dispute
διαλογίζομαι	debate
διαλογισμός, ο	reasoning, questioning
διαμαρτύρομαι	testfy solemnly
διαμερίζω	divide, distribute
διάνοια, η	mind, understanding, thought

διατάσσω	command
διατρίβω	continue
διαφέρω	differ
διδασκαλε N-VSM	See διδάσκαλος
διδασκαλία, η	teaching
διδάσκαλος, ο	teacher
διδάσκω	teach
διδαχή, η	teaching
δίδωμι,	give
διερχομαι, deponent	go through
δίκαιος, -α, -όν, adj	righteous
δικαιοσύνη, ἡ	righteousness
δικαιόω	justify
δικαίωμα, -ατος, το	righteous deed
δίκτυον, το	net
διό, adv.	wherefore
διότι, adv.	because
δισχίλιοι	2000
διψάω	thirst
διωγμός, ο	persecution
διώκω	pursue, persecute
δοκέω	think
δοκιμάζω	prove, approve
δόλος, ο	guile, deceit
δόξα, η	glory
δοξάζω	glorify
δοξαν N-ASF	See δόξα
δουλεύω	serve
δοῦλος, ο	servant
δράκων, -οντος, ο	dragon
δύναμαι	able
δύναμις, δύναμεως, η	power
δυναται V-PNI-3S	See δύναμαι
δυνατός,-η, -ον, adj.	powerful, possible
δύο	two
δώδεκα	12
δώδεκα χιλιάδες	12000
δωδέκατος, η, ον	twelfth
δωμεν V-2AAS-1P	See δίδωμι

δωρέα, η gift
δῶρον, το gift

Ε, ε, Έψιλόν

ἐάν if
ἑαυτοῦ, ἧς, οὗ, relexive pronoun of himself, of herself, of itself.
ἐάω permit
ἑβδομήκοντα 70
ἕβδομος, η, ον seventh
ἐγγίζω come near
ἐγγύς, adv. near
ἐγείρω I raise up
ἐγένετο, V-2ADI-3S See γίνομαι
ἐγεννήθησαν, V-API-3P See γεννάω
ἐγίνετο, V-IDI-3S See γίνομαι
ἐγκαταλείπω forsake, leave behind
εγνω V-2AAI-3S See γινώσκω
ἔγνωκα, V-RAI-1S See γινώσκω
εγραψεν V-AAI-3S See γράφω
ἐγώ, pron. I
εδοθη V-API-3S See δίδωμι
ἔδωκεν, V-AAI-3S See δίδωμι
ἐθεασάμεθα, V-ADI-1P See θεάομαι
ἔθνος, το nation
ἔθος, το custom
εἰ, Cond if
ει V-PAI-2S See εἰμί
ειδεν V-2AAI-3S See ὁράω
εἶδόν, V-2AAI-1S See ὁράω
ειδον V-2AAI-3P See ὁράω
εἶδος, τό form, external appearance, kind
εἴδωλον, το image, idol
ἔικοσι (ν) 20
εἴκοσιτέσσαρες 24
εἰκών, -όνος, η to watch
εἰμί I am
ειναι V-PAN See εἰμί

ειπεν V-2AAI-3S	See λέγω
εἶπόν, V-2AAI-1S	See λέγω
ειπον V-2AAI-3P	See λέγω
εἰπών, V-AAP	See λέγω
εἰρήνη, η	peace
εις, prep. with accusative	into, to, toward, for
εἷς, μία, ἕν	one
εἰσάγω	lead in
εἰσέρχομαι, dep.	enter, go in
εἰσπορεύομαι	enter
εἰστήκει, pluperfect, V-LAI-3S	See ἵστημι
εἶτα	then
εκ, prep. (εξ before vowels) with genitive	out, out of, of
ἑκατόν	100
ἑκατοντάρχης or -αρχος, ο	centurion
ἐκβάλλω	cast out
ἐκεῖ, adv.	there
ἐκεῖθεν, adv.	thence, from that place
ἐκείνην D-ASF	See ἐκεῖνος
ἐκεῖνος, η, ο, pron.	that
ἐκκαίδεκα	16
ἐκκλησία, η	assembly, church
ἐκκόπτω	cut off
ἐκλέγομαι	choose, pick out
ἐκλεκτός, -η, -ον, adj.	elect, chosen
ἐκπίπτω	fall away
ἐκπλήσσω	astonished, amazed
ἐκπορεύομαι	go out, depart
ἐκπορεύσονται, V-FDI-3P	See ἐκπορεύομαι
ἐκτείνω	stretch forth; reach out
ἕκτος, -η, -ον, adj.	sixth
ἐκχέω or ἐκχύνω	pour out
ἑκών, -α, -ον, adj	willing
ἐλάβομεν, V-2AAI-1P	See λαμβάνω
ελαβον V-2AAI-3P	See λαμβάνω
ἐλαία, η	olive tree
ἔλαιων, το	olive oil
ἐλάσσων, -η, -ον, Adj.	worse

ἐλάχιστος, -η, -ον, adj.	least
ἐλέγχω	reprove, convict
ἐλεέω	mercy on, I have; to pity
ἐλεημοσύνη, η	alms
ἔλεος, το	mercy, pity
ἐλευθερία, η	liberty
ἐλεύθερος, -α, ον, adj.	free
ἐλήλυθα, V-RAI-1S	See ἔρχομαι
ἐλθών, V-AAP-NSM	See ἔρχομαι
ἐλπίζω	hope, I
ελπις, ελπιδος, η	hope
ἐμαρτύρησεν, V-AAI-3S	μαρτυρέω
ἐμαυτοῦ, ῆς, reflexive pronoun	of myself
ἐμβαίνω	go into, step into, embark
ἐμβὰς, V-2AAP-NSM	See ἐμβαίνω
ἐμβλέπω	look upon or at
ἐμβλέψας, V-AAP-NSM	See ἐμβλέπω
εμειναν, V-AAI-3P	See μένω
ἔμεινεν, V-AAI-3S	See μένω
ἐμός, ή, όν, poss. adj.	belonging to me, my
ἐμπαίζω	mock
ἔμπροσθεν, adv. , also used as prep with gen	in front of, before, in the presence of
ἐμφανίζω	manifest
εν, prep. with dative	in, by, among, near, with
ἐνακόσιοι	900
ἔνατος, η, ον	nineth
ἐνδείκνυμι (Mid. ἐνδείκνυμαι)	show forth
ἔνδεκα	11
ἐνδύω	put on, clothe
ἕνεκα or ἕνεκεν, prep. with gen.	on account of
ἐνενήκοντα	90
ἐνενήκονταεννέα	99
ἐνεργέω	work, effect
ἐνιαυτός, ο	year
εννέα	9
ἐννεακαίδεκα	19
ἔνοχος, -η, -ον, adj.	danger, guilty, subject to
ἐντέλλομαι	command

ἐντολή, η	commandment, law
ἐνώπιον, adv. with Genitive	before, in the sight of, in the presence of
ἕξ	6
ἐξ, PREP	See ἐκ
ἐξάγω	lead out
ἐξακόσιοι	600
ἐξαποστέλλω	send forth
ἐξελθεῖν, V-AAN	See ἐξέρχομαι
ἐξέρχομαι	I go out, I go forth
ἔξεστι	lawful, it is
ἐξηγέομαι, deponent	I declare
εξηγησατο V-ADI-3S	See ἐξηγέομαι
ἑξήκοντα	60
ἐξίστημι and ἐξιστάω	amaze, am amazed
ἐξομολογέω	confess, profess
ἐξουθενέω	despise
ἐξουσία, η	power, authority
εξουσιαν N-ASF	See ἐξουσία
ἔξω, adv.	outside, without
ἔξωθεν, pron with gen.	from without
ἐοπτή, η	feast
ἐπαγγελία, η	promise
ἐπαγγέλλομαι	promise
ἔπαινος, ο	praise
ἐπαίρω	lift up
ἐπαισχύνομαι	ashamed
ἐπάνω, adv.	above
ἐπάνω, prep. with gen.	over
ἐπαύριον, adv	next day, day following
ἐπεί, adv.	when, since
ἐπειδή, conj.	since, because
ἔπειτα, adv.	then
ἐπερωτάω	ask, question
ἐπί, prep. with acc (ἐφ before rough breathing)	on, to, against
ἐπί, prep. with dat(ἐφ before rough breathing)	on the basis of, at
ἐπί, prep. with gen(ἐφ before rough breathing)	over, on, at the time of

ἐπιβάλλω	lay upon
ἐπιγινώσκω	come to know
ἐπίγνωσισ, -εως, ο	knowledge
ἐπιδίδωμι	give to
ἐπιζητέω	seek for
ἐπιθυμέω	covet, desire, lust after
ἐπιθυμία, -ἡ	passion, eager desire
ἐπικαλέω	call, I; name, I; middle, invoke, appeal to
ἐπιλαμβάνομαι	take hold of
ἐπιμένω	continue
ἐπιπίπτω	fall upon
ἐπισκέπτομαι	visit, have a care for
ἐπίσταμαι	understand
ἐπιστολή, η	epistle, letter
ἐπιστρέφω	turn to, return
ἐπιτάσσω	command
ἐπιτελέω	complete, perform
ἐπιτίθημι	lay upon
ἐπιτιμάω	rebuke, warn
ἐπιτρέπω	suffer (permit)
ἐποίει, V-IAI-3S	See ποιέω
ἐπουράνιος, -η, -ον, adj.	heavenly
ἑπτά	7
ἑπτακαίδεκα	17
ἑπτακισχίλιοι	7000
ἑπτακόσιοι	700
ἐργάζομαι	work
ἐργάτης, ο	workman
ἔργον, το	work
ἔρημος, ἡ,	wilderness, desert
ερημω A-DSF	See ἔρημος
ἐριθεία	contention, strife
ἐριθείας	See ἐριθεία
ερμηνευεται V-PPI-3S	See ἑρμηνεύω
ἑρμηνευόμενον, V-PPP-NSN	See ἑρμηνεύω
ἑρμηνεύω	Interpret, translate, explain
ἔρχεσθε, V-PNM-2P	See ἔρχομαι
ερχεται V-PNI-3S	See ἔρχομαι
ἔρχομαι, dep.	come, go

ἐρχόμενον, V-PNP-ASM	See ἔρχομαι
ἐρχόμενος, V-PNP-NSM	See ἔρχομαι
ερχου V-PNM-2S	See ἔρχομαι
ἐρωτάω	ask, request, entreat
ερωτησωσιν V-AAS-3P	See ἐρωτάω
ἐσθίω	I eat
ἐσκήνωσεν, V-AAI-3S of σκηνόω	See σκηνόω
ἔστηκεν, perf. V-RAI-3S	See ἵστημι
εστιν G1510 V-PAI-3S	
ἐσχάτῃ A-DSF-S	See ἔσχατος
ἔσχατος, -ή, -ον, adj	last
ἔσωθεν, adv.	from within, within
ἕτερος, -α, -ον, Adj	other, another
ἔτι	yet, still, even
ἑτοιμάζω	prepare
ἕτοιμος, -η, -ον, adj.	ready, prepared
ἔτος, το	year
εὐαγγελίζομαι, dep.	to preach the gospel
εὐαγγελίζω, η	preach the gospel
εὐαγγέλιον, το	gospel
εὐαγγελίῳ	See εὐαγγέλιον
εὐδοκέω	well pleased with
εὐθέως	straightway, immediately
ευθυνατε, V-AAM-2P	See εὐθύνω
εὐθύνω	make straight, steer
εὐλογέω	bless
εὐλογία, η	blessing
εὐρήκαμεν, V-RAI-1P	See εὑρίσκω
ευρισκει V-PAI-3S	See εὑρίσκω
εὑρίσκω	to find
εὐσέβεια, η	godliness
εὐφραίνω	rejoice
εὐχαριστέω	thanks
εὐχαριστία, η	thanksgiving
εφ PREP	See ἐπί
εφη V-IAI-3S	See φημί
ἐφίστημι	stand over, come upon
ἔχθρος, -α, -ον, adj.	hating (as noun-enemy)

ἔχω	have
ἔχων, V-PAP-NSM	have
εωρακα V-RAI-1S-ATT	See ὁράω
ἑώρακε, perf. V-RAI-3S	See ὁράω
ἕως, prep. gen.	until, as far as

Ζ, ζ, Ζῆτα

ζάω	live
ζεστός, -ή, -όν, adj.	hot
ζεῦγος, -εος, τό,	yoke
Ζεύς, ὁ	Jupiter, Zeus
ζῆλος, ο	zeal, jealousy
ζηλόω	zealous, I am
ζημία, ἡ	damage, loss
ζημιόω	harm
ζήσονται, V-FDI-3P	See ζάω
ζητειτε V-PAI-2P	See ζητέω
ζητέω	seek
ζήτημα, ατος, τό	question, subject of debate
ζόφος, ὁ	darkness, gloom
ζύμη, η	leaven
ζωγρέω	catch, take prisoner
ζωή, η N-NSF	life
ζώννυμι	gird
ζωογονέω	live, preserve, life, stay alive
ζῷον, το	living creature, animal
ζωοποιέω	make alive

Η, η, Ἔτα

ἤ, conj.	or
ἤ, conj.	than
ηγαγεν V-2AAI-3S	See ἄγω
ἡγεμών, ο	governor, leader
ἡγέομαι	chief, I am; think, regard
ᾔδειν, V-LAI-1S	See εἴδω
ἤδη, adv.	already
ἠθέλησεν V-AAI-3S	See θέλω

ἠκολούθησαν, V-AAI-3P	See ἀκολουθέω
ηκολουθησαν V-AAI-3P	See ἀκολουθέω
ηκουσαν V-AAI-3P	See ἀκούω
ἦλθε, V-2AAI-3S	See ἔρχομαι
ἦλθον, V-2AAI-1S	ἔρχομαι
ηλθον V-2AAI-3P	ἔρχομαι
Ἠλίας	Elias
ἥλιος, ὁ	sun
ημας P-1AP	See ἐγώ
ημεις P-1NP	See ἐγώ
ἡμέρα, η	day
ἡμέρα, N-DSF	See ἡμέρα
ημεραν N-ASF	See ἡμέρα
ἡμέτερος, -α, -ον, adj.	belonging to us, our
ημιν P-1DP	See ἐγώ
ἦν, V-IAI-3S	See εἰμί
ηρνησατο V-ADI-3S	See ἀρνέομαι
ἠρώτησαν, V-AAI-3P	See ἐρωτάω
Ἠσαίας	Isaiah
Ἠσαίας, ὁ	Esaias, Isaiah
ησαν V-IAI-3P	See εἰμί

Θ, θ, Θῆτα

θάλασσα, η	Sea
θάνατος, ὁ	death
θανατόω	death, I put to
θάπτω	bury
θαυμάζω	marvel, wonder, wonder at
θεάομαι, dep.	see-look at
θεασάμενος, V-ADP-NSM	See θεάομαι
θέλημα	desire, wish, will, want
θελήματος, το N-GSN	See θέλημα
θέλω	to want, to will
θεμέλιος, ὁ	foundation
Θεὸν N-ASM	See Θεὸς
Θεὸς, ὁ	God
θεου N-GSM	See Θεὸς
θεραπεύω	heal

θερίζω	reap
θερισμός, ο	harvest
θεωρέω	look at, see
θεωροῦντες, V-PAP-NPM	See θεωρέω
θήρα, η	door
θηρίον, το	wild beast
θησαυρός, ο	storehouse, treasure
θλίβω	press, oppress
θλῖψις,-εως, η	tribulation
θρίξ, τριχός, η	worm
θρόνος, ο	throne
θυγάτηρ, -τρος, η	daughter
θυμός, ο	wrath
θυσία, η	sacrifice
θυσιαστήριον, το	altar
θύω	sacrifice, kill

Ι, ι, Ἰῶτα

ἰάομαι	heal
ἴδε V-AAM-2S	See ὁράω
ἴδετε, V-AAM-2P	See ὁράω
ἴδῃς, V-AAS-2S	See ὁράω
ιδια A-APN	See ἴδιος
ιδιοι A-NPM	See ἴδιος
ιδιον A-ASM	See ἴδιος
ἴδιος, α, ον adj	belonging to one's self; one's own
ἰδού, particle	behold, lo, see, look
ἰδών, V-AAP	See ὁράω
ιερεις N-APM	See ἱερεύς
ἱερεύς, ο	priest
ἱερόν, το	temple
Ἱεροσόλυμα, το	Jerusalem
ιεροσολυμων N-GPN	See Ἱεροσόλυμα
ιησου N-DSM	See Ἰησοῦς
ιησου N-GSM	See Ἰησοῦς
ιησουν N-ASM	See Ἰησοῦς
Ἰησοῦς, ο	Jesus

ἱκανός, -ή, -όν, adj.	sufficient, worthy, considerable
ιμαντα N-ASM	See ἱμάτιον
ἱμάς, ο	shoe latchet
ἱμάτιον, το	garment
ινα, conjunction	in order to/ that, to
'Ιορδάνης, ο	Jordan
ιορδανου N-GSM	See 'Ιορδάνης
ιουδαιοι A-NPM	See 'Ιουδαῖος
'Ιουδαῖος, ο	Jew
ἵππος, ο	horse
'Ισραήλ N-PRI	Isreal
'Ισραηλίτης N-NSM	Israelite
ἵστημι	stand
ἰσχυρός, -α, -ον, adj.	strong
ἰσχυρότερος, -α, -ον, adj.	stronger, comp. of ἰσχυρός, α, ον, strong
ἰσχύς, -ύος, η	strength
ἰσχύω	strong, I am; able
ἰχθύς, -ύος, ο	fish
'Ιωάννης, ο N-NSM	John
'Ιωαννου N-GSM	'Ιωάννης
ιωνα N-GSM	See 'Ιωνᾶς
'Ιωνᾶς	Jona
'Ιωσήφ	Joseph

Κ, κ, Κάππα

κἀγώ	and I, I also
καθάπερ	even as, as
καθαρᾶς	See καθάρος
καθαρίζω	cleanse
καθαρός, ά, όν, adj	clean, pure
καθεύδω	sleep
κάθημαι	to sit, to be sitting
καθίζω	to sit, to be seated, to cause to sit
καθίστημι	set, constitute
καθώς, adv.	as, even as
και, conjunction	and, also, even
καινός, -ή, -όν, adj.	new
καιρός, ο	time

καίω	burn up
κἀκεῖ (=καὶ ἐκεῖ)	and there
κἀκεῖθεν (=καὶ ἐκεῖθεν)	and from there, and then
κακία, η	malice, evil
κακός, -ἡ, -όν, adj	bad
κακῶς, adv.	badly
κάλαμος, ο	reed
καλέω	call
καλός, -ἡ, -όν. adj	good, beautiful
καλῶς, adv.	well
καπνός, ο	smoke
καρδία, η	heart
καρπός, ο	fruit
κατά, Prep. with Acc.	according to, throughout, during
κατά, Prep. with Gen.	down, from, against
καταβαῖνον, V-PAP-ASN	See καταβαίνω
καταβαίνοντας, V-PAP-APM	See καταβαίνω
καταβαίνω	go down
καταβάς, V-2AAP-NSM	See καταβαίνω
καταβολή, η	foundation
καταγγέλλω	proclaim
καταισχύνω	put to shame
κατακαίω	burn up
κατάκειμαι	lie down
κατακρίνω	condemn
καταλαμβάνω	comprehend
καταλείπω	leave
καταλύω	destroy, lodge
κατανοέω	observe
καταντάω	come to
καταργέω	bring to naught, abolish
καταρτίζω	mend, fit, pefect
κατασκευάζω	prepare
κατειχετο, V-IPI-3S	See κατέχω
κατέλαβεν, 2AAI-3S	See καταλαμβάνω
κατεργάζομαι	work out
κατέρχομαι	come down, go down
κατεσθίω	devour, eat up
κατέχω	have, hold back, hold down

κατηγορέω	accuse
κατοικέω	inhabit, dwell
κάτω, adv.	down, below, less than
καυχάομαι	boast
καύχημα, -ατος, το	boasting, ground of boasting
καύχησις, -εως, η	boasting
κεῖμαι	lie, am laid
κέκραγε, perf. V-2RAI-3S	See κράζω
κελεύω	order
κενός, -η, -ον, adj.	vain, empty
κέρας, -ατος, το	horn
κερδαίνω	gain
κεφαλή, η	head
κηρύσσω	preach
κηφας, N-NSM	Cephas
κλάδος, ο	branch
κλαίω	weep
κλάω	break
κλείω	shut
κλέπτης, ο	thief
κλέπτω	steal
κληθηση V-FPI-2S	See καλέω
κληρονομέω	inherit
κληρονομία, η	inheritance
κληρονόμος, ο	heir
κλῆρος, ο	lot
κλῆσις, -εως, η	call, a divine, invitation
κλητός, -v, -ον, adj.	called
κοιλία, η	womb, belly
κοιμάομαι	sleep, fall asleep
κοινός, -η, -ον, adj.	common, unclean
κοινόω	make common, defile
κοινωνία, η	fellowship, contribution
κοινωνός, ο	partner, sharer
κολλάομαι	join, cleave to
κολπον N-ASM	See κόλπος
κόλπος, ο	bosom
κομίζω	receive
κοπιάω	toil

κόπος, ὁ	labor, trouble
κοσμέω	adorn
κοσμον N-ASM	See κόσμος
κόσμος, ὁ	world
κοσμου N-GSM	See κόσμος
κοσμω N-DSM	See κόσμος
κράβαττος, ὁ	bed, pallet, mattress
κράζω	I cry out
κρατέω	grasp
κράτος	power, dominion
κρείσσων, ον	better, comparative of ἀγαθός
κρίμα, -ατος, τo	judgement
κρίνω	Judge, decide
κρίσις, κρίσεως, ἡ	Condemnation, damnation, judgement
κριτής, ὁ	judge
κρυπτός, -η, -ον, adj.	hidden
κρύπτω	conceal
κτίζω	create
κτίσις, -εως, ἡ	creature
κυλλος, adj.	maimed
κύριος, ὁ	Lord
κύριον, N-ASM	See κύριος
κύριου N-GSM	See κύριος
κωλύω	forbid, hinder
κώμη, ἡ	village
κωφός, -v, -ον, adj.	deaf, dumb

Λ, λ, Λάμβδα

λαλέω	I speak
λαλοῦντος, V-PAP-GSM	See λαλέω
λαμβάνω	take, receive
λαός, ὁ	people
λατρεύω	serve, worship
λεγει V-PAI-3S	See λέγω
λεγεις V-PAI-2S	See λέγω
λεγεται V-PPI-3S	See λέγω
λέγῃ, V-PAS-3S	See λέγω
λέγω	I say

λέγων, V-PAP-NSM	See λέγω
λευιτας N-APM	See Λευίτης
Λευίτης, ο	levite
λευκός, -η, -ον, adj.	white
ληστής, ο	robber
λίαν, adv.	greatly
λίθος, ο	stone
λίμνη, η	lake
λιμός, ο	famine, hunger
λογίζομαι	recon, count, account
λόγος, ο	word
λόγου, N-GSM	See λόγος
λοιπός, -η, -ον, adj	remaining, the rest, henceforth, furthermore
λυπέω	grieve
λύπη, -ης, -η, adj.	pain, grief
λύσω, V-AAS-1S	See λύω
λυχνία, η	lampstand
λύχνος, ο	lamp
λύω	loose
μαθηται N-NPM	See μαθητής
μαθητής, ο	disciple
μαθητων N-GPM	See μαθητής
μακάριος, α, ον adj.	blessed
μακράν	far away
μακρόθεν	afar, from afar
μακροθυμέω	patient, I am
μακροθυμία, η	longsuffering, patience, forebearance
μάλιστα	especially
μᾶλλον, adv.	more, rather
μανθάνω	learn
μαρτυρει V-PAI-3S	See μαρτυρέω
μαρτυρέω	witness
μαρτυρήσῃ, V-AAS-3S	See μαρτυρέω
μαρτυρία, η	record, testimony, witness
μαρτυριαν N-ASF	See μαρτυρία
μαρτύριον, το	testimony, witness, proof
μάρτυς, -υρος, ο	witness
μάχαιρα, η	sword

Μ, μ, Μῦ

με P-1AS	See ἐγώ
μέγας, μεγάλη, μέγα, adj	great
μεθερμηνευόμενον, V-PPP-NSN	See μεθερμηνεύω
μεθερμηνευομενον V-PPP-NSN	See μεθερμηνεύ
μεθυσθῶσι, V-APS-3S	See μεθύω
μεθύω	over drink
μείζον, ον,	greater, comparative of μέγας, great
μειζω A-APN	See μέγας
μέλει	care, it is a
μέλλω	about to
μέλος, -ους, το	member
μεμαρτύρηκα, V-RAI-1S	See μαρτυρέω
μενει V-PAI-3S	See μένω
μενεις V-PAI-2S	See μένω
μένον, V-PAP-ASN	See μένω
μένω	abide, remain
μερίζω	divide
μεριμνάω	anxious, distracted
μέρος, το	part
μέσος, adjective	middle (midst), among
μεσος A-NSM	See μέσος
Μεσσίας	Messiah
	See Μεσσίας
μέτα, prep. with accusative	according to, throughout, during, after
μέτα, prep. with genitive	down, from, against, with
μεταβαίνω	depart
μετανοέω	repent
μετάνοια, η	repentance
μέτρον, το	measure
μέχρι or μέξρις (before vowels), conj.	until, as long as
μέχρι or μέξρις (before vowels), prep with gen	as far as, even to, until
μή, conj. and adv.	lest, so that not, not, no

μηδέ	and not, nor, not even/ μηδέ...μηδέ - neither ... nor
μηδείς, μηδεμία, μηδέν Adj.	no one, nothing
μηκέτι	no longer
μήν, μηνός, ο	month
μήποτε	lest, perchance
μήτε	neither ... nor
μήτηρ, μητρός, η	mother
μήτι, interrogative particle	(expects negative answer)
μιδθός, ο	wages, reward
μικρός, ή, όν, adj	small
μιμνήσκομαι	remember
μίσεω	hate
μνῆμα, -ατος, το	grave
μνημείον, το	tomb
μνημονεύω	remember
μοι P-1DS	See ἐγώ
μοιχεύω	commit adultery
μονογενής	only begotten
μονογενης A-NSM	See μονογενής
μονογενους A-GSM	See μονογενής
μόνος, η, ον, Adj.	only, alone
μου P-1GS	See ἐγώ
μυρίας	10000
μύρον, το	ointment
μυστήριον, το	mystery
μωρός, -α, -ον, adj.	foolish
Μωσεύς	Moses
μωσεως N-GSM	See Μωσεύς
μωσης N-NSM	See Μωσεύς

Ν, ν, Νῦ

Ναζαρέθ	Nazareth
Ναθαναήλ	Nathaniel
ναί	yea, truly, yes
ναός, ο	temple
νεανίσκος, ο	youth
νεκροὶ A-NPM	νεκρός

νεκρός, νεκρά, νεκρόν, adj	dead
νέος, -α, -ον, adj.	new, young
νεφέλη, η	cloud
νήπιος, ο	infant, child
νηστεύω	fast
νικάω	conquer
νίπτω	wash
νοέω	understand
νομίζω	suppose
νομικός, -η, -ον, adj.	pertaining to the law
νόμος, ο	law
νόμῳ N-DSM	See νόμος
νόσημα, το	disease, sickness
νόσος, η	disease
νοῦς, νοός, ο	mind
νυμφίος, ο	bridegroom
νῦν, adverb	now
νυνί, adv. (Attic)	now (strengthened form)
νυξ, νυκτος, η	night

Ξ, ξ, Ξῖ

ξενία, η	lodging
ξενίζω	entertain (a stranger)
ξενοδοχέω	entertain strangers
ξένος, -η, -ον, adj.	strange, foreign
ξηραίνω	dry up
ξηρός, -ά, -όν, adj.	dry, withered
ξύλϊος, -η, -ον, adj.	wooden, made of wood
ξύλον, το	wood, tree
ξυράω	shear, shave

Ο, ο, Ὀμικρόν

ὁ / ἡ / τό	The definite article
ὅς, ἥ, ὅ, relative pronoun	who, which, what, that
ὀγδοήκοντα	80

ὄγδοος, η, ον	eighth
ὅδε, ἥδε, τόδε	this (here)
οδον N-ASF	journey, way, highway
ὁδός, ἡ	journey, way, highway
ὀδούς, -οντος, ὁ	tooth
ὅθεν	whence, wherefore
οἱ T-NPM	See ὁ / ἡ / τό
οἵ R-NPM	See ὅς, ἥ, ὁ
οἶδα	I know
οἴδατε, perf. V-RAI-2P	See εἴδω
οἰκία, η	house
οἰκοδεσπότης	householder
οἰκοδομέω	edify, build
οἰκοδομή, η	edification, building
οἰκονόμος, ὁ	steward
οἶκος, ὁ	house
οἰκουμένη, η	world, the inhabited
οἶνος, ὁ	wine
οἷος, -α, -ον, adj.	such as
ὀκτακόσιοι	800
ὀκτώ	8
ὀκτωκαίδεκα	18
ὀλίγος, η, ον, adj	few, little
ὅλος, η, ον, Adj	whole
ὀμνύω or ὄμνυμι	swear, take an oath
ὁμοθυμαδόν, adv.	with one accord
ὅμοιος, -α, -ον, adj.	like
ὁμοιόω	liken
ὁμοίως, -α, -ον, adj.	likewise
ὁμολογέω	confess, profess
ον R-ASM	See ὅς, ἥ, ὁ
ὀνειδίζω	reproach
ὄνομα, ονοματος, το	name
ὀνομάζω	name
οντα V-PAP-ASM	See εἰμί
ὄντως, adv,	really
ὀπίσω, adv	after, back, behind
ὀπίσω, prep. with Gen.	after, behind
ὅπου	where, whither

ὅπως	in order that- used similar to ἵνα
ὅραμα, -ατος, το	vision
ὁράω	see with eyes or mind
ὀργή, η	anger
ὅρια, η	boundaries
ὅρκος, ο	oath
ὅρος, το	mountain
ὅς, ἥ, ὅ relative pronoun	who, which
οσοι K-NPM	See ὅσος
ὅσος, -η, -ον, adj.	as great as, as much as, as many as
ὅστις, ἥτις, ὅτι	whoever, whichever, whatever
ὅστις, ἥτις, ὅτι, pron.	whoever, wich ever, what ever
ὅταν, Conj	when, whenever
ὅτε, adverb	when (relative)
ὅτι, conjunction	that, because
οὗ	where
οὐ (ουκ before vowels; ουχ before rough breathing)	no, not
ου R-GSM	See ὅς, ἥ, ὅ
ου PRT-N	See οὐ
οὐαί	Woe! Alas!
οὐδε … οὐδε	neither … nor
οὐδέ, conj.	not. nor. not even
οὐδείς, οὐδεμία, οὐδέν, Adj.	no one, nothing (in indicative)
οὐδέποτε	never
ουκετι, adv.	no longer
ουν, conjunction	accordingly, therefore
οὔπω, adv.	not yet
ουρανον N-ASM	See οὐρανός
οὐρανός, ο	heaven
οὐρανοῦ, N-GSM	See οὐρανός
οὖς, ὠτός, το	ear
οὔτε	not
οὔτε … οὔτε	neither … nor
οὗτος / οὗτοι / αὕτη / αὗται/ τοῦτο, pron.	this, he, her, it
ουτος D-NSM	See οὗτος / οὗτοι / αὕτη / αὗται
οὕτως, adverb	thus, so
οὐχί	not, a strong form of οὐ

ὀφείλω	owe, ought
ὀφθαλμος, ὁ	eye
ὄφις, -εως, ὁ	serpent
ὄχλος, ὁ	crowd, multitude
οψει, V-FDI-2S	See ὁράω
οψει V-FDI-2S-ATT	See ὁράω
ὄψεσθε, V-FDI-2P of ὁράω	See ὁράω
ὀψία, η	evening

Π, π, Πῖ

πάθημα, -ατος, το	suffering
παιδεύω	teach, chastise
παιδίον, το	child, babe, infant
παιδίσκη, η	maid servant
παῖς, παιδός, ὁ or η	child, boy, girl, servant
παλαιός, -α, -ον, adj.	old
πάλιν, adv.	again
παντα A-ASM	all
παντα A-NPN	all
παντες A-NPM	all
παντοκράτωρ, -ορος, ὁ	almighty, ruler of all
πάντοτε, adv.	always
παρά, prep with dative	beside, with, in the presence
παρά, prep. with accusative	at, more then, along side of
παρά, prep. with genitive	from, of, by, with
παραβολή, ης, η	parable
παραγγέλλω	command, charge
παραγίνομαι	come arrive
παραδίδωμι	hand over, betray
παράδοσις, -εως, η	tradition
παραιτέομαι	excuse, I make, refuse
παρακαλέω	beseech, comfort, exhort, intreat
παράκλησις, -εως, η	exhortation, comfort
παραλαμβάνω	take, receive
παραλυτικός, ὁ	paralytic
παράπτωμα, -ατος, το	trespass
παράχρημα	immediately
παρέλαβον, V-2AAI-3P	See παραλαμβάνω

παρεμβολή, η	camp, army, fortress
παρέρχομαι	pass by, pass away, arrive
παρέχω	offer, afford
παρθένος, η	virgin
παρίστημι	present, stand by
παρουσία, η	presence, coming
παρρησία, η	boldness, confidence
παρτίθημι	set before; middle, entrust
πᾶς, πᾶσα, πᾶν, adj	all, every
πάσχα, indeclinable, το	passover
πάσχω	suffer
πατάσσω	smite
πατήρ, πατρός, ο	father
παύομαι	cease
πείθω	pursuade
πεινάω	hunger
πειράζω	tempt
πειρασμός	temptation
πέμπτος, η, ον	fifth
πέμπω	send
πέμψαντός, V- AAP-GSM	See πέμπω
πεμψας V-AAP-NSM	See πέμπω
πεμψασιν V-AAP-DPM	See πέμπω
πενθέω	mourn
πεντακισχίλιοι	5000
πεντακόσιοι	500
πέντε	5
πεντεκαιδέκατος, η, ον	fourteenth
πεντήκοντα	50
πέραν, prep. with gen.	beyond
περι, prep. with accusative	around
περι, prep. with genitive	concerning, about, to. of
περιβάλλω	put around, clothe
περιπατέω	walk
περιπατοῦντι, V-PAP-DSM	See περιπατέω
περισσεύω	abound, am rich
περισσος, -η, -ον, adj.	excessively abundant
περισσοτέρως, adv.	more abundantly
περιστερα, η	dove

περιστεραν N-ASF	See περιστερα
περιτέμνω	circumcise
περιτομή, η	circumcision
πετεινόν, το	fowl, bird
πέτρα, η	rock
Πέτρος, ο	Peter
πετρου N-GSM	See Πέτρος
πηγή, η	spring, fountain
πιάζω	take
πίμπλημι	fill
πίνω	drink
πίπτω	fall
πιστευεις V-PAI-2S	See πιστεύω
πιστεύουσιν, V-PAP-DPM	See πιστεύω
πιστεύσωσι, V-AAS-3P	See πιστεύω
πιστεύω	believe
πίστις, πίστεως, η	faith, belief, trust
πιστός, ή, όν, adj	faithful
πλανάω	lead astray
πλάνη, η	error, wandering
πλατεῖα, η	street
πλείων, ον	more comp. of πολύς
πλεονεζία, η	covetousness
πληγή, η	wound, blow, plague
πλῆθος, το	multitude
πληθύνω	multiply
πλήν, adv.	however, but, only
πλήν, prep. with gen.	except
πλήρης, adj	full, filled up
πληρόω	I fill
πλήρωμα, -ατος, το	fullness
πλησίον, adv.	near
πλησίον, το	neighbor
πλοῖον, το	ship, boat
πλούσιος, -α, -ον, adj.	rich
πλουτέω	rich, I am
πλοῦτος, ο	wealth
πνευμα, πνευματος, το	Spirit, spirit
πνευμα N-ASN	See πνευμα, πνευματος

πνευματι N-DSN	See πνευμα, πνευματος
πνευματίκος, -η, -ον, adj.	spiritual
πόθεν, Adv.	whence (from where), from which
ποιέω	do, make
ποιήσατε, V-AAP-2P	See ποιέω
ποικίλος, -η, -ον, adj.	manifold, varied
ποιμαίνω	shepherd, rule
ποιμήν, -ένος, ο	shepherd
ποῖος, -α, -ον, adj.	what sort of, what
πόλεμος, ο	war
πόλις, πόλεως, η	city
πολλάκις	often
πολύς, πολλή, πολύ, adj	much, many
πονηρος, α, ον, adj.	evil
πορεύομαι, deponent	go
πορνεία, η	fornication
πόρνη, η	harlot, prostitute
πόρνος, ο	fornicator
πόσος, -η, -ον, adj.	how much? how great?
ποταμός, ο	river
πότε, interrogative adv.	when?
ποτέ, particle	ever, once, at some time
ποτήριον	cup
ποτίζω	drink, I give
ποῦ, adverb	whither, where
πούς, ποδός, ο	foot
πρᾶγμα, -ατος, το	deed, matter
πράξαντες, V-AAP-NPM	See πράσσω
πράσσω	perform habitually, do
πραΰτης, -ητος, η	gentleness, humility
πρεσβύτερος, -α, -ον, adj	elder
πρεσβύτεροι, N-NPM	See πρεσβύτερος
πρίν, adv.	before
πρό, prep with gen.	before
προάγω	lead forth
πρόβατα	See πρόβατον
πρόβατον	sheep, lambs
προέρχομαι	precede, go in front
πρόθεσις, -εως, η	setting forth, a purpose

πρόπος, ο	manner, way
προς, prep. with accusative	toward, to, against, with
προς, prep. with dative	at, by, near, on, by means of
προς, prep. with genitive	for, concerning
βπροσδέχομαι	receive, wait for
προσδοκάω	wait for
προσέρχομαι	come to
προσευχή, η	prayer
προσεύχομαι	I pray
προσέχω	take heed, attend to
προσκαλέομαι	summon
προσκαρτερέω	continue in or with
προσλαμβάνω	receive
προστίθημι	add, add to
προσφέρω	bring to
πρόσωπον, το	face
πρότερος, adv.	before
πρότερος, -α, -ον, adj.	former
προφηται N-NPM	See προφήτης
προφητεία, η	prophecy
προφητεύω	prophesy
προφήτης, ο	prophet
προφητῶν	See προφήτης
πρωί	early, in the morning
πρῶτος, adj.	first, chief
πρῶτος, -ή, -όν, adj	first
πτωχός, -η, -ον, adj. or noun	poor, as noun-poor man
πύλη, η	gate, porch
πυλών, -ῶνος, ο	gateway, vestibule
πυνθάνομαι	inquire
πῦρ, πυρός, το	fire
πωλέω	sell
πῶλος, ο	colt
πώποτε, Adv.	at any time
πως, a particle	at all, somehow, in any way
πῶς, adv.	how; in what manner? by what means?

Ρ, ρ, Ρῶ

ῥαββί, ὁ	master (rabbi)
Ῥαβδίζω	beat with rods
Ῥάβδος, ἡ	rod
Ῥάπισμα, -ατος, τό	strike, slap
Ῥαφίς, ίδος, ἡ	needle
Ῥέω	flow
ῥῆμα, -ματος, το	word, speech
ῥίζα, η	root
Ῥιζόω	root, cause to take root
Ῥίπτω	cast, cast down
ῥύομαι	deliver, rescue
Ῥυπᾰρός, -ά, -όν, adj.	filthy, dirty
Ῥώννυμι	strengthen, render firm

Σ, σ, ς, Σίγμα

σάββατον, το	sabbath
σαλεύω	shake
σάλπιγξ, -ιγγος, η	trumpet
σαλπίζω	sound a trumpet
σάρξ, σαρκός, η	flesh
σάρκα	(N-ASF) See σάρξ
σε P-2AS	See σύ
σεαυτοῦ, ῆς reflexive pronoun	of yourself (thyself)
σέβομαι	reverence, worship
σεισμός, ο	earthquake
σένδέκατος, η, ον	eleventh
σημεῖον, ον	miracle, sign
σιγάω	silent, I am
σιμωνα N-ASM	See Σίμων, Σίμωνος
Σίμων, Σίμωνος, ο	Simon
σῖτος, ο	wheat
σιωπάω	silent, I am
σκανδαλίζω	stumble, cause to
σκάνδαλον, το	stumbling, cause of
σκεῦος, ο	vessel, plural, goods
σκηνή, η	tabernacle, tent

σκηνόω	dwell
σκοτία, η	darkness
σκοτια N-DSF	See σκοτία
σκότος, ο	darkness
σοι P-2DS	See σύ
σός, ή, όν, poss. adj.	belonging to you (thee), your (thy)
σός, σή, σόν	thy, thine
σοφία, η	wisdom
σοφός, -η, -ον	wise
σπείπω	sow
σπέρμα, -ατος,το	seed
σπέρματος	(N-GSN) See σπέρμα
σπλάγχνα, η	bowels, heart, compassion
σπλαγχνίζομαι	compassion, I have
σπουδάζω	hasten, am eager
σπουδή, η	haste, diligence
στάδιον, το (τὰ στάδια)	furlong-about 606 ft.
σταυρός, ο	cross
σταυρόω	crucify
στέφανος, ο	crown (Stephen)
στήκω	stand, stand fast
στηρίζω	establish
στόμα, στόματος, το	mouth
στρατηγός, ο	commander
στρατιώτης, ο	soldier
στραφεὶς, V-2APP-NSM	See στρέφω
στρέφω	turn
σύ, pron. P-2NS	you
συγγενής, -ης, -ες, adj.	kindred, relative
συζητέω	discuss, dispute
συκῆ, η	Fig tree
συκην N-ASF	See συκῆ
συκης N-GSF	See συκῆ
συλλαμβάνω	take, conceive
συμφέρω	bring together
σύν, Pron Dat.	With
συνάγω	gather
συναγωγή, η	synagogue
σύνδουλος, ο	fellow servant, fellow slave

συνέδριον, το	council, Sanhedrin
συνείδησισ, -εως, η	conscience
συνεργός, ο	fellow laborer
συνέρχομαι	come together
συνέχω	hold fast, oppress
συνίημι	understand
συνίστημι or συνιστάνω	commend (tr.), stand with, consist (intr.)
σφάζω	slay
σφόδρα, adv.	exceedingly
σφραγίζω	seal
σφραγίς, -ἴδος, η	seal
σχίζω	split
σώζω	save
σωμα, σωματος, το	body
σωτήρ, -ηρος, ο	Savior
σωτηρία, η	salvation

Τ, τ, Ταῦ

τα T-APN	See ὁ, ἡ, τό
τάλαντον, το	talent
ταπεινόω	humble
ταράγω	pass by
ταράσσω	trouble
ταραχή, η	trouble, disturb
τάρειμι	present, I am; arrived, I have
τάσσω	appoint, arrange
ταυτα D-NPN	See οὗτος, οὗτοι, αὕτη, αὕται
ταχέως, adv.	quickly
ταχύ, adv.	quickly
ταχύς, -α, -υ, adj	wift
τε	particle, and often not translated
τεθέαμαι, perf. V-RNI-1S	See θεάομαι
τεκνα N-NPN	See τέκνον
τέκνον, το	child, son
τέλειος, -α, -ον, adj.	complete, perfect, mature
τελειόω	fullfill, make perfect
τελευτάω	die

τελέω	fulfill, finish
τέλος, το	end
τελώνης, ο	tax collector
τέρας, -ατος, το	wonder
τεσσαράκοντα	40
τέσσαρες, τέσσαρα	four
τεσσαρεσκαιδέκατος, η,	thirteenth
τέταρτος, η, ον	fourth
τετρακισχίλιοι	4000
τετρακόσιοι	400
τη T-DSF	See ὁ, ἡ, τό
την T-ASF	See ὁ, ἡ, τό
τηρέω	keep
της T-GSF	See ὁ, ἡ, τό
τι I-ASN	See τίς, τι
τι I-NSN	See τίς, τι
τίθημι	place, put
τίκτω	give birth to
τιμάω	honor
τιμή, ης, η	honor, price
τίμιος, -α, -ον, adj.	precious, honorable
τίς, τι, indefinite pronoun	someone, something, a certain one, a certain thing
τίς, τί, interrogative pronoun	who, which, what
το T-ASN	See ὁ, ἡ, τό
το T-NSN	See ὁ, ἡ, τό
τοιοῦτος, η, ον, adj	such
τοις T-DPM	See ὁ, ἡ, τό
τολμάω	dare
τον T-ASM	See ὁ, ἡ, τό
τόπος, ο	place
τοσοῦτος, -αύτη, -οῦτον, -οῦτο, adj.	so great, so much, so many
τότε, adv.	Then, at that time
του T-GSM	See ὁ, ἡ, τό
του T-GSN	See ὁ, ἡ, τό
τους T-APM	See ὁ, ἡ, τό
τουτο D-ASN	See οὗτος, οὗτοι, αὕτη, αὗται
τουτων D-GPN	See οὗτος, οὗτοι, αὕτη, αὗται

τράπεζα, η	table
τρεῖς	three
τρεισκαίδεκα	13
τρέχω	run
τριάκοντα	30
τριακόσιοι	300
τρίς	thrice
τρισχίλιοι	3000
τρίτος, η, ον	third
τροσκυνέω	worship
τροφή, η	food
τυγχάνω	obtain, happen
τύπος, ο	mark, example
τύπτω	smite
τυφλός, ὁ	blind man
τω T-DSM	See ὁ, ἡ, τό
των T-GPM	See ὁ, ἡ, τό

Υ, υ, Ὑψιλόν

ὑγιαίνω	good health, I am in
ὑγιής	whole, healthy
ὕδατι N-DSN	See υδωρ
ὕδωρ, ὕδατος, το	water
υἱόν N-ASM	See υἱός
υἱός, ο	son
υἱοῦ, N-GSM	See υἱός
ὑμεις P-2NP	See σύ
ὑμέτερος, α, ον, poss, adj.	belonging to you, your
ὑμιν P-2DP	See σύ
ὑμων P-2GP	See σύ
ὑπάγω	depart
ὑπακοή, η	obedience
ὑπακούω	obey
ὑπαντάω	meet, go to meet
ὑπαρχω	exist
ὑπέρ, prep. acc.	above
ὑπέρ, prep. gen.	in behalf of
ὑπηρέτης, ο	servant, assistant

ὑπό, prep. gen.	by, of
ὑπό, prep. acc.	under
υποδημα, -ατος, το	shoe, sandal
ὑποκάτω, adv	under, underneath
ὑποκριτής, ο	hypocrite
ὑπομένω	tarry, endure
ὑπομονή, η	steadfast endurance
ὑποστρέφω	return
ὑποτάσσω	put in subjection
ὑστερέω	lack
ὕστερος, -α, -ον, adj.	afterwards, later
ὑψηλός, -η, -ον, adj.	high, lofty
ὕψιστος, -η, -ον, adj.	highest
ὑψόω	lift up, exalt

Φ, φ, Φῖ

φαινει V-PAI-3S	See φαίνω
φαίνω	shine
φανερός, -α, -αν, adj.	manifest
φανερόω	make manifest
φανερωθῇ, V-APS-3S	See φανερόω
Φαρισαῖος, ο	Pharisee
φαρισαιων N-GPM	See Φαρισαῖος
φαῦλος, το	evil, foul
φείδομαι	spare
φέρω	bear, bring, carry
φεύγω	flee
φημί	say
φιάλη, η	cup bowl
φιλέω	love
φιλιππον N-ASM	See Φίλιππος
Φίλιππος	Philip
φίλος, -η, -ον, adj.	loving
φίλος, ο, noun	friend
φοβέομαι	to fear
φόβος, ο	fear
φονεύω	kill, murder
φωνή, η	noise, sound, voice

φωνῆς, N-GSF — See φωνή
φρονέω — think
φρόνιμος, -η, -ον, adj. — prudent
φυλακή, η — guard, prison
φυλάσσω — guard
φυλή, η — tribe
φύσις, -εως, η — nature
φυτεύω — plant
φωνέω — call
φωνή, η — voice
φωνησαι V-AAN — See φωνή
φῶς, φωτός, το — light
φωτιζει V-PAI-3S — See φῶς
φωτίζω — light

Χ, χ, Χῖ

χαίρω — rejoice
χαρά, η — joy, delight
χαρίζομαι — freely give, forgive
χαριν N-ASF — See χάρις
χάρις, χάριτος η — grace
χάρισμα, -ατος, το — spirituai gift
χείρ, χειρός, η — hand
χείρων, -ων, -ον, adj. — worse, more severe
χήρα, η — widow
χιλίαρχος — captain
χιλιάς, -αδος, η — 1000
χίλιοι — 1000
χιτώς, -ῶνος, ο — tunic
χοῖρος, ο — pig
χορτάζω — eat to the full
χόρτος, ο — grass, hay
χπεία, η — need
χράομαι — use
χρηστότης, -ητος, η — goodness, kindness
Χριστός, ο — Christ
χριστου N-GSM — See Χριστός
χρόνος, ο — time

χρύσεος, -α, -ον, adj.	golden
χρυσίον, το	gold
χρυσός, ο	gold
χωλός, -η, -ον, adj.	lame
χώρα, η	country
χωρίζω	separate, depart
χωρίον, το	place, field
χωρίς, prep. with gen. and Adv.	without, apart from, beside

Ψ, ψ, Ψῖ

ψεύδομαι	lie
ψευδοπροφήτης	false prophet
ψεῦδος, το	lie
ψεύστης, ο	liar
ψυχή, η	soul

Ω, ω, Ὠμέγα

ὦ	O!
ὧδε	hither, here
ωμολογησεν V-AAI-3S	See ὁμολογέω
ὤν, οὖσα, ὄν V-PAP-NSM	See εἰμί
ὥρα, η	hour
ὡς, adverb	as, like, even as, how, about
ὡσαύτως, adv.	likewise
ὡσεί, ADV	as, like, about
ὥστε	so that
ὥστερ	just as, even as
ὠφελέω	profit

ABOUT THE AUTHOR

Dr. Steve Combs is an ordained minister. He spent his early years in Kentucky, Virginia, and finally Ohio. He was not raised in a Christian home. He had some Christian influence from his grandmother, but that had little effect on him. Due to discussions with a Baptist preacher and a Sunday School teacher, who visited his home, he began to read the Bible. The Word of God had its effect. He came under strong conviction of his sins. A friend invited him to a nearby church during revival meetings. As a result, he received Christ as his Savior.

Since then, there have been major transformations to his life. God called him to preach and enabled a backward shy individual suffering from an inferiority complex to stand before crowds and confidently proclaim the Word of God. God gave him a business background as a CPA. God put him in several ministry positions. He has served as a Bible Institute teacher and Dean, a youth pastor, assistant pastor, and a senior pastor. He holds a Doctor of Theology from Covington Theological Seminary.

Currently Steve Combs is Assistant Director and a Global Translation Advisor for Global Bible Translators/ Bearing Precious Seed Global, www.bpsglobal.com, a ministry of Plantation Baptist Church in Plantation, Florida. Global Bible Translators starts and assists Bible translation projects around the world.

He is married and has four married children.

INDEX

Abstract Nouns, 7, 254, 256, 257
Accent marks, 9, 99
Accusative Case, 113, 125, 137, 138, 148, 158, 160, 167, 169, 170, 172, 178, 201, 231, 233, 234, 235, 237, 239, 241, 243, 257, 305
Active Voice, 5, 115, 116, 117, 118, 120, 121, 122, 123, 143, 144, 146, 148, 149, 154, 175, 176, 177, 182, 183, 185, 196, 197, 204, 205, 212, 213, 214, 215, 218, 219, 228, 229, 230, 246, 247, 248, 268, 273, 277, 284, 291, 306, 307, 308, 310
Adding To or Taking Away from Scripture, 8, 292, 294
Adjective used as a substantive, 165
Adjectives, 6, 7, 61, 125, 139, 140, 152, 153, 158, 162, 163, 164, 165, 167, 168, 169, 171, 172, 173, 188, 191, 196, 197, 198, 199, 204, 235, 236, 254, 257, 261, 262, 310, 311,
  Adjective used as a substantive, 165
  Attributive Adjective, 140, 257
  Positive Degree of Adjectives, 163
  Possessive adjectives, 168, 172
  Predicate Adjective, 162, 164, 165, 254, 257
  Superlative degree of Adjectives, 163, 169, 170, 172
Adverbs, 6, 136, 139, 140, 168, 171, 172, 173, 196, 207, 231, 235, 236, 263, 310, 311
Alphabet, 5, 96, 104
  accent marks, 9, 99

Article, 5, 7, 113, 114, 116, 125, 127, 137, 140, 148, 149, 152, 153, 156, 164, 165, 198, 199, 230, 231, 232, 233, 234, 239, 243, 254, 255, 257, 260, 265, 283, 295, 305, 311, 312
breathing marks, 72, 98
Consonant Combinations, 97
Diaresis, 97, 145
Diphthongs, 97, 98, 99, 145, 146, 214, 243
Enclitic, 150, 151
Iota Subscript, 99
Long and Short Vowels, 99
Open and closed vowels, 99
Postpositive, 141
Pronunciation, 5, 18, 90, 96, 99, 104
Proclitic, 150
Punctuation, 99, 100
Rules of Contraction, 97, 145
Ambiguities, 8, 290, 292, 297, 298,
Anachronisms, 8, 292, 302
Aorist active, 174, 175, 176, 185, 203, 204, 205, 218, 219, 228, 229, 230, 291
Aorist middle, 175, 177, 204, 219, 229, 230
Aorist participle, 6, 7, 197, 204, 205, 206, 254, 311
Aorist passive, 176, 177, 178, 183, 205, 219, 229, 230, 247, 248, 310
Aorist Tense, 6, 7, 116, 117, 118, 174, 175, 176, 177, 178, 183, 185, 195, 197, 203, 204, 205, 206, 213, 218, 219, 220, 226, 229, 230, 231,

358

Aorist Tense, cont. - 246, 247, 248, 254, 255, 291, 306, 307, 310, 311
Article, 5, 7, 113, 114, 116, 125, 127, 137, 140, 148, 149, 152, 153, 156, 164, 165, 198, 199, 230, 231, 232, 233, 234, 239, 243, 254, 255, 257, 260, 265, 283, 295, 305, 311, 312
Aorist active, 174, 175, 176, 185, 203, 204, 205, 218, 219, 228, 229, 230, 291
Aorist middle, 175, 177, 204, 219, 229, 230
Aorist participle, 6, 7, 197, 204, 205, 206, 254, 311
Aorist passive, 176, 177, 178, 183, 205, 219, 229, 230, 247, 248, 310
Attributive, 6, 7, 140, 152, 162, 164, 165, 197, 198, 199, 206, 254, 257, 311
Attributive Adjective, 140, 257
Authority of the Scriptures, 5, 21, 22, 26, 30, 31, 32, 33, 35, 76
Bible
  Authority of the Scriptures, 5, 21, 22, 26, 30, 31, 32, 33, 35, 76
  Inspiration of the Scriptures, 5, 21, 22, 23, 25, 26, 29, 34, 35, 36, 64, 76, 80, 81, 82
  *Preservation of the Scriptures***,** 5, 16, 21, 26, 27, 28, 29, 35, 67, 76, 80, 81, 82
  Sufficiency of Scripture, 33
Breathing marks, 72, 98
Case, 5, 6, 7, 18, 19, 39, 47, 61, 86, 94, 99, 105, 113, 114, 124, 125, 126, 127, 129, 130, 131, 132, 137, 138, 139, 148, 151, 152, 153, 155, 156, 160, 164, 170, 172, 178, 188, 190, 196, 200, 201, 202, 203, 207, 209, 213, 214, 225, 227, 230, 234, 235, 237, 241, 243, 251, 255, 257, 259, 272, 273, 278, 290, 298, 302, 305, 306, 307, 308, 310, 311, 312
  Accusative Case, 113, 125, 137, 138, 148, 158, 160, 167, 169, 170, 172, 178, 201, 231, 233, 234, 235, 237, 239, 241, 243, 257, 305
  Dative Case, 5, 6, 7, 18, 99, 113, 125, 129, 130, 131, 132,133, 134, 137, 138, 139, 154, 160, 178, 190, 202, 218, 227, 234, 235, 241, 242, 243, 260, 270, 272, 305
    Dative of Advantage or Disadvantage, 132
    Dative of Cause, 133
    Dative of Indirect object, 132
    Dative of Manner, 134
    Dative of Means, 7, 133, 241, 242
    Dative of Measure, 134,
    Dative of Personal Agency, 133
    Dative of Place, 132, 133
    Dative of Possession, 6, 182, 218, 227
    Dative of Sphere, 133
    Dative of Time, 133
  Genitive Case, 6, 7, 113, 125, 130, 131, 137, 138, 151, 154, 160, 168, 170, 171, 172, 189, 195, 200, 202, 203, 209, 210, 228, 232, 239, 240, 241, 243, 255, 274, 278, 305
    Genitive absolute, 209
    Genitive and the Articular Infinitive, 232
    Genitive and the Expression of Agency, 228, 239
    Genitive of Comparison, 170,
    Genitive of Content, 210
    Genitive of Person with παρά, 274, 278

Case, cont. -
  Genitive of Place, 209
  Genitive of Separation, 210
  Genitive with ὑπό, 241
  Nominative Case, 5, 6, 113, 114, 122, 123, 124, 125, 126, 127, 130, 146, 148, 149, 151, 152, 153, 154, 158, 163, 169, 188, 189, 190, 195, 196, 200, 201, 202, 205, 248, 257, 283, 305
    Nominative of Apposition, 127
    Predicate nominative, 113, 122, 123, 125, 127, 146, 148, 149, 283, 305
  Vocative Case, 113, 125, 190, 305
Collocational Clash, 7, 266
Compound Verbs, 139
Conditional Clauses and the Subjunctive, 223, 224
Conjunctions, 5, 6, 7, 136, 141, 218, 225, 231, 255, 259, 274, 276
  Conjunction δε, 276
Consistency in Bible Translation, 7, 254, 258
Consonant Combinations, 97
Constructions with πιστευω, 6, 174, 178
Cultural Substitutes, 8, 292, 298, 300
Dative Case, 5, 6, 7, 18, 99, 113, 125, 129, 130, 131, 132, 133, 134, 137, 138, 139, 154, 160, 178, 190, 202, 218, 227, 234, 235, 241, 242, 243, 260, 270, 272, 305
  Dative of Advantage or Disadvantage, 132
  Dative of Cause, 133
  Dative of Indirect object, 132
  Dative of Manner, 134
  Dative of Means, 7, 133, 241, 242
  Dative of Measure, 134,

Dative of Personal Agency, 133
Dative of Place, 132, 133
Dative of Possession, 6, 182, 218, 227
Dative of Sphere, 133
Dative of Time, 133
Declension, 5, 6, 114, 124, 125, 126, 127, 129, 130, 131, 134, 150, 151, 156, 157, 158, 159, 160, 162, 163, 164, 165, 166, 169, 172, 188, 189, 190, 191, 192, 196, 200, 204, 205, 215, 218, 243, 254, 260, 261, 306
  First Declension, 5, 129, 130, 131, 134, 196, 204,
  Second declension, 5, 6, 124, 125, 127, 162, 163, 169, 172, 188, 189, 196, 204, 261, 262
  Third declension, 125, 188, 189, 190, 191, 196, 204,
Deliberative Subjunctive, 221
Demonstrative Pronoun, 6, 150, 155, 156, 157, 161, 312
Deponent, 122, 123, 178, 183, 195, 226, 310
Diaresis, 97, 145
Diphthongs, 97, 98, 99, 145, 146, 214, 243
Direct discourse, 6, 228, 237, 238
Emphatic Negative Subjunctive, 221
Enclitic, 150, 151
E-Sword, 5, 12, 13, 15, 17, 18, 86, 101, 105, 106, 115, 185, 249
Figures of Speech, 7, 8, 48, 82, 266, 269, 279, 287, 288, 289, 290
First Aorist, 6, 7, 174, 175, 176, 204, 205, 254, 255, 307
First Declension, 5, 129, 130, 131, 134, 196, 204,

Flexibility in Translation, 7, 138, 139, 141, 246, 252, 258, 270, 272
Future tense, 6, 116, 117, 118, 176, 181, 182, 183, 184, 185, 223, 224, 246, 247, 248, 269, 306, 307, 310
Gender, 18, 61, 113, 114, 116, 125, 126, 151, 152, 155, 160, 163, 164, 190, 196, 227, 230, 305, 306, 310, 311, 312
Genitive Case, 6, 7, 113, 125, 130, 131, 137, 138, 151, 154, 160, 168, 170, 171, 172, 189, 195, 200, 202, 203, 209, 210, 228, 232, 239, 240, 241, 243, 255, 274, 278, 305
  Genitive absolute, 209
  Genitive and the Articular Infinitive, 232
  Genitive and the Expression of Agency, 228, 239
  Genitive of Comparison, 170,
  Genitive of Content, 210
  Genitive of Person with παρά, 274, 278
  Genitive of Place, 209
  Genitive of Separation, 210
  Genitive with ὑπό, 241
Grammar and Meaning, 274, 277, 283, 305
Historical Present, 7, 266, 269, 290
Hortatory Subjunctive, 220,
Imperative Mood, 6, 116, 178, 208, 221, 228, 229, 230, 234, 236, 247, 255, 306, 309
Imperfect Tense, 5, 116, 117, 118, 119, 120, 121, 122, 123, 127, 148, 175, 178, 182, 197, 246, 247, 306, 307
Implied Information, 7, 260, 264, 265, 295, 298
Indefinite Pronoun, 6, 113, 150, 155, 157, 158, 161, 312

Indicative Mood, 5, 6, 116, 120, 121, 122, 123, 143, 144,146, 147, 148, 149, 154, 162, 175, 177, 178, 181, 182, 183, 184, 185, 197, 199, 200, 204, 205, 206, 212, 213, 215, 216, 220, 222, 223, 224,225, 237, 242, 243, 246, 247, 254, 255, 268, 273, 291, 306, 307, 309
Indirect discourse, 6, 228, 237, 238,
Infinitive, 6, 228, 230, 231, 232, 233, 234, 235, 236, 237, 242, 248, 255, 310
Inspiration of the Scriptures, 5, 21, 22, 23, 25, 26, 29, 34, 35, 36, 64, 76, 80, 81, 82
Interrogative, 6, 155, 157, 158, 160, 161, 312
Iota Subscript, 99
Lexicon, 8, 18, 83, 86, 103, 104, 120, 125, 127, 134, 176, 183, 185, 187, 249, 250
Long and Short Vowels, 99
Method of Bible Translation, 8, 279, 281
Middle Voice, 5, 6, 116, 117, 121, 122, 143, 147, 174, 175, 176, 177, 178, 181, 182, 183, 184, 196, 203, 205, 214, 215, 216, 219, 228, 229, 230, 231, 247, 248, 306, 308, 310
Mood, 116, 120, 148, 188, 193, 196, 204, 213, 218, 220, 222, 223, 224, 226, 229, 230, 237, 2402, 243, 247, 306, 307, 309, 312
Moveable Nu, 144, 190
Negative Subjunctive, 221
Nominative Case, 5, 6, 113, 114, 122, 123, 124, 125, 126, 127, 130, 146, 148, 149, 151, 152, 153, 154, 158, 163, 169, 188, 189, 190, 195,

Nominative Case, cont. - 196, 200, 201, 202, 205, 248, 257, 283, 305
  Nominative of Apposition, 127
  Predicate nominative, 113, 122, 123, 125, 127, 146, 148, 149, 283, 305
Noun, 5, 6, 7, 18, 19, 61, 62, 83, 114, 116, 118, 124, 125, 126, 127, 129, 130, 131, 132, 134, 137, 139, 140, 145, 148, 150, 152, 156, 157, 163, 164, 165, 170, 171, 188, 189, 190, 191, 196, 197, 198, 199, 207, 209, 210, 230, 231, 235, 236, 240, 250, 254, 256, 257, 305, 310, 311
  Abstract Nouns, 7, 254, 256, 257
Accusative Case, 113, 125, 137, 138, 148, 158, 160, 167, 169, 170, 172, 178, 201, 231, 233, 234, 235, 237, 239, 241, 243, 257, 305
Case, 5, 6, 7, 18, 19, 39, 47, 61, 86, 94, 99, 105, 113, 114, 124, 125, 126, 127, 129, 130, 131, 132, 137, 138, 139, 148, 151, 152, 153, 155, 156, 160, 164, 170, 172, 178, 188, 190, 196, 200, 201, 202, 203, 207, 209, 213, 214, 225, 227, 230, 234, 235, 237, 241, 243, 251, 255, 257, 259, 272, 273, 278, 290, 298, 302, 305, 306, 307, 308, 310, 311, 312
Active Voice, 5, 115, 116, 117, 118, 120, 121, 122, 123, 143, 144, 146, 148, 149, 154, 175, 176, 177, 182, 183, 185, 196, 197, 204, 205, 212, 213, 214, 215, 218, 219, 228, 229, 230, 246, 247, 248, 268, 273, 277, 284, 291, 306, 307, 308, 310
Dative Case, 5, 6, 7, 18, 99, 113, 125, 129, 130, 131, 132,133, 134, 137, 138, 139, 154, 160, 178, 190,
202, 218, 227, 234, 235, 241, 242, 243, 260, 270, 272, 305
Dative of Advantage or Disadvantage, 132
Dative of Cause, 133
Dative of Indirect object, 132
Dative of Manner, 134
Dative of Means, 7, 133, 241, 242
Dative of Measure, 134,
Dative of Personal Agency, 133
Dative of Place, 132, 133
Dative of Possession, 6, 182, 218, 227
Dative of Sphere, 133
Dative of Time, 133
Declension, 5, 6, 114, 124, 125, 126, 127, 129, 130, 131, 134, 150, 151, 156, 157, 158, 159, 160, 162, 163, 164, 165, 166, 169, 172, 188, 189, 190, 191, 192, 196, 200, 204, 205, 215, 218, 243, 254, 260, 261, 306
  First Declension, 5, 129, 130, 131, 134, 196, 204,
  Second declension, 5, 6, 124, 125, 127, 162, 163, 169, 172, 188, 189, 196, 204, 261, 262
  Third declension, 125, 188, 189, 190, 191, 196, 204,
Gender, 18, 61, 113, 114, 116, 125, 126, 151, 152, 155, 160, 163, 164, 190, 196, 227, 230, 305, 306, 310, 311, 312
Genitive Case, 6, 7, 113, 125, 130, 131, 137, 138, 151, 154, 160, 168, 170, 171, 172, 189, 195, 200, 202, 203, 209, 210, 228, 232, 239, 240, 241, 243, 255, 274, 278, 305
  Genitive absolute, 209

Noun, cont. -
   Genitive and the Articular Infinitive, 232
   Genitive and the Expression of Agency, 228, 239
   Genitive of Comparison, 170,
   Genitive of Content, 210
   Genitive of Person with παρά, 274, 278
   Genitive of Place, 209
   Genitive of Separation, 210
   Genitive with ὑπό, 241
Mood, 116, 120, 148, 188, 193, 196, 204, 213, 218, 220, 222, 223, 224, 226, 229, 230, 237, 2402, 243, 247, 306, 307, 309, 312
Moveable Nu, 144, 190
Nominative Case, 5, 6, 113, 114, 122, 123, 124, 125, 126, 127, 130, 146, 148, 149, 151, 152, 153, 154, 158, 163, 169, 188, 189, 190, 195, 196, 200, 201, 202, 205, 248, 257, 283, 305
   Nominative of Apposition, 127
   Predicate nominative, 113, 122, 123, 125, 127, 146, 148, 149, 283, 305
Number (singular or plural), 7, 18, 33, 113, 114, 116, 117, 125, 152, 155, 160, 164, 196, 305, 306, 310, 311, 312
Person, 116, 117, 118, 120, 121, 122, 123, 132, 144, 150, 151, 154, 156, 159, 175, 176, 182, 183, 212, 218, 220, 221, 228, 237, 240, 246, 268, 269, 306, 309, 312
Predicate nominative, 113, 122, 123, 125, 127, 146, 148, 149, 283, 305
Subject, 113, 117, 121, 122, 125, 126, 127, 133, 137, 148, 150, 152, 153, 157, 159, 183, 198, 201, 209, 231, 234, 235, 257, 277, 282, 283, 298, 305, 308, 310, 312
Vocative Case, 113, 125, 190, 305
Numbers, 260, 261, 262
Only begotten, 250, 251, 257
Open and closed vowels, 99
Optative tense, 116, 226, 306, 309
Parsing, 101, 114, 118, 120, 122, 123, 125, 126, 127, 134, 137, 141, 142, 144, 149, 151, 154, 161, 167, 205, 212, 240, 312
Participle, 6, 7, 171, 188, 194, 195, 196, 197, 198, 199, 200, 203, 204, 205, 206, 207, 208, 209, 212, 214, 215, 234, 238, 242, 248, 254, 255, 277, 281, 284, 310, 311
Passive Voice, 5, 6, 116, 117, 121, 122, 123, 143, 147, 176, 177, 178, 181, 182, 183, 184, 195, 196, 198, 203, 204, 214, 215, 216, 219, 229, 230, 231, 241, 247, 248, 277, 281, 306, 308, 310
Perfect tense, 5, 176, 188, 195, 196, 206, 212, 213, 214, 215, 218, 231, 246, 247, 248, 250, 269, 273, 306, 307, 308, 310
Person, 116, 117, 118, 120, 121, 122, 123, 132, 144, 150, 151, 154, 156, 159, 175, 176, 182, 183, 212, 218, 220, 221, 228, 237, 240, 246, 268, 269, 306, 309, 312
Pluperfect Tense, 6, 116, 212, 215, 216, 306, 308
Pointers for Translation, 256, 264, 268, 276, 281
Polysemy, 7, 185, 241, 245, 258
Positive Degree of Adjectives, 163
Possessive adjectives, 168, 172
Possessive Pronoun, 152, 227, 312
Postpositive, 141

363

Predicate position, 7, 153, 162, 164, 165, 198, 199, 254, 257
Predicate Adjective, 162, 164, 165, 254, 257
Predicate nominative, 113, 122, 123, 125, 127, 146, 148, 149, 283, 305
Prepositions, 5, 7, 113, 125, 131, 132, 133, 134, 136, 137, 138, 139, 140, 141, 142, 148, 152, 171, 208, 209, 210, 232, 233, 234, 241, 242, 253, 254, 255, 257, 272, 273, 278, 305, 310, 312
Compound Verbs, 139
Present Participles, 6, 195, 197, 200, 205, 207, 208, 255, 310
Present Tense, 117, 118, 119, 120, 123, 144, 147, 175, 178, 181, 183, 197, 213, 219, 231, 269, 290, 306, 307, 308, 310
Preservation of the Scriptures, 5, 16, 21, 26, 27, 28, 29, 35, 67, 76, 80, 81, 82
Principle Parts of Verbs, 176, 183
Principles of Translating:
  Adding To or Taking Away from Scripture, 8, 292, 294
  Ambiguities, 8, 290, 292, 297, 298,
  Anachronisms, 8, 292, 302
  Collocational Clash, 7, 266
  Consistency in Bible Translation, 7, 254, 258
  Cultural Substitutes, 8, 292, 298, 300
  E-Sword, 5, 12, 13, 15, 17, 18, 86, 101, 105, 106, 115, 185, 249
  Figures of Speech, 7, 8, 48, 82, 266, 269, 279, 287, 288, 289, 290
  Flexibility in Translation, 7, 138, 139, 141, 246, 252, 258, 270, 272
  Grammar and Meaning, 274, 277, 283, 305
  Historical Present, 7, 266, 269, 290
  Implied Information, 7, 260, 264, 265, 295, 298
  Italics in Translation, 6, 228, 239
  Method of Bible Translation, 8, 279, 281
  Only begotten, 250, 251, 257
  Pointers for Translation, 256, 264, 268, 276, 281
  Polysemy, 7, 185, 241, 245, 258
  Preservation of the Scriptures, 5, 16, 21, 26, 27, 28, 29, 35, 67, 76, 80, 81, 82
  Role of Teachers, 8, 292, 303
  Shifts in Verb Tense, 8, 279, 290
  Source Language, 277, 282, 283, 284, 295, 296, 297, 313
  Target Language, 283
  Translating Idioms, 8, 279, 284
  Word Order, 6, 7, 141, 148, 184, 228, 239, 265, 274, 277, 278, 283, 305
Proclitic, 150
Pronouns, 5, 6, 7, 114, 126, 132, 137, 140, 150, 151, 152, 153, 154, 155, 156, 157, 158, 159, 160, 161, 162, 163, 166, 170, 172, 197, 198, 199, 207, 209, 224, 227, 241, 244, 255, 259, 260, 265, 266, 268, 269, 311, 312
  Demonstrative Pronoun, 6, 150, 155, 156, 157, 161, 312
  Indefinite Pronoun, 6, 113, 150, 155, 157, 158, 161, 312
  Interrogative, 6, 155, 157, 158, 160, 161, 312
  Possessive Pronoun, 152, 227, 312

Pronouns, cont. -
Reciprocal pronoun, 155, 160, 161, 312
Reflexive pronoun, 6, 152, 155, 159, 161, 312
Relative pronoun, 6, 150, 152, 160, 161, 255 259, 312
Pronunciation, 5, 18, 90, 96, 99, 104
Proper Names, 7, 241, 243,
Punctuation, 99, 100
Reciprocal pronoun, 155, 160, 161, 312
Reflexive pronoun, 6, 152, 155, 159, 161, 312
Relative pronoun, 6, 150, 152, 160, 161, 255 259, 312
Role of Teachers, 8, 292
Rules of Contraction, 97, 145
Second Aorist, 6, 7, 174, 175, 176, 177, 178, 185, 204, 205, 206, 219, 230, 231, 246, 254, 255, 307
Second declension, 5, 6, 124, 125, 127, 162, 163, 169, 172, 188, 189, 196, 204, 261, 262
Shifts in Verb Tense, 8, 279, 290
Simple Subjunctive, 220
Source Language, 277, 282, 283, 284, 295, 296, 297, 313
Subject, 113, 117, 121, 122, 125, 126, 127, 133, 137, 148, 150, 152, 153, 157, 159, 183, 198, 201, 209, 231, 234, 235, 257, 277, 282, 283, 298, 305, 308, 310, 312
Subjunctive, 6, 7, 116, 188, 193, 218, 219, 220, 221, 222, 223, 224, 225, 226, 230, 254, 255, 284, 306, 309
   Conditional Clauses and the Subjunctive, 223, 224
   Deliberative Subjunctive, 221
   Emphatic Negative Subjunctive, 221
   Hortatory Subjunctive, 220,
   Negative Subjunctive, 221
   Simple Subjunctive, 220
   Subjunctive showing purpose, 222
Sufficiency of Scripture, 33
Superlative degree of Adjectives, 163, 169, 170, 172
Target Language, 283
Tense of Verbs, 23, 116, 117, 118, 119, 120, 123, 144, 147, 174, 175, 176, 178, 181, 182, 183, 188, 196, 197, 205, 209, 212, 213, 215, 218, 219, 220, 223, 224, 229, 230, 237, 246, 248, 269, 273, 279, 290, 291, 306, 307, 308, 310, 312
The Negatives οὐ **and** μή, 242, 243
The Role of the Teacher, 8, 292, 303
Third declension, 125, 188, 189, 190, 191, 196, 204,
Translating Idioms, 8, 279, 284
Use of Italics in Translation, 6, 228, 239
Verbs, 5, 6, 7, 8, 116, 117, 118, 119, 120, 121, 122, 123, 125, 126, 132, 137, 139, 140, 143, 144, 146, 148, 149, 152, 153, 154, 165, 174, 175, 176, 177, 178, 181, 182, 183, 185, 196, 197, 198, 199, 200, 204, 205, 206, 207, 208, 209, 212, 214, 218, 226, 230, 232, 233, 234, 235, 236, 237, 241, 243, 246, 248, 249, 250, 254, 255, 257, 268, 269, 279, 290, 305, 306, 308, 309, 310, 311, 312
   Active Voice, 5, 115, 116, 117, 118, 120, 121, 122, 123, 143, 144, 146, 148, 149, 154, 175, 176, 177, 182, 183, 185, 196, 197, 204, 205,

Verbs, cont. -
212, 213, 214, 215, 218, 219, 228, 229, 230, 246, 247, 248, 268, 273, 277, 284, 291, 306, 307, 308, 310
Aorist Tense, 6, 7, 116, 117, 118, 174, 175, 176, 177, 178, 183, 185, 195, 197, 203, 204, 205, 206, 213, 218, 219, 220, 226, 229, 230, 231, 246, 247, 248, 254, 255, 291, 306, 307, 310, 311
Aorist active, 174, 175, 176, 185, 203, 204, 205, 218, 219, 228, 229, 230, 291
Aorist middle, 175, 177, 204, 219, 229, 230
Aorist participle, 6, 7, 197, 204, 205, 206, 254, 311
Aorist passive, 176, 177, 178, 183, 205, 219, 229, 230, 247, 248, 310
Compound Verbs, 139
Constructions with πιστευω, 6, 174, 178
Deponent, 122, 123, 178, 183, 195, 226, 310
First Aorist, 6, 7, 174, 175, 176, 204, 205, 254, 255, 307
Future tense, 6, 116, 117, 118, 176, 181, 182, 183, 184, 185, 223, 224, 246, 247, 248, 269, 306, 307, 310
Imperative Mood, 6, 116, 178, 208, 221, 228, 229, 230, 234, 236, 247, 255, 306, 309
Imperfect Tense, 5, 116, 117, 118, 119, 120, 121, 122, 123, 127, 148, 175, 178, 182, 197, 246, 247, 306, 307
Indicative Mood, 5, 6, 116, 120, 121, 122, 123, 143, 144, 146, 147, 148, 149, 154, 162, 175, 177, 178,

181, 182, 183, 184, 185, 197, 199, 200, 204, 205, 206, 212, 213, 215, 216, 220, 222, 223, 224, 225, 237, 242, 243, 246, 247, 254, 255, 268, 273, 291, 306, 307, 309
Infinitive, 6, 228, 230, 231, 232, 233, 234, 235, 236, 237, 242, 248, 255, 310
Middle Voice, 5, 6, 116, 117, 121, 122, 143, 147, 174, 175, 176, 177, 178, 181, 182, 183, 184, 196, 203, 205, 214, 215, 216, 219, 228, 229, 230, 231, 247, 248, 306, 308, 310
Mood, 116, 120, 148, 188, 193, 196, 204, 213, 218, 220, 222, 223, 224, 226, 229, 230, 237, 2402, 243, 247, 306, 307, 309, 312
Optative tense, 116, 226, 306, 309
Participle, 6, 7, 171, 188, 194, 195, 196, 197, 198, 199, 200, 203, 204, 205, 206, 207, 208, 209, 212, 214, 215, 234, 238, 242, 248, 254, 255, 277, 281, 284, 310, 311
Passive Voice, 5, 6, 116, 117, 121, 122, 123, 143, 147, 176, 177, 178, 181, 182, 183, 184, 195, 196, 198, 203, 204, 214, 215, 216, 219, 229, 230, 231, 241, 247, 248, 277, 281, 306, 308, 310
Perfect tense, 5, 176, 188, 195, 196, 206, 212, 213, 214, 215, 218, 231, 246, 247, 248, 250, 269, 273, 306, 307, 308, 310
Pluperfect Tense, 6, 116, 212, 215, 216, 306, 308
Present Participles, 6, 195, 197, 200, 205, 207, 208, 255, 310
Present Tense, 117, 118, 119, 120, 123, 144, 147, 175, 178, 181,

Verbs, cont. -
183, 197, 213, 219, 231, 269, 290, 306, 307, 308, 310
Principle Parts of Verbs, 176, 183
Second Aorist, 6, 7, 174, 175, 176, 177, 178, 185, 204, 205, 206, 219, 230, 231, 246, 254, 255, 307
Subjunctive, 6, 7, 116, 188, 193, 218, 219, 220, 221, 222, 223, 224, 225, 226, 230, 254, 255, 284, 306, 309
   Conditional Clauses and the Subjunctive, 223, 224
   Deliberative Subjunctive, 221
   Emphatic Negative Subjunctive, 221
   Hortatory Subjunctive, 220,
   Negative Subjunctive, 221
   Simple Subjunctive, 220
   Subjunctive showing purpose, 222

Vocative Case, 113, 125, 190, 305
Voice, 116, 117, 121, 122, 196, 241, 277, 306, 307, 308, 310, 312
 Active Voice, 5, 115, 116, 117, 118, 120, 121, 122, 123, 143, 144, 146, 148, 149, 154, 175, 176, 177, 182, 183, 185, 196, 197, 204, 205, 212, 213, 214, 215, 218, 219, 228, 229, 230, 246, 247, 248, 268, 273, 277, 284, 291, 306, 307, 308, 310
 Middle Voice, 5, 6, 116, 117, 121, 122, 143, 147, 174, 175, 176, 177, 178, 181, 182, 183, 184, 196, 203, 205, 214, 215, 216, 219, 228, 229, 230, 231, 247, 248, 306, 308, 310
 Passive Voice, 5, 6, 116, 117, 121, 122, 123, 143, 147, 176, 177, 178, 181, 182, 183, 184, 195, 196, 198, 203, 204, 214, 215, 216, 219, 229, 230, 231, 241, 247, 248, 277, 281, 306, 308, 310
Tense of Verbs, 23, 116, 117, 118, 119, 120, 123, 144, 147, 174, 175, 176, 178, 181, 182, 183, 188, 196, 197, 205, 209, 212, 213, 215, 218, 219, 220, 223, 224, 229, 230, 237, 246, 248, 269, 273, 279, 290, 291, 306, 307, 308, 310, 312

Word Order, 6, 7, 141, 148, 184, 228, 239, 265, 274, 277, 278, 283, 305

NOTES

1 Wikipedia. *The Greek Language*. June 2020.

2 Larry Pierceon. *In the Days of Peleg*. Answers in Genesis. Dec. 1, 1999. Web. Jan. 16, 2019.

3 The 1689 Baptist Confession of Faith. https://www.the1689 confession.com/1689/chapter-1. Jan. 19, 2019.

4 H.D. Williams. The Miracle of Biblical Inspiration. (The Old Paths Publications: Cleveland, GA) 2009. PDF download. Jan. 2019.

5 Merriam-Webster Dictionary online. Merriam-webster.com. Web. 5-2019

6 Gary La More. Thou Shalt Keep Them: ABiblical Theology of the Perfect Preserrvation of Scripture. Cited. David Brown. Providential Preservation: the Doctrine that Virtually Disappeared. Print. Jan. 23, 2019.

7 Andy Stanley. At Exponential a conference. 2014. Cited. *God's Word: The Authority over Us*. Answers in Genesis. 2017. Web. Jan. 24, 2019.

8 Christianity Today. *Should Pastors Stop Saying 'God says?'* 2014. Cited. *God's Word: The Authority Over Us*. Answers in Genesis. 2014. Web. Jan. 24, 2019.

9 Burgon, John William. The Traditional Text of the Holy Gospels (p. 29). Kindle Edition.

10 Edward F. Hills

11 Ibid

12 Dr. Jim Taylor, *In Defense of the Textus Receptus*. theoldpathspublications.com. 2016. Nook Edition. P. 260. 4-2019.

13 Biblical Archaeology. www. la-via.es/english/archivo/ MagdalenEN.htm. Web. 2014.

14 Dr. Edward Hills.

15 Dr. Jim Taylor, p. 180.

16 Burgon, John William. *The Traditional Text of the Holy Gospels* (p. 18). Kindle Edition.

17 Burgon, John William. The Traditional Text of the Holy Gospels (pp. 21-22). Kindle Edition.

18 Burgon, John William. The Traditional Text of the Holy Gospels (p. 41). Kindle Edition.

19 Burgon, John William. The Traditional Text of the Holy Gospels (p. 44). Kindle Edition.

20 Burgon, John William. The Traditional Text of the Holy Gospels (p. 43). Kindle Edition.
21 Burgon, John William. The Traditional Text of the Holy Gospels (p. 45). Kindle Edition.
22 Dr. D. A. Waite. *Summary of the Traditional Text.* Deanburgonsociety.org. 1997. Web. 4-2019.
23 Burgon, John William. The Traditional Text of the Holy Gospels (pp. 45-46). Kindle Edition.
24 Dr. Wilbur Pickering. *In Defense of the Objective Authority of the Sacred Text.* Walkinhiscommandments.com. 2009. Web. 4-2019.
25 Wikipedia. *Byzantine text-type.* Web. 4-2019.
26 Dr. David L. Brown. *Early Witnesses to the Received Text.* Logosresourcepages.org. Web. 4-2019.
27 Burgon, John William. The Traditional Text of the Holy Gospels (p. 91). Kindle Edition.
28 IBID
29 IBID
30 Frederick H. A. Scrivener. *A Plain Introduction to the Criticism of the New Testament.* Ed. iv (1881), Vol. II. pp. 264-265. Cited. Burgon, John William. The Traditional Text of the Holy Gospels (p. 37). Kindle Edition. 4-2019.
31 John Foxe. Fox's Book of Martyrs Or A History of the Lives, Sufferings, and Triumphant Deaths of the Primitive Protestant Martyrs: The Original Classics - Illustrated (pp. 43-44). Unknown. Kindle Edition
32 James Snapp, Jr. *Byzantine Manuscripts: Where Were They Before the 300's?*thetextofthegospels.com. 2017. Web. 4-2019.
33 Burgon, John William. The Traditional Text of the Holy Gospels (pp. 49-50). Kindle Edition.
34 Burgon, *Tradional Text*, p. 62.
35 Burgon, *Tradional Text*, p. 65.
36 Edward F. Hills
37 Maurice Robinson and William Pierpont. "Introduction." *The New Testament in the Original Greek According to the Byzantine / Majority Textform.* Skypoint.com. (Published in print by: The Original Word Publishers: Atlanta. 1991). Web. 4-2019.
38 IBID
39 Edward F. Hills, The King James Version Defended. (Des Moines, Iowa: Christian research Press. 1973). Print. p. 197.

40 J.H. Merle D'Aubigne, *History of the Reformation of the Sixteenth Century*, New York: Hurst & Company, 1835, Vol. 5, p. 157; cited by, David Cloud, *Is the Received Text Based on a Few Late Manuscripts?* Way of Life Literature. Web. Mar. 18, 2004.

41 Edward F. Hills, *The King James Version Defended*, 1956, 1979, pp. 198-199

42 Wikipedia, Juan Ginés de Sepúlveda, Web. This is also attested to by Chris Thomas, *Erasmian Myths: Codex Vaticanus.* confessionalbibliology.com. May 16, 2016, wherein the actual ccorrespondence between Sulpeveda and Erasmus is given (in Latin), taken from Thomas Horne. *Introduction to the Textual Criticism of the New Testament*, which was edited by Samuel Tregelles, London: Longman, Brown, Green, Longmans, and Roberts. 1856. pp xv, xvi, available in Google Books

43 Samuel Prideaux Tregelles, *An Account of the Printed Text of the Greek New Testament with Remarks on Its Revision upon Critical Principal Together with a Collation of Critical Texts*, (London: Samuel Bagster and Sons, 1854), p. 22. / Marvin R. Vincent, *A History of the Textual Criticism of the New Testament,* (New York: MacMillian, 1899), p. 53/ F.H.A. Scrivener, *A Plain Introduction to the Criticism of the New Testament*, 4th ed., ed. Edward Miller, 2 Vols., (London: George Bell and Sons, 1881), Vol I, p. 109. All cited by www.av1611, com in *Why Then are New Translations Thought Necesssary?* Web.

44 Charles Ellicott, The Revisers and the Greek Text of the N.T. by two members of the N.T. Company, pp. 11-12. Cited by, David Cloud, *Is the Received Text Based on a Few Late Manuscripts?* Way of Life Literature. Web. Mar. 18, 2004.

45 Frederick H. A. Scrivener, *Scrivener's Annotated Greek New Testament.* 1881. (Dean Burgon Society Press: Collingswood, New Jersey. 1999). Print. pp. vii-viii.

46 (1689 Baptist Confession of Faith, Chapter 1, section 8. http://www.arbca.com/1689-chapter1. 8-23-18.

47 Jonathan Petersen. Billy Graham: 1918-2018. Bible Gateway. 2018. https://www.biblegateway.com/ blog/ 2018/ 02/ billy-graham-1918-20. Web. Feb. 2019.

48 The Bible Societies. Trinitarian Bible Society Quarterly Record. Jan-Mar 1979. Pgs. 13-14. Cited: The UBS Greek New Testament. Prophets-See-All. http://prophets-see all.tripod.com/46645.htm. Web. 17 August 2017.

49 Brown, Andrew, The Word of God Among All Nations: a Brief History of the Trinitarian Bible Society, 1831-1981. P.122. 1981. Trinitarian Bible Society. Cited: The UBS Greek New Testament. Prophets-See-All. http://prophets-see-all.tripod.com/46645.htm. Web. 17 August 2017.

50Brown, Andrew, The Word of God Among All Nations: a Brief History of the Trinitarian Bible Society, 1831-1981. P 12. 1981. Trinitarian Bible Society. Cited: The UBS Greek New Testament. Prophets-See-All. http://prophets-see-all.tripod.com/46645.htm. Web. 17 August 2017.

51Metger, Bruce. Cited: Brooks, James. Bible Interpreters of the Twentieth Century. p. 64. Cited: "Aren't Newer Translations Based on a Better Greek Text." KJV Today. 2017. Web. 17 August 2017

52"Aren't Newer Translations Based on a Better Greek Text." KJV Today. 2017. Web. 17 August 2017.

53Westcott and Hort. The New Testament in the Original Greek, the Text Revised by B.F. Westcott and F.J.A. Hort. (Cambridge: MacMillan & Co., 1882), p. 20. Cited: "Aren't newer translations based on a better Greek text?" KJV Today. 2017. Web. 17 August 2017.

54La More, Gary E, Ph. D. (in Greek Philosophy and M. Div. in Greek and Hebrew). Bruce Metzger: a Princeton Apostate. Pastor's Helps. Grace Missionary Baptist Church. Web. 22 July 2017.

55La Moore

56La Moore

57La Moore

58 A. Hembd, MACS. The Doctrinal Views of Dr. Kurt Aland, Textual Critic. Quarterly Record of the Trinitarian Bible Society, Issue 579, April to June, 2007.http://standardbearers.net/uploads/The_Doctrinal_Views_of_Kurt_Aland__A._Hembd-TBS_2007_.pdf. Web. Feb. 2021.

59 Wikipedia. Carlo Maria Martini. 2021

60Introduction, Nestle-Aland: Novum Testamentum Graece , 27th revised edition. 2006. Cited. Aren't Newer Translations Based on a Better Text? The King's Bible. www.kingsbible.org.Web. 14 July 2017

61Fowler, Everette W. Evaluating Versions of the New Testament. (Watertown, WI: Maranatha Baptist Press, 1981) p. 28-66. Print. 19 August 2014.

62Charles V. Turner, Biblical Bible Translating (Lafayette, Indiana: Sovereign Grace Publishers, 2001). Print. 11-12.

63Turner. 12

64 "Family," New World Dictionary of American English, 1988 ed. Webster, Noah. "Webster's Dictionary of American English." 1828 edition. E-Sword. Rick Meyers. Version 10.2.1. Franklin, Tn.: 2013. Downloaded computer software.

65 "Nation." New World Dictionary of American English, 1988 ed. Webster, Noah. "Webster's Dictionary of American English." 1828 edition. E-Sword. Rick Meyers. Version 10.2.1. Franklin, Tn.: 2013. Downloaded computer software.

66 Winter, Ralph D. and Koch, Bruce. Finishing the Task: the Unreached People Challenge. Mission Frontiers. June 2000. Web. 14 June 2000.

67 Winter and Koch

68 Winter and Koch

69 Global Research. International Mission Board. (www.peoplegroups.org). 2020. Web. January 2020.

70 JP Deutillo. The Toulambi. http://jpdutilleux.com/ the work/toulambi/index.html. Web. 2004, 2005

71 Global Research. International Mission Board. (www.peoplegroups.org). Web. Web. March 2020.

72 Global Research. International Mission Board. (www.peoplegroups.org). 2019. Web. January 2019.

73 Wycliffe. Scripture and Language Statistics 2018. http://www.wycliffe.net/statistics Web. July 2017

74 Global Research. International Mission Board. (www.peoplegroups.org). Web. Web. March 2020.

75 J. Gresham Machen. *New Testament Greek for Beginners.* (Toronto: The Macmillan Company. 1951) Print. P. 41, 42.

76 Dr. Jim Taylor. Comment to the author.

77 H. E. Dana and Julius R. Mantey. *A Manual Grammar of the Greek New Testament.* Ontario: The Macmillian Company. 1955. P 102. Print.

78 Theologians say He is three *persons* in one God. I agree that the Father, Son, and Spirit are persons. However, to say that there is one God in three persons makes it sound like they are all *separate* persons. They are not. They are ONE. I am not sure that the way theologians describe the Trinity is adequate. Perhaps nothing is. Nevertheless, the Lord our God is one Lord (Deut. 6). He is one person consisting of the Father, the Word, and the Holy Spirit (1 Jn. 5:7).

79 The Complete Word Study Dictionary. *E-Sword*. Rick Meyers. Version 10.2.1. Franklin, Tn.: 2013. Downloaded computer software.

80 Lawrence, Nathan. *Is Yeshua "the only begotten" or "the one of kind, unique" Son of Elohim?* https://hoshanarabbah.org. 9/9/2017. Web.

81 G. Abbot-Smith, *A Manual Greek Lexicon of the New Testament.*

82 Word Study

83 Thayer

84 Strong. *Strong's Exhaustive Hebrew and Greek Dictionaries*. E-Sword. Rick Meyers. Version 10.2.1. Franklin, Tn.: 2013. Downloaded computer software.

85 Word Study

86 American Heritage® Dictionary of the English Language, *5th Edition*. (2016: Houghton Mifflin Harcourt Publishing Co.) Cited, The Free Dictionary. 2003-2020. Web. 10/28/2020.

87 Beekman, John and Callow, John. *Translating the Word of God*. Grand Rapids: Zondervan Publishing House. 1974. Print. Pg 221.

88 H. E. Dana and Julius R. Mantey.

89 Webster

90 *American Heritage Dictionary of the English Language. 5th Edition*. (2016: Houghton Mifflin Harcourt Publishing Co.) Cited, The Free Dictionary. 2003-2020. Web. 10/28/2020.

91 As I am indebted to many authors for most of the information and concepts in this book, I will mention two, to whom I referred for most of the information in this section on Figures of speech: 1) Dr. Charles Turner and his book, *Biblical Bible Translating*, and 2) my friend, editor, and publisher, Dr. H. D. Williams, *Word-for-Word Translating of the Received Texts*.

92 American Heritage® Dictionary of the English Language, Fifth Edition. Copyright © 2016 by Published by Houghton Mifflin Harcourt Publishing Company. Cite. Litotes - Cited, The Free Dictionary. 2003-2020. Web.

93 Purdue Online Writing Lab. *Verb Tense Concistency*. https://owl.purdue.edu/owl/general_writing/grammar/verb_tenses/verb_tense_consistency.html. 10/28/2020. Web.

94 Word Study

95 Webster, 1828.

96 Charles V. Turner. *Biblical Bible Translating*. (Sovereign Grace Publishers: Layfayette, In. 2001) Print. P 36.

97 *Collins English Dictionary. Complete and Unabridged, 12th Edition*. (Harper Collins Publishers. 2014.) Cited, The Free Dictionary. 2003-2020. Web. 11/2/2020.

98 Beekman and Callow

99 Dr. Jim Taylor. Comment to the Author.

100 Dr. Charles Turner, P 140.

101 The first two examples are from Dr. Charles Turner, P 146.

www.ingramcontent.com/pod-product-compliance
Lightning Source LLC
Chambersburg PA
CBHW071313150426
43191CB00007B/606